To Mr. Gunther E. Pohl with,
my compliments and best wishes!

JEW AND MORMON

Historic Group Relations
and Religious Outlook

By

DR. RUDOLF GLANZ

Published with the help of the
Lucius N. Littauer Foundation

New York
1963

Library of Congress Catalogue Card Number 63–16229

Printed in the United States of America
WALDON PRESS, Inc.
150 Lafayette Street, New York 13, N. Y.

To Yoram and Raanan
my grandsons

On historic group relations the following
studies by the author have appeared:

JEW AND YANKEE: A HISTORIC COMPARISON
Jewish Social Studies, vol. VI, No. 1, 1944

JEWS IN RELATION TO THE CULTURAL MILIEU OF THE
GERMANS IN AMERICA UP TO THE EIGHTEEN EIGHTIES
New York 1947

JEWS AND CHINESE IN AMERICA
Jewish Social Studies, vol. XVI, No. 3, 1954

THE "BAYER" AND THE "POLLACK" IN AMERICA
Jewish Social Studies, vol. XVII, No. 1, 1955

ACKNOWLEDGMENTS.

I want to express my gratitude to Dr. Gladys Rosen for editing the manuscript. Her keen interest in Mormon history moved her to take on this task.

Furthermore, my thanks are due to the following institutions which have made possible my research: the Archives of the Church of Jesus Christ of Latter Day Saints in Salt Lake City, the Coe Collection at Yale University, Berrian Collection at New York Public Library, Perkins Collection at Harvard, Huntington Library, National Archives, Library of Congress, University of Utah, Brigham Young University, Western Reserve University, Bancroft Library, the Public Libraries in San Francisco, Los Angeles, San Bernardino and Salt Lake City, the New York Historical Society, American Jewish Historical Society, American Jewish Archives and Library of the Hebrew Union College in Cincinnati, the Jewish Theological Seminary and the Local History Center there.

In planning this book biography was considered outside the scope of the work. The interested reader will find most valuable biographical sketches of Utah Jews in Leon Watters, The Pioneer Jews of Utah, New York 1952, pp. 107–174. Some older ones are to be found in: Sketches of the Inter-Mountain States. Salt Lake City 1909, pp. 73, 117, 263 and: Salt Lake City. Past and Present . . . by E. V. Fohlin . . . Salt Lake City [1908], pp. 147–150.

This writer has endeavored to allow the original spelling in sources to remain unchanged. Exceptions have been made only in cases of obvious printer's errors.

I want to express my gratitude to Mr. Harry Starr for procuring the financial help of the Lucius N. Littauer Foundation for this publication.

TABLE OF CONTENTS

INTRODUCTION

Awareness of the present minority problem of a special and unique sort in American history grew out of studies of the history of immigration and historic group-relations of immigrants. The fact was duly recognized that in the continuing westward-movement the immigrant met two new and entirely different societies, in Utah and California—both resulting from the crossing of the continent—and had to make his adjustment to them.

The Mormon Society and all economic and social intercourse between the Mormons and the Jews can be regarded as an expression of American life formed by religious teachings and the effects of pioneer environments upon a newly formed society. In this the new California Society was no match for the "State of Deseret" because it lacked any leading religious principles at its founding. The results of all the contacts between Mormon and Jewish Society are therefore more impressive than in any other region of the United States successively populated by immigrant waves.

This peculiarity of founding a religious society—so it was recognized from the beginning—was correlated with special religious principles in relations with the Jews. In itself such recognition led to a study of the whole position of the Jew in Mormon creed and doctrine.

The holy writings originating in Mormonism insofar as they were instrumental in the founding of a new religious society—were recognized as historic factors which were able to produce effective ideas about the Jews and to form historic group-relations between the Mormons and the Jews, or at least to influence them. These writings retain their effectiveness as religious ideas and remain valid no matter what historical textual criticism of these writings may teach us as to the origin of Mormonism. The Prophecy and Revelation asserted in these writings become especially important factors in the history of ideas insofar as the position of the Jew

1

in Mormon creed and doctrine is concerned and—to whatever extent it can be proven—for the historic group-relations of the Jews and the Mormons too.

Yet, while fully acknowledging the history-creating power of these holy writings, it is more important to take them, not so much in their original form, but rather in the various authoritative interpretations given to them in the later Mormon literature. Even according to Mormon concept a later revelation supersedes a prior one, if it accords with the necessities of life; and various theological positions of the founding-period appear to have been changed by the interpretations of the followers.

In all this, it is important to note that the position of the Jew in Mormon creed and doctrine did not undergo any basic change as a result of such later transformations by Mormon interpretative writings. Occasionally there were small accommodations in minor features of the historic image of the Jew especially when the Mormon concept of their own community changed. Their consciousness of their role as a community of historic destiny deepened and the comparison with the fate of the Jewish people was forced upon them by the persecutions they suffered. As a result, the picture of the Biblical Jew expanded and the appearance of post-Biblical Judaism changed only to a small degree. It is significant that this can be said of the position of the Jew in the minor Mormon Churches' doctrines as well as in its main (Utah) branch.

This peculiar religious position of the Jew in Mormon creed and doctrine is not matched by any of the non-Mormon religious communities of the time. In its transformation of the Biblical picture of the pagan world surrounding God's chosen people all these non-Mormon communities were considered by the Mormon as "Gentiles."

But life and doctrinal position could not concur. Important interests in Mormon society in Utah forced all non-Mormon elements in the territory to line up in one adverse front—the Jews included. Isolation from this front was to be sought by the Mormon people as in the Biblical example of the Gentiles of Old. One of the most widespread witticisms of the contemporary world originated from this, namely that Utah is the only place in the world where the Jew is a Gentile. Actually the role of the Jew in

2

the relations among the various religious groups constituting the Mormon-Gentile problem needs a thorough clarification. The character of the Jewish community as an independent non-Christian community endured in Mormon doctrine and was never lost. Even the religious promise given to the Jews was entirely different from the promise given to the Christian non-Mormons. Mormonism, at that time the only religion founded on American revelation, taught that "Zion" could be built in America by the revival of old Israelitic priesthood and prophecy. Yet, the Jews would be restored to their old homeland, Palestine, without any special promise in the new American "Zion" of the Latter Day Saints. According to this concept the Jew in Utah was not merely part of the non-Mormon front but his quality as non-Christian was expressly asserted. (Apparently it was in accordance with this concept that later invitations by the Mormons to settlement in Utah were directed to all who acknowledge Christ.)

In reality the position of the Jewish religious group in Utah was in between the Christian denominations of old and the new American (Christian) believers, styled Mormons. In the Mormons' fight for independent statehood and an exclusive Mormon Society, the rising Jewish community experienced an economic crisis together with all Christian Gentiles as a result of the founding of the "Zion Cooperative." Such tendencies brought the Jews in Utah in line with the political party of the Gentiles which was not without influence on all developments leading to definite statehood for Utah.

All this notwithstanding, the basic facts remained unchanged. Three of the basic factors in the Jewish-Mormon relationship set it apart as unique in American history and in Jewish history the world over: First, a general Christian united front was formed in the religious conflict against the Mormons to which, of course, the Jews did not belong. This differs sharply from many a European country where for over a thousand years there had been a united front only in the religious conflict against the Jews. Second, in the territory of Mormon colonization all those not adhering to the Saints were treated as Gentiles by them and in this category the resident Jews were also included. Third, notwithstanding occasional friction, there was no basic Jewish-Mormon quarrel. The Jewish people who, through their own basic position, stood

3

outside the Mormon conflict were best equipped to appreciate the real significance of a historic process which was controversial for American Christians. The Mormon group was formed by the events of that very same historic period which was also decisive in shaping American Jewry. The Utah century of the gathering of the Latter Day Saints represents for the Jewish people the period of the transference of the last great center in Jewish history, in Eastern Europe to the New World.

How this process was mirrored in the public opinion of the Jews in America and the world over is therefore a necessary adjunct to the whole picture of Mormonism in the world. This includes articles—by early Jewish travelers—writers and Utah residents—which are not to be found elsewhere.

Due to the unique character of the present problem, its treatment and clarification reveal aspects of American history not found in any of the other historic group-relations in America. In this way it is hoped that this study will make a necessary contribution to knowledge in the field of American history. In the same way the study of Mormonism—so well developed in American historiography—should be enlarged by an essentially new and thus far unrecognized aspect.

4

CHAPTER 1

Contemporary Interest in Mormonism

Mid-Nineteenth Century Europe, in the full grip of its Atlantic migration, was learning many strange new things about America. Outstanding was the story of the rise of an entirely new religion with many Biblical overtones. The past of the Jews, so well known to the European peoples, appeared in a new light. Once again the historical wanderings of the ancient Biblical people were discussed, and it was asserted that golden tablets had been found in America, containing the reports of these migrations. But most important for the believer was the fact that the chain of revelation, broken since Bible days, had been renewed in America. Revelation had been received on American soil. A new prophet, actually the first since Mohammed, had risen there and was gathering his believers into a new church. Important changes were imminent because the gathering of the faithful went hand in hand with migrations across the American continent. This was of interest to all the world, but it was of special importance to the relatives of emigrants who stayed on in Europe. It was even more important to all prospective emigrants whose decision had yet to be made, since it added still another interesting feature to their image of America.

Finally, with the revelation of the great secret which the Mormons had so carefully hidden in the beginning, i.e., the practice of polygamy, curiosity and tension in Europe reached its peak. The desire to reduce the unknown at least partly to the known excited greater interest in the asserted Biblical trend of the Mormons. The discussion of Biblical conditions and their potential influence on the New World through the new religion suddenly brought old questions to life again.

Deeper thought about this new American phenomenon could

5

not miss the relation to Biblical tendencies in Europe during the last centuries. But the closeness to these events prevented a proper deliberation and proper perspective. The task of realistically surveying the effect of European Biblicism on Mormonism was reserved for the science of our days.

Entirely different and almost diametrically opposed to this general European interest in Mormonism were the interests of the European Jews. To them, America was the great hope of emigration, the only door to liberty, the last chance to escape discrimination of all kinds. The sharpened historical sense of the European Jewry might well have foreseen that wherever Jewish matters were placed in the forefront of general interest, Jewish hopes were truly in danger. The interest of the Jews in Europe in all these speculations about their past, the migrations of the Lost Tribes and their identification with living peoples could, in the best case, only have been a paper interest. The Jewish newspapers in Europe took note of all such news items as curiosities and used them as space-fillers for lack of anything better. Whether Englishmen or Indians were to be considered the descendants of the Lost Tribes left the European Jews entirely cold. This feeling hardly changed in the course of the following decades and in 1873 in America it was just as psychologically wrong as in Europe earlier, to imply that the Jews themselves should be the first to examine the Indian theory of the Lost Tribes: "Whatever may be the truth, as a problem, still to be solved, it would seem to be of special interest to the Jews themselves, and of more moment, perhaps, for them, to disprove the conclusion, than for any other persons to confirm it." (*Overland Monthly,* v. X (1873), p. 291.) Such recommendations did not reflect the actual spiritual life of European Jews nor their interest in immigration. The talk of a Judaized America—every Yankee spiritually a Jew with an affinity to the Jews in Europe—could only create difficulties for the emigrating Jews and even more for those who had to stay on in their European communities. The insinuation that the Jews should in any way participate in an endeavor to force world opinion to link America with them appeared especially absurd to them. Indeed, the flow of writings about these matters emanated at the time exclusively from non-Jews. The place of this question in older Jewish literature was forgotten; and any discussion of this whole complex was simply beside the point to the European Jews of this period.

But the picture changed at once when the news of Mormon polygamy, traced by them to its Biblical origins, reached Europe. The apathy of the Jews in Europe generally turned to hostility toward a situation which forced the Jews into a discussion of the true Biblical situation. Underlying this sentiment was the feeling that a discussion of this nature was very likely to disrupt the process of unrestricted emigration. The extent to which this feeling was real was later experienced by the American Jews on the other side of the ocean. Their reaction to this reality forms an important part of the historic Jew-Mormon problem.

Whatever the later developments were, this viewpoint played no role in the initial stage of Mormonism. No European movement of Biblicism had officially sanctioned polygamy and Mormonism could not have learned it from Europe. The Biblical movement there revolved in entirely different circles, whose influence on Mormonism will now be determined.

CHAPTER 2

European Influences: Biblicism and Mormonism

Certain spiritual developments in modern European history came about when the peoples of Europe, having become Protestant, turned back to the Old Testament. This movement reached its peak in 17th Century England which, it is to be noted, was at that time entirely without Jews. However, it took place to a greater or lesser degree in nearly all of the Protestant countries. We subsume all such developments under the term *Biblicism*.[1]

Among all these peoples there arose sects which as free churches opposed the established church and often the government as well. Such historical conditions forced them to work out a spiritual image of life for individuals and the community for which they could find no basis in the New Testament. In contrast to this, however, the books of the Old Testament offered parallel situations with which these peoples could find a meaningful relationship. Intensive study and deep penetration into the books of the Hebrew Bible were not difficult for members of the lower classes of society from which the sects and their leaders were recruited. They felt no need for scholastic theological discussions which characterized the study of the New Testament during the Middle Ages. Free interpretation was an integral part of this new religious experience. The popular mind was thus able to attain a far reaching identification with events in the Old Testament which were regarded as the pattern of individual and national life. This spiritual movement of Biblicism reached its peak with the application of the idea of the Covenant to personal life and to the State, as a social organism existing under a covenant with God.

From this historic situation in Europe two points basic to the investigation of Mormonism emerge. First, the Biblicism which flourished among the nations of Western Europe, which contributed to the first big wave of Atlantic migration to America. This immigration was continually fed by new emigrants from those countries in which early Mormon missionary efforts were most effective in producing new adherents. (For instance, among 85,220 persons brought to Utah by the Perpetual Emigrating Fund, approximately half were English Mormons.[2]) Secondly, the new religious community was formed mainly from the same lower classes from which the free Protestant churches of Europe had drawn their adherents. Their leadership also rose from within as was the case with the European sects. The only difference—in itself without great importance—was that on American soil the task of governing the new church fell naturally to men who, although they had come from these lower classes, were no longer emigrants themselves. Although their forebears had already been transplanted to America, their families still belonged to the same relatively low station in life.

To measure the scope of Biblicism achieved by European free churches and possibly brought by them to America essential criteria have been set up. These criteria are not so much concerned with the leading ideas of the entire spiritual movement, such as the covenant and its application to person and state. Rather, they are based on precepts of law in the Hebrew Bible which—despite the fact that they were in opposition to the concepts of the New Testament which decreed their non-observance—were nevertheless observed by the sects to a greater or smaller degree. One author[3] summarizes these criteria as follows: Biblical personal names given; Observance of Biblical dietary laws; Circumcision, Sanctification of the Seventh Day of the Week as the Sabbath according to Biblical law and British Israelism.

Although, with the exception of British Israelism, most of the other points are non-existent in Mormonism a full evaluation of their role is in place at this point. Because all these elements of European Biblicism had been transplanted to America at least in some rudimentary form, proof of their absence in the formation of the Mormon church would make the role of transformed Anglo-Israelism even more decisive. It then appears that most things which were strong enough to inspire religious conscience in Europe had, in the American situation which created Mormonism, either already found expression or proven their ineffectiveness. All these elements may then be eliminated as factors in the origin of Mormonism.

a. *The giving of personal Biblical names.* Vis-à-vis their popularity among the Puritans and most other sects transplanted to America, the use of Biblical personal names by the Mormons was not new. Indeed, such names were less represented among the Mormons than among other sects. We base this on the list of names of participants in the Centennial trek to Utah which indicated that these names were given by the Utah pioneers themselves to their children and should be remembered by their grandchildren. We find the following result: among 143 persons not even 20 bear a Biblical personal name, including 5 Josephs and 4 Davids, I Ruth and 1 Abraham. The giving of these names is far from the original meaning of the new process of Biblical name-giving in the free churches of Europe. Furthermore, the name Joseph in the specific case of the Mormons must be ascribed to a special relationship to the founder of Mormonism, Joseph Smith.[4]

Name-giving for the first generation born Mormon came at a time when Biblical names in America had already begun to lose popularity. This process was so much faster among the Mormons because they lacked the tradition of Biblical naming which had contributed so much to the founding of the English sects. In addition, the transition to new names was actually accomplished by the Mormons in *one* generation, whereas the same process within other denominations took several generations, judging by the enumeration of names in the First American Census of 1790. True Biblical name-giving as in England under Mary when all the refugees had English or New Testament names whereas their children bore Biblical names never took place among the Mormons.[5] There is an occasional tendency to give Biblical names at least to Indian converts. But even in those cases the name of Abraham, father of all faithful is not used as a rule. Jewish tradition which gives this name to all male proselytes had no influence here. Among 58 Indians of the Piute nation converted in 1855 by the Las Vegas Mission, we do not find one Abraham, although 20 of them, men and women, were given other Biblical names.[6]

The Mormons have rarely used the Biblical protest-names of the radical Puritan wing of the English Church. Names like

10

Adoniram, Ezekiel and Nehemiah were historically a reaction to situations wherein a parallel to Biblical events was sought. Therefore, the Biblical names of the Mormons consist mainly of those which are embedded in their doctrine and church organization, i.e., Aaron and Melchisedek from their priestly orders, Joseph and Ephraim from their interest in the Lost Tribes. Occasionally the name Moses is given as a Biblical image.

The basic stock of American-born adherents of the new church hailed from the Eastern states in which the Biblical name-giving tradition had been strong ever since Puritan days. We learn this from the First Census of 1790 and American-born first generation Mormons were similarly named. The more remarkable, therefore, was the abandonment of such nomenclature for their children. Only 56 Biblical names, among them 16 Josephs and 2 Ephraims, are found in a biographical dictionary of 1919 listing 781 Utah personalities, the clear majority of whom had been born in Utah.[7]

In 1901 among 231 Mormons with names from A to G there were still 39 Biblical names.[8] The diminution of Biblical name-giving which began before the founding of the church by those who later became its adherents had thus become increasingly more evident in the next Mormon generation. Of the 31 Smiths in Jenson, only 10 have Biblical names whereas in the first Vermont Census (1790), two-thirds of the Smiths had Biblical names.

Among Scandinavian people the Reformation did not establish an extensive tradition of giving Biblical names. The Mormons there were the first grand-style dissenters from the established Lutheran church who emigrated to America. Consequently, they did not bring many Biblical names with them and were not eager to continue with them in their new homeland. This became important for the general stock of Mormon personal names since a considerable number of their immigrants were Scandinavians. For instance, we find no Bible names among 3 Petersens, 3 Knudsens, 8 Jensens and 1 Jenson, 10 Andersens and Andersons, 9 Larsens and Larsons and only one David among 6 Christensens.[9]

The lack of an effective name-giving tradition is proof that the post-Reformation European religious struggles did not live on in the historical consciousness or literary tradition of the Mormons.

This absence of a real Biblical names tradition among the

Mormons weakened their relationship to the Bible, at least in this one respect. It was strengthed only later by the Moses comparison in their Exodus.

The giving of Bible names to localities was practiced rather sparingly by the Puritans. This fact was noted with praise in later times when Biblical place-names appeared more often:

"Nonsense in Names.

"There is, it is true, abundant reason for gratitude that the Puritans let us off as easily as they did. It is remarkable that they were content with bestowing ordinary names upon their settlements, when there was nothing to prevent their using unlimited moral precepts or text of Scripture. . . ."[10]

The scarcity of Biblical place-names in Utah is even more noteworthy because Mormons sought a geographic analogy between Utah and Palestine and managed to convey this impression to their contemporaries as well:

"Utah reproduced to their imaginations a new and enlarged type of Canaan. As they emerged from the defiles of the Rocky Mountains they beheld a vast basin in which lay a Dead Sea, with a shoreline of 290 miles, in a frame of treeless mountains, its sullen waves lapping a snow-white beach. From a second sea of Galilee— the beautiful Utah Lake another Jordan poured down, along whose green banks the Mormon, in his mind's eye, saw set the cities of the Lord."[11]

Only 4 Utah place-names originate in the Bible, only 5 in the Book of Mormon, most of the others are names of Utah pioneers.[12] This scarcity is remarkable also because in contrast to the decrease in personal Biblical names, Biblical place-names increased during the 19th century in America. The fact that most of them were to be found in other states and not in Utah, is further proof that Biblical associations connected with localities were not very strong in the minds of the Mormon people. This contrasted with other religious groups whose nearness to the Bible brought Biblical names onto the landscape. Aside from Ephraim and Joseph with their special relationship to Mormon creed, we find only Moab and Mt. Carmel in Utah (the latter existed in Pennsylvania even before the American Revolution). In particular, the Biblical names

12

Goschen, Sharon and Lebanon, often found in other states, are missing in Utah.

Observing Biblical Dietary Laws

In general, these laws remained without any decisive influence on Mormonism. This is especially remarkable because Mormonism introduced its own precepts concerning drinks, even forbidding stimulants like tea and coffee. Nevertheless, certain insights into the meaning of Biblical dietary laws as observed by the Jews came about. We can read: "Meat should be butchered as nearly as possible in conformity with the Mosaic Law. City meat inspectors declare the Jewish markets the ideal ones in respect to the sale and manipulation of all meat."[13] In the Mormon press, articles from other newspapers praising Biblical dietary laws were reprinted.[14] But sympathetic sentiments of this kind had no relationship to abstaining from food forbidden to Jews. The Mormon did not thereby become a pork-hater, no more than did those sects which obeyed other Biblical precepts. For instance, in Sabbatarian Ephrata "two Judaizing brothers" with "a fear of pork" were accused of being disturbers of the spiritual peace.[15]

Circumcision

The sign of the covenant, circumcision, was considered by most European nations the most significant difference between Jew and Christian. Consequently, circumcision made little headway among the sects even during periods of expanding Biblicism. Nevertheless, we find some examples of it in Europe and in single cases in America as well. In literary form we learn of a case in the Ephrata monastery-community in Pennsylvania: ". . . then soon after that A. W. de Olny and D. G. circumcised one another according to the Jewish rite. And they abused Paul with words very much because he had revoked circumcision."[16] Indeed, even in the first phases of the new church it had been stated that circumcision "might be done away."[16a]

In a Mormon sermon the insignificance of the circumcision is cited as the most important case of the ineffectiveness of the Mosaic Law:

"Elder Orson Pratt . . . showed that the law of Moses and the law of circumcision never could save men and women in the kingdom of God. . . ."[17]

The Mormons' non-observance of the rite of circumcision wherein they conformed with other Christian communities in America became a target of derision for their adversaries, who ironically accused them of inconsistency. At the first circumcision of a Jewish boy in Salt Lake City, the circumciser who had been brought into the city from a great distance, was harangued by an anti-Mormon paper in the following words:

"We advise the reverend gentleman not to be in a hurry to leave, there is a large field for him hereabouts. We know, at least, fourteen thousand in Salt Lake City alone, who claim to be of Israel, but have never complied with this regulation of Abraham, 'their father.' We advise Mr. Levenberg to attend to their case, or compel them to own up that they are 'uncircumcised Gentiles,' like the rest. Brethren, walk up to your privileges."[18]

Observing the Biblical Sabbath

The Biblical Sabbath, too, can hardly be considered an important factor in the origins of Mormonism. Strict observance of the Sabbath as the seventh day of the week was not accepted by the main church Mormons although it did exist at least in a minor Mormon sect on Beaver Island, Spring 1850, in this strict form. Resultant troubles brought on by Gentiles were reported and the Sabbath prayer-meeting was kept under guard:

"But as the Mormons began at this time to keep Saturday as the Sabbath, the Gentile teamsters generally found some opportunity to work their oxen that one day of the week hauling past the place of meeting. For this annoyance there was no legal remedy, and the Mormons were compelled to submit."[19]

The non-observance of the main church is the more remarkable because at the time of its founding organized communities of American Sabbatarians already existed. Their numerical strength compared with the Mormons in the first two decades of their existence was relatively large. For instance, the Seventh Day Baptists already had 6,032 communicants in 1846 and their church buildings were scattered over all of America.[20]

14

At this point, we may not overlook rumors that in the Utah Church, observance of Biblical Holidays were considered for a future time. The traveler, Benjamin, reports this as a result of his talks with leading Mormon personalities in Salt Lake City.[21]

Again, it is an exaggeration to see in the serene mode of the observance of Sunday by the Mormons anything which did not already exist in the idea of the English Sunday with its avoidance of certain worldly pleasures. Indeed, this kind of Sunday observance may be considered a direct influence from the Jews.[22]

From all we have learned about European Biblicism, it may be said with certainty that there is no causal connection between it and Mormonism. The latter must be understood from entirely new American motives which became dynamic enough to produce a new religion on new soil. Nevertheless, the European situation produced one factor which thrust itself into an American creation of religion and became decisive for it, Anglo-Israelism. This concept named after the English, the people with the strongest faith penetrated various people in Europe. It was based upon the thought that a people striving to live according to the Bible also has the right to consider itself the descendants of the old Bible nation, the Israelites. This idea had brought with it speculation about a connection with the Lost Ten Tribes even in Europe. This relationship later became fateful for America with the origins of Mormonism.

Nowhere in Europe had the principle behind Anglo-Israelism been likely to result in the founding of a new religion. It had become rather a confirmation of the legality of different religious societies which could reap proven descent from the Bible nation as the divine reward for its orthodoxy. Among the great English people it brought ou a kind of national pride which sought to connect the possession of an empire with the inheritance of the true religion. It was regarded as a disgrace that the American cousin had sold his right as the first born to the Indian and had left for the Anglo-Saxon nation only a pottage of lentils. In 1874 the "Anglo-Ephraim Association" turned with moving words to America to get rid of this impossible situation: ". . . are you, with all those Scripture directions set before you, to go to 'perhaps the Red Indians, perhaps the Afghans,' to account for Joseph-Ephraim, the

15

ten tribes? With all we have learned of Joseph, and the prominence given to the latter-day Ephraim, as compared to Judah, are you really satisfied with this, 'the Jews everywhere, and the stick of Joseph in the hand of a Red Indian; in fact Judah the head, and Ephraim-Israel not even the tail?' "[23]

And later, even when persuasion was deemed too weak, an invasion of America was attempted:

"The apostle of Anglo-Israelism, Mr. Edward Hine, will . . . arrive in this country next month, to deliver lectures showing that the British race is descended from the lost ten tribes. . . ."[24]

By that time, however, the matter had already been decided for America by its new religion. The identification of the Lost Tribes with the Indians by the "Book of Mormon" remained the only representative of the Anglo-Israel principle in America. Although the original thought of Anglo-Israelism may still exist in England among the masses of the people, it no longer lives on in America, outside of the position taken by Mormonism.

In a survey of European Biblicism the idea of founding new priestly orders or renewing the old Biblical priesthood plays no role. Indeed, the priestly orders of the Mormons represent a new American creation. Since the extinction of the Melchisedek sect in the early Christian period until modern times, it had seemed unlikely that the Biblical figure of Melchisedek might found any sect or order. The innovations binding the administering of the spiritual welfare of a church exclusively to the members of a Melchisedek order was entirely a Mormon creation. In contrast to this, the members of the Aaronic order, which includes all the people who became priests, minister to the temporal welfare of the church members only. This turning away from the Bible where the priestly tribe only had to care for the holy things and was removed from all temporal matters becomes clear. Its roots lie in the Christological interpretation of the Melchisedek figure which will be further discussed below. But it may be noted here that the Mormon approach came at a time when the old Israelitic priesthood was mainly a memory in the spiritual life of world Jewry. It is characteristic that the most forceful Jewish religious movement in modern times—Chassidism—did not attempt to renew the role of the priestly group in ancient Israel.[25]

16

CHAPTER 3

The American Situation—As Seen by Mormonism

For many men, the new continent and its conquest by westward movement was in itself a religious experience. There were those who saw in it the realization of everything Europe might have given to its peoples but had not. One great hope remained upon the spiritual height of the new power-consciousness which the vast American continent with its advancing conquest of nature gave to these people. It was that America would in the end crown all this new accomplishment with the best Europe had to offer: historical religion. In their eyes America was capable of creating everything beautiful and good by its own power. There was only one approach to be transplanted from Europe—religion. Even those who were adherents of the cult of America's inevitable progress, as, for instance, Walt Whitman, in his later years, reached this conclusion. With or without such high-flown opinion of the new continent, it was the conviction of organized European religious societies that America could never effect this necessary transplantation by its own power. They therefore became mother churches which had to accomplish this task on virgin soil by means of active help, namely by dispatching religious leaders to America.

The religious experience of those who ultimately succeeded in creating Mormonism by their own power was quite different. In order to approach the historical event and how it evolved through the inner force of an idea, we must first clear away the irrelevant material which obscured the real phenomenon for its contemporaries. Not one among the deluge of contemporary writings about Mormonism yielded a sober evaluation of what America as a whole had contributed to the creation of the Mormon creed. Undoubtedly the new religion was regarded as a vast disturbance at a time when all American churches were taking shape as organized communities. Little wonder that a disproportionate outburst of arguments and pamphlets clouded the general American aspect of the new religious movement.

Furthermore, European transcontinental travelers of various levels of education were not even willing to apply European yardsticks to the Mormons. They were even less willing to see in Mormonism a characteristic expression of an American situation. On their way to the gold land of California, they had to visit Utah and give some news about the Mormons because without it their travel books would not have been considered complete. Such Europeans were quite willing to concede to the entire European continent a period of impetuous adolescence whose spirit found expression in European literature. This exuberance, they said, had created beautiful and good things and was to be given credit for that. However, the same process in America was seen with different eyes. There, impetuous development was only raw nature and exuberance of any kind merely mad boasting. How could any understanding for what the "Book of Mormon" meant in the total American situation of the early 19th century have developed from such a point of view?

The American, however, experienced the awakening of his continent in an entirely different fashion from the descriptions of him. He felt that in addition to the physical force to conquer the new earth, he also possessed the spiritual powers to encompass the vast continent and to be superior to nature or at least to tame it. He created his own image of a giant childish ego which was strong enough to play with nature. The American hero of the tall tales stemmed from the closeness of daily folklore to nature and from observing life in nature. The Indian was a pioneer in this area. Not only did he learn the paths of the wilderness but he was also able to interweave natural phenomena into the human soul. How far was it then from an exuberance which allowed the American man to play with the unbound nature of a new continent to a new word of God on American soil, an American promise to the new fighting inhabitant crossing the unknown continent? Yet this exuberance might not have been enough if some individual had not tried to bring about a new revelation on American soil with the intention of connecting it with the founding of a new positive

18

religion. In any case, some of those who observed the efforts of European churches on the virgin American soil did not approve America's taking over ready-made European models of religion. Such men were ready to see America's manifest destiny in the field of founding a new religion as well. It was only a short step from this to a personality who felt himself to be so predestined, presenting himself as one who had to accept the new revelation from God. Furthermore there were many who felt that they would do better than those in the old religions if they could only find a community willing to accept their revelations. The Mormon report of its beginnings points out that its founder received the new revelation only after trying to find which of the numerous competing churches was the right one. He was convinced, as were those who created Mormonism, that none of them could fill the American man with heavenly light.

Indeed it took decades after the appearance of the "Book of Mormon" to formulate these convictions so that they might guide us through a world of ideas long since past. However, although convinced that America was the highest goal of this new revelation, its founder did not forget the groundswell of human longings springing from the historical religions of Europe. From the beginning the American member of the new religion was not cut off from his spiritual origin, the Bible. On the contrary, he had to be protected in his future as a new "Saint" from the danger that, as a member of a nation essentially without a history, he would not be esteemed by those who placed all important religious experiences in Biblical times. Consequently America had to be given a proper religious past closely connected with the realm of th Bible. However, the Biblical genealogical tables of peoples did not suffice for this purpose. It was necessary to find a supplement covering the period from the Biblical writings until our days. This could come about only by revealing a previously hidden history which would bring Biblical history up to the events of our days. Also the peoples accounting for the time in between must have had holy writings and prophets and must have emigrated to America in olden times. Furthermore, in order to be equal to the people of the old covenant with God, these peoples must also have been given tables and must have recorded promises given to them. The prophet of our days finally found both.

What the "Book of Mormon" basically undertook to accomplish was only the first religious seed laid in the new American earth. It grew into a large tree of life for religious Americanism under whose shadow all nations of the earth were invited to come. But the main idea was and remained American even though it was expressed in Biblical language and imagery:

"Divine Authority

"If America is not the land given to a branch of Joseph, where or in what part of the globe shall that tribe receive the fulfillment of Jacob's prediction? Where, if not in America, has a land been peopled by a multitude of the nations of Joseph? Can a multitude of the nations of Joseph be found in Europe, Asia, or Africa, or in any of the adjoining islands? If not, then America seems to be the only place where that great prediction could receive its accomplishment. The Book of Mormon testifies that America is 'the land of Joseph,' given to them by promise."[1]

Such words used by the Mormon mission to Europe and spoken to prospective emigrants to America expressed as a religious vision the fact that America's future would be built up by a multitude of emigrant nations. This vision also united this "multitude" with the Biblical past of the new continent revealed by the eye of a seer in the multitude of the Indian tribes in America, all of "Israelitish origin," just as in the "Book of Mormon." At the same time it transformed the Anglo-Israelism so well known to the European peoples and claimed it for America by the identification of the Indians with the "lost tribes."

Now that Mormonism has lived long enough in America to allow for historical perspective this step, connecting the Biblical past with America, is seen to be the decisive factor which the established religions had nothing to equal or oppose. For instance one of the apostles of the Mormon church declared in the dark times of the early persecutions of practicing polygamists:

"We think that our revelation treats of matters if possible more important to human nature than the Old Testament. It solves the problem of the past history of America. It has the only new gospel and indigenous prophet and seer on this hemisphere. It has grown more rapidly than the Jewish power, and if it were not for our notion on the subject of marriage, I believe we would have more converts in the United States than any other sect."[2]

Such proud words remained good Mormon opinion even at a much later time after the persecutions had shaken the core of church believers much more strongly. The Mormon found his consolation in the uniqueness of his values compared to everything ecclesiastical Christianity had offered up to his time and in the confidence that no other religion was likely to take over America:

"You have nothing to offer the American people, while we represent its historic connection with the only living past, the Bible story, by proving it is the Bible people, physically surviving through the ten lost tribes."[3] The renewed Bible-story remained his greatest treasure, "pro foro interno" as well as his stock-in-trade in missionary activity.

The convincing power and full validity of the new Bible-story of the descendants of the "Lost Tribes" in America is immediately followed up by its dynamics. The biblical and post-biblical migrations revealed in the "Book of Mormon" are given from the beginning in a broad parallelism to the unique Westward-Movement of the American population over the new continent. Even before the persecutions had forced the Mormons into their long trek into the Intermountain Basin the prophet's effort to transfer the seat of the new church to the West was compared with a Biblical image —"leaving New York as Moses left Egypt—wandering over the wild prairies of the West, as the great lawgiver wandered over the wilderness of Zion—."[3] The "Book of Mormon" linked its conviction of the greatness and destiny of America to the wanderings of its chosen pioneers over the infinite vastnesses of the West, and intended its new post-Biblical genealogical table of peoples as a background suited to the wandering of these newly revealed peoples. This in itself enables us today to read it as a frontier tale filled with the political convictions of the pioneers of its time as indicated by modern scholarship.[4] But this merely touches upon the proper dynamics of the new religion. The basic feeling that all these wanderings came about and will be undertaken in the future by religious destiny gained substance in the firm conviction that only religious colonization and its concomitant wanderings could settle the broad expanse of America. This is even more important because at that time there was an opportunity to observe various socialistic secular settlement-experiments in America based on principles imported from Europe. Their failure gave the concept of religious colonization as realized by the Mormons its shining crown. The following harangue of secular Socialism is characteristic and undoubtedly remained pertinent:

"Mormonism and Socialism. Poor, timid, cautious Socialist! You were too much alarmed at your spectral illusions! You should have sought the apostle of Latter Day *Saints*, Orson Pratt, and by his miraculous gifts he would have inspired you with sufficient *courage* to declare your real belief in God's material existence! But there, it could not be! Your 'rational system' was the result of mere induction, but here is one of *revelation*! Your Robert Owen possessed not the claims of Joseph Smith! He laboured with his mind—Joseph Smith had it made *ready* to *hand*! Robert Owen could not produce by *reason* what Orson Pratt knows by revelation. Ah, poor, poor Socialist! You could arrive at *doubt*; but the Mormon arrives at *certainty*! He is your superior! At his shrine you must burn your incense!"[5]

In any case at the midst of the 19th century the complete failure of the rationalistic-communistic settlements in America was recognized by progressive minds. In contrast to this, the religious colonization of the Mormons was acknowledged as a convincing success.[6] This achievement was even more highly regarded because of the special circumstances under which it was accomplished, in spite of the lures of the near-by gold land, California: "a Kingdom of Saints settles itself in nearest contiguity to what would seem to be exclusive territory of Mammon."[6] Jewish community leaders of America who later saw Utah were just as much impressed by the religious power of Mormon colonization.

Much earlier, before the Utah period, even those enemies who spoke most sharply about the "Mormon delusion" had to give expression to their great astonishment at the power of Mormonism to colonize. They expressed it in sad warnings to those who, in view of the power of faith to bring people to new settlement areas, could nevertheless believe that they could easily get rid of this new religion. The following words are reported as the sayings of Bishop Chase of Illinois:

22

"You smile at the insignificance of the influence of the Mormon prophet and the disciples of Mormonism. You feel here as it might be brushed away like dust with a feather, but I tell you that 30,000 of these deluded people now with their preachers roam round and over Illinois, and deceive, and continue to deceive, thousands more; that our lands must often be ploughed by Mormons."[7]

However, the very success of this religious colonization soon produced the "Biblical" argument of the adversaries of the Mormons. They compared this success with the occupation of Canaan by the Israelites, thus imputing to the Mormons hostility against the rest of the population from the very beginning.[8]

In this manner, a way was opened for opposing opinions to solidify and to forge the historical fate of the Mormons by evaluating the new phenomenon in a serious vein. Friend and foe as well as some impartial people stressed the fact that Mormonism was an American tree which could have grown only on the soil of the new continent. European travel books about America had already failed to point this out. The first enlightenments about the American character of Mormonism were still filled with the intellectual contempt with which American phenomena were generally treated in European literature:

"The fact is that there could scarcely be a more likely place in the whole world than America for getting afloat a scheme like Mormonism... There are a class of persons in America that are rather fond of inventing things and these matters have long passed among us as "Yankee jokes"—their invention of tales is now as notorious as the wit of the Irish. Besides, America being a new country, greatly favored such a thing. The invention, therefore, is not so much a wonder, taking this view of the matter, for many things which Mormonism pretends to reveal (as the origin of the Indians), are matters of speculation with respect to America. . . ."[9]

In contrast to this the situation was already pragmatically evaluated at this time by impartial American thinkers:

"It was urged by Smith himself that the New World was as deserving of a direct revelation as the Old; and his disciples press upon their hearers that, as an American *revelation*, this system has peculiar claims upon their regard and acceptance. The feeling of nationality being thus connected with the new sect, weak-minded native-born Americans might be swayed by patriotic motives in connecting themselves with it."[10]

Altogether the Mormons became more and more firmly convinced that their new religion was the natural expression and ultimate meaning of America. This conviction was repeatedly expressed as for instance in a statement as late as in 1877:

"That America should bring forth a peculiar people, like the Mormons, is as natural as that a mother should bear children in the semblance of the father who begat them. Monstrous, indeed, would it be if, as offspring of the patriarchs and mothers of this nation America brought forth naught but godless politicians."[11]

CHAPTER 4

Indian-Israel in Mormonism

Mormonism's identification of the Indians with the lost tribes of Israel became a link with the world of the Bible on American soil. But this function was not easily effected in Mormonism although it may seem that it simply marked the close of a discussion, based purely on the centuries old concept of faith as revealed history. A complex of other facts was a necessary precondition to accomplish this end. Some of the facts had been recognized by the founders of the new religion and some had to be created as religious facts by a purposeful act of religious will through expedient revelation.

Speculation about the fate of the lost tribes of Israel which, according to old Jewish tradition, were still in existence had for many centuries been almost exclusively a concern of Jewish literature. This phase ended at the beginning of the seventeenth century when the lost tribes were identified with the Indians. Speculation was then transferred nearly exclusively to the Christian world and discussion of the truth of this theory flowered into a vast literature. At the same time, belief in the continued existence of the lost tribes and their identification entered a legendary literary phase in Jewish popular consciousness.[1] The situation was in no way changed by an occasional eccentric like Mordecai M. Noah who was impelled by contemporary discussions in the Christian world to speculations of his own. He was inclined to accept the descent of the Indians "in all probability" from the lost tribes in accordance with current ethnological views.[2] Most of Noah's Jewish contemporaries who witnessed the founding of Mormonism regarded all discussions concerning the Jewish aspect of Indian descent as mere journalism. Such items served to satisfy the curiosity of the average reader who, though occupied with entirely different interests, also wished to learn something about the curiosities of the New World. The history of the Indians was no more important to the average reader of Jewish newspapers, especially in Europe, than any of the current Indian tales making the rounds. In any case this theme was usually treated as a "space filler" in newspapers and yearbooks.[3] The Jew who was fully aware of his past could not take such theories seriously. The American Jew had the same reaction to the various versions of Mormon creed having to do with individual Hebrew tribes—Ephraim, Joseph, Benjamin—with which he was later confronted.

Among the early American Christian theories about this matter, Samuel Sewall's was outstanding. He regarded the Indians as Jacob's posterity and located the New Jerusalem of the future somewhere in Mexico.[4] At a later stage, the emphasis was upon ethnological signs: "The opinion that many of the Samaritan Israelites had settled here [in America] is not to be discarded. The mores of the Americans, their habits and many ritual acts are proofs up to this date of their Jewish origin."[5] In the nineteenth century a survey of all these American Christian speculations was already available:

"For the solution of this ethnological problem in connection with this people Professor de Vere cites some authorities tending to prove that the American Indians were of Jewish origin. William Penn adopted that view and James Adair, an Englishman of learning and enterprise, himself well acquainted with Hebrew, after living thirty years among the Chickasaws, where he had frequent intercourse with the Cherokees, the Choctaws, and the Muscogees, was firmly convinced that the Red men of the South at least were descendants of one of the lost tribes of Israel."[6]

At one time, when an "antique" Hebrew inscription was found in Ohio, American Jewry's experts in Hebrew were actually confronted with this research.[7]

It may appear strange that an originally old Jewish literary tradition could be divested so entirely of its relationship to Jewish reality. However, this is not the only case in Jewish history in which popular concepts lost their value for the Jewish people at the very moment they were taken over by the Christian world.

Mordecai M. Noah, whose concept of a sovereign Jewish State

26

of Ararat was gloriously attractive to the European Jews, longing for emigration, was regarded as eccentric by his fellow-Jews in America. His opponents relied upon derision rather than serious arguments which did not seem to pay in his case. Furthermore his statement that "measures will be adapted to make them [Indians] sensible of their condition and finally re-unite them with their brethren, the chosen people,"[8] affirming the concept of a special Jewish mission to the Indians, was anathema to the American Jews. Although historians may now regard this as a superficial imitation of the contemporary Evangelical mission to the Indians, it was no more aware of the potentialities of the Indian descendancy-theory than was the Evangelical mission. It remained for the Mormons to develop this aspect.

Still there are some isolated cases in which this theory was accepted by Jews. Significantly such individuals seem to have spent their lives isolated from fellow-Jews, as, for instance, Abraham Mordecai, a Jew of Dudleyville, Tallapousa County.[9] Furthermore, they had no influence on the organized Jewish community in America.

In contrast to this, the concept that the descent of the Indians from the lost tribes was a proven fact, became increasingly popular in the American-Christian community. Such consciousness resulted firstly in a sharp separation between American and European thought. In Europe the Anglo-Israel theory had blossomed during the 19th century. It developed the principle that a people living according to the precepts of the Bible may trace its origin to the old Bible folk. In America, however, Biblical origins were brought into relationship to the Indians who would only now be accepting Christianity with its Biblical orientation. Such a discrepancy could be eliminated only by means of the idea and activity of the mission to the Indians. Hand in hand with these needs a working hypothesis of the evangelical mission to the Jews was developed which held that the Indian had only to be shown his descent from the Jews to move him to accept Puritan Christianity which represented life under the Biblical covenant. Such a scheme was better in theory than in practice. In real life, it exploded like a soap bubble as witnessed by the rather eloquent creations of contemporary popular American humor. Thus the fact that the theory

27

of the descent of the Indians from the Jews of old was already rooted in Puritan thought does not in itself explain the spiritual situation of Mormonism.

In contrast to these conversionist illusions, Mormonism created in its Indian-Israelism a new dynamics, setting itself an entirely new goal, the creation of Zion in America. It declared its mission to the Indians to be a constitutive part of this goal and the Indians themselves as the basic mass of the new American Israel. Thus, the previous type of conversionist activity among the Indians receded into the background insofar as the Mormons were concerned. The number of Indian converts was of small importance in view of the Indian-Israel kinship which linked Biblical genealogical tables to an American Zion, and at the same time forged an unbreakable chain between the peoples of America and Biblical life and landscape. The urge to give all these new peoples their own ancient history, to achieve a complete spiritual self-identity for the American continent was diametrically opposed to the erudite literature concerning the descent of the Indians from the lost tribes. Learned speculation about how these old Israelites had come to America—essentially speculation in historical geography—was confronted by revelation. Of course expedient revelation[10] did not exclude the historical geographical notions then current. These theories, particularly those dealing with routes to America, were woven into such purposeful revelations. Together with the original speculations about the existence of the lost tribes the mystical element dealing with their concentration in a specific place was fostered. Further proofs of all these notions concerning the Jews were later added as they developed from the specific historical fate of the Mormons. The following is a classical example of how these notions and currents were combined.

"We have before stated that the Latter-Day Saints believe that the Ten Tribes still exist, and that their home is the Far North. That they still exist is absolutely necessary to fulfill the unfailing promises of Jehovah to Israel, and to all mankind. The presence of the remnants of Judah, in every land today, is an uncontrovertible testimony that the covenant made with Abraham has not been abrogated or annulled. The vitality of the Jewish race is proverbial, and can we reasonably expect that when one branch of a tree shows such native strength, the other branches will not be

28

proportionally vital? Is it not more consistent to believe that, as the Jewish race under the curse of the Almighty and suffering centuries of persecution, still survives, so is it, with the rest of Jacob's seed, rather than that they, ages ago, were blotted out of national existence?"[11]

This is indeed a remarkable reversal of the Pauline image of Judaism as the dried up branch, which must be cut down so that the new branch of Christianity could grow better. It is particularly noteworthy, since it was stated two thousand years later, by a Christian offspring of the old Judaic tree which was being used for further grafting!

The above declaration that Indian-Israelism was an absolute prerequisite for Mormonism deserves special consideration. It must be indicated at this point that not one of the heresies which led to the founding of separate Mormon churches ever denied this concept. This, like other views on Biblical and Jewish matters, remained a point of agreement despite all the differences among Mormon communities.

The following statement by a Mormon community split from the main church indicates that revealed history is so indestructible that even greater stress is placed upon universal confirmation of this revelation:

"In fact it has now become a settled point by all efficient antiquarians and American historians, who have written at length on the habits, language, customs, maxims, manners and religious character of the Indians of America, that they are truly descendants of old Israel, and that it is a matter of impossibility that their peculiarities in so many respects of *manners, language* and *religious ceremonies* should be so consonant with the *manners, language* and *religious ceremonies* of old Israel by mere accident."[12]

However, in order for Indian Israelism to become a dynamic basis for purposeful revelation, the descendency-theory first had to have penetrated deeply into American popular consciousness. Only then could this theory be absorbed by the basic religious feeling of the American population. Mormonism's historic decision was successful because it rightly assessed the given situation and announced its revelation at the proper moment.

That this was so was clearly indicated by the literary creations of American humor which reflected popular thought better than

29

learned treatises. The intense concern with this theme indicated that interest in it was widespread. Indeed, the subject was not purely literary even if occasionally literati adhering to the Indian descendancy theory were laughed at. Such ridicule was to be expected since the theme was a general one and the literati served only as scapegoats.

Popular humor treated this subject on various levels, from simple derision to the elaborate presentation of complete satirical scenes. In one case the first families of Virginia were laughed at because they had become related to the Jews by Indian blood.[13] Another time the typical humorous figure of the Irishman was enriched by this new feat:

"O'Flaherty—if it is as yez say that the Oirish bees wan av th' Troibes av Ishrael that left the other troibes an' settled in Oireland, how comes it that yez noses be so large while the Oirish have hardly any noses at all, at all?

"Hockenheimer—Dos vas soon egshplained. Ven your dribe left our dribes dey cut off dere noses to spite dere faces."[14]

Sometimes the humor dealt directly with details of the Indian descendancy discussion of the time. For instance, the following discusses how the Indians might have reached the New World:

"But taken for granted that the Indians really are the remnants of those mislaid Israelites, the difficulty next arises as to how the dickens they got here, for when the Israelites were first missed there was as yet no railway communication between this country and Asia, and unless they tunneled their way up through, via China, it is difficult to account for their presence here."[15]

The ethnological elements of comparison between Indians and Jews dealt with in contemporary discussions were also the subject of derision. Even the writers of travel books brought home an echo of this humor: "Especially reminiscent of the Jews is also the eloquence . . . of the Indians. . . ."[16] This influence is even more evident when the actual use of this eloquence is described: "It also entered my mind that those scholars who are firm in their belief in the descent of the Indians from the Jews, certainly have never compared an Indian scene with a Jewish scene on the market in bargaining."[17] Another refutation of the comparison is supplied by a more anecdotal description: "This theory was exploded in a laughing way when a Jew remarked that if they were members of his race, they never would have let Manhattan island slip through their fingers for a paltry twenty-four dollars."[18]

Nor did literature overlook the deeper meaning of this satire involving the Indian in the historical fate of the Jewish people, without his consent. No less a writer than James Fenimore Cooper, the master of all Indian stories, whose descriptions of Indian life captivated Europe and its adolescents, gives us a deep insight into the spiritual attitude of the Red Man to the descendancy-argument of the missionary propagandizing him:

"I know little about them, Parson Amen; not being certain of ever having seen a Jew in my life. Still, I will own that I have a sort of grudge against them, though I can hardly tell you why. Of one thing I feel certain—no man breathing should ever persuade me into the notion that I'm a Jew, lost or found, ten tribes or twenty. What say you, corporal, to this idea:

"Just, as you say, Bourdon. Jews, Turks and Infidels, I despise: so was I brought up, and so I shall remain."[19]

And, at another place an outburst of true feelings against the real enemy states: "If any are lost, it is the Yankees. The Yankees are Jews, they are lost."[20] Only a deeply depressed creature could hold such a belief and he would consequently stand out as a black sheep among the Indians:

"Some thought that he believed himself lost, and a Jew, and not an Injin."[21]

Another description tells how the missionary developed the basis of his conversionist effort vis-à-vis the Indian:

". . . many Christians see the great truth which makes the Indians of America and the Jews beyond the great salt lake one and the same people."[22] But the Indian catches only one thing in the story: "Why did not the Son of the Great Spirit kill the Jews? Why did he let the Jews kill him? Will my brother say?"[23] And with this he arrived at the root of the historical problem.

We find variations of this Indian dialogue in other places. Some of them depict the mental struggle of the Red Man when faced with the crucifixion story:

"Indian—Was it the Indians who killed Him?

"Preacher—No, it was the Jews.

"Indian—Are the Jews Boston-men?

"Preacher—Yes, the Jews are Boston men.

"Indian—Did it happen in our country?

"Preacher—No, it happened away beyond the *salt creek* (ocean).

"Indian—Well, then, Mr. P., I hope you are not trying to drag us Indians into *that difficulty*."[24]

Such real or imagined difficulties of the Red Man in accepting the Jewish origins imputed to him was actually the headache of the evangelical Indian mission, which derived no direct advantage from this theory. It was essentially different with the Mormons who had devised Indian Israelism as an instrument for converting the Bible-believing white population to Mormonism. The rich fruits of this revelation had been furnished with mystical elements even before their own mission to the Indians had begun. The success of the Mormons' Indian-Israelism later proved to be entirely independent of the Mormon mission to the Indians. On the contrary, if we later hear reports of individual Christian Indians who believed in their descent from the lost tribes, it indicated that they had acquired the idea only after whole Indian tribes had already become Christian.

Chapter 5

"Mormon Bible"

At the root of the Biblicism of European emigrant nations lay the conviction that religion had first begun with the Bible and was unthinkable without it. Founding a new religion without a new Bible would therefore have appeared a hopeless task. Thus, in accordance with this basic condition of the New World, Mormonism had to create a "Bible" of its own, a "Mormon Bible," in order to address a new revelation to the American people. The difficulty lay only in the fact that mankind already had the Bible and a new Bible would have to meet great obstacles. A religious historian has already shown that the "Book of Mormon" itself envisaged the resistance against a new Bible as a consequence of the argument that the Bible had already been given to mankind.[1]

The new religious establishment overcame these difficulties by accepting the Bible and supplying it with interpretations to fit the special events to be revealed as an addition to the Bible by the "Book of Mormon." Then the new Bible could no more exist without the old than the old could achieve its full meaning for the new continent without the new. The basic formula thus created has remained unchangeable: "the Bible and Book of Mormon are both to be taken together."[2]

So the one has to support the other and for this purpose the "Book of Mormon" has been given to the Gentiles "and also to the Jews, proving to them that the holy scriptures are true."[3]

This mutual interdependence is further elaborated in relationship to its various parts:

"The Book of Mormon, however, declares that the Bible is true and it proves it; and the two prove each other true. The Old and the New Testaments are the stick of Judah. You recollect that the tribe of Judah tarried in Jerusalem and the Lord blessed Judah, and the result was the writings of the Old and New Testaments. But where is the stick of Joseph? Can you tell where it is? Yes. It was the children of Joseph who came across the waters to this continent, and this land was filled with people, and the Book of Mormon or the stick of Joseph contains these writings and they are in the hands of Ephraim."[4]

A further elaboration of the tenet that the two stand together is clarified by stressing the similarity in the way in which both were given as an invisible gift of Heaven: "Moses . . . never showed those stone tables any more than Joseph Smith showed the golden plates. . . . Our people out here believe equally in the tale of Moses and in that of Joseph."[5]

The outside world immediately grasped this Mormon claim and the expression "Mormon Bible" soon became current replacing the older "Golden Bible." The word was applied to the "Book of Mormon" exclusively although other inspired writings by the founder of the religion appeared later and were also considered holy by his adherents.[6]

The basic relationship of the "Book of Mormon" to the Bible was already revealed by the statement that the "plates of brass" containing the first historical record of an old people revealed by the "Book of Mormon" also contained the five Books of Moses.[7]

The Mormons acknowledged the notion prevailing among those people who had experienced European Biblicism, i.e., that the Jews had been destined by Providence to bring the Bible into the world. It is said that in Bible times the Book had to come "out of the mouth of the Jew" and that at that time "the things which were written were plain and pure."[8]

That these requisites were not fulfilled by the "Book of Mormon" was pointed out by the literary opponents of the new religion. However, literary criticism of the "Mormon Bible" points out that this book was not read by the faithful Mormons as the Bible was read by other people, and was indeed less known to them than other holy writings of Mormonism. The fact that it was certainly not studied thoroughly was revealed in the following statement by an ex-Mormon:

"Mr. Stenhouse, who was for many years one of their leading men, and probably the most intelligent man that they ever had among them, once told me that he never read 'The Book of Mormon' through in his life and that he did not believe anybody else ever did."[9] The same conclusion was reached by a critic in his analysis of the literary creations of the Mormons:

"In the published discourses, and in the Catechism of the sect, the word Mormon very rarely occurs. Indeed, the appeal is to the Jewish and Christian Scriptures rather than to the new revelation, and the sacred plates dug up from the hill Cumora are quite subordinate to the tables of stone which Moses received on Sinai: The word brought to light by the angel Moroni is almost as unknown to the faithful in Deseret as the Sybilline oracles were to the citizens of Rome. It is joined to their history, rather than to their faith."[10]

There was truth in this analysis that the "Book of Mormon" was not as closely related to Mormon life as was the Bible. Indeed, they derived examples and maxims for daily behavior from the Bible rather than from the "Book of Mormon." Also, the Mormons saw their historical fate in Biblical terms and the "Book of Mormon" added nothing to the image of the contemporary Jew as seen by the Mormons. Nevertheless it remained the "Mormon Bible" for the contemporary world at large as well as among America's various immigrant peoples because it was only under the mantle of the Bible that simple people could be made to understand what had taken place in America.[11] European discussion of the new American religion also referred to the "Book of Mormon" in this manner.

Even more significant is the fact that the "Book of Mormon" has never been compared with the holy book of any other religion, not even with the Koran, although such a comparison could have yielded a point in respect to polygamy. There were some rudimentary parallels between Mormonism and Islam but the only actual comparison was exclusively linguistic. The "Book of Mormon" was defended against the accusation of stylistic inferiority by comparing it to the Koran.[12] Mormon life was never regarded as closely related to any other great religious book.

The Bible as the "good book" has always been identified with truth. By contrast the expression "true as the Book of Mormon" indicated untruthfulness whether projected seriously or jokingly.[13]

The expression, especially in a jocular vein, was widespread, often in the form of an oath on the "Mormon Bible." People who used the expression intended to criticize those who dared to set an untruthful book against the "true Book." Contemporary evaluations of the relationship between the "Book of Mormon" and ancient Jewish literature produced expectedly critical sentiments:

"[It] . . . consists of a series of professedly historical books—a desultory and feeble imitation of the Jewish chronicles and prophetical books—in which, for the poetry and warnings of the ancient prophets, are substituted a succession of unconnected rhapsodies and repetitions, such as might form the perorations of ranting addresses by a field preacher to a very ignorant audience."[14] In time such literary evaluations were related to stereotypes of the contemporary Jew in America in the manner of the Jew-Yankee comparison.[15] Significantly this approach found expression in the German press of America:

"Also to this day no German has been found insolent enough to translate this scribbling, although curiosity might bring him a sufficient sale. . . . In addition, it is noteworthy that much is prophecied of American liberty and nearly all of Isaiah is quoted. His words were interpreted as well as possible as relating to this American branch of Jews. To show the follies and improbabilities of the fable would be doing too much honor to this book because to people in their right mind the genuineness of the Book is out of the question. The only plausible aspect of this history of the early population of America is that up to this day the Americans are the greatest *Jews* of the world."[16]

The above remarks are significant in that here already the accepted connection with the contemporary Jew was singled out before discussing any of the other points with which Jews were later troubled in their relationship to the Mormon creed. (Polygamy appears to be still forbidden in the "Book of Mormon.")

In deriding the Mormons, the phrase "rich as a Jew" found a corresponding echo there: "Mammon and Mormon are alike in sound, and their principles and creeds are not, it is presumed, dissimilar."[17] In further applying this theme to the Book of Mormon the Biblical comparison reached a new dimension:

"The gold plates, it is said, no longer exist; their loss seems to be irreparable. Could they be seen and examined by the world, and their contents again be deciphered, we have no doubt they would attract the attention of many thither, if for no other purpose than to see religion and gold so admirably blended. The law delivered to Moses was written on tables of stone—how much more valuable must that be written on plates of gold!"[18]

But, in time, other voices rose, in contrast to this contempt. Significantly a voice in the same German newspaper quoted above had already printed an article containing an entirely different literary evaluation of the "Book of Mormon":

"To put up a well supported theory that the original inhabitants of the American continent were descendants of Israel without revealing any weak spot by any assertion or description possibly proven false, shows a degree of talent and gift of penetration which appears a miracle in itself for an uneducated youth."[19] And, more distant in time, admiration is spoken out in general terms for the achievements of the Book:

"Whatever may be the truth in respect to the real origin and authorship of the book of Mormon, there can be no doubt of its wonderful adaptedness to the purposes to which it has been applied. We cannot agree with those who would deny the work either genius or talent."[20]

This suitability, it is stated, is clearly related to the concept of Indian Israel:

"Instead of presenting a new dispensation growing out of an old ecclesiastical history to which it assumes to impart a new life, it has actually created a past history of its own, which, though severed from the main currents of our common traditional Christianity, connects it back, through passages never before suspected or explored, with the early Jewish revelation."[21]

It was precisely this decision which had to be made in the American situation: Transplanting of European religion through a new branch or entirely new revealed religion on new soil. And the result held no doubt for these contemporary critics:

". . . for the first time since the days of Mohammed . . . distinctly a new religion. It claims a new revelation, and a new prophet. It has a new law, a new spiritual polity, and a new mission."[22] The spiritual basis of this entire religious creation was the privilege of new prophecy as posited in the Book of Mormon with the rise of a new nation on a new continent. Contemporaries paid little attention to this kind of argumentation. In this case the "Book of Mormon" spoke for itself summarizing all the essential elements of the new prophetism: It defied those who denied the possibility of a new Bible because the old one was already in existence. In this regard it was demonstrated that the ancient people received their Bible only through the Jews and that it was impossible that the Jews should remain forever the only people of God receiving revelation. Furthermore a new nation on a new continent had been created just because the old revelation had not yet been terminated. This new nation could prove its nearness to God by receiving a new revelation. Therefore the Old Bible could not contain all the words of God. As the intercourse between God and mankind was renewed by a new prophet, a new Bible would surely originate by inner force:

"Thou fool, that shall say, A bible, we have got a bible and we need no more bible.

"Have ye obtained a bible, save it were by the Jews?

"Know yet not that there are more nations than one....

"Wherefore, because that ye have a bible, ye need not suppose that it contains all my words; neither need ye suppose that I have not caused more to be written."[23]

In the purposeful obscurity of these words there is room for everything, the personal demand of the prophet and the mystical interpretation of the text by his adherents. The definite meaning of the words, though not clearly expressed, states again that only America could be considered for receiving the new revelation and bringing the new Bible into the world.

But one thing is clear in all Mormon declarations about the new revelation: that it came about entirely in the Spirit of the old Prophets:

"Now behold this is the Spirit of revelation—behold this is the Spirit by which Moses brought the children of Israel through the Red Sea on dry ground."[24]

The period of the growth of Mormonism in America was also characterized by the importation of rationalistic thought which was already firmly established among the Germans. Thus Mormonism

38

was under fire from two directions—the established religions and rationalism. It is for the latter reason that we find so much anti-Mormon material in the German-American press. But both the Christian Bible believers and the radical adherents of enlightenment did not discuss the essence of the claim to new revelation, the nature of revelation itself. A question of this kind could be raised in the human soul only if the revelation of the Bible as the true word of God could be separated from all the rationalistic elements used by those critics who found the "Book of Mormon" so distasteful. Otherwise these same rationalistic criticisms would have to apply to the Bible too.

The very fact that the discussion of this basic problem took place in connection with the Book of Mormon was deeply significant in strengthening Judaism among American Jews.

"Moses and Joseph Smith. A correct rendering of the first verse of Leviticus is this:

"And he called to Moses, and the Lord spake to him from the tabernacle of the appointment for meeting, saying..."

The rationalists, when they trample this verse under their feet, are compelled to find themselves occupying this ground, or at least occupying ground very near to it, that Moses was an older brother of Joseph Smith, founder of Mormonism.

This Smith concealed himself in a room behind a curtain drawn across the room, and there he dictated the Mormon bible to his scribe on the other side of the curtain, which he professed to be translating from the golden plates which had recently been exhumed from a hill in New York. What he really possessed behind the curtain was a production of the pen of Solomon Spaulding, prepared about twenty years before, which was a sort of romance of ancient times among the Indians. But if Moses published the picture of his own enthusiastic imagination as direct revelations from the Lord, which they were not, he was likewise a deceiver. If Moses, by the power of his own intellect, constructed a Deity, and located his Deity in the holy room above the mercy-seat, and made this Deity such a machine that it would utter the words which Moses had previously given it to utter, who does not see that Moses and Smith were a noble pair of brothers? If Moses prepared the tabernacle in the name of God of Heaven, and gave it a false painting of holiness, and made the blood and lives of the two sons of his brother Aaron sacrifices to that false holiness, who does not see him in the light of a murderer? If Moses placed his own speaking machine in the holy room of the tabernacle and honored it with the name of God, and gave it his own words to utter, he dreadfully trampled on one of the most holy of the ten commandments, which is, that man should make no image of the Lord to worship it and receive its words as the utterance of God.

The first verse of the third book of Moses has an importance in religion to which our grandest conceptions fail to do justice. One view of it gives us the Bible as the true word of God; the other view gives us the Bible or the Pentateuch as the most wonderful web of false statements. . . ."[25]

Such thoughts of an awakening Judaism in America could only characterize the situation of a Jewish people contented with the Bible and viewing Sinai as the uniquely given opportunity for existence under the lasting covenant with God. But to the Christian denominations the situation looked quite different. Those who could not find the "fullness of the Gospel" in the writings holy to the Christians could only search for fulfillment, for additions through new revelation, new prophetism and writings "caused more to be written" by the Lord. From this there developed a branch of Mormonism concerned with this religion only insofar as believers sought revelation in it. But the changing form and content of Mormon revelation as gathered in the course of time should gain new meaning and importance during the course of this investigation insofar as the position of the Jew in Mormon creed and doctrine is concerned.

CHAPTER 6

Zion in America

The mission bestowed upon the American continent by the "Mormon Bible" was the creation of a center by means of a new religious establishment. From the beginning it was referred to as the founding of Zion. In the Book of Mormon the bliss of the new revelation was already dispensed to those who undertook this task:

"And blessed are they who shall seek to bring forth my Zion at that day."[1] The special revelations received by the Prophet Joseph Smith relating to the location of the new Zion and giving the orders to go there, were an early development. The frequent renewal of blessings for those who obeyed accompanied the various phases and stages of the new church.[2]

All the basic notions of this religious center had a common kernel: that it had to be in America because America was the only land fit for it. Furthermore it would not be established by mere radiation from the main site of a church, but only by the labor of the faithful who would come there with their wives, children and property. The development of Zion must become a "literal gathering" of the Saints of the Latter Days who took on this task. This concept of the gathering-in of believers was in accord with the basic idea of the new continent, i.e., that America would be built up only by moving into the new unsettled areas of land. The association became even stronger when prophetic revelation decreed that the "Far West" was the area for the in-gathering of the inner circle. American migration across the continent, the Westward movement, became the dynamic element of the new creed and of the way the faithful had to go to build Zion.

The name "Zion" was also used in the Westward movement of non-Mormon American pioneers. However, in these cases it merely referred to the religious community and its good life in the newly settled West:

"On the whole, our Zion seems to have an onward tendency in Oregon, notwithstanding the many opposing barriers the enemy raises in our way."[3] Or as it is stated in relationship to a new location: ". . . taking into prayerful consideration the entrest [sic] of Zion in relation to said location."[4] In most other cases it referred to the church organization as a whole as "our beloved Zion"[5] or in a particular region:

". . . as we very much need a few hundred dollars, to settle ourselves comfortably, educate our children and to aid in promoting all the interests of Zion on the Pacific Coast."[6]

The Zion of the Mormons represented an essentially different aspect. It was the religious concentration of native settlers and new immigrants in a region of new settlement brought about by the rebirth of the Bible people in America, and as a preparation for the millenium.

However, the function of the millenium as conceived by other religious groups receded entirely into the background in the face of the Mormon vision concerning America. It was a concrete announcement that Zion was located in America and, depending upon the specific situation of the Mormon community, it stated exactly where in America Zion was to be found.

But the faith in America was unchangeable: "Here then, in America, is the land conferred upon Jacob. . . ."[7] Or as formulated by Brigham Young: "This American continent will be Zion . . . this continent of America is the continent of Zion."[8]

This all-American enthusiasm and certainty continued throughout the years in the writings of the Mormons: "The West is the future world. . . . All America, then, is Zion!"[9]

In the last formulation of Mormon creed which the Prophet gave to contemporary America before he was murdered, he decreed:

"We believe in the literal gathering of Israel, and in the restoration of the Ten Tribes. That Zion will be built upon this continent."[10] After the death of the prophet, the church leaders preparing a new settlement-area for the faithful in the Inter-mountain Basin, issued a circular from winter quarters in Nebraska stating: "Should any ask, Where is Zion? tell them in America. . . ."[11]

42

The idea of expansion to the West, which inspired all America at that time, was closely woven into the instructions concerning how Zion was to be built up and in the prophecies about the expansion of the new realm of God: "therefore it is wisdom that the lands should be purchased by the saints; and also every tract lying westward, even unto the line running directly between Jew and Gentile."[12] (This line was the boundary between Indian Territory and settled land of the pioneers.)

Years later when it had already been decided where Zion was to be located in America, Brigham Young asserted in reference to Utah: "These valleys are the place of gathering for the Saints,"[13] and the designation "Mormon's Zion in the Great Salt valley"[14] became a recurrent phrase. Indeed the general feeling of the Mormons for the American West was strongly manifested not only in the main church but also in the smaller Mormon churches stemming from the split.

"The Saints of the Western continent will gather into the western part of the United States, beginning at the state of Missouri. . . ."[15]

As a beaten man always returns to the scene of his suffering, Mormon writings refer again and again to Missouri, the scene of their tragic expulsion. The Prophet goes so far as to promise the return of the Mormons to Jackson County, Missouri, and the restoration of Zion there, before the last triumphal scene of the millenium.

This Westward movement took a peculiar turn during the first years of the gold rush to California. It was only a short episode resulting from proper revelations within a group split from the main church. It declared California to be the promised land and ordered preparations for the emigration there:

"In the land of California shall my people find refuge from the evils and troubles that afflict the nations of the earth; there they shall have peace. . . ."[16] Other utterances such as: "that the land of Bashan represents the whole of California in the description given by Esdras, and that the river Bashan is the Rio Colorado, that empties in the Gulf of California"[17] attempt to preserve the same spiritual connection with the Biblical landscape which proved so helpful to the main church in Utah.

43

There are additional promises of this new Zion which depart in essence from the millenial concept of the main church: " . . . we have only to say that after the Saints are established in the land of California, the Lord says they shall keep the seventh day, but we have no liberty given us to neglect the observance of the first day, until we are permitted to keep the seventh."[18]

This return to the Sabbath of the Jews was characteristic of European Biblicism but this group had no chance to realize it in California. Nevertheless we do hear of public meetings[19] for this purpose and of an "Organization of the Emigrating Society."[20] Furthermore "the Saints who go to Bashan"[21] are in no case willing to take with them adherents of the Utah Church,[22] although some were willing to go to California. The trek there was seen as a "task of encountering the difficulties of pioneering the way to Zion in a new wilderness and mountainous country."[23] (The final meeting of Jew and Mormon in California came about in San Bernardino, a settlement of Utah Church adherents who did not view California as Zion.)

The road to building Zion, according to Mormon concepts, had been constructed by prophecy which joined together the basic elements of their eschatological ideas of the millenium with those which past experience led them to regard as inevitable. In this structure the contemporary Jewish people, for the first time, played a decisive role. The main theme here was the continuation of prophecy. In order for the prophecies of our time to come true the promises of the ancient prophets must be fulfilled. The most important of these promises had been the restoration of the Jewish people. Consequently "Zion" could not be built by the Saints without this restoration of the Jews to their old homeland, a prerequisite to "Zion" in America. These two elements together form the essence of Mormon millenial creed. However, it was first of all necessary for this belief to prove itself strong:

"The Latter Day Saints believe in prophecies before they take place. We have just as much confidence in returning to Jackson country and the building of a great central city that will remain there a thousand years before the earth passes away, as the Jews have in returning to Jerusalem and re-building the waste places of Palestine. In fact we have more faith than they have; for they have been so many generations cast out of their land that their

44

descendants have almost lost their faith in returning. But the Latter Day Saints are fresh, as it were."[24]

The interdependency of the two events was constantly stressed: "The conversion of the Gentile people is dependent in no inconsiderable degree upon the restoration of the Jews..."[25] The Gentiles would have to witness the fulfillment of the prophecy regarding the Jews after which the signs for the in-gathering of the Gentiles would become clear:

"The point being very clear that God's ancient covenant people, the Jews, must and will assuredly soon be gathered home, it remains only to show what is to become of the Gentiles, or what we have to do is the premises. For none will deny but that the fullness of the Gentiles is nearly come in..."[26] As a result of this basic Mormon idea, the Mormon position *vis-à-vis* attempts to convert Jews to Christianity differed entirely from the traditional attitude of other Christian denominations. According to this concept, Mormon church government could not be made authoritative for the Jew in the meantime. He had to insist on the promise of his return to his homeland Palestine and to institute his own government under the house of David there. He also had to think in terms of the renewal of the ancient priesthood which had been suspended during the exile and diaspora. No wonder therefore that the conversionist activities of the Mormons so conspicuously directed against various nations of the Gentiles appeared inconsequential in regard to the Jews. Due to the Spirit of Mormonism the conversion of individual Jews could not lead to the final end because the Jewish people had to be gathered in to Palestine. The recognition of Jesus by the Jews was not due before this. But the Jewish commonwealth in Palestine which was yet to be created later had to recognize the American Zion created by the Latter Day Saints as the future Kingdom of God. This Zion, representing the highest level of all promises given until our days, will also have to incorporate the promises already fulfilled until that time. Therefore it will also have to effect the union of the restored Palestine with Zion, the universal American community of peoples:

"This being the case, I know of no further promise for the Gentiles than the general invitation which is given in this last call, the gathering call of both Jews and Gentiles into one fold.

And all the remnant among us have to do is to prepare the way for the Jews' return, that we may in Abraham be blessed."[27]

The world will see the two processes actually as one:

"By and by the Jews will be gathered to the land of their fathers, and the ten tribes, who wandered into the north, will be gathered home and the blood of Ephraim, the second son of Joseph, who was sold into Egypt, which is to be found in every kingdom and nation under heaven, will be gathered from among the Gentiles, and the Gentiles who will receive and adhere to the principles of the gospel will be adopted and initiated into the family of Father Abraham. . . ."[28]

The duty of furthering the gathering of the Jews into Palestine was equated by the Mormon with the obligation to preach the gospel to them:

"It is obligatory upon us to see that the House of Israel have the gospel preached to them; to do all that is in our power to gather them to the land of their fathers, and to gather up the fulness of the Gentiles before the gospel can go with success to the Jews."[29]

Prayer for divine intervention in the gathering of the Jews into Palestine was expected to be successful because it came from the Mormons:

"But from what branch or part of the house of Israel will the Lord look for this petition or request to issue, if not from the Latter Day Saints, for we are out of the tribe of Joseph through the loins of Ephraim, who have been as a mixed cake among the Gentiles, and are the first fruits of the Kingdom, and the Lord has given unto us the kingdom and Priesthood and keys thereof. Hence the Lord will require us to ask for those blessings which are promised unto Israel, and to labour for their salvation."[30]

The task of bringing the Jews back to Palestine might, according to divine plan, supersede any other mission in importance:

"The word of the Lord will be—'O ye, my servants, I have a new commission for you. Instead of going forth to convert the Gentile nations, go unto the remnants of the house of Israel that was scattered in the four quarters of the earth. Go and proclaim to them . . . that the time has arrived for my people Israel . . . to gather unto their own homes again, and to build up old Jerusalem

46

on its former heap. And then will commence the gathering of the Jews to old Jerusalem.' "[31]

Not only is the concept of the return of the Jews an essential precondition for the Mormon millenium, but, according to Mormon creed, without it other things lose in value:

"I thank God that the day is at hand when the Jews will be restored. I have felt to pray for them; I feel interested in their behalf, for they are of the seed of Abraham and a branch of the house of Israel and the promises of God still remain with them. It is true they fell through unbelief, and the kingdom was taken from them and given to the Gentiles. . . . But they, like the Jews, have fallen through the same example of unbelief, and now, in the last days, the kingdom of God has to be taken from the Gentiles, and restored back to every branch and tribe of the house of Israel; and when it is restored to them, it must go back with all its gifts, and blessings, and Priesthood which it possessed when it was taken from them."[32]

Within the frame of this total complex of the destiny of all nations that of the Jews and the promise to them remained unique: ". . . we are a nation of Gentiles. We who have come here what are we? We are called from the Gentile nations. The promises are not made to us that are made to people who are the unmixed descendants of Israel."[33]

The Mormon's faith in a Zion in America should be of the same intensity as the Jews' belief in their return to Palestine: ". . . our eyes are fixed upon a land on the western boundaries of the State of Missouri and the boundaries of the State of Kansas. We expect to go there just as much as we expect the sun will rise and set. We have no other expectation. We expect to return there just as much as the Jews expect to return to old Jerusalem in the latter days. Perhaps you may inquire if we expect to return as a majority. Yes. Do we expect to return as a great people? Yes . . . "[34] The Mormon also had a place which corresponded to the old Jerusalem of the Jews: "Zion is built in Jackson County, and after the Temple is built upon that spot of ground where the cornerstone was laid in 1831. . . . "[35]

The position of the Jew in the Mormon millenium was the same for the minor Mormon churches as for the main church. How-

47

ever, the latter formulated the promise to the Jew as an article of faith: "And we further testify that the Jews among all nations are hereby commanded, in the name of the Messiah, to prepare to return to Palestine and to rebuild that city and temple unto the Lord"[36]

The two tasks, of building old Jerusalem as well as Zion in America, appear to be one work undertaken by the Mormons to bring on the millenium:

"A great, a glorious, and a mighty work is yet to be achieved in spreading the truth and kingdom among the gentiles—in restoring, organizing, instructing, and establishing the Jews—in gathering, instructing, relieving, civilizing, educating, and administering the salvation to the remnants of Israel on this continent—in building Jerusalem in Palestine, and the cities, states, temples of Zion in America; and in gathering the Gentiles into the same covenant and organization—instructing them in all things for the sanctification and preparation, that the whole Church of the Saints, both, Gentile, Jew, and Israel, may be prepared as a bride for the coming of the Lord."[37]

The eschatological aspect of this image envisioned a Jerusalem built up by the Jews, beleaguered by the occidental nations, defended by the Lord and emerging victorious. Ultimately it would be recognized by all western nations.[38] The prospective role of the conversion of the Jews to Jesus in this process, was not treated uniformly in Mormon literature. Sentences recommending the "ministry of the salvation of Zion . . . unto the Gentiles first, and then . . . unto the Jews"[39] were contradicted by utterances requiring the recognition of Jesus as the precondition to the fulfillment of the divine promise of the return of the Jews to Palestine.[40] In any case the belief in a "second coming of the Son of Man, as first observed among the Mormons[41] by the surrounding world, effected a link with the belief in the return of the Jews.[42] In the older Mormon writings the concept that the Jews' return did not depend on their conversion was predominant. In any event, the images depicting this return did not mention conversion. The main element in these descriptions was America as the scene of the return:

"The great day is hastening on when the whole house of Israel will be gathered home from their long dispersion, to Zion

48

and Jerusalem. The United States is a witness to the gathering at Mount Zion, if her population will look at things as they are; and the old world in the East may soon hear record, also, of the gathering at Jerusalem."[43]

The image of Palestine as the place where after all persecutions in their history the Jews would find refuge influenced the image of the American Zion as a refuge where the persecuted Saints would enjoy their longed-for freedom:

"Oh, may the day soon hasten on
When scatter'd Israel will go home,
And all the Saints they might be free,
And taste the sweets of liberty
In upper California...."[44]

And even the future of Zion in Utah was made uncertain by persecutions of the Saints:

"Zion's Future.
"... Oh Zion! Gentiles hate thee;
They fain would drive thee still."[45]

American Zion as a refuge from persecution was the first historical analogy between the fate of the Mormons and the Jews. The main scriptural analogy was based on Utah's geographic situation. Its landscape was able to fulfill the requirement that the new Zion must correspond to the letter of Isaiah's Biblical prophecy that Zion would be built on high mountains:

"Many of the children of Zion have fulfilled this exhortation of Isaiah; and I now say to the balance of her children, 'Get thee up into the High Mountain....'"[46]

In later discussion with secessionist Mormon churches established in other regions this argument was refuted by demonstrating that Salt Lake City is not located on mountains.[47]

Indeed, it was recalled much later that the prophet had originally sought an entirely different mountain region, his only directive being that these mountains must be situated in the West:

"Salt Lake City, August 20, 1869. The following extracts I have taken from Joseph Smith's Journal ... Tuesday, Feb. 20, 1844. I instructed the Twelve Apostles to send out a delegation and investigate the locations of California and Oregon, and hunt out a good location where we can remove to *after the Temple is completed* and where we can (like the Israelites) build a city in a day, and have a government of our own; get up into the mountains where the Devil cannot dug us out, and live in a healthy climate, where we can live as long as we have a mind to. . . . The foregoing extracts . . . set forth clearly the fact that he had an eye to the West. Yours respectfully, Joseph F. Smith."[48]

And indeed, the general concept of the West continued to be recognized as the main achievement of the religious colonization of the Mormons. This emphasis was even good enough for another religious community, Oneida, which had not settled in the Far West. We read in its paper:

"Mormonism . . . shows on a small scale the attractive power under which men with living faith in God unite to subjugate the wilderness; and brings the joys and comforts of a civilized life to thousands from the abject classes of Europe, who are induced to immigrate to this country under their inspiration."[49]

From the beginning of Mormonism there was also a non-territorial interpretation of Zion. It was reiterated after Joseph Smith's death in the General Epistle of the Church of December 1847: ". . . . if any asks, What is Zion? tell them the pure in heart."[50]

Thus, by substituting the Saints for the territory an opportunity was afforded for the word to maintain its religious significance in the Mormon religion after the influx into Utah had actually ended. The use of the word in designating Church undertakings such as the Zion Cooperative was followed by its use as a component of Utah business firm names. The same use was also made of the word *Deseret*, which also had a religious connotation originally (Book of Mormon). This usage, independent of its original territorial meaning,[51] parallels a similar use of the word Zion as a name component in many Jewish businesses in America.

However, it is clear that Zion was more than a concept or a convenient designation; it was the longed for home territory of the Latter Day Saints, the Center of Mormonism and the world.

CHAPTER 7

Self-Identification with Israel

The metaphor equating religious communities on American soil with Israel was a favorite way of characterizing people or situations for which the prototype was assumed to be in the Bible. Religious spirit was so full of Old Israelitish glory that the heart overflowed. These people felt that they were justified in designating other people as "true Israelites" just as they could recognize a woman as a "mother in Israel few of her sex have done more for a holy walk to live."[1]

New England theocracy placed the spiritual Puritan nation under the covenant of the same Bible as the Jew who stood under the covenant of Abraham with God. It thereby extended the comparison with Israel of old to the fundamentals of political life. However, it was Mormonism which endeavored to reach full identification of the new Saints in spirit with old Israel and to induce them to openly call themselves Israel. The biblical concept of a holy people, a nation of priests, had an irresistible influence upon the name chosen for the new spiritual nation on American soil. They called themselves Saints and were conscious of a unity based on their entirely new task on the new continent. This self-consciousness about being new, and the American freedom to undertake a new spiritual task, had transferred Israel's name to the new community. At the beginning the acceptance of this name did not imply any exclusiveness. Such exclusiveness was engendered by the united offensive front of all Christian denominations against the Mormons. To them, Mormonism appeared to be a kind of artificial extension of adolescence. It was painful to them to see that this American child, having grown into an impetuous adolescent, could not mature sufficiently to be a grownup. Finally when the corrective rod applied by history did not help and when, despite all persecutions, the Mormons refused to return to the fold of positive Christianity, even the parable of the lost son was forgotten. They could only warn others not to become entangled in the ways of evil. Meanwhile, the bad son driven out into the wilderness had created his own communal life, and had found an answer to this by developing his consciousness of a special kind of exclusiveness. Its classical formulation appeared in a sentence used as a motto for a social meeting in the "Social Hall" in Salt Lake City: "Israel should unite alone with Israel."[2] The religious concept of a new task for America had been transformed into a rule of social intercourse for the Mormons.

This final product of the religious laboratory America represented at that time gave added meaning to the process whereby the historical notion of old Israel developed among the Mormons, making of it a cornerstone of the concept of the American "Zion."

"Israel" was conceived as the totality of all nations, insofar as they accepted the new dispensation and were united in the new task of the in-gathering to America. However, the special promise received by the Jews was not forgotten. "Every sentiment and feeling should be to cleanse the earth from wickedness, to purify the people, sanctify the nations, gather the nations of Israel home, redeem and build up Zion, redeem Jerusalem and gather the Jews there, and establish the reign and kingdom of God on earth."[3] This process of leading mankind to its destination, the in-gathering of the millenium was referred to as the "literal gathering."

"We believe in the literal gathering of Israel, and in the restoration of the Ten Tribes."[4] Thus this universal process had a special significance only for the Jews because of the promise that they would be restored to Palestine. The idea that God rules over all nations of the earth by the word of his prophet and that this was the ultimate fate of the Mormons was expressed by Joseph Smith in this way:

"He stated . . . that God had appointed and ordained that he, with his descendants, should rule over all Israel, meaning the Latter Day Saints or Mormons, the Indian tribes and ultimately the Jews and Gentiles."[5]

But it is stressed strongly that the new "Israel" means a spiritual nation which must first be built on American soil. In this process of building the new nation the selective moment would prove itself decisive, but the elected must first prove that they are worthy of bearing the name "Israel": "As to our right to call the world Gentile, because we are Israel by blood, it is a more reasonable view than some, but it will take some help from God to prove that lineage for thousands of us yet; and if it is not proved for us, the limits of that house are undefined—the sun has not yet risen on the day that defines the extent of that literal race."[6]

But there were occasions when the entire Israel could be seen: "Israel had assembled to exercise a God given privilege, that of choosing . . . a Presidency of the High Priesthood. . . ."[7]

The polarity of the concept "Israel," past and present, was created by a religious analogy concerning America: "The United States is an anti-type of ancient Israel as well as a type of modern Israel when they shall be restored "to their fatherland according to the predictions of their prophets. When the Hebrews were first organized as a confederacy they were composed of thirteen tribes. . . . When the American confederacy was organized it consisted of thirteen original states."[8]

However, the adversaries of the Mormons did not seek a comparison far away in time and space regarding ancient and modern Israel. They sought it in the contemporary life of Jews and Mormons in Utah: "Modern and Ancient Israel. . . . Indeed, our Hebrew brethren are amongst our most substantial citizens. Independent of their own resources, which are by no means limited, they can claim (if they like) that they reside in a community where all the law makers and the chief landholders are of the 'blood of Israel' the same as themselves. They do not seem inclined, however, to boast anything on this head. We are afraid there is very little affinity between the ancient house and the 'modern Israel' inhabiting these valleys. And yet with all their differences there are two striking points of resemblance: both know where to put their hand upon a dollar; and neither seem in a violent hurry to get back to the promised land."[9]

The spiritual identification with ancient Israel gave rise to Mormon temples consecrated "to the name of the God of Israel."[10] The virtues of Mormon soldiers were evaluated according to the image of the host of Israel as was the case with the Mormon battalion

53

in the Mexican War: "Who shall say that the same God who sent terror into the camps of the enemies of ancient Israel did not have an eye over the little modern Israelitish force then crossing the great desert by his Divine command through the Prophet Brigham who had said, "There will be no fighting, except with wild beasts."[11] As the virtues of the combatants were evaluated in the image of old Israel, so were the spoils to be given to the Mormon conquerors according to the Biblical model, as stated on the occasion of the founding of the "Danites" (1838), the secret Mormon order pledged to follow the dictates of the Prophet: ". . . Know yet not brethren, that it soon will be your privileges to take your respective companies and go out on a scout on the borders of the settlements, and take to yourselves spoils of the goods of the ungodly Gentiles? For it is written, the riches of the Gentiles shall be consecrated to my people, the house of Israel."[12]

From this point of view "Gentile, Jew and Israel"[13] may exist side by side with Mormonism and hear its pronouncements. But, as in the Book of Mormon, where "Israelites" mean old Israel only in one case,[14] the pronouncement may be entirely reserved for the inspired new nation. For the action on the new continent this made no difference. The task "to fish out and hunt up Israel"[15] remained the main object of the search of the "Latter Days," during which the Saints would be found.

Nearly one hundred years later a hundredth church conference imprecisely stressed once again that Israel was not limited to the ancient Jewish people: "It has become common usage to associate the word Israel with the Jewish people only, which is a great error. While it is true that all Jewish people are Israelites, it is equally true that there are Israelitish people that are not Jews."[16]

It was said of the "Mormon women—religious empire founders, in faith and fact"[17] that with them there arose "An Israelitish type of woman in the age."[18]

Mormon exclusiveness was often regarded by their adversaries in terms of the religious clannishness of Israel in ancient times. Brigham Young defined it once as a matter of faith:

"As weak and frail as we are, the Latter-day Saints are my delight; their society is sweet to me; I crave no other; they are the only people I wish to see and associate with. Unless in the line of my duty, I do not wish ever to associate with any people who do not believe in the gospel of the Son of God."[19]

The Church paper once embodied this principle of exclusiveness in a story from the old Jewish lore:

"Sound Advice

". . . Gamaliel gave very good advice . . . which some 'doctor of the law' might with propriety and with good results give in these days . . .' Refrain from these men, and let them alone; for if this counsel or this work be of men, it will come to naught; but if it be of God, you cannot overthrow it." . . . Public men will find that "Mormonism" is of God; and they cannot overthrow it . . . best policy to pursue in regard to "Mormonism" is to let it alone."[20]

The happy life that this self-satisfied Mormon Society was already leading during the first decade of its mountain empire was reported by a trustworthy Jewish witness who stated frankly that he had never met people as happy as they.[21]

CHAPTER 8

The Gentiles, and the Jew as a Gentile

The Biblical division of the nations into those faithful to God and the surrounding heathen peoples, Jews and Gentiles, was completely taken over in Mormon literature. This is true of all their holy writings accepted as authoritative or inspired as well as of theological works, writings and talks by church leaders. In the actual application of these notions, first to nineteenth century America and then to the whole world, Biblical literary expression encountered the same obstacles to transplanting Biblical life to America as had other Mormon ideas. An additional difficulty was the shift in meaning which the word *Gentile* had undergone in the Christian world during the course of 2000 years. Also decisively important were the historic experiences of the Mormons on American soil. These helped forge their own unique notions of the "Gentiles" and forced them to a clear delineation of the Mormon world *vis-à-vis* the world of the "Gentiles." No wonder therefore that the one word *Gentile* contains so many connotations on various levels of semantic development. Even more confusion stemmed from the fact that the Biblical antinomy "Jew and Gentile" was frequently used in non-Mormon literary tradition in America with a meaning basically different from what it had been in ancient days.

Leo Spitzer[1] has already demonstrated the abyss, the split in the entire cultural unity of Judaism and primitive Christianity resulting from the changed meaning of the word "Gentile." Originally the antinomic pair of notions "Jew—Gentile" meant the faithful world opposed to the heathens. The order of the two words followed the dynamic process whereby the word of God should be brought by missi (apostles) to the heathen. However, in 19th-century America Gentile connoted something entirely dif-

56

ferent. Gentiles stood for the united Christian world now opposed only to the Jews. Non-Christian peoples, heathen or other non-Christians, were no longer referred to by the word "Gentile" and there is no antinomic pair of words for the notions implicit in this kind of contrast. Furthermore this word "Gentile" was used for the Indian, Negro or even the "heathen Chinese" only in the most exceptional cases.

"Jew and Gentile" as an expression was at first used in the Anglo-Saxon cultural milieu to achieve a higher unity. Haliburton, the provincial Tory, having become satirist on American soil, makes the phrase a humorous point of attack upon English conditions:

"So the little man, Lord Bunkum, when he opens Oxford to Jew and Gentile, and offers to make Rothschild Chancellor instead of Lord Derby."[2] In an example from the period of early migration to the Far West we find the phrase "bond and free," as current at the time as "Jew and Gentile," connected with the latter in a significant way. The agent in promising his services "will also extend that magnanimity to all classes of people, to Jew or Gentile, bond or free ... "[3]

In the same way the praise of the centenarian Moses Montefiore may be sung by "Jews and Gentiles in a hundred tongues"[4] in the ballad of an American poet, in full unity of the notions expressed by it. Even the American Jews finally adopted such use of the word for their own needs and they found nothing unseemly in it. In an appeal to the Polish Jews in America to take over preparatory work for the immigration of additional compatriots we find:

"If our Polish coreligionists will move in this matter, they will find ample sympathy and support among Jews and Gentiles of all denominations."[5]

Such adaptation for internal Jewish use had become psychologically possible because the "Gentile," the condensed Christian world, had become a collective noun of different Christian denominations. This collective noun still contained, it is true, the separation of the Jew from the Christian world as it existed in Europe. Nevertheless it was no longer regarded in the sense of a united front of the Christians against the Jews as in Europe.

Everywhere in America, the use of this word in the Christian, Mormon and finally also in the Jewish world depended on the matter under consideration. If the same or similar things were involved, the phrase "Jew and Gentile" was only an affirmation of this sameness in an appropriate literary figure of speech. If, on the other hand, a contrast was felt to be involved, the same phrase meant something entirely different. Such differentiations start with the mildest forms, if for instance the Jews may be called "Gentiles from Jerusalem."[6] They increase into sharper contrast according to the experiences of the moment or, as in the case of the Mormons, static facts in their environments.

We should now examine the racial theories which arose in Europe during the nineteenth century, especially the theories of superior races in regard to their influence upon the Mormon concept of the Gentiles. The answer is decidedly negative. These theories had not yet played any role in religious America.

"If an attempt be made to derive any light from a distinction between Jew and Gentile, and to show that the latter included the races who had been previously excluded, the argument is not advanced one step, for we know that many of the gentile nations were descended from the family of Noah. Indeed one irrefragable proof of the futility of the doctrine of separate races is that two of the supposed races, namely the Caucasian and Mongolian, inhabiting Europe and Asia, are distinctly traced through history to their Jewish origin."[7]

The new "Gentile" concept of the Mormons was thus not influenced by contemporary race theories. It actually emerged from those new American experiences which helped shape the basic common feeling of this newly formed religious society.

The pairing of Jew and Gentile by a mutual relationship already appeared in early holy Mormon writings after the "Book of Mormon" had decreed that it had been given to both of them. The new gospel must be given in the same way as in ancient times, that is to both:

"And now behold, there are others which are called to declare my gospel, both unto Gentile and unto Jew: Yea, even unto twelve."[8]

And in a later revelation the order in which the new faith

58

was to be brought to the world was instituted in the same way as before, when the apostle went from the Jews to the heathen, sparing the former for later endeavors:

"The twelve are a travelling, presiding high council . . . to build up the Church, and regulate all the affairs of the same, in all nations: first unto the Gentiles, and secondly unto the Jews."[9]

The same position was already taken in the prophecy of the church to be founded, as given in the Book of Mormon: "Wherefore, these things go forth from the Jews in purity to the Gentiles, according to the truth which is in God."[10] The Jews, already in possession of a promise, have time to deal with the new gospel. The first Jew who published a detailed description of Utah had this same impression. "The Gospel is first to be preached unto the Gentiles, secondly, to the Jews."[11] In the same way this order of coming events penetrated the consciousness of the Mormon people and found eloquent expression in the following hymn:

> "First to the Gentiles sound the news,
> Throughout Columbia's happy land;
> And then before it reach the Jews,
> Prepare on Europe's shore to stand
> . . . The nations catch the pleasing sound,
> And Jew and Gentile swell the strain;
> Hosanna o'er the earth resound;
> Messiah soon shall come to reign."[12]

To the ideas about the order of coming events were added others concerning the circumstances under which the world would near the millenium. Here the order was reversed, firstly the Gentiles will experience grave upheavals but at the same time the restoration of th Jews will take place:

" . . . the Lord according to his word has set his hand to recover the Jews, and as the Gentiles go down the Jews will rise and prosper, and return to their promised land of Palestine, and rebuild Jerusalem. . . . there are certain bounds set as a limitation to the times of the gentiles, and also for the Jews to remain in their states of unbelief, after which they will receive the gospel which will be in the time of the 'fullness of the gentiles.' "[13]

But such ups and downs in the fate of the two served to

59

strengthen the feeling that they belong to one another in their religious destiny. The basic belief that the new gospel was given to both was not changed by their later experiences. The Book of Mormon stands completely changeless as in the hymn:

> "And the book of Mormon, true,
> With its covenants ever new,
> For the Gentile and the Jew,
> He translated sacredly."[14]

And the mission of the apostles was directed to both: ". . . they were to go into all the world, to both Jew and Gentile, and preach . . ."[15]

Optimism concerning activities of the special messenger of the new Church to Palestine, Orson Hyde, was expressed in a commentary to his reports:

". . . we humbly trust that his labors will be a lasting blessing to Jew and Gentile . . ."[16]

Good literary use of the Jew-Gentile phrase without stressing the contrast in it was as common among the Mormons as in the rest of America. An example of it is to be found in the area of educational endeavors:

"Our people, in Sampete, are considerably anxious about schools . . . We would like young or middle-aged men of good character, not particular whether they are Jews or Gentiles, if they are morally upright men whose orthography and pronunciation are correct—yho can pass an examination in reading, writing, geography, arithmetic and grammar. . . .

Orson Hyde."[17]

The phrase was used by the Mormons along with other literary slogans then current in America: "All eyes—Jews and Gentiles, Saint and sinners, bond and free . . . are turned to the West . . . the Mormon War . . . remember the fate of Jerusalem. . . ."[18]

In contrast to this, however, there are many cases in which these two words clearly refer to two different groups and this difference, just as well known to Mormons as to the rest of America, was stressed.

"San Bernardino, Los Angeles County, Feb. 6th, 1852. . . . People have continued to arrive at this place up to this time, by

60

way of Salt Lake and the upper country, both Gentiles and Jews."[19]

Or in a more actual way expressed by Brigham Young in so practical a matter as in municipal elections:

"The Jews and Gentiles have of late brought some of their difficulties before the High Council in Salt Lake City for adjudication, in preference to going to the District Court; and the High Council, I believe, has invariably given satisfaction when such cases have been brought before it. This is a step in the right direction—to settle all matters without having recourse to law, which would do away with the necessity of employing lawyers, court fees, etc."[20]

Again Brigham Young bringing into even sharper relief the diversity of the two groups in the matter of their daily intercourse: "Shall we deal with Jews? Yes. With those who call themselves Gentiles? Certainly."[21]

There existed another phrase, ascribed to the Mormons as early as in 1842 *("Milking the Gentiles* is a kind of vernacular term to the Mormons . . .").[22] There is no report of a version of this phrase dealing with the Jews.

In non-Mormon America "Jew and Gentile" as a purely literary phrase, with or without broadening it by the use of other popular words, was used often and by preference. "Saints and scoundrels, Jews and Gentiles" figure as characters in a "modern Yankee fable" of 1856.[23]

In the matter of equal treatment of everyone with the Mormons: "No," said I, "if you can show me a breach of the law, Jew or Gentile will get the same deal the Mormons get."[24] Theodore Roosevelt gave the phrase its broadest application by connecting it with most modern terms in an utterance about the public schools: "Exactly as we welcome to them alike the children of Jew and Gentile, of Catholic and Protestant, so we insist that in their management no one creed shall have any special jurisdiction. . . ."[25]

The non-literary use of this word-pair was sometimes avoided by the non-Mormons when it might mean open conflict with the Mormon. In this case the phrase was circumscribed by the substitution of more categories as in the following example:

". . . we have not, and will not, interfere with that right [to

61

convene in masses] in any religious sect, whether Jewish, Pagan, Mormon or Christian. . . ."[26]

Jus as early, non-Mormon sentiment against the application of the term "Gentile" to all non-Mormons in Utah Territory developed: "The Mormons call everybody *gentiles,* except themselves. That is, they are separatical in the completest sense."[27]

And this could flare up in anger as when United States soldiers were denied admission to public places of entertainment in Salt Lake City: "When it comes to this that a man is debarred from a place of public entertainment . . . on the mere fact that he wears the uniform of his country's service, it is high time that loyal men, whether soldier, Jew, Gentile or Mormon, should resent the uncalled for insult. . . ."[28]

An article in a paper in Utah Territory (1864) titled "Mormon and Gentile" states: "Thousands of good-meaning people would come here and make their homes with us, but they cannot, unless they will allow themselves, by some at any rate, to be treated as the Jew of old treated the leper in Israel."[29]

When emotions on both sides were crystallized in linguistic expression, the Mormon community's conception of the character of the Jews as a group became clear. To illustrate this there is no better way than to read their concept of the gypsies who were also compared by others with the Jews:

"The Gypsies.—Who are they? Are they Jews? They tell you they are not. Are they Gentiles? No. Like the Jews they are wanderers without a home. Like the Jews, they are mingled among all people, and yet distinct from all, despised. . . .

"But the Jew is a worshiper of Jehova—the Gritana, or Rhoma, knows him not. . . ."[30]

There was no doubt that the Jews were a spiritual nation of God. Consequently the term "Jews" continued to be in their favor whatever their fate might be in relationship to the new Mormon community. And in regard to the big joke of the century, that in Utah the Jew is a Gentile, there are two aspects to be considered, the word designation and his actual position. The latter includes his relationship as a group to the Mormon community and vice versa.

The joke aside, we soon learn that there is little to prove that

62

the Jew was referred to as "Gentile." Declarations like: "Utah is the only spot on earth where the Hebrew is termed a 'Gentile,' "[31] prove nothing as to word usage even if they come from persons in Utah. They are rather the expression of a reality elsewhere summarized in this way: "Circumstances alter cases. Jews are Gentiles in Utah."[32] We could rather read out a warning against such generalizing of the language term "Gentile" from the following: ". . . As we apply the term Gentile, it is more than likely that thousands more Israelitish by extraction than ourselves are falsely branded."[33] In any case, no matter how an outsider's notions of the treatment of the Jews by Mormons might differ from other contemporary opinion, he had a clear impression that they were separated from other non-Mormons by their designation: ". . . [They] call . . . with the sole exception of the Jews all persons of different faith . . . 'Gentiles,' that is to say heathens. . . . The Jews are no 'heathens' because they were the first to whom God revealed himself and for the reason that they stick to their old faith."[34]

The Jew was linguistically separated from the image connoted by "Gentile" as indicated by the fact that there was also a cordial term for him *"Brother Jew,"* used by the Mormons on occasions when friendly words were directed only to him and not to the Gentiles.[35] Surely this linguistic differentiation between the Jew and the "Gentile" affirmed the generally friendly basic attitude of the Mormons to the Jews—Benjamin who reported this usage calls the attitude extraordinarily friendly. However, since the hard laws of life in Utah, whereby the Jew stood economically in the camp of the Gentiles, were not to be changed by this attitude, the Jew was treated economically like a Gentile. The far-flung concept of the Jew as a Gentile originated in Utah from this kind of treatment. Jew and Gentile were economically considered a unity: "Among the leading merchants were a number of Abrahamic descent, for it is one of the anomalies of this anomalous community that all the Jews are Gentiles."[36]

The same identification is found in another report from Salt Lake City: "On Main . . . Walker Brothers, Ramshoff & Co., Gilbert & Sons, are the principal Gentile merchants, but the last named *Gentile* firm are also *Jews*. There is known no distinction between Jew and Christian by the Mormon—they are both Gentile to him."[37]

63

A German missionary who reported that the Jews enjoy preferred economic treatment from the Mormons for religious reasons was therefore entirely inaccurate.[38]

Naturally American popular humor made much of this originally economic identity, deriding the confusion brought about by the Jew becoming a Gentile. The following was printed by a Utah Gentile journal, one of whose founders had been a Jew:

"Clear as Mud"—We lately heard the following dialogue between two persons who had just left the Bowery:

Lady—Were those persons *Gentiles* that sat on our right this morning?"

Gentleman—"Certainly, they are *Jews* that have lately arrived!"

After having this profound metaphysical distinction, Quiz fell into a series of cogitations, which resulted in leaving him in the following perplexing condition:

If a Jew is a Gentile, what is a Gentile but a Jew? And if a Gentile is not a Jew, how is it that a Jew is a Gentile? And again, if the Jew really is a Gentile, how is it that he really is a Jew? Is he really a Jew because he is a Gentile or really a Gentile because he is a Jew? Then, if the Jew—that is if the Gentile—or more properly speaking, the Jew, that is, of course the Gentile Jew be really and truly a Gentile, what kind of Gentile must he be that is so much a Jew that he is no Gentile at all? Will somebody explain?"[39]

In the face of all these outbursts of popular humor, the Mormons never lost sight of the relationship of the community of peoples in the world to the historic Jewish people. They also did not forget that they themselves belonged to these peoples although they had their own spiritual attitude to the Jews: "We are all Gentiles by nationality, we are of the Gentile nations who hold the sway of the earth."[40] And at another place:

"Says one—'Whom do you call Gentiles?' Every nation excepting the literal descendants of Israel. We, the Latter Day Saints, are Gentile; in other words, we have come from among the Gentile nations, though many of us may have the blood of Israel within our veins. . . ."[41]

The difference between the Mormons who recognized that they were Gentiles by birth and the other Gentiles, lay in their concept of the Millennium in which the Jews played such an important role:

64

"Tens of thousands among the Gentile nations will receive the Gospel, but the majority of them will reject it, and the Jews will receive it; and it will go to them with all the gifts, blessings, and powers it possessed when it was taken from them."[42] At least, the tradition of the Jews would always stand as a blessing of God peculiar to them vis-à-vis everything the Gentiles might be able to achieve:

"In many respects, when they come into the covenant and are baptized, and the power of God rests upon them, you will see a different work than you see at the present time. It is just as much as we, with our Gentile traditions, an inheritance we have received from our fathers, which have come down through generations—it is as much as many of us can do, with all the power we can exercise, to remain in the Church."[43]

But all this rational consciousness that all peoples to be gathered into the new Zion were Gentiles could not prevent historical events from effecting a transformation of the Gentile concept among the Mormons.

The way from the new promise to a new theocratic community was a flight from the old community of peoples. New experiences resulted in a new evaluation of this existing community of peoples. The seceding Mormon now looked at the American people, from which he was descended and from whom he was fleeing across a thousand miles of wilderness. He saw a strange people toward whom he had to seek a new spiritual attitude and from whom he had to flee further. The latter had already been accomplished by allowing the enemy to pursue him in his new State of Deseret. He thus created anew all the problems of a strange surrounding to be mastered only by statesmanship. All these conflicts were essentially social. Religious motives were pushed into the foreground although hardly touched upon in the encounter. The story of their development makes the growth of Utah into a laboratory of all the contemporary social forces in the new America. But the decisive factor remained the spiritual attitude to the surrounding world as it grew out of historical events. Just as without an exodus from already settled spaces "Zion" could not have originated, there could not have been a true "Gentile" problem in Utah without the development of the image of a spiritual secession. With every mile further into the wilderness the differentiation between the Mormons and the great mass of the American people grew more pronounced. This same American people in its irresistible urge toward the West was again destined to overtake the Mormons who were drawing away. These other Americans met the Mormons again in Utah. There they found themselves facing a church community separated from the "Gentiles" and trying by self-sufficiency to create a new theocratic state.

New spiritual yardsticks gained through great historic experiences created the Mormon attitude toward the rest of American society. The "Gentile" of Biblical oratory had become the adversary, the active enemy population of the surrounding world, the obstacle in daily life.

If not for this, Mormon history might have taken an entirely different turn. Had the Mormon stood on holy ground on a hill in Western New York with a spiritual Zion of his own, he might have been able to live on in American dispersion. He might have been able to escape a too literal interpretation of the injunction to gather round a newly built Temple. Perhaps individual Mormon communities could have assembled around local temples, and eventually they could have formed a union of religious communities.

However, such developments were prevented by the Mormon persecutions which awakened a new historical consciousness among the Mormons, and rallied them into a front opposed to the Gentiles.

But how did the Jew fit into this rather odd Mormon image of the American "Gentile" which sealed off from them their own American brethren, the same Yankees as their church leaders? How did the Jew become a part of these encirclements of enemies, a "Gentile" in Utah? As it was so often the case in Jewish history, in Utah, too, the "Jewish" question became the barometer of the situation and a guide to the true nature of the "Gentile" conflict in Utah.

There simply was no anti-Jewish conflict in Utah. The Jew's role in the image of Utah's Gentile was like part of a puzzle. Whenever it behooved the Mormons, he was treated separately and with such friendly greetings as 'Brother Jew." However, the sharpness of the Mormon Church and the measures it directed against him resulted from his penetration into Utah in pursuit of his economic goal in American life. He thereby became a carrier of the "Gentile" principle. In this case the "Gentiles" acted through him and would be hurt by his being treated as a "Gentile."

As a logical consequence of its origin, the term "Gentile" began to lose its sharpness as the Mormon Empire opened up to the rest of America. At the time when this developing tendency was becoming stronger, the gradual disappearance of the term "Gentile" was predicted:

"The term 'Gentile' will therefore pass away. . . . All trading or social relations with people, in or out of the Church, will decide themselves upon grounds of acquaintance, experience and individual judgment. All wholesale prohibitions of classes or creeds, commercially or religiously, are opposed to the spirit of the age, and must cease."[44] A criticism of this seclusion by a Mormon splinter group included as its high point a comparison with Israel of old:

". . . Elder W. L. Godbe said . . . Like the ancient Israelites we had been accustomed to regard all Gentiles as our enemies, and had built up a wall of bitterness and hate between them and ourselves, which must be broken down before we can reach them to do any good. . . .[45]

Such self-criticism on the part of the Mormons was certainly also an echo of the outside Christian world which regarded the Mormons simply as modern Judaizers. Indeed the contemptuous use of the term "Gentile" had been condemned much earlier: "The man that originated the term a "Damned Gentile," is brother to him who invented the equally indiscriminate one of a 'damned Mormon."[46]

Finally Brigham Young himself enacted a reformulation of the "Gentile" concept equating Gentile with the unbeliever only. He also took this opportunity to authoritatively interpret the historic origin of the word among the Jews: ". . . Gentile, or 'gentilism,' applies only to those who reject the gospel and will not submit to and receive the plan of salvation. Will you remember this? It does not apply to any only those who are opposed to God and His Kingdom. When the Jews, as a nation, were in their glory they called the nations around them Gentiles. Why? Because they were opposed to the laws and precepts that the Lord, through Abraham,

67

Isaac, Jacob and Moses, had revealed for the guidance of Israel. But it does not apply to this or any other nation, simply because they are not of our faith; and in fact, in these days, on account of their conduct, the term could be more properly applied to the Jews than to any other people; but it does not apply to them for they are of the chosen seed. Among the nations of the earth there is a great mixture, but there are many millions that we shall yet gather into this Church.

"Remember this, O, ye Elders of Israel, and do not apply the term 'Gentile' to a man because he is not baptized."[47]

In time the term, after lingering on for some decades, became obsolete for all practical purposes. It lived on only in literary usage. With peace in Utah the word "Gentile" was generally superseded by "non-Mormon."[48]

CHAPTER 9

Ephraim: Mixed Among the Nations

The extraordinary position of Ephraim in the Biblical blessings (Gen. 48, 14–19) and the prophecy that this tribe would be
the seed of many nations, had become part of the Anglo-Israel
theory in various respects.[1] The echo of this Biblical position was
even stronger in the popular imagination of the Anglo-Saxon cultural milieu and it also found expression in eloquent literary expressions in America.

The mere assertion of having descended from Ephraim made
the claimant appear to be eccentric:

*I am one of those of the tribe of Ephraim who refused to
cross the Red Sea:* we were not to be humbugged by *that damned
fellow, Moses—no, sir, we were not."*[2]

Such ideas were combined with notions of the Messiah and
other abstruse historical constructions. Speculation about all such
matters likewise formed the subject of literary descriptions:

"Lair Gawain

". . . This was 'Zion'—Lair Gawain's earthly Zion—much
smaller than the heavenly city, as he reverently explained, with the
old open Bible in his hand; and, instead of twelve gates, one for
each of the twelve tribes of Israel, the laird's New Jerusalem had
but two doors, by ignoring the ten tribes that had revolted from
the house of David. I used to remonstrate with him, with a child's
pity and earnestness, on this point: the ten tribes that had gone
out with Ephraim may repent some day, it were well to have the
doors ready.

" 'No,' he said, 'they are, as their fathers, a stubborn and
rebellious generation. . . .' "[3]

69

In this case the direction of thought was entirely formative, thus creating an archeological toy based on the image of Ephraim's role in the future. But other notions go much further and in their adventurous spirit delve into the preparation for the millennium. The following speculation surpassed everything else in this field in its boldness. It was also remarkable because it made eschatological predictions as did an already established Mormonism. It was even more remarkable because it was published in an American Jewish newspaper:

"What Is Coming

"Messrs, Editors:

"I feel it my duty to ask you this time to be so kind as to insert these few lines in your *Messenger,* on my own responsibility, as it is of great importance to all Israel, and whether you do it or not, I discharge my duty as an honest believer in Moses and the Prophets, of Israel's God, who is a God of revelation.

"Be it known to all of the house of Judah, who are scattered all over the world, that the tribes of Ephraim and of Menasseh, who have been carried away captives to the land of Assyria and have been lost from the knowledge of the world, are on the way from beyond the Arctic Ocean, and these two tribes will appear in a few months from now, to the sight of the public of this continent of America. They are coming by way of Deserts, and they will come through Canada. They have a prophet of God to lead them. These two tribes are one of a city, and two of a family who are coming to build up Zion, of whom the prophet Jeremia had stated, in Chapter III, verses 12, 14 and 15, and also in Chapter L, verses 2, 3, 4 and 5, and they will gather up most of the Canadian Indians and also Chief Sitting Bull with his hand and they will come here to Utah first.

"They will be a peaceably civilized and intelligent people, for to civilize their brethren, the red Indians, who are also of the tribe of Manasseh and they will teach them to become an honest and a peaceful race; to forsake hunting, theft and murder, and to begin to get an honest and industrious livelihood, so that the Lord, God of Israel, shall become their father and friend again, and they all will begin to obey the laws of God and also the laws of the land.

"And they will dethrone the Mormon apostles and bishops from their offices and from their Legislation and organization and they will get organized by the voice of Israel's God into an Israelite kehilah, and they will have Uncle Sam to be their good friend, and they will go up to Camp Douglas and kindly ask General Smith if he will let them have one of his largest guns for a few minutes, and they will charge it with a good strong charge of the best gunpowder and then will they put in the gun the present system of polygamy and the Mormon doctrine of blood atonement and the secret oaths and combinations which are practiced in the endowment house, and also priestcraft and the living oracles, which they profess to be in the name of the Lord, and all their false doctrines, etc., etc., and they will take a very good aim and fire off all the above toward the deepest part of Salt Lake, and it will sink into it, never, nay never, to rise again.

"Then will commence the morning star of Jacob to shine bright, and then comes 'the day break' to shine forth with its glorious rays, even the light and glory of Zion, and from here in the West, it will spread and it will lighten the whole world, and kings and queens, with their nations, will begin to come to her light, as our holy prophets have predicted.

"The other eight lost tribes are, or will, march towards Palestine, and they will come by the way we read in the latter part of the 11th chapter of Isaiah: and they will let all the house of Judah know who the true Messiah is, and they have also a prophet to lead them; then will the house of Judah hear those Israelites cry a tone: Come out our brethren and sisters from the mystical Babylon, even the corrupted Christendom. Astronomers and astrologers are predicting that they can see in the heavenly stars and planets that great destructions are coming, just as our holy prophets have predicted thousands of years ago that it will come to pass just previous to our redemption, and at the coming of our glorious Messiah, our King and Saviour.

"The above received by the glorious power of revelation on the 11th inst. from our God, who has lifted up his powerful hand to gather together and to restore the outcast of Israel and the dispersed of Judah, even us, his covenant people, and He is about to give us the promised lands. America, to Ephraim and Manasseh,

71

the sons of Joseph, and Palestine to the house of Judah, and the eight tribes of Israel. M. G.

"Salt Lake City, June 29th."[4]

As we can see Jews were also speculating about such matters.

One of the strangest features of the Ephraim images was their notorious drunkenness:

"The Drunkards of Ephraim. Drunkenness being a great characteristic of the British race it has been suggested that this one of the features which identify them with the descendants of Ephraim; they were for drunkenness in Isaiah's time."[5]

It was also expressed in popular humor:

"By the way, if this Anglo-Israel or Anglo-Ephraim Theory be true, do you not see a fitness in this sad reminiscense of the old sin of Ephraim, when you remark that drunkenness is the besetting sin of our own nation? Of course this is no proof that we are of Ephraim. . . ."[6]

To the British nation the Biblical blessing meant the concentration of power in one, not in many nations as in their own case: "The 'beginning of strength,' the increase, the large possession, was given to *Joseph*. . . .[7] [id est Ephraim as the preferred of the two sons of Joseph]. But to the Mormons applying a new genealogical table of Biblical peoples to America the meaning of Ephraim lay only in its dispersion over many nations:

"You Latter-day Saints . . . know who the children of Ephraim are, Ephraim who was mixed among the nations, the descendants of Joseph. You know that they are, the ones who hold the keys of the patriarchal blessings—the power to bless all the tribes of Israel. It is limited to the House of Ephraim or Joseph. The other tribes may have their prophets . . . but they have not the patriarchal priesthood and power to pronounce blessings upon the tribes of Israel. Why? Because it belongs to him who holds the keys of the firstborns . . . the Lord took away the keys from Reuben who was the firstborn of Israel and transferred them to Joseph. . . ."[8]

The dispersion of Ephraim's seed over the nations was commonly accepted by all Mormons, including groups split from the main church:

"Minutes of a Conference of the Church . . . City of James, Beaver Island, on the 6th, 7th, 8th and 9th of July, 1849. . . . That

72

the seed of Jacob are the sons of Ephraim, on whose head Jacob named his name; and that this seed, in fulfillment of the predictions of the prophets, by intermarriage became mixed among the nations of the earth, and the Elders of this church are said seed, chosen of God by revelation and prophecy to 'push the people together to the ends of the earth' and that the Lamanites or Indians are of the house of Joseph, and mostly of the tribe of Manasseh, as the prophet Ezekiel has declared concerning the Book of Mormon, that it is the 'stick or record of Joseph in the hand of Ephraim.' "[9]

This descent from Ephraim also formed the personal legitimation for the prophet Joseph Smith:

"He stated that Emma his wife was of Indian descent, in a line from one of the tribes of Israel. That he (Joseph) was a descendant from Joseph of old through the blood of Ephraim. And that God had appointed and ordained that he, with his descendants, should rule over all Israel, meaning the Latter Day Saints or Mormons, the Indian tribes and ultimately the Jews and Gentiles."[10]

The transition from dispersion to gathering leads then to America: "It has been proven that Ephraim dwells in America, consequently the Book of Mormon would be taken out of the earth in America."[11]

According to the Mormon image of the in-gathering into Zion, the following is the over-all situation:

The places of assembly are America and Palestine, the former . . . as the gathering of "Ephraim and his fellows," while the "dispersed of Judah" will migrate to and rebuild Jerusalem."[12]

This picture appears in the language of the hymn as early as 1849:

"A last dispensation . . .

. . . The Jews will go forth and the ten tribes shall come

From a land in the north, to inherit their home,

While Ephraim's loved children, who roam in the west,

Shall gather round Zion, and with her be blest."[13]

There was a need to explain America as the theatre of the in-gathering "of the blood of Ephraim"[14] and the assertion of the Mormons "we are out of the tribe of Joseph through the loins of Ephraim."[15] It was also necessary to elucidate Ephraim's being singled out from among the nations and the forces which enabled it to fulfill a historical task only the Mormons could undertake: "The Book of Mormon came to Ephraim, for Joseph Smith was a pure Ephraimite. . . ."[16]

And "Where are the Ephraimites? They are mixed through all nations of the earth. God is calling upon them to gather out, and He is uniting them and they are giving the gospel to the whole world."[17]

Not all Gentiles gathered-in into Zion would be the legitimate offspring of Ephraim, but Ephraim was the elite taking over the leadership in this process:

"Ephraim has become mixed with all the nations of the earth, and it is Ephraim that is gathering together. . . . Take a family of ten children, for instance, and you may find nine of them purely of the Gentile stock, and one son or one daughter in that family who is purely of the blood of Ephraim. It was in the veins of the father or mother, and was reproduced in the son or daughter, while all of the rest of the family are Gentiles. . . ."[18]

We have knowledge of the discussion the Jewish traveler Benjamin had with Brigham Young concerning his assertion of Mormon descent from Ephraim. Benjamin states that he had proven to Young its falsehood and adds: "He, in answering, could only refer to divine revelation received."[19]

Mormon blessings were given in accordance with Gen. 48, 20 in the name of Ephraim not only for men, but also for women. The formula used included "thou art of the blood of Ephraim" and "Thou are of the lineage of Ephraim and therefore art entitled unto the blessings conferred upon Joseph the father of Ephraim and Manasseh. . . ."[20]

Charles B. Thompson, a leader of a splinter group, was called "Father Ephraim by his adherents who thought him to be an incarnation of Ephraim."[21] The Biblical reference to the "mountains of Ephraim" also fitted well into Utah's geophysical picture and the abode of the Mormons was called the "valleys of Ephraim."

In the general call to the Saints Ephraim represents Providence insuring the success of God's work as undertaken by the Mormons. The free will of becoming saints to accept this call is fortified by the inheritance of Ephraim's divine blessings, superior to all other

74

blessings in the Bible. Therefore, they can never fail. To the new Israel appointed by God's will for a new task, comes Ephraim as the self-selected elite with its own blood line of divine inheritance.

As seen from the historical viewpoint: Mormons would not relinquish any Biblical aspect in their claim to succession on the road to the millennium.

CHAPTER 10

The Mormon Mission to the Jews

The Mormons' basic conception of their mission was directed especially toward the Indian and the Jew, entirely neglecting the Negro. Yet, their enemies sometimes cast suspicion on them precisely in relation to their position vis-à-vis the Negro. In Jackson County, Missouri, a citizen's committee reported a diabolical Mormon design: ". . . one of the means resorted to by them is an indirect invitation to the free brethren of color in Illinois, to come like the rest to the land of Zion."[1]

The fact that the actual situation differed entirely from the purport of this accusation brought about a tragic turn in Mormon history. Indeed, the dynamic principle of Mormonism fell short precisely when social trends in America required dynamism. In the country's critical problem of free or slave labor, Mormonism showed itself no less a captive of the *status quo* than other forces which took no part in this conflict. It paid for this indifference with subsequent stagnation and loss of influence. It can be shown from contemporary comments of Mormons that they were just as fearful of a schism in the Church because of the slavery issue as the Catholic Church, which had just begun its organization out of Baltimore. The diversion of Mormon missionary propaganda to the Indians instead of the Negroes may be compared with the Jesuit missions to the Mississippi at a time when the most favorable prospects were to be found precisely among the Negroes of the South. After Emancipation, the Negroes streamed into those frontier Churches which had at least participated to a degree in the fight for their liberation, with the Baptists, the typical Western frontier Church, taking the lion's share through the Negro Baptist Church. Just as the Catholic Church was bypassed entirely, with decisive effects upon the subsequent distribution of religious strength in America, so the Mormons, too, remained without an "issue" during and after the Civil War. The misguided mission to the Indians resulted in failure, the way to the Negro was practically barred, and the European immigration, interrupted by the Civil War, provided only reduced missionary opportunities afterward. The Mormon political debacle brought about by skillful enemy strategists who concentrated upon the polygamy issue merely gave expression to the fact that the Mormons had long before lost a much greater stake.

The fact that the Negro was actually denied admission to the new American Zion required a theological construction of his position *sub specie aeternatis* which could justify his exclusion from the priesthood. To the outside world the very existence of such a theological argument similar in its construction to the Biblical argument used in the slavery issue, was monstrous. Actually, a religious group such as theMormons could not take a secular position in such a situation. This position, which regards the Negroes as descendants of rebels in Heaven or of Cain still being punished for his crime, has become a grave onus upon the conscience of many individuals in the Mormon Church. They are unable to reconcile this position with being communicants in this Church.[2] There was even a difference in the two pro-slavery arguments based on the Bible. The first defended slavery as an ancient human institution; the other took the issue out of the Bible story directly to the realm of Heaven and the eternal questions of reward and punishment. The schismatic "Reorganized Church" tried to solve the problem with a new revelation of Joseph Smith III. Even this, however, makes half-hearted reading: "Be not hasty in ordaining men of the Negro race to offices in my church . . . *there are some who are chosen instruments* to be ministers to their own race."[3]

Hence there was no active, effective Mormon Mission to the Negroes.

The Mormon mission to the Indians followed the traditional paths of the other Christian denominations. They had already gone ahead in attempts to apply the theory of Indian descent from the Ten Tribes to their mission work among the Indians. However, the dynamic transformation of the Indian-Israel theory by the Mormons was effective only among white people searching for a connection between America and the Biblical past. This theory rounded out their religious image of the world. However, it meant nothing to the world outlook of the Indian tribes in America which were only slowly transforming their world-image in the light of Christianity. The fact that Zion in Utah was surrounded by Indians and had to solve many practical questions of everyday living resulted in many conflicts. Consequently, the conceptually important idea of an Indian mission retreated before the need to find a means of living together with the Indians. Eventually, the theoretical importance of the Indian mission also shrank.

In contrast o this, the idea of the mission to the Jews which began with the traditional Christian-Jewish propaganda approach, created a highly developed and unique structure. In it, the expression of their own religious concepts very soon proved superior to the actual conversionist goal. On its highest level the Mormon mission to the Jews was a religious diplomatic representation rather than an agency for winning new souls.

However, certain individuals, who formed an insignificant minority, stuck to the old line, as did Orson Pratt, who said: "If those Jews would repent and turn to be converted . . . they had a hope of having their sins blotted out . . . but until they must remain in torment. . . ."[4]

Indeed, it is noteworthy that, wherever the early Mormon mission to the Jews was based on conversionist goals, it proved to be entirely futile. On the other hand, wherever it strengthened and confirmed belief in the in-gathering of the Jews into Palestine and offered the spectacle of representatives dispatched to the Jews in Palestine and throughout the world, it set a record in expanding the faith. Furthermore, the dispatched missionaries were given the first opportunity to witness real Jewish life and to bring this knowledge to their fellow-Mormons. This created a sense of closeness to all world events affecting the Jews. In time, an enduring atmosphere was created in which the Mormon people continued to live even after the Mormon mission to the Jews had obviously lost any importance. In fact, the coverage of Jewish news in the Mormon press began to expand at that time. In addition, in Utah's Gentile conflict, the Mormons had seen real Jews, and as a result of the existing situation, had classified them as Gentiles and treated them as such. Beyond all that the Jewish people so peculiar in its situation continued to live on in the thoughts of the Mormon people.

There was no organic relationship between the two sides of the Mormon mission to the Jews—the conversionist activity and the external representations of the church. The desire for the one put the other into the shadow. The issue here was not degree of development nor consecutive phases, but rather the fact that the importance of the one—representation of the Church—caused the other, conversionist activity, to fall apart. Thus the strengthening of one idea resulted in the weakening of the other. If there was a desire to win Jewish masses for a new religion, Parestine certainly was not the right place; the urge to convert Jews should rather have led missionaries to Eastern Europe. If it was nevertheless decided to dispatch a Jewish mission to Palestine this meant that it was deemed necessary to obtain representation for the new faith in the religious world ot all Western countries which maintained representatives in the Holy Land. This being the case, the need to establish a connection with the Jews superseded any conversionist activity among them.

In connection with the Mormon missionary work the old comparison of Jew-Mormon was revived: "In order to effect this conversion from Gentilism to Mormonism, more pains were taken than were ever employed in making a proselyte by the hypocritical Jews of old."[5] The Mormons were thereby warned not to follow the example of the Jews who had not bothered with proselytes for a long time. On the contrary, in order to promote conversion, Mormons publicly praised their promised land pointing out that "Zion" is really a country where even in America milk and honey flow: "A more successful way of proselyting than by preaching the ridiculous tenets of their theology, is the extravagant praise of the Mormon's Zion, in the Great Salt Valley. . . . It is portrayed as equal in all respects to the Canaan which the Jews so long sought while journeying in the wilderness."[6] Naturally, praising Utah in this way couldn't have made sense either to American Jews or to potential Jewish emigrants to America. The former assessed their chances in the opening of the West according to existing economic trends and various other points of view independently. They came to Utah as merchants just at the time when the great rush to Cali-

79

fornia had already ceased and the Intermountain basin seemed to be promising mainly because of Salt Lake City's favorable location on an important traffic route. The latter had already formed their image of America from the experience of other immigrants who had preceded them. To the extent that, while still in Europe, they had thought of going to the American West, upon their arrival, the Intermountain Basin had not entered their thoughts. Likewise, the few later Jewish converts, in contrast to the immigrant masses won over in the West and North of Europe, were not influenced by the idea of going to Utah. Thus, the most successful approach for the Mormon Mission to the Gentiles from the beginning had no meaning for the Jews. With this, however, the actual interest in conversionist activities among the Jews died out.

The first reports on the appointment of a Mormon mission to Palestine clearly expressed the authoritative viewpoints of the church leadership. The letter in which the prophet commissioned Orson Hyde as missionary to Jerusalem stated in imperative terms: "It is highly important, in our opinion, that the present views and movements of the Jewish people be sought after, and laid before the American people for their consideration, their profit and their learning."[7] It is thus expressly stated that such a step will result in the spiritual strengthening of the American people who are to be converted to Mormonism. The mission to the Jews was thereby declared an official representation of Mormonism on behalf of the American people; they went to Palestine to show the whole world that the American people were ready to accept the old promise given to the Jews, and also to announce to the American people that the confirmation of its new Mormon faith was near. The news of this appointment already appeared in the Mormon press in England in 1840:

"Late from America.

". . . Elder O. Hyde and John E. Page, started on their mission soon after the Conference, to visit the Jews. They go first to the Jews in New York, and then on to Palestine. They will call upon you in England, as it will be on the way."[8]

This report was immediately taken up and commented on by the enemies of the Mormons:

"*The Mormons*—These religious humbugs have deputized

80

twelve of their members (answering we suppose to the twelve Apostles) to go to the Holy Land, and preach the Gospel to the Jews. John Page and Orson Hyde are two of the number. The headquarters of the Mormons are now at Commerce, Illinois, on the Mississippi River. Their number is increasing."[9]

The prophet still took pride in this mission to Palestine in the last formulation of the new faith destined to be given by him to the outside world. It contains a statement: "Missionaries of this church have gone to . . . Palestine. . . ."[10]

The first Mormon mission to Palestine entered the Holy Land in 1841. It had already made its mark by announcing that Orson Hyde would bless Palestine's earth, as a result of which the in-gathering of the Jews would take place. This conception later became common belief among the Mormon people. It is therefore no wonder that the reports of the missionaries were already working in this direction. They saw the imminent gathering of the Jewish people in signs and situations which became known to the missionaries only during their travels. This journey produced an important document which showed how the Mormon missionaries approached the Jews in England. A letter by Orson Hyde to the prophet, dated June 15, 1841, reported on the circumstances he encountered in this area. But this letter also served to illuminate the inner drive which led this remarkable man to become a missionary to the Jews and to Palestine:

"I have just received a note from Dr. S. Hirschell, President Rabbi of the Hebrew Community in this country, in reply to a very polite note which I sent to him, requesting the indulgence of a personal interview with him. But in consequence of a very severe accident which befell him, he is confined to his room, and unable at this time to grant the asked indulgence. (His leg is broken.)

"I have addressed to him a communication upon the subject of my mission, a copy of which I transmit to you. It may not be altogether uninteresting to the Saints and friends in America.

". . . Since I have arrived to years of more mature reflection, and become religiously inclined, the writings of the Jewish prophets have won my affections; and the scattered and oppressed condition of that people has enlisted the finest sympathies of my heart

. . . in the early part of March 1840, I retired to my bed one night as usual; and while meditating and contemplating the field of my future labors, the vision of the Lord, like clouds of light burst into my view (see Joel II, 28). The cities of London, Amsterdam, Constantinople, and Jerusalem, all appeared in succession before me; and the spirit said unto me: 'Here are many of the children of Abraham whom I will gather to the land that I gave to their fathers; and here is also the field of your labors. . . .' "[11]

Thirty years later the Church leaders dispatched their second mission to Palestine under the same theological auspices, as indicated by the instruction given to George A. Smith, on October 15, 1872: ". . . When you go to the Land of Palestine, we wish you to dedicate and consecrate that land to the Lord, that it may be blessed with fruitfulness, preparatory to the return of the Jews in fulfillment of prophecy, and the accomplishment of the purposes of our Heavenly Father. . . ." Brigham Young. Daniel H. Wells."[12]

Mormon reportage of this voyage was extensive. It began with a report of the departure:

"Bound for Palestine.

"Miss Eliza R. Snow and Elders George Dunford and Jacob Weiler of this city, Elder Anson Call of Bountiful, and Elder Lorenzo Snow of Brigham City, members of President George A. Smith's party, took their departure today, bound for New York, Europe, Egypt and Palestine."[13]

After their arrival the following letter, signed George A. Smith, was printed:

". . . Brother Schettler and I then called on the Rabbi of the Portuguese congregation to whom I presented a letter of introduction from the rabbi of San Francisco. He said the letter was a good one, and that he liked the look on my face. I talked to Brother Schettler, he to a German Jew, and the Jew to the Rabbi, as the latter could only speak in Hebrew, Portuguese and Turkish. He offered me a cigar; I told him I did not smoke. He said he was glad I had called on him, and brought a glass of water and some preserves, also cups of coffee for each of us. He remarked that the Jerusalem Jews were very poor, but if they had control, they would make great improvements. He said the Mosque of Omar was on the site of Solomon's Temple, but not in the centre; also that no

Jew goes inside the Mosque enclosure. He believed the God of Hosts would some day redeem the land. He introduced me to two of his friends, who showed us some ground they had bought from the Turks, and were erecting upon it a hospital and some dwellings for the poor Jews, with funds from abroad. We then went to their synagogue, and found it a plain, well furnished building; ... the Rabbi very courteously said he would call upon me in camp.

"March 4, at 10 a.m., we received a visit from Abram Askenasi, chief Rabbi in Jerusalem; we understand he is selected by the Turkish Sultan, and has received some titular orders from him. They express a firm faith in the redemption of Israel and the return of the ten tribes. They say there are no springs here now, but used to be in the day's of Israel's prosperity, and there will be again. Rain water is now their only supply, and later in the season it sells at a farthing a bottle. Europeans have been boring for water, but unsuccessfully, it not being time for it. The interview was very pleasant and interesting, and the Rabbi and three of their principal men who accompanied him appeared to be men of intelligence.

"We visited Mr. Shapiro's collection of ancient parchments, some of them very old, dug from beneath the ruins of synagogues both in Palestine and Arabia; they possess much interest. These writings are on various kinds and qualities of parchment, one of which, found in the mountains of Moab, discloses the idea that the Gods were male and female. . . ."[14]

In a later discourse based on the report from the Palestine mission, Brigham Young asserted that the desolation of the country and the situation of the Jews there indicated that the restoration of the Jews was imminent.[15]

On the other hand, a lesson for the Mormon people was also derived from this desolation: "The Jews are broken up into sects and parties, and in almost every town in Palestine you find a few of them, oppressed, poor and despised as elsewhere, living monuments of prophecy . . . He will do with us precisely as he did with Israel if we fail to observe the law of tithing and offerings. . . ."[16]

Later the rise of the modern Zionist movement was also felt to be the outcome of Orson Hyde's blessings over the land and people of the Jews.[17]

The second Mormon mission did not arouse any great public excitement any more, and no wonder! Thirty years had passed and the country's curiosity as to what events might follow the Mission had been dispelled. Critics now summarized both missions with a single negative evalution: "Palestine was first visited by Orson Hyde in the year 1841 and, as the Mormons themselves say, without any success at all. In February 1873, another mission, led by George A. Smith, the first counsel of Brigham Young, arrived. But it seems that this mission was intended not so much for conversionist efforts as for the achievement of other hitherto unknown goals."[18]

The inexplicability of the decision to dispatch a second mission to Palestine even produced rumors that Mormons intended to emigrate to Palestine.[19]

The world literature of missionary reports contains reports of living conditions among various peoples throughout the centuries in many languages. These have enriched our knowledge of other peoples in many ways. But there is certainly nothing in all this literature to match the Mormon missionaries' descriptions of the Jewish people. This was primarily an outcome of the fact that the Christian mission to the Jews in the nineteenth century used, in contrast to the Mormons, Jewish converts almost exclusively. The reports of these men, highly colored by their personal interests, rarely contributed anything genuine and truthful about Jewish living conditions. But a second, and perhaps more important reason for this uniqueness, was the fact that in this case the missionary found the confirmation of his message in the belief already existing among the people to whom he was sent. The big news which he reported home was that the Jews everywhere in the world believe in the restoration of Palestine. Such an approach is unheard of in the entire missionary literature. The missionary himself became in a sense an observer of existing beliefs rather than a propagandist for a new faith. Seen in this light the Mormon missionary reports, even when stripped of all nonessentials, contain the essence of what concerned the Mormons.

Of course, there are many other important items beside the will to restoration among the Jews in these reports. First of all, there was the search for signs of the times which might confirm the imminent restoration of the Jews. Even more important for posterity was the ingenuous, fresh approach in the descriptions of the living conditions of the Jews everywhere in the world. This contrasted pleasantly with the lack of understanding on the part of other Christian missionaries to the Jews, especially the exaggerations and bland insincerities of the Jewish converts so often involved in such missionary work.

For the whole Mormon community in America and in other parts of the world, the missionary effected the first awareness of the life of Jews in the world. He created a new, unique source of knowledge for the Mormon people by relating everything to the final purpose, the confirmation of the restoration belief. But he also gave realistic news about conditions in various countries, the system of the Halukka (support of the Jewish poor in Palestine), their general situation in the Holy Land and the continuing emigration there:

"They are very different from the Jews we have seen in France and Italy; they are far from being infidels; on the contrary, they are superstitious Jews. They have a real expectation of the Messiah's coming, and this feeling is waxing stronger and stronger. . . . They are counted as dogs by the Moslems. . . . Almost all the male Jews here spend their time in reading. There are six synagogues in Jerusalem, and thirty-six reading places. These latter are established by individuals that they may attain some merit to their souls."[20]

Or the following news about imminent emigration directly from Palestine: "Going to Jerusalem— It is said that several thousands of Polish and Russian Jews, at Berlin and elsewhere, have entered into an engagement to proceed on the first favorable opportunity to Jerusalem, to await in prayer and fasting the coming of the Messiah."[21] In this way currents in Jewish life were rendered to life for the distant reader as the expressions of a living Jewish People. This reader had up to then known the Jew only from his role in Bible-readings, but he had no knowledge of the historical fate of the Jew in the dispersion. Things heard, seen and read were now combined to confirm the great hope:

"Restoration of the Jews. . . . A letter of Jerusalem says. . . . The English Consul endeavors to engage the Jews to cultivate the

85

land of their fathers, under the favor of Mehemet Ali, and considerable quantities of land have been purchased for foreign immigrants. It is said there is somewhere a Talmudic saying that when there shall be 25,000 Jewish inhabitants in the Holy Land, the laws and regulations must be again enforced which prevailed when Palestine was a Jewish state. The Rabbis in Turkey are endeavoring to complete the above number by colonists which, doubtless, will not be difficult under the powerful protection of England. Some rich Jews in London and Italy intend to establish factories and manufactures in Jerusalem, and some other considerable towns under the protection of England. The English Government has appointed a Vice-Consul at Jerusalem for all Palestine."[22]

Even thirty years later, during the second Palestine mission, a report from Jerusalem to Brigham Young stated that the Jews there: ". . . express a firm faith in the redemption of Israel and the return of the tribes."[23] This time, however, little was reported about the signs of the time and much about the sad conditions of the Jews in Palestine.

Mormon missionaries were also the ones who brought the first realistic message about the Jews of Europe to the Mormon people, thereby insuring for the future a continuing interest in the Jews everywhere in the world and in America as well. Again it must be stressed that in contrast to the reports of other Christian missionaries to the Jews, the Mormons emphasized the lofty aspects of Jewish religious community life. Thus, Heber Kimball sent the following report from his stay in England. His meeting with English Jews in the London Synagogue revealed unexpected inner riches:

"From thence we visited the Jewish Synagogue to see their order of worship, which was all performed in Hebrew. We stayed during the whole ceremony in their worship . . . all of which passed off with great solemnity and order; there were no females present at the meeting, and no one permitted to enter their place of worship without a hat on. At the door we were requested to put ours on, which we accordingly did; but passing farther into their synagogue, the beauty and splendor thereof caused us again to take them off. A second request to put them on rather embarrassed us, and perhaps to them we might have appeared a little *clownish*."[24]

After a detailed description of the London Jewish quarter, he exclaims enthusiastically: "They are the most spirited, ambitious and persevering people I ever saw. They believe the gathering of Israel . . . is near. . . ."[25]

At another opportunity another Elder, Edward Stevenson, described the services in the synagogue of Gibraltar: "Visited the Jews' synagogue with Mr. Delamar, a learned Jew of six languages. As I entered I was informed it was customary to wear hats, which I soon saw was the case, for all kept their hats on during worship. The pulpit was in the center. The ark being opened, parchments were taken out, rolled on two sticks, with bells on the top, which passed around the congregation, each kissing it, keeping up a continuous chanting. A portion is read from the pulpit in a singing tone, and then returned to the ark, where there are several; each one sings and bows to the arks, and are soon dismissed."[26]

It was also the observer-missionary whose insight into Jewish sufferings in view of Jewish steadfastness, gave shape to his belief that for all its sufferings this people was destined to be restored. In addition to recognizing the deeper meaning of suffering, he interpreted the frame of mind of the Jews: "The imperial consul of Austria, at Galatz, . . . to whom I had a letter of introduction from his cousin at Vienna, told me that in consequence of so many of their Jewish subjects being inclined, of late, to remove to Syria and Palestine, his government had established a general consul at Beirut for their protection. There are many Jews who care nothing about Jerusalem, and have no regard for God. Their money is the God they worship; yet there are many of the most pious and devout among them who look towards Jerusalem as the tender and affectionate mother looks upon the home where she left her lovely little babe."[27]

A search for the lost tribes was also ascribed to the second Palestine mission which tried to determine the opinion of the Jews about this matter: "Rabbi Askenasi, speaking of the ten tribes, said he had no idea where they were, but he believed they were preserved, and that their posterity would return, and the time would come when God would bless Israel, and when water would be abundant in Jerusalem."[28]

Since everything reported by the Mormon missionaries was

87

transmitted immediately to the Mormon press, it became familiar news to all members of the church. Thus the missionary, insofar as he did not deal with matters related to the sacred aspects of church doctrine, became simply a special news reporter when he wrote about the Jewish situation in specific countries. Together with such news, the Mormon press printed numerous other notices of Jews and things Jewish gathered from other sources.

Only the Missionary's reports about meeting with Jews, and how he was received by them, contained a personal note. This then led to the second part of his work, the actual conversionist activity. But here, too, it was remarkable that Mormon missionaries always mentioned that they were received by the Jews with respect and friendliness. This was strongly in contrast to numerous reports of missionaries of other Christian religious societies, who complained about unfriendly reception by the Jews. The same friendliness to them was shown by the spiritual leaders of the Jews; for instance, the rabbi of the Portuguese congregation in Jerusalem received the Mormon mission at his home and returned the visit: "I had a letter of introduction, procured by Mr. James Linforth, from the Rabbi of San Francisco, to Rabbi Askenasi! He is a very venerable-looking man—tall, heavy-set and a good supply of beard, like the Apostles in the picture. He seemed very much pleased with my visit, treated me with courtesy, showed me their synagogue and the building they were erecting, and returned the visit, accompanied by several of the Jewish elders, at my tent, where we had a pleasant interview."[29] As previously noted, the Mormon missionaries employed a linguistic triangle of English, German and Hebrew for such discussions.[30]

Although Mormon missions to various countries had already met Jews, the special mission to the Jews was actually the first real experience with them on a larger scale. Undoubtedly when it started this mission had carried with it some of the usual conversionist baggage and in the beginning its eagerness to convert Jews might not have been weak. However, all this receded as soon as their experiences revealed an amazing new world, the inner life of the Jews. The need to give their own faith its meaning within the framework of this new world of experiences grew the more they saw of the Jews. Nevertheless, they did attempt some form of con-

88

version which must be compared with the original concept of the conversion of the Jews held by their spiritual authorities.

The declaration in the "Book of Mormon" that it was written so that Jews might acknowledge Jesus as the Christ, was still under the influence of the traditional conversionist activities of Christian religious societies.[31] We know nothing about an eventual distribution of the "Book of Mormon" among Jews by the mission to the Jews. The few references to the thoughts of the first mission concerning actual conversionist activity are found in Orson Hyde's two letters from his journey, titled "Highly Interesting News from Jerusalem."[32] In these letters conversionist attempts recede into the background in view of all the new items of interest. But in his quest for information, Orson Hyde had to contact baptized Jews who were Christian missionaries themselves. He was in the house "of Mr. Simmons, a very respectable Jew . . . converted." This person belonging to the "English Church" had also as a guest another "minister of the Church of England . . . a German and a Jew by birth." He obtained missionary literature of this Church to read, but didn't find anything interesting in it and consoled himself with his own hopes based on additional information heard elsewhere: 'But there is more hope of those Jews receiving the fullness of the gospel, whose minds have never been poisoned by the bane of modern sectarianism. . . . Mr. Whiting told me that there had been four Jewish people in Jerusalem converted and baptized by the English minister, and four only. . . ."[33] These were the only actual missionary experiences the Mormon messenger had to report of himself and others. Nevertheless, the newspaper adds: "We humbly trust that his labors will be a lasting blessing to Jew and Gentile."[34]

During the second mission to Palestine, so many years later, things already looked quite different. The hope to convert Jews was actually already given up in the course of this undertaking: ". . . there is no infidel in the face of the earth who can disbelieve the mission of the Saviour more than they do."[35]

An all-time curiosity in this area was Elder John Taylor's conversation with one of the Rothschilds. On the occasion of the latter's presence in Salt Lake City, he showed him the Temple and presented him with a 'French copy, he being a Frenchman," of the "Book of Mormon." "This conversation took place in the Townsend house." The Baron was confronted with the tenets of Mormon faith: ". . . You Jews have quite a role to perform in the latter days. . . ." and 'that you will be gathered to old Jerusalem.. .." We may readily believe the Mormon representative's statement that Baron Rothschild did not allow such statements to go undisputed.[36] Naturally the Mormon press during this period, like the press elsewhere in the world, was impressed by the numerous discussions of colonization schemes. In these discussions, including one involving Palestine, Rothschild's financial help was speculated upon.

Certain experiences of the Mormon missionaries indicated how precarious was their own situation even in comparison with the corresponding situation of the Jews in the same country. For instance, in Prussia, where "the Jews also have some shadow of religious privilege,"[37] but Mormon propaganda is not tolerated. Mr. Bromberg, the American consul in Hamburg is "a native German." "Mr. Bromberg [apparently a Jew] expressed some surprise at our presumption in undertaking to carry the Gospel to the Kingdom of Prussia. Says he, Prussia . . . setting you out of their kingdom immediately."[38]

Nevertheless, vestiges of conventional conversionist thoughts relating to the Jews occasionally turned up even in later Mormon literature. Treatises on the "restoration of the Jews" sometimes ended with repentant acceptance of Christianity on their part.[39] At the beginning, the Mormon press even contained typical articles such as "The Conversion of Israel,"[40] which read like borrowings from contemporary conversionist literature. Christian martyrological notions associated with the Jews of old, were even found expressed in the appearance of the prophet: "On Sunday, Joseph Smith, Jr., in his discourse. . . . He supposed the prejudices of the Jews and Pharisees were so great against the Saviour, that they would give them nothing to eat, and they took that method to get it."[41] But how little of all this remained in force was epitomized in the person of Brigham Young. He laughed off all conventional conversionist activities relating to the Jews based upon such images and when the occasions arose, he even told typical current jokes concerning Jewish conversions by force.[42]

The Mormon press also sometimes reported actual news about

Jewish conversions: "A letter of Jerusalem says . . . of 400 Jews, 100 have embraced Christianity,"[43] a figure not altogether convincing for that locality.

The Mormon mission to the Jews and to Palestine and its outcome underwent the detailed criticism of their neighbors. This criticism was expanded to an assessment of all conversionist tendencies and activities vis-à-vis the Jews. In addition, there were generalizations about the conversionist success of the Mormons among various non-Jewish groups which may be useful in connection with the Jewish theme of conversion. Finally, the Mormon heretics also made use of this promising opportunity.

Contemporaries like J. W. Gunnison regarded the episode of attempted conversionist activity among the Jews mainly as the failure of a concept originally deemed especially important by the Mormons: ". . . The grand scheme was to convince the Jews in all the world. . . . The Indians throughout the length and the breadth of the land were to be informed of their origin. . . . Even now the Mormon missionaries apply to Jewish Rabbis, and ask them to listen to the voice of the Gentile prophet. . . . We have lately seen the account of such a meeting at Amsterdam, but the Jew stands unconvinced, and holds to his traditions; the Indian listens to 'the talk' about the Great Spirit and returns to the chase unconverted; all these seem to view the matter as the fiction of an enthusiast."[44] Another historian not personally involved in the events in the same way as Gunnison summarized his opinion as follows:

"Also there was no success in winning over Jews and Indians in any greater number, although the Mormon missionaries were especially attentive to both and also dispatched a mission to Palestine."[45]

In time this criticism, mixed with ironical anti-Mormon sentiment, also sharpened: "The Jews have still to be gathered together, and 'the nations from the north country' whose coming according to the Bible, is to be so terrible, are to find the Mormons, 'the children of Ephraim,' ready prepared with such rites, and such tabernacles, that the 'sons of Levi,' the Jews, can perform their old worship, and thus refreshed continue their progress to the Holy Land."[46]

Such derisive comment upon the failure of the blessings of the first Palestine mission may have resulted from the long lapse of time since the criticized event. But the second mission found its detractors at once: "The Salt Lake Tribune says: 'The Mormon missionaries from Zion under Apostle Smith have arrived in the Holy Land, and the Corresponding Secretary writes a very interesting letter dated: In camp before Jaffa Gate of Jerusalem, Feb. 25, 1873. This mission will, perhaps, correct in some points the Mormon history of America. The Garden of Eden has been located in Jackson County, Missouri, and Adam's bones were buried in that State by the Prophet Smith. But these Jerusalem missionaries have now found the place where the skull of Adam was buried in Palestine—also the tomb of Melchisedek. So America has got rid of that much of Mormonism.' "[47]

But it was pointed out even by these adversaries that the first mission after much talk had found among the Jews in Palestine, many who were tremendously interested in the idea of the return of the Jews to their homeland.[48] Indeed, the failure of the Mormon Indian mission fitted in with an old puritanical concept connecting it with the fate of the Jews:

"A reason offered by some why the gospel was not prevalent among the Indians was that 'it is not probable that any nation more can be converted till the calling of the Jews; till the seven plagues finished, none was able to enter the temple, that is, the Christian church.' "[49] And adversaries of the Mormons placed the Indian mission in the same unwanted category as conversionist activity among the Negroes, which was falsely ascribed to them: ". . . impertinent and mischievous interference of the Mormons with the slaves of the country. Their threatened association with the neighboring tribes of Indians was a serious subject of alarm; . . ."[50]

The true situation of the Indian mission was pointed out by Brigham Young himself: "Our missionaries have labored among them, and what effect has it had? But little."[51]

Information concerning the real position of the Negro in the Mormon church was given to the world at large by outsiders: ". . . a black man cannot be ordained a priest according to their code as we have already mentioned. Everywhere, also in the Hereafter, he has to occupy a servant's station and has in heaven only a small part of happiness and glory. . . ."[52] Outsiders also reported that the black color of his skin and being reduced to the lowest class of mankind was the consequence of crimes by his forebears.[53] For the Indians a better future was envisaged: "The red men are damned to their nasty color only for a time and the day will arrive when they will be restored to all their rights and will be worthy of their descent from the seed of Abraham."[54]

The concept of the Jewish mission, when given a satirical turn, was a weapon in the hands of the heretic fighting against the established Mormon Church." Barnet Moses Giles, a literal descendant of the House of Israel" introduced himself to the inhabitants of Utah as "New prophet, quite a sensation; quite a strange thing; and a Jew in the bargain."[55] He demonstrated to them the consequences of a mission to the Jews firstly in its spiritual aspects. He then declared that the church leaders, because of their minimal knowledge of the Hebrew language of the Bible, were not qualified for this purpose: ". . . the Book of Mormon and the Book of Doctrine and Covenants will have to be translated in the Hebrew language and carried to the Jews. I say who will and can do it? Can Brigham Young do it? No! He ought to be qualified for it."[56]

"B. M. Giles the Israelite" then turned to a satirical exposition of the consequences for Utah of the successful conversion of Jews. The Jews "begin to build up the holy city Zion, here on this continent of America, which belongs to the sons of Joseph, the sons of Jacob."[57]

Consequences were fearful indeed, because in fulfillment of the revelation given to Joseph Smith, Utah belongs, lock and stock, and especially the "Deseret News," to which this ironical letter was directed, to the Jews:

"Then, my dear sir, your printing office is a part of your Gentile gospel embracers, and it is a part of your riches and it is Church property, and it belongs to Jesus Christ—then that will become consecrated unto the poor Israelites. Sir, I am an Israelite. . . . And not the printing office only will be ours, I mean the literal Israelites, but a great many more things will also be ours very soon. Be it known to you all that a great many Jews will shortly come here by voice of Jesus Christ and not by the voice of Gentile Mormon Elders. First to the Gentiles, then to the Jews, and then you will see me stand in the river Jordan, and I will baptize the repenting Jews here in the wilderness of Joseph, . . . the Father will clothe them with good clothing, and he will tell them to help themselves in the large Z. G. M. I. [Mormon Cooperative], which belongs to the rich Gentiles, even Mormons, who call themselves 'the Church'—and it is Church property. . . . And then we will take the tabernacles for our worship."[58]

And the answer of the apostles of the Mormon Church to all this is likewise anticipated by the "Israelite Prophet":

"Take no notice of the half-crazy Jew; he is touched in his head."[59] In passing, the "literal Israelite" teased the Mormon Church, which was so abhorrent to him, once again, because of its attitude to the Negroes:

"A Negro is excluded from having the priesthood in this church. . . . Is a Negro not a creature? Yes," and the suggestion of Shylock's question is plastered with evangelical Christianity. "If he is black through the curse which Cain or Ham received, is not the gospel the power of God unto salvation, unto every one that believeth, white or black, no difference."[60]

During the period of such satirical presentations of the Mormon mission to the Jews by a heretic there also appeared literary examples of American humor in which Jews go on to teasing Christians for their own aggressive conversionist activities. One of them was the aforementioned newspaper notice of J. F. Cooper, "inviting the Jews to meet to concert means of converting."[61]

Jewish reports concerning the activities of the Mormon mission among the Jews are non-existent. Occasionally, however, a remark about Mormon missionary work has come to us from the Jewish press, such as the following: "Mormon missionary work still continues, and with great success in Christendom. . . . In Boston they complain strongly of the illiberality of Evangelical clergymen who having been permitted to preach in the Temple of Salt Lake City, refuse them admission into their own pulpit."[62]

When reading these remarks we must bear in mind that frequent interchange of guest-sermons between Jews and Christians was already popular at that time. We will then understand the amazement of the Jewish newspaper reader who was accustomed to equate bad relations among Christian denominations with the achievements of "Interfaith" among Christians and Jews, as symbolized by guest sermonists.

94

CHAPTER 11

Restoration of the Jews

Belief in the imminent gathering of the Jews into their old homeland, Palestine, was one of the basic concepts of Mormonism. It grew from what was originally the general sentiment of the American population to an article of faith in the new dispensation. Again, as with the descendancy theory of the American Indians it can be proven that considerable contemporary and even pre-Mormon basic feelings of this kind existed in America among persons of different religious denominations. But again the essentially new contribution of the Mormons was in transforming this general feeling into a written article of faith. Once more, what had been mere individual speculation often connected with political expediency became dynamic and effective in a religious society.

Even before Mormonism, the restoration of the Jews had been announced in America too as the great imminent event destined to be experienced by this generation. The appearance of Napoleon had raised this hope to a political level:

"Yes, gentlemen; among other great and wonderful events, which we foretold, but which never happened, and moreover, never will happen, was the restoration of the Jews by the intervention of that renowned pacificator, Bonaparte. We first prophecied, and many men of our cast who had a knack of prying into futurity, echoed our prediction, that the pious emperor of the Gauls would make Jerusalem the headquarters of the Millennium and under our auspices many a wandering Jew was recruited, and stood in readiness to march at a moment's warning to take possession of his patrimonial property."[1]

But even after the great meteor had vanished and it had become clear that even Napoleon could not have fulfilled this hope, the thread of political speculation centering on this event continued to be spun by the American people. This was done, as in the case of a simple person in Ohio (1845) by combining the realities of the time with a firm belief in a political composite image in the following manner:

"I feel great interest in the prosperity of Jacob, and have full faith in their restoration. I know not else how the Scriptures can be fulfilled. Have you read the latest discourse of M. M. Noah? He is an Israelite; would to Heaven we could add—'In whom there is no guile.' But this discourse from an Israelite is well worth attention. The restoration, we suppose, will be Jewish, not Christian. What will occur after it is entirely another question. Is not the way preparing? The Jews, it is fully understood, *expect* to be restored. They are waiting. The Russian Autocrat is said to be expelling them. Palestine, to a great extent, remains vacant. Egypt *may* become a dependency of Britain. A friendly power in Palestine may then be vastly important to her. Turkey is imbecile. France is swallowing the Mohammedan realms of Northern Africa. Turkey, in Europe, may soon become the prey of Austria and Russia. To sustain the balance of power, England (possibly) may seek to hand over Hanover to Prussia, and indemnify herself by serving Egypt and replanting Palestine. But I pretend to no gift of prophecy; yet the signs of the times are surely of great and singular significance.

K."[2]

However, such political combinations formed only a rivulet. The mainstream of the deep religious feelings in this area was shaped by the conviction of the simple soul that by miracle and divine destination the restoration of the Jews would come to pass during the lifetime of this generation. Therefore, voices expressing the hope of experiencing this in person or during the lifetime of children, are much more important and much greater in number. For instance, the New York citizen, John Pintard (1828), wrote to his daughter: ". . . the Jews be once more restored to their ancient Kingdom. Your children may see these great events."[3]

And in troubled times as, for instance, after the upheaval of the American nation by the Civil War, this hope showed all the signs of a preparation for the millennium:

". . . We live in troubled times, gentlemen, and I never expect to see peace again. It seems, sir, as if our times were the latter days which we are taught to expect, when there shall be wars and rumors of wars. I believe that we shall see the Jewish people led up to Jerusalem and gathered in from all the corners of the earth, according to the promise, and all the other promises made to the chosen people will be fulfilled. But there will be no more peace for the rest of the nations. That's the way it looks to me. I may be mistaken. . . ."[4]

But in quiet times, or at least when the religious mood had calmed down to a certain degree, the same conviction continued and found expression in poetical, consoling images and words. It sometimes was related to existent situations of the times, but remained on the whole the timeless expression of imminent religiosity, as, for instance, the following poem (1836):

> ". . . But, Oh! Judea, there shall come
> For thee another glorious morn;
> When thy retreats shall be a home
> For thousands pining now forlorn
> In distant lands; no more to roam
> The objects of disdain and scorn."[5]

Expressing the hope of the restoration of the Jews became a favorite theme of those literati who wrote about religious matters, especially in anything related to the Jewish cult. For instance, a certain author wanted to stress this in a description of the services in the Chicago synagogue:

"The Jewish synagogue is a large temple, and filled on occasions, to overflowing with the posterity of Abraham. In their worship they revere and respect the Old Testament, and are waiting with the utmost confidence, that the Messiah, a temporal King, will be sent to them, who will assemble them again into the Holy Land, the Turks to the contrary, notwithstanding, and make them once more a great nation."[6]

And in some cases this was connected with an evaluation of the Jewish people in its present state which must be regarded as an important expression of the opinions of the times:

". . . we know of no reason why a numerous and severely oppressed people should not rise up and attempt to shake off the yoke of their obdurate tyrants—it is a political incident naturally growing out of the state of things. And as, in the wonderful dispersion of this people, the decrees of God, as made known by His prophets, were literally fulfilled, there is not wanting those who look to their gathering again with confidence and hope.

"This singular and interesting people, scattered all over the world, and everywhere despised and maltreated, have continued a *separated* race of men in all nations, having a home in none. It is easy to imagine that, under such circumstances, they may be more easily gathered to a given point than any other class or sect under heaven—as well to obtain for themselves the rights and privileges which they see enjoyed by others, as to fix themselves in a *home* and a country. . . .

"The deserts of Palestine, brought into cultivation by patient industry may again blossom as the rose—and *Jerusalem,* miserable as it is, speedily rival the cities of the world for beauty, splendor and wealth. . . ."[7]

In contrast or rather as a supplement to the political speculations about outside factors favoring the return of the Jews, it was pointed out that it was also dependent on inner, spiritual movements among the Jews themselves:

"Gathering of the Jews—

"It is affirmed that a remarkable change is in progress among the Jews in every country, owing to a manuscript being largely circulated by an influential Rabbi proving from the Scriptures that the time has come when the Jews must set about making preparations for returning to the land of their fathers. . . ."[8]

The conflict, seemingly entirely modern, between the demand of the Jews to return to Palestine and their right to total equality in all the countries in which they lived by preference, was treated in America as early as in 1792. The religious speculators worried lest the equal treatment of the Jews might not finally grow to be an obstacle to their return to Palestine:

"America has also shewn the world, that to admit the Jews to all the privileges of natural-born subjects, is far from being a dangerous experiment, as has been generally supposed. I cannot see that allowing them such privileges destroys our prophecy, or will in the least hinder their return to their own land when the time

98

shall come. And I am far from being afraid, that God will be angry with the United States for giving to Jews, in common with other nations, the equal blessings of protection, liberty, property, etc. I find threatenings in Scripture against those nations that have afflicted the Jews, but none against those who afford them rest and peace. . . ."[9]

Such a far-reaching identification of religious consciousness with faith in the restoration of the Jews could not but result in the exploitation of that theme by the American popular humor. In this it shared the fate of the theory of Indian descendancy from the Jews. The products of this humor were thought to promise literary success especially when they dealt with contemporary events. And the image of a would-be restorer could evoke laughter even after Napoleon:

"I inquired of my mother whether there were not some Jewish blood in the family? Possibly I might be a Hebrew of the Hebrews; nay a lineal descendant of David; perchance the intended restorer of the Jews—nay the very Messiah! or, at least, a very near connection—a sort of right-hand man, an earthly instrument, his sword-arm—destined to overthrow kingdoms and achieve the victory of Armageddon."[10]

Little wonder therefore that inventive minds planned to exploit this widely disseminated belief financially and to arrive at schemes which would serve this purpose.

We learn from press reports that in 1864 an anonymous "Hebrew Government" for Palestine was founded in America purporting to have set itself the goal of bringing the Jews there. A bond issue on the American market was its first step. The Jewish community reacted quickly and sharply to this venture as we see from a notice in the "American Israelite":

"A Humbug—The New York Times is responsible for the following humbug: 'A Hebrew Government—. . . the executive is about to call for loans, and issue bonds, in the name of the Israelitish Government, bearing seven per cent interest."[11]

But reports of the imminent return of the Jews were everywhere, for instance, among the Freemasons: "The Jews are returning, in great numbers, to the land of their fathers; and already are they preparing to erect another temple."[12] And a reflection of

Mormon speculations is to be seen in the following: "Thus the Mormonite speculations on the Restoration of the Jews and on the Millennium, are the same which may sometimes be heard in Puritan pulpits. . . . Even the date assigned to the Restoration of the Jews is the same in both systems. 'It shall come to pass in the nineteenth century,' says the official organ of Mormonism, 'that the great trumpet shall be blown, and they [the Jews] shall come who are ready to perish in the land of Assyria, and the outcast in the land of Egypt, and shall worship the Lord on the holy Mountain of Jerusalem.' "[13]

With the same eagerness the Mormons publicized news about this theme from other papers.

In contrast to all these disparate widely dispersed sentiments of the American population, the restoration of the Jews, as a written article of Mormon faith, meant something essentially different. It effected a working dynamics of faith within the realms of this religious society as well as renewed vitality in its external propaganda. Thus, the restoration of the Jews became a function of the concept of the millennium not dissimilar to the effect Ephraim, the "mixed cake" would have among the nations of this earth. Ephraim had to urge the gathering of the Gentiles, to bring about the fermentation. But the return of the Jews to their homeland by its wonderful example was to influence all peoples and signal the removal of all nations to Zion. This crucial role was assigned to the restoration by the Mormons from the very beginning. It was steadfastly maintained in all Mormon writings including those of our day."[14]

Already mentioned in the "Book of Mormon," this point was stressed again and again by both friend and enemy:

". . . The Book of Mormon is a sacred instrument . . . to bring in the gathering dispensation of the Saints, the return of the Jews, and the ushering in of the fullness of the Gentiles."[15] And as seen by the opponents of the Mormons: "They (the elders) claimed, among other things, that simultaneously with the coming of the Book of Mormon the Jews began to gather back to Palestine, and that the Lord *restored the rains to Palestine* that had been denied it for nearly nineteen hundred years. . . ."[16]

Such an event, logically, could come about only by divine in-

100

tercession. Human plans and even the illusions of societies, created to achieve this by converting the Jews are of no avail:

"In vain may attempt be made, by the organization of societies, for the amelioration of the condition of the Jews; in vain will societies be organized for their restoration to their own land and the rebuilding of Jerusalem, until the Lord's time arrive . . . a proclamation must come from Heaven and be sounded in their ears: namely, that an angel must come from Heaven and bring the everlasting gospel, not for the Jews, the descendants of Israel alone, but for every nation, kindred, tongue and people."[17]

We read of it in the Nauvoo-period of the Mormons as an early declaration of the prophet: "The Jewish nation have been scattered abroad among the gentiles for a long period; and in our estimation, the time of the commencement of their return to the Holy Land, has already arrived. . . .

Joseph Smith"[18]

And after the tragic murder of the prophet which wrote finis to that period, the apostles made the following pronouncement in their proclamation:

"And we further testify, that the Jews among all nations are hereby commanded, in the name of the Messiah, to prepare to return to Jerusalem in Palestine, and to rebuild that city and temple unto the Lord."[19] The same was preached to the faithful at the time when the new location of the Zion in America had already been found. Brigham Young made the following statement from Utah, the new locale: "Jerusalem will be rebuilt and will be the place of gathering, and the tribe of Judah will gather there; . . ."[20]

Naturally, the belief in the restoration of the Jews was also combined by the Mormons with current events. Political hopes were also connected with such combinations. Numerous reports about Jews in the Mormon press were meaningful only insofar as they effected a certain spiritual closeness between the faithful and Jews all over the world. In all such news items political moments which might somehow have a connection with the imminent gathering of the Jews were strongly emphasized. And yet, in the emergent religious picture the Mormon creed remained pure and unmarred by its actual relationship to daily political events. But the concept of the Restoration of the Jews was influenced not only by political considerations but to an even greater degree by thoughts concerning the millennium. It would take place accompanied by awesome fighting but final victory would be with the Jews:

". . . the nations of the old world . . . will send a great army to Palestine against the Jews. . . . This signal victory on the part of the Jews . . will change the whole order of things in Europe and Asia, in regard to political and religious organization and government.

"The Jews as a nation become holy from that day forward, and their city and sanctuary become holy."[21]

This prediction of new holiness for the historical Jewish people resulting from their restoration brought up the question of whether the Jews would then have to acknowledge Jesus. This concept, like the Christian propaganda of other denominations, finally won out in Mormonism too, although it remained, in a certain sense, controversial. There would be splits among the Jews: "Many of them, however, will not receive the gospel, but seeing that others are going to Jerusalem they will go also. . . . At the same time they will have their synagogues, in which they will preach against Jesus of Nazareth, 'that impostor,' as they call him, who was crucified by their fathers."[22]

The majority held that the gathering of the Jews would come about while they were yet in a state of unbelief: "They will be gathered to their own lands in unbelief. Many societies of Christendom overlooking this fact, or, if seeing it, not believing that it would be so, are making strenuous efforts to convert the Jews. . . ."[23]

Restoration was similarly regarded by Orson Pratt, who, in contrast to the majority opinion, maintained that the gathering would take place only after the realization of the American Zion. He, too, believed that it would come about under catastrophic circumstances:

"The Jews, or many of them, will gather back to Jerusalem in a state of unbelief in the true Messiah. . . . And they will rebuild Jerusalem after the times of the Gentiles will be fulfilled. While in that state of unbelief Gog and Magog, the inhabitants of Russia and all those nations in northern Europe, will gather against

102

the Jews before Jesus comes. . . . For you know when the Rothschilds and the great bankers among the Jewish nation shall return back to their own land to rebuild the city of Jerusalem, carrying their capital with them, it will almost ruin some of the nations, and the latter will go up against Jerusalem to take a spoil. . . . This great calamity comes upon the Jewish nation in consequence of their unbelief in the true Messiah."[24]

It should be noted in this connection that the preface of the "Book of Mormon" declares that it was written so that the Jews might acknowledge Jesus as the Christ.[25] Later statements followed the same line of reasoning, as, for instance, that of Wilford Woodruff: "Take the Jews today anywhere in the world, and they do not believe in Jesus. I do not say this because I wish to find fault with them. I have a great love for them as a people. But they have rejected the Messiah, and they will remain in unbelief until they go back and rebuild Jerusalem—which they will do in this generation—and until the Messiah comes. The day will come when Juda will know who Shilo is, and that day is not very far distant."[26]

Such a vision of a repentent Jewish people also appeared in an early vision of the prophet: "And then shall the Jews look upon me and say, What are the wounds in thine hands, and in thy feet? ... I am Jesus that was crucified. I am the Son of God. And then shall they weep because of their iniquities; then shall they lament because they persecuted their king."[27]

However, the few widely scattered utterances of this kind did not result in any basic change in the existing dynamics of the restoration theory because they did not alter the basic religious situation. The great innovation of the Mormons was not a rehash of the old mission to the Jews of other Christian religious societies; nor was it their own mission to the Jews which later proved to be misdirected. It was rather their announcement that the return of the Jews was imminent and that this event would give the signal for the gathering of the Gentiles in the American Zion. Therein lay the dynamics of the Mormon approach. At the same time, the Jewish missions of other denominations, particularly unrealistic in America, were unable to come to new life, because the genuine religious forces required were no longer potent. The true situation of the Jews as evoked by the thoughts of restoration

103

among the faithful, led in just the other direction: the heroism of the old Jewish people experiencing these great days of in-gathering must have been given by divine election. This sounded quite different from old missionary talk:

"May we not naturally conceive that a people thus preserved without advance or recession; dispersed and combined; broken, yet firm; without a country, yet dwellers in all, everywhere insulted, yet everywhere influential, without a nation, yet united as no nation, ever before or since; has not been appointed to offer this extraordinary contradiction to the common laws of society, and even the common progress of nature, without a cause, and that cause one of final benevolence, universal good and divine grandeur."[28] And this uniqueness of the Jewish people was sought everywhere and explained by "mysterious operations which have preserved Israel a separate race through eighteen hundred years."[29]

But the Mormons did not disregard the play of political forces whenever it was possible that the hope of restoration might be founded on them. It was even rational to expect that this hope might be realized in the natural course of political events, just as the destruction of the independence of the Jewish homeland had been a political event: "It was by political power and influence that the Jewish nation was broken down, and her subjects dispersed abroad; and I will here hazard the opinion, that by political power and influence they will be gathered and built up; and further, that England is destined in the wisdom and economy of heaven to stretch forth the arm of political power, and advance in the front ranks of this glorious enterprise.

"There is an increasing anxiety in Europe for the restoration of that people. . . . Special ambassadors have been sent, and consuls and consular agents have been appointed. . . ."[30]

Consequently every detail of events in the world arena apt to bring about the final goal of the restoration of the Jews was heeded, and the situation in Palestine itself was closely observed. The reports of the emissaries of a mission dispatched to the Jews for this purpose fulfilled this function. Such a mission, within the framework of the over-all ends of the Mormon Church became a diplomatic mission. In talks with consular officers and with personalities in the political and financial world the missionaries

104

sougt information about the basic facts which future developments might make decisive for the fate of Palestine. Most important was the knowledge that the traditional Christian mission to the Jews had failed in Palestine itself as elsewhere. It was reproached for not having been able to effect the return of the Jews to their homeland:

"A great deal has been done by the religious world, so far as dollars and cents, and the formation of societies are concerned, for the amelioration of the condition of the scattered Jews. But what are the results of all the labors of the various Christian sects in this direction? Have they succeeded in gathering the Jews from the nations of the earth? Not at all. A very few Jews at the present time are residents of Palestine, and they are not converted to the truth. They believe in the religion of their ancient fathers, and all of them who dwell there are very poor, many of them are what may be termed beggars, being sustained principally by the charity of travelers and other visitors to that land, and by donations from charitable Christians and Jews abroad. But all the Jews dwelling in Palestine are but a very small handful, compared with the immense numbers of their brethren who are scattered to the four winds of heaven."[31]

In the assessment of the real situation of the conversionist societies, the Mormon press went to extremes as, for instance, in the following "Editorial Summary":

"The Rev. R. Laird Collier, a noted minister at Chicago, preached a sermon early in this month, in which he made statements about the futility of the efforts to convert the Jews that the Secretary of the Hebrew Christian Brotherhood, Rev. E. Van Noorden, himself a converted Jew, felt it necessary to controvert in a sermon. To strengthen his argument, the latter said that, 'Twenty thousand Jews in Europe join in worshiping the great king.'

"This assertion a Jewish minister disputes and declares it to be positively untrue. . . . He thinks these stories about converted Jews is one of the disreputable means whereby good and unsuspecting Christians are induced to come out with their quarters and dollars for the benefit of the Jewish missionaries. . . .

"This is rather hard upon the reverend Secretary and the Society he represents. We are inclined to believe, however, that the Jewish minister is correct in his statements. These missionary societies, in too many instances, consider 'the ends sanctify the means,' and the stories about their operations, which in a less pious cause, would be called harsh names for the purpose of swelling their funds. The people who believe that the Jews can be converted to Christianity, at present, know but little about their Bibles. It may be to the interest of the 'Hebrew Christian Brotherhood' and its Secretary to make the credulous, pious people believe that they are converting Jews with the donations they receive; but they cannot deceive the Jews, and those who know what is predicted concerning them, by such statements."[32]

In contrast to this sad situation, The Mormon vision of the future of the Jews in their homeland was retained:

"When the time shall have arrived for the fulfillment of the prophecy recorded by Ezekiel the Prophet, when the Jews and the ten tribes shall return and they shall no more be divided into two kingdoms, Jerusalem will be redeemed from the hands of the Gentiles, and it will be again inhabited by the Jews as a nation; not by a poor miserable remnant, dependent upon the charity of foreign nations for subsistence, but hundreds of thousands of the twelve tribes will return to Palestine, and their capital city will be Jerusalem, not Samaria."[33]

The greatness of the imminent task also appeared in Mormon poetry:

"Juda's Return
"The chosen ones of Israel, are scattered far and wide,
Where flows the lordly Tiber, where rolls the Atlantic tide;
By Danube's winding water, and Hudson crystal springs,
Dwells the myri'd descendants, of the Prophets and the
    Kings."[34]

It is clear that for the Mormon creed a territory other than Palestine could not be considered for the in-gathering of the Jews. The following was a characteristic manifestation of this view which was also noteworthy from the viewpoint of American Jewish history. It was directed against the man who wanted to convoke the Jews of the whole world to his "Ararat" in America. This manifestation was no less convincing because it appeared in the framework of a polemic against an inimical article in Noah's "New York Evening Star." The attitude remained pertinent even when "Ararat" was declared a mere real estate speculation. It was in-gathering of the Jews which was under consideration: "This much from M. M. Noah, a Jew who had used all the influence in his power to dupe his fellow Jews."[35]

The religious earnestness of this position contrasted sharply with the reactions of other Americans to this position of the Mormons. Indeed, when the connection between the belief in the in-gathering of the Jews and the Mormons became generally known by the American public, it had repercussions among the American Jews. They had to suffer at least a part of the derision assigned to the Latter Day Saints. The thought that the same Jews who were energetically engaged in a daily struggle for success in an expanding American economy, should be gathered in a far country soon had a comical reaction. Indeed, the simple person was so susceptible to this effect that he confronted the Jew with this picture of the in-gathering and enjoyed the effect of this image on those who would be gathered.[36] The American press occasionally pointed out the irresponsibility of news reports vis-à-vis the imminent in-gathering of the Jews:

"Every few years we hear of some important move being made relative to the return of the Jews to their native land, all of which we presume to be the coinage of some idle brain that has but little else to do."[37]

The above example of contempt for the in-gathering idea—both literary and actual—in its relation with the Indian descendancy theory and the "mixed cake" Ephraim which impelled the in-gathering in the American Zion attained an even more derisive meaning by incorporation into what the world held improbable and unimaginable—the system of Mormon creed and doctrine.

107

CHAPTER 12

The Mormons and the Jewish People of Old

The establishment of a spiritual Biblical landscape was conditioned by the image of ancient Israel as envisioned by the Mormons. The comparison of Biblical events, such as the exodus from Egypt with corresponding events in Mormon history and of the Biblical leader figure Moses with the leader of the Mormons who met a similar challenge, resulted from enthusiasm for the historic record of ancient Israel. There was an overwhelming desire to achieve a renewal of ancient Israelite ways of life, first of all through the administration of the new religious community by a modern priesthood formed in accordance with the Biblical idea of a holy people, a people of priests. The reintroduction of such institutions as the Biblical tithe to cover the expenses of the church bears witness that the existence of ancient Israel was felt to be a manifestation of the divine will to make this people His instrument.

The seriousness of the Biblical tasks taken over by the Mormons was shown by a warning to heed the example of the Jews: ". . . The Israelites were required merely to bring or send their tithes into the Lord's treasury. It was made an act of conscience with them, but they did not obey this commandment any more than the rest, and they suffered for their disobedience. . . ."[1]

The delineation of the Biblical elements in Mormonism will always remain an indication of the strength of Jewish ideas and the telling power of ancient Jewish life. It will show the inspiration and motivation the new American derived from the ancient Jewish past as well as the confidence he had in the future. Even if the new American Saint added so many other elements to this that it often became unrecognizable to contemporaries, its origins in ancient Jewish sources was always evident to people of under-

108

standing. The faith of this new American in the source of Jewish life is to be admired also because it had arisen in a nation lacking a long history of its own. Whatever may have been the history of the former inhabitants of the continent as revealed by the prophet, the only history this new American wanted to make a part of his own past was the history of ancient Israel. This was the true basis for the spiritual landscape of the Bible in the American Zion.

The children of the new religion were very ready to learn and to apply customs of ancient Israel which seemed to have been forgotten or neglected. The subsequent development of ideas of this kind could even lead to an attempt by a minor Mormon church to renew the kingdom in Beaver Island.* Furthermore, if institutions in Biblical times were considered timeless, then the marriage institution might also be renewed in the form which had existed in Biblical times. It is on this point that the Biblical argument for Mormon plural marriage was based: what was right before God so many years ago did not stop being so even in our times. Later especially this experiment with Biblical ways proved crucial for the new religion. But the heavy blows suffered by the Mormon church in regard to the practice of polygamy were only one aspect of the Mormons' basic historical problem, which was their persecution by the rest of Christian America.

The original concept of the new religion did not give the slightest indication that it would ultimately be only the common fate of the persecuted which would cement the new religion. According to the Founding Fathers of the new religion, the new truth had but to be revealed to the American people and to the world. In the enthusiastic search for good it was easy to syncretize many different elements of faith; life would eventually have to create a new organic synthesis from what was originally a recognizable syncretism. However, in this respect the unique example offered by the Jewish people as a historic community based on religion, was not observed at all by the Mormons. The founders of this new religion could not imagine that even in free America, a new faith under the conditions of the times, could endure in the hearts of men mainly because its adherents were persecuted. Later when the transition of Mormonism to a religion based on a common historic fate had already been sealed by the blood of so many martyrs including the prophet, the memory of the sufferings of the Jewish people in all periods of its history became the consoling companion of the Mormon people. These Jewish sufferings were related to the people by the church leaders as an illustration of the strength of faith. In this manner the American Saint, too, had been enabled to accomplish his historic achievements.

The area of identification between the Mormon people and the existence of the Jewish people thus became much broader than it had been at the beginning. It was no more merely the renewal of ancient Israel as a source of life, but rather the similar fate, community by common fate, and exodus as an aftermath of oppression. Their exodus was also accomplished under an elected leader, into their own promised land. After having accomplished this and after wandering through the deserts, they went on to the necessary defense against a pursuing enemy in "Zion." "We are situated as the Jews [Hebrews] were at the Red Sea; our enemies are pressing us . . . none but God can save us."[2]

In the first phase of Mormonism, some basic components of ancient Israel developed which gave to it its enduring appearance:

"The Hebrew symbol is not the cross, but the sceptre. The Hebrews know nothing of the cross. It is the symbol of the heathenism, whence Rome received her signs and her worship. . . . The reign of Messiah! Temples to the Most High God! The sceptre, not the cross!"[3]

If it is not the cross of suffering but the authoritative staff of the priesthood which should give the answer to the problems of modern life as to those of ancient times, then an old Israelitic idea has once again emerged victorious. In brief, the Mormon conception of priesthood was simply the Biblical idea of the holy people, a nation of priests. The priests, according to the words of the Bible, should clothe themselves in righteousness and sanctify their lives. This process was dramatized by the Mormons who permit each individual to rise to priesthood during his lifetime. Furthermore, there are two grades of priesthood, the different orders of Aaron and Melchisedek, the old class of priests by birth having disappeared. The first Jew to describe the Mormons extensively recognized this identification with the old Jewish ideal of a nation of priests: ". . . they call themselves 'Ancient Israelites of the order of the Melchisedek priesthood.' "[4] With the Mormons Biblical priesthood starts with Abraham, the father of all the faithful:

"Abraham was faithful to the true God, he overthrew the idols of his father, and obtained the priesthood after the order of Melchisedek...."[5] The far-reaching Christological interpretations of the Melchisedek figure to be dealt with elsewhere play no role at all in the establishment of the Mormon priesthood which stems only from the Bible:

"The Melchisedek, and Aaronic, are the only priesthoods that God ever has acknowledged; therefore, if the Christian word have neither of them, it is solemn mockery for them to administer the ordinances of the kingdom of God; for they have no authority to do it."[6]

Again, we have an example of Mormonism's success in making dynamic an element which existed in other religious communities where it did not result in anything essentially new or creative. For instance, in Ephrata a consecration "to the priesthood, by the laying on of hands; after which they were admitted to the ancient Order of Melchisedek by having the degree conferred on them in ancient form" is described.[7] But such single cases of self-identification of individuals with the old priesthood of Israel created nothing new, whereas the Mormons succeeded in evoking a religious mass-consciousness by means of the same idea, including a new responsibility in the new faith. The sacrifice which the priest of old had to offer was thus spiritualized into a sacrifice for the new community. Rightfully our aforementioned Jewish observer regarded this transformation as a sign of a community full of religious spirit:

"These Mormons are certainly the most earnest religionists I have ever been among. It seems to be a constant self-sacrifice with them, which makes me believe the masses of the people honest and sincere."[8]

Such a concept of folk-priesthood, could conceivably give rise to the idea that the requirements of theocracy and democracy were both satisfied:

"They delight to call their system a government, a 'Theo-Democracy'; and that, in a civil capacity, they stand as the Israelites of old under Moses."[9]

111

In bringing the great vision of folk-priesthood to life, the idea of a central location for the cult, as was the case with the ancient Jewish temple, exercised considerable influence on the faithful. Indeed it appears equal in strength to the power of the priesthood concept. With people dispersed over the vast spaces of a new continent, there was an urgent need to concentrate around a spiritual center of the cult: "The West is the future world. Yet how shall there be the new civilization without its distinctive temples? Certainly there shall be no Abrahamic dispensation and covenant unless symbolized by temples raised to the name of the God of Israel!"[10] The Mormons' love for their Nauvoo temple which had been built at so great a sacrifice, was compared by their friend, Thomas Leiper Cane, with the love the Jews of old had for their temple: "All had worked for it and it was the building of all and it had come to be loved by them with a passion in which the love of an artist for his fair creation was mixed with a semi idolatry as could find no parallel except that of the Jews toward their temple."[11]

With the idea of the temple, paradoxical as it may sound, we enter for the first time a broader plain of historical discussion between Mormonism and the American Christianity. In the last analysis, this conflict concerned the evaluation and incorporation of certain old Jewish cultural elements. It was epigramatically expressed by a contemporary cultural critic: "Mormonism is Judaism grafted on Christianity, instead of Christianity grafted on Judaism."[12] This inverted process had to be combatted. On the other hand, the fact remains that in their pioneer period, the American churches likewise had the vision of the temple before their eyes. This fact, however, helps us to reach the right conclusions about this period and the ideological battleground between the Mormons and the Christian denominations which later came into existence. Even the Christians of the formative period of the American churches had nothing to say against this spiritual "Judaizing," but were themselves enthusiastic about the temple. One has only to compare the derision poured out on the Mormons because they built a Temple in imitation of the old Jewish Temple with a remark written by Bishop Francis Asbury, in the eighteenth century, about a meeting of the faithful held in a large temporary tent:

"Some of our assemblies resembled the congregation of the Jews at laying the foundation of the second temple in the days of Ezrah —some wept for grief; others shouted for joy; so that it was hard to distinguish one from another: So it was here: . . ."[13]

The accusation of subservience to the Jewish spirit because of their temple could hardly be made against the Mormons by these same men, even in another generation. Furthermore, American exuberance would not have been so fervently branded paganism or even worse by later anti-Mormon literature if only it could have been incorporated into the life pattern of American Christianity. To be sure the formative period of American churches was full of dramatic moments. This battle against the wilderness and the frontier spirit was especially lively for the circuit riding clergymen who continually had to create new outposts for the church. It was, indeed, the Mormon's actual tearing away from the mother-churches which finished the matter.

Bishop Asbury's comment comparing the Temple in Jerusalem to his tent of assembly was the description of a situation which lasted only for a short time and came to an end with the dismantling of the big tent. In contrast to this, as soon as the Mormons set foot in a place, they dreamed of a real temple as the only lasting center. They built this temple, thus realizing a historical closeness to Israel of old. The Temple gave a unique appearance to the entire Mormon settlement:

"The Mormons have but one temple or own chapel for each town or village, and it would appear that this is always to be so. Joseph Smith felt that a multiplicity of churches would be prejudicial to earnestness of faith, which he proved by saying that in New York, London, Paris, Rome, cities where temples swarm, faith is more thinly than elsewhere, while the Jews, after a lapse of eighteen centuries, have never forgotten their only temple at Jerusalem."[14]

The identification of the Mormons with their unprecedented building of a Temple held the excited interest of the American public for a long time. To what extent the Jewish public was also stirred by it may be seen by a voice in a Jewish newspaper, as late as in 1880: "The Mormons are still pegging away at their new temple. It is now twenty years since it was commenced; D.

4,000,000 has been expended and it is one-fourth completed. The building is being constructed of Utah granite, and when finished will be the finest church edifice, if not the finest building of any kind, in America. It will require D. 28,000,000 to complete the temple."[15]

The mere question of a temple, therefore, was in no case the subject of dispute between the Mormons and other Christians. To understand this, the entire discussion must first be divested of its anti-Mormon intent and afterwards it must indicate the areas where Judaism-Christianity-Mormonism overlap one another. Exactly this was accomplished by a Christian contemporary:

"Judaism has been praised, honored, imitated, kept alive in the Christian teaching of the age, until it has at last found disciples to reconstruct it as a living institution. . . . Mormonism is intended to be a theocracy like the Jewish. . . . The Mormons have shown what can be made of the old Puritan idea carried out consistently to its ultimate conclusions. If the Jewish notions of theology are good for the nineteenth century, they have reasoned, why not the Jewish theory of government."[16]

In fact it was both a paradox and a logical consequence: the Biblical spirit was cultivated in America during the first two centuries of its spiritual life and now it was involved in a merciless fight against a group in which this Bible spirit had found only too trusting imitators. However, the situation was serious enough to eliminate any possibility of pardon. The same strong-willed independent folk-spirit which had seen in the Bible the pattern for proper decisions in modern life, was now called upon for a defense against Mosaic invasion. In addition many were of the opinion that only by turning away from Judaism could the Mormon people be saved, because in the end the battle of Christianity against Judaism would be fought on Mormon ground. This is nowhere more strongly stated than in the heresies which arose in Utah at the time:

"Now it is this Germanic or Anglo-Saxon mind which is bursting into mighty activity among the Mormons—mightier because so long suppressed—bursting from absolution into the genius of republicanism which will save the Priesthood and save Utah from a collision with the nation. You possess the Asiatic not the Germanic

114

or American mind, and therefore, you work upon the old theocratic ideas of Moses in the wilderness and not of a Christ grandly moving through a world's affairs. The one destroys priesthood in time, the other perpetuates it for ever; the one dies in Hebraism and Mosaic economics, the other lives in a universal civilization and everlasting Christ. Moreover, the former would bring any religious community into conflict with modern governments, and therefore, not even in America do the Jews attempt to reestablish their ancient theocracy. Indeed, the modern Jews would never permit its reestablishment, for even they are more Christian than Mosaic. It is left to the priesthood of Utah to attempt to bring back the days and economy of Moses, for you, the leaders of the people, are Mosaic in your priesthood and as before observed, Asiatic in your type of mind."[17]

In this way the "caveat consules" was given to the Mormon leaders. The cry for the extirpation of this Mosaism made an impressive reply necessary. This reply came in an entirely new effort, also the result of new experiences. It was an attempt to call on the image of the Eternal Jew as a witness for the martyrdom of their faith.

Chapter 13

The Image of the Jew Through the Ages

As a minority, continuously in danger, the Mormon people were naturally sensitive to other persecutions in the world. This in itself would have heightened Mormon interest in the Jewish people, even if the consciousness that the descendants of the ancient Biblical people were involved, had not been so strong. The closeness to the conditions of life in Bible times resulted in an even closer relationship to the life of the Jewish people in all countries. Consequently, the Mormon press reports gave detailed descriptions of Jewish life, written with unique warmth and underlying sympathy. Many of these reports were also given a theological significance because according to the Mormon concept, they were part of the preparation for the millennium. However, and in this respect the Mormons are not less realistic than other Americans, the situation of the Jewish people in the world was seen in dry facts and sober statistics. Organizational activities in Jewish life and general Jewish news are more frequently reported in the Mormon press than in other general American newspapers and magazines.

Nevertheless for the ultimate image of the Jew through the ages, it was the history of his persecutions which proved decisive. The Mormon people firmly believed that these persecutions recorded its own fate with all the sufferings to which it was destined during the decades of the formation of its community.

Out of this grew the first insight, the knowledge of the steadfastness of the post-Biblical Jew:

"In the history of the world there can be found nothing more remarkable than the records of the Jewish race. Few, and insignificant, as they have even been so far as numbers are concerned, they have yet been the center of an interest to the civilized, and especially the Christian races of the world which completely eclipses that attached to the mightiest nations. The 'peculiar people,' through the darkest ages of the Christian era, while enduring cruelty the most horrible and suffering the effects of the exterminating and bloodthirsty edicts of tyrants have preserved their identity, and have excited the wonder of all the rest of mankind by the extraordinary tenacity with which they have clung to their ancient traditions and to their religion. These have been their life and their fidelity to them the Jews undoubtedly owe their preservation as a distinct nationality. Fire and sword have in vain been used to induce the race to forsake the traditions and hopes of ancient Israel and terrible as have been their sufferings, caused at different epochs, through religious intolerance, the persecutions and trials endured by any sect, or partly, and by all combined, pale into insignificance when compared with what the Israelites have endured for their religion. Their steadfastness has seemed as immovable as the pillars of heaven."[1]

The fate of the Mormons proved that there is no escaping history, especially when it becomes a copy of Jewish history. Those who name themselves "Jews" suffer the Jewish fate through persecutions that generally befall Jews alone, but which on American soil by a strange concatenation became the essential history, the capacity to experience history of another group. Those afflicted by the fate of ancient Israel, through persecutions became "Jews." The Yankee, persecuted in America, thereby became "the Jew of the New World."

Thus the Jewish people, as an example of continuous persecution in history, had an entirely different value for a church fighting for its existence. Judaism as the uncontested community of suffering of all generations had become a guide to the future. The Jew's attitude to his persecutors merely had to be indicated; its useful application to the church members followed as a matter of logical course.

In a pedagogical sketch designed for the youth, the result of an insight into Jewish existence is given with an explanation of contemporary facts:

"Like the Latter-Day Saints, the Jews have suffered from the falsehoods told about them by apostates from their faith. For some time past there has been an intense feeling of hatred

117

shown to the Jewish people in Russia and many parts of Germany. This has broken out into acts of bitter persecution. . . . This spirit of persecution has not raged so much of late; still, it is with difficulty that it can be repressed or kept within bounds. For a while it seemed that it would carry on its cruel and inhuman work until the Jews would all be compelled to flee to other lands. Numbers were brought to the United States, and many persons were in favor of their settling here; but the tide was checked. This country was not found to be so desirable; and latterly there has been considerable talk of the Jews going to Palestine.

"Latter-day Saints cannot fail to be interested in the Jews and their movements. We cannot forget the promises which the Lord has made to them. Ancient prophets have predicted that they should yet rebuild and inhabit Jerusalem. In our day the Lord has confirmed the prophecies by revealing that the time is near for the Jews to be gathered to their ancient lands."[2]

The Jew had now assumed an entirely different role in the task of conversion. Indications of this, connected with criticism of the traditional endeavors to convert the Jews, are to be found in the Mormon press, as early as Kirtland:

". . . A Jew once said to me, says Adam Clarke, 'There are some of you Christians who are making wonderful efforts to convert the Jews. Ah, there is none but God Almighty that can convert a Jew, Adam Clarke remarks. Truly I believe him . . .

"*Remarks*—Neither the house of Joseph in America, nor the Jews among all nations, nor the ten tribes which went out to that country, 'where never mankind dwelt,' can be converted by ministers though the Gentiles are. . . . "[3]

This was clearly stated after the Mormon people had risen much higher on the ladder of persecution. Brigham Young, after the Utah trek, addressed the assembled members of the church on "August 8th, 1852 in the following words:

"There are the Jews—and recollect that they are a very religious people to this day; a more religious people never lived than they, that is, the Tribe of Judah, and the half tribe of Benjamin, that were left in Jerusalem; they are as tenacious as any people can be, to this day, for the religion of their fathers; and where can you see them among the nations of the earth, without seeing a hunted, driven, and persecuted people? The laws of nations have been framed for the express purpose of killing and destroying them from the earth. Yes, in the midst of nations that profess to adhere to the doctrines of Christianity—that legislate, and make laws, and put them in force—laws have been made to exterminate them; they cry out against them, and raise mobs to persecute and destroy, and clear the earth of the Jews.

"Notwithstanding all this, will they forsake their religion? No. They have suffered themselves to be stoned in the streets of the cities, their houses to be burned over their heads; but will they forsake their religion? No! they will perish rather."[4]

Such views of the Jewish people's firmness were especially stressed during critical moments of Mormon history. We find a reference to the Jews even in that most spectacular extra-edition of any newspaper in the world, the one which revealed the concept of plural marriage to the inhabitants of Utah. The firmness of the Jews is conspicuously featured in this celestial message.[5]

As a result of this new position of the Jew in Mormon creed something had to be created which, in contrast to other conversionist endeavors, theologically defended the right of the Jew to remain unconverted. This right was part of the interdependence of all the promises made to mankind. The Jew had to insist on being let alone until the promise to his forefathers would be fulfilled. This viewpoint was pronounced at a church meeting on January 30th, 1853 by Parley Pratt:

"If I were a Jew you might cry to me, and preach to me to dooms-day, and then take a sword, and hold it over me to sever my head from my body, but I would not move one step to the standard that is not Abraham's, nor from the everlasting covenant in which My Fathers Abraham, Isaac and Jacob, and all the holy prophets, will come and sit down in the kingdom of God, upon the same principles with their modern children. I am a Jew and my hope is in the covenants of the Fathers."[6]

For the sake of this hope the Jewish people had been preserved as a group and had emerged united from every persecution.

"They have been hunted down with dogs, and the time has been when it was perfectly lawful in some nations for every Christian child who was disposed to do so to stone a Jew while passing through the streets; and it is not long since they were not permitted to own a foot of land in any of the Gentile nations ... Their history is not lost, neither are they, and the simple reason they are not is because they were chosen of the Lord ... A remnant of the people of Israel are to be saved, and they will yet be gathered together."[7]

Occasionally, the unity of the Jewish people in spite of all persecutions, is explained by its spiritual and cultural values, in addition to the promise given to the Jews:

" ... terrible judgments fell upon the Jewish nation, yet they were not utterly destroyed, a remnant was all the time preserved, and today, in every nation under heaven is found a remnant of the seed of Israel, retaining the Hebrew language, many of their ancient manners and customs, their old law written on parchment, which is read in their synagogues every Sabbath day. In nearly all the countries in which they have been scattered they have been subject to the most extreme abuse. They have been in constant fear, they have been permitted to reside only in certain quarters, and have had imposed upon them the most fearful exactions . . . notwithstanding all the oppression . . . from generation to generation, they still maintain their identity as the seed of Abraham. [Babylon and Nineveh perished.] But the Jews are still a distinct race, and they are a living record of the truth of the revelations of God."[8]

At this point, when the continuing existence of the Jewish people filled all hearts with strong emotions, concern about the future existence of the Mormon people sought in the example of

120

the Jews a moral guaranteeing its continued existence. In order to put the Jewish example to practical use, it had to include the purification of the faithful along the lines of the Jews' firm adherence to the faith, but persecution as a fate in itself had to be given a deeper theological significance.

This concept was a historical turning point reaching far beyond any single religious community, for it concerned mankind as a whole. The historical question was now: How does persecution effect the continued existence of human ideological communities? Is it possible that such communities would have long since died out if they had not been transformed into actual communities by persecutions? And was the Jewish people the first example of an extended existence caused only by martyrdom? And could this also be true of the Mormons? Subsequent times and general historiographical endeavors have greatly strengthened such points of view and have attempted to compare them with all types of human communities of ideas. But a solution to such problems of historical science is not in sight and has certainly not been found for the Jews or Mormons. Yet voices of all ages have assured us that the blood of martyrs is the seed of faith.

It was not necessary for the Mormons to construct such a general theory of the function of persecution in history but for their own use sentiments of this kind served well as explanations of their fate. Thus says Brigham Young:

"If we had received no persecution in Nauvoo, would the gospel have spread as it now has? Would the Elders have been scattered so widely as they are now, preaching the Gospel? No, they would have been wedded to their farms, and the precious seed of the word would have been choked."[9] Without these persecutions there would have been no exodus and they would not have found their promised land; Zion would not have materialized in the "State of Deseret." Without it, also, significant points of contact with ancient Israel would not have been made. Brigham Young would not have been compared with Moses and the various elements of the Biblical Exodus could not have been transferred to Mormon tradition. There could not have been talk of the golden calf and many other matters which had a purposeful, visible influence upon the faithful in "Zion."

121

Here too it may be pointed out as has been previously indicated in other elements of the Mormon creed, that the firmness of the Jew was highly regarded by other Christian denominations in America. However, the question of historic fate was not involved for them and it did not affect their doctrine or create special traditions among them. Furthermore, with the Mormons the doctrine of Jewish restoration became part of the experience of Mormon persecutions in the memory of later generations. In contrast to this, other early Christian voices raised in America in regard to the persecution of the Jews elicited no change in Christian belief other than a general better understanding of the Jew; nor did they bring about any association with their own denominational history.

Nevertheless, doubt about the moral qualities of conversionist activities in respect to the Jews was expressed by a traveler in America who in 1824 already reproached his European countrymen:

> "The Jews, instead of being respected for the firmness with which, even under the most horrible persecutions, they have adhered to the faith of their forefathers, have been oppressed, and almost placed out of the pale of the law, in nearly every country of Europe. I recollect when at school at Eton, asking an old Jew who sold oranges, why he had never embraced Christianity; and his reply made a great impression on me, and induced me to look upon the Jews with much more respect than before. 'I despise,' said he, 'any man who quits the faith of his fathers, merely because it is abused by the ignorant and bigoted.'"[10]

Despite such enlightened sentiment, conversionist activities went on in Europe and in America.

But the Mormons elaborated their position further. When the Jew remained firm in the faith of his fathers due to divine will it was clear that all efforts to convert him must be without success. The Jew received his revelation from God and only God Himself can by His divine will determine the time the Jew will accept a new gospel:

> "The Lord knew how to preach to the Jews, and told them what the truth was. You may as well undertake to

122

command the most degraded of these Indian tribes, and give them arms and accoutrements, and try to put them through the regular military exercise, as to preach to the Jews to make them believe in the Lord Jesus Christ.

"Jerusalem is not to be redeemed by the soft still voice of the preacher of the Gospel of peace. Why? Because they were once the blessed of the Lord, the promised seed. They were the people from among whom should spring the Messiah; and salvation could be found only through that tribe. The Messiah came through them, and they killed him; and they will be the last of all the seed of Abraham to have the privilege of receiving the New and Everlasting Covenant. You may hand out to them gold, you may feed and clothe them, but it is impossible to convert the Jews until the Lord God Almighty does it."[11]

However, some individual Jews did accept the Mormon faith. Before there was any experience concerning their devotion to the the new faith, the Mormons first had to separate the wheat from the chaff. They developed a theory of spiritual self-selection on the basis of change of blood much like the self- selection of Ephraim, the "mixed cake" among the nations. It was formulated by Brigham Young:

"Can you make a Christian of a Jew? I tell you, nay. If a Jew comes into this Church, and honestly professes to be a Saint, a follower of Christ, and if the blood of Judah is in his veins, he will apostatize. He may have been born and bred a Jew, have the face of a Jew, speak the language of the Jews, and have attended all the ceremonies of the Jewish religion, and have openly professed to be a Jew all his days, but I will tell you a secret—there is not a particle of the blood of Judaism in him, if he has become a true Christian, a Saint of God; for if there is, he will most assuredly leave the Church of Christ, or that blood will be purged out of his veins. We have men among us who were Jews, and became converted from Judaism. For instance, here is brother Neibaur; do I believe there is one particle of the blood of Judah in his veins? No, not so much as could be seen on the point of the finest cambric needle, through a microscope with a magnifying power of two millions. This is a secret that you will perhaps find out, in a coming day, to your satisfaction."[12]

Conversion had thus become what it had been according to the oldest Jewish conception, an inversion in which man tried to find God in his own soul. Understandably Alexander Neibaur as the avowed representative of the true process of finding a new faith, wrote with pride in his diary [December 1st, 1854]:

". . . Brigham Young preached concerning the Jews no Jew coming in this Church would remain faithful. Br. Neibaur as a Jew has changed his Jewish Blood there is not a smallest particle of the Blood of a Jew in him——"[13]

Jews who bore out this theory of apostasy by falling away from their new Mormon faith could also be found in time.

CHAPTER 14

The Jew-Mormon Comparison

The position of the Jew in Mormon creed and doctrine was gradually developed and interpreted by the Mormon leaders in their authoritative statements about ancient Israel and the Jew through the ages. Thus, the way was opened to a contemporary Jew-Mormon comparison. This development paralleled that of the Jew-Yankee analogy which was dominant in America at the time. The latter was used by various immigrant peoples to establish the image of the native American by comparing him with the image of the Jew, which was well-known to them from their European past.[1] The unanimous answer to the question which troubled so many Europeans as to: "What actually was the native American?" was, "The Yankees are the Jews of the New World."

And now the Mormon, who was himself so often the Yankee from Vermont, stepped to the side of the Jew. The image of a new Yankee standing upon the sacred soil on an American hill where he had found his own Tablets of the Law absorbed some features of the Jew-Yankee comparison and added new ones entirely in the religious sphere into which the old Jew-Yankee comparison intruded only occasionally. ("Six days of the week the Yankee deceives his fellow man, and on the seventh day he deceives God," a demonstration against the "Puritan Sabbath" as a "vestige of patriarchal Judaism.")

Now a vast field had been opened for the new Mormon comparison with the Jew, a Mosaic priesthood, Zion to be built in America and the entire genealogical table of Biblical peoples, lost and found. In a word: anything could go.

Nowhere could we find a comparison between the Mormon and, let's say, the sufferings of the early Christians or between the Mormon way of life and that of primitive Christianity or later

125

Christian sects who were persecuted. In this respect, there was no difference between the Mormon's self-comparison and that of the Gentiles. No matter who made it, the comparison was limited to the relationship to the Jew.

From the Mormon's point of view, the contemporary situation not only favored self-comparison with the Jew, but also furthered it in the ways of life, the spiritual climate, and the imagined Biblical landscape. A lack of understanding of these processes is shown by later critics of Mormonism who called the Biblical landscape concept an artificial product of the Mormon mind. To thoughtful observers, the image of the Bible landscape arose spontaneously, as was noted while they moved about in Utah:

"It is curious to see how the very physical circumstances of Mormonism are a copy of the Jewish. The parallel is not a fanciful or accidental one. The Mormons acknowledge, in some points intend it,themselves. Kirtland and Nauvoo were their settlements in Egypt; Joe Smith was their Moses; and when he died too early for a sight of the promised land, Brigham Young became the Joshua who led them all the way home. They have founded their Jerusalem in a Holy Land wonderfully like the original. Like Gennesareth, Lake Utah is a body of fresh water emptying by a river Jordan into a Dead Sea without outlet and intensely saline. The Saints find their Edomites and Philistines in the Indians . . . and in the Gentile troops of Uncle Sam. The climate is a photographic copy of the Judaean; the thirsty fields must be irrigated through long seasons of rainless, cloudless heat, while the ridges of Lebanon, here called the Wahsatch, are covered with snow."[2]

Enough Biblical images came to the mind of the outside observer to make the most essential features of the Jew-Mormon comparison common to Mormon self-comparison and the comparison made by the Gentile outsider. With this accord between the two, the importance of this comparison as a whole for the illumination of American folk-consciousness during the formative years of Mormonism, increased tremendously. For it was deemed natural by the Gentile that whenever the Mormon compared his fate with that of Israel of old, this comparison also had to be considered from a third point of view, with the addition of an illustration from the non-Mormon surroundings. It was thought that the

126

peculiar significance lay in the fact that the Mormon himself made comparisons of this kind. In this way, the contemporary Jew as well as ancient Israel, together with the Mormon, were presented to the American public through common characteristics.

In addition, the entire American atmosphere before the Civil War was saturated with Biblical images regarding the slavery question. A wider search for Biblical likenesses was entirely in the spirit of the times but all this was overshadowed by the opportunity offered by the Mormons. A true orgy of Biblical analogies and comparison with the Jews generally inundated America. This flood rose even higher and the Jew-Mormon comparison reached its peak when the Mormons adopted a Biblical argument for their polygamy which had, in the meantime, been revealed by them to America. The polygamy furor is not easily understandable to later times. However, in contemporary America, which had no literature on sex, either native or imported, the Biblical descriptions of ancient family conditions presented an opportunity to discuss concealed contemporary social life.

In considering the entire scope of the Jew-Mormon comparison, it is necessary first of all to separate the Biblical elements from the post-Biblical. The former were experienced by the Mormon people at first; the others followed as an afterthought.

The consciousness of expulsion from their homes and the search for a new homeland was central to the Mormons' experience. They worked out a complete analogy with the narration of the Exodus of the children of Israel from Egypt to Canaan. The comparison went into all the details given by the Bible, slavery first, then the rise of the leader Moses, the wanderings through the desert, the golden calf episode and finally reaching the promised land. For each phase, a parallel to the historic life of the Mormon was effected. This approach penetrated the consciousness of the Mormon people so thoroughly that every attempt to fabricate other analogies paled into insignificance. For example, the life of the primitive Christians and Christian martyrology proved to be without any influence compared to the Exodus story. The Christian story appears only in the demand for the traitor—here the apostate from the Mormon faith—thereby further strengthening an analogy to the treatment the Jew received from the Christian world generally:

127

"Apostasy and its causes.

". . . William Law, who Judas-like, while sitting at the Council Board, and on terms of intimate friendship with the prophet of God, was secretly plotting with his enemies to destroy him."[3]

This extreme interpretation of the Exodus story by the Mormons was the most influential element in causing America to regard them as the Jews of the New World.

As in the theory of the Indian descent from the lost tribes and other matters, we again have an opportunity to compare Mormons and Puritans. This time, it is in the way in which they applied the Exodus story to their own spiritual experiences. As the result of such a comparison, we find that Puritan America, with its founders and epigones, created a spiritual atmosphere based on this theme in many aspects. Yet they never experienced the essence of this comparison as historical events. In contrast to this, the Mormons relived the entire Biblical narrative in their own history, during the course of one generation in America. (No Puritan generation in America met these criteria.)

Individual phases of the application of the Exodus comparison to the Mormons mirrored the historical events whether the Mormons applied the comparison to themselves or others applied it to them. In the first example the Mormons' own comparisons dealt with the separation of the new religious society from the surrounding world. But soon, and in this we find a resemblance to the Puritan use of the Exodus story, the analogy was to the emigration from Europe of the masses which Mormon missionary efforts brought to America. The following part of a prayer composed in Nauvoo expresses this clearly:

". . . We thank thee, that as thou didst formerly raise up thy servant, Joseph, to deliver his brethren in Egypt, so thou hast raised up another Joseph to save his brethren from bondage to sectarian delusion, and to bring them into this great and good land—a land flowing with milk and honey, which is the glory of all lands, and which thou didst promise to be an inheritance for the seed of Jacob for evermore. . . . Bring the son from afar, and the daughters from the ends of the earth, and let them bring their gold and their silver with them."[4]

As the Westward Movement on the American continent be-

128

came part of Mormon fate, the Exodus comparison switched from an image of emigration from Europe, to the historic migration of the Mormons across the continent as the most vital phase of Mormon history. Contemporaries pointed out that this migration was initiated by native Americans and not by immigrants:

"They were not 'the ignorant masses from Europe.' They were mostly men and women of New England blood. . . ."[5] This point was made with pride by contemporary Mormons who illustrated it by depicting circumstances and giving genealogical details:

"The Mormons submitted to be driven from their homes. Yet they are chiefly American-born citizens; for the community has not in Nauvoo been swelled, as now in Utah, with floods of emigration. The modern Israel, who left under their Moses, were sons and daughters of America, whose sires had fought in the Revolution, and some, as, for instance, Apostles Parley and Orson Pratt, could trace their parentage to the Pilgrim Fathers. It was these men who consented, by a regular treaty (in which Douglas and others had a hand), to be driven from the country their sires had settled and the national family their Revolutionary ancestry had formed. Nothing in history since the Exodus of Israel from Egypt equals this Mormon exodus."[6]

Those who witnessed the beginnings of Mormonism viewed the impulse to go West as an expression of a general American tendency as did Kane in a letter to Horace Greeley: 'Driven westward by the uncontrollable impulse which Providence has given to the American Citizen, with the wandering Jew . . . he will move onward. . . .'[7] But anyone who followed their religious literature could, from the beginning find mystical hints about the West accompanied by Biblical images:

"The Far West.
". . . reader, stop and pause at the greatness of God; and remember that even Moses, when on top of Pisgah, lifted up his eyes and looked westward first, to view the promised land."[8] Or in another passage:

"The West.
"When Moses climbed up to view the heritage of God, he lifted up his eyes westward. . . . And by an article in our next No.

129

it will be seen, that the Jews continue to pray to God upon the ruins of the west wall of Jerusalem."[9] Their very first choice of western land for settlement was greeted by an outsider with the following remark: ". . . Their great prophet Jo has selected a part of Geouga county, Ohio, and pronounced it to be 'the promised land' and thither the deluding people are flocking, chiefly from New York. . . ."[10]

But all these Biblical echoes pale into insignificance before the serious decision to lead the Mormons leaving Nauvoo into an entirely uninhabited land. The full scope of the Biblical story in all its details now became applicable—the wandering through the desert including the episode of the golden calf, the final occupation of the land and its defense against enemies from without. And when all this was accomplished, the Mormons continued to transmit their living historical record to all later immigrants and to the next generation. An outsider observing this historical sense of the Mormons found the following words for it: "Moses could not repeat more diligently to Israel the story of their Exodus, than the Mormon prophets repeat to the Saints the story of their woes."[11]

Modern wanderings in the desert become a unique phenomenon, and newspapers of a great nation followed its phases and published the decrees of the leaders of such an Exodus. And it becomes even more newsworthy in that the desert wanderers themselves published a newspaper—the first ever issued in the territory of what was later Nebraska:

"The Mormons are about to issue a newspaper from their camp in the wilderness."[12]

The sufferings of the trek were endured because the great vision of the promised land was ever before their eyes: "Slowly and painfully they journeyed forward, as the Israelitish host had journeyed through the wilderness of Kadesh and Tein. . . . It seemed that, like the Hebrews of old, the generation which had left the land of bondage would perish by the way. . . . This Promised Land lay before them."[13]

If one compares Puritan and Mormon as to which better deserved the designations "Pilgrims" and "Israelites," the decision must fall to the Mormon by virtue of his wanderings in the desert:

130

". . . The Pilgrim Fathers of the East contend for a title which falls inevitably to these peers of the old Israelites, the Wanderers over the Wilderness of the West. They have been literally strangers and pilgrims, have had their cruel Pharaos on waters sometimes compared with the Nile—the Mississippi. . . . The mountain-locked lakes of the Rocky Mountains, with the connecting Jordan, are their Palestine, where they sit down to build up in great prosperity their new Jerusalem. . . ."[14]

The first sight of the Promised Land reported by the American press as 'the new Mormon location,"[15] was later dramatically underlined ("This is the place").

According to the Mormons, the land was given to them by the same divine promise which gave Canaan to the ancient Israelites. They regarded their right to occupy the Land and their duty to make it fruitful as entirely equal to the task set for Israel of old: ". . . Our creed is the good old Jewish creed, which tells us to occupy the land, to till it and dress it, and make it bud and blossom and bear fruit, and become a sign of the Kingdom of God. We have come here to stay here; . . . And his interpreter, the soft-tongued Pratt, shows, in the great highway through the mountains, a fulfillment of the words of the Hebrew seers, and a proof that God holds guard over the Saints of the Latter Day."[16]

In the whole complex of the Mormon Exodus story, the figure of the leader and his irresistible capacity to influence human souls, stands out, and the Moses-Brigham Young comparison completes the story:

"This is a greater work than that performed by Moses, of redeeming the children of Israel from Egyptian bondage; yet it is done on the same principle. The voice of God to Moses was to deliver His people from their bondage and he would be with him and assist him. The command is now for the people to be delivered from their bondage, poverty and distress, and come to the valleys of the mountains, where they can sustain themselves. . . . Had Moses presented himself in the same way as Washington or William Tell . . . had he, I say, appeared in his own name, and presented before the people as a person of superior powers and ability and [not] claimed power greater than that he possessed as a man, all would have been well. But when he went before them in the name

131

of the Lord Almighty, he experienced some difficulty in performing the work which had been assigned him."[17] Other enlightened Americans also regarded the deed embodied in the Mormon exodus —even if there were no divine call—as a peak of human achievement—particularly when compared with the Biblical exodus:

". . . The Israelites entered the land of promise by arms, and established themselves by the force of military prowess. But this is not quite the land of promise, nor are these Israelites who stream over the Rocky Mountains. But they are a sturdy band, whose enterprise will cover these fertile hills with golden harvests."[18]

To all those who believed that historical events reach their culmination in the rise of a truly great man, "Brigham Young, a new Moses"[19] was the epitome. The "Mormon Moses"[20] became a Bible comparison *sui generis* and was even immortalized as an inscription on one of the "Graphic Statues" of contemporaries.[20] The concept of leadership among the Mormons was in time patterned entirely upon the figure of "Mormon Moses."

"Intimately connected with them from their exodus from Illinois, this man has indeed been their Moses, leading them through the wilderness to a remote and unknown land, where they have since set up their tabernacle, and where they are now building their temple." (1856)[21] And the justification of the new term was exemplified in a polemical outcry: "Brigham is Moses, and we are Korah a. Co."[22]

That American Jews too were mightily impressed may be seen from a fictional speech of a Jewish educator inserted in a journal dedicated to the edification of Jewish youth:

"Mr. Young, in you I behold a second Moses only you have been more successful; my ancestor was only allowed to bring the children of Abraham, Isaac and Jacob to the confines of the Holy Land, he could only take a peep at it, and then laid himself down to rest in the wilderness. You, a second Moses, are far more successful, you brought your followers to this blessed country, you made this land bloom and flourish. . . ."[23]

Nevertheless, the opposition did not tire of stressing what in their eyes was the basic difference between the Biblical and the Mormon Moses. The following poem expresses the view of the enemy:

132

Crossing Weber River

... The Castellated rocks; the Mormon Pisgah.
... Upon those heights the Mormon Pilgrims stand
And from them first discern their promised land;
... So Moses saw from Pisgah's top the shore
Where Israel's weary wandering should be o'er.
But oh! how different was the ancient seer
From him who led his blinded followers here!
Yet doth the scene resemble that of old,
Where God with Moses did communion hold—
Those flaming forests that on high we see
To fancies vision might a Horeb be;
No further similes my pen would try,
Since Moses' creed was truth, and Smith's a lie.[24]

Tragedy touched the "Mormon Moses" only at the end of his life when persecution endangered his life-work. This introduced the only sad feature of the comparison with the Biblical Moses:

"Brigham Young is a Moses whose hands will not much longer be staid. But if he should die now of a broken heart, as the result of what the Mormons would consider persecution of an illegal character, he would die a martyr."[25] And in this contemplated martyrdom the "Mormon Moses" assumed a resemblance to the post-Biblical version of Moses, as interpreted by oral post-Biblical Jewish tradition.

At the same time the general exodus comparison became more specific: ". . . The journey of Moses and the Israelites pales into insignificance compared with this. Accepting Jewish revelation while we ridicule that of the Mormons, we see Jehova on the side of the Israelites, leading them. . . . At last, ungrateful as they were, they came to a land of plenty, prepared by the hands of strangers to their occupation. Not so with the "Latter Day Saints. . . ."[26]

For the people who came to Utah later, the Exodus had already become oral tradition. This was important for the immigrant masses in order to give them a substitute for actual participation in the Utah trek. They were indoctrinated, as contemporaries saw it, "to regard England as Egypt and their old dwelling-place as exile from a brighter home. America is to them Canaan, Salt Lake City a new Jerusalem."[27] This applied to the English Mormons;

133

other immigrant peoples contributing adherents to Mormonism easily created their own sayings along the same lines.

But not everything said in the course of the Exodus comparison was a positive recognition of historic achievement. The enemies of the Mormons seized the opportunity to strengthen their position by stressing unsympathetic aspects of the Biblical story in their comparisons. There was, first of all, the fact that Canaan had been occupied by the Israelites after a struggle with other peoples. Significantly this Biblical moment was retroactively applied to the Mormons to justify their having been driven out of earlier places of settlement in America. By occupying the land in the same way as the Israelites did, they had occasioned their own expulsion by their neighbors: "They were charged . . . of overturning the government, driving out the old population and taking possession of the country, as the children of Israel did in the land of Canaan."[28] These were the words of the former governor of Illinois at the time the Mormons had already left Nauvoo. But the argument already existed at the time that Nauvoo was settled by them. "In the times of Moses it was enough to say, 'the Lord has given us this land for an inheritance.'—in our days it has to be paid for. . . ."[29] The German who wrote this did not understand that a blood-price could not be set on the right to settle on empty land.

The vital instinct that the land had to be taken from the Indians was renewed vis-à-vis the Mormons. It grew even stronger since Mormon land was already cultivated and the elimination of enemies under such favorable circumstances seemed a good thing. The feeling was that might makes right.

The Mormon reconstruction of the Biblical episode of the golden calf resulted from the curious parallel development of two diametrically opposed societies: California and Utah. The first was founded by the gold rush, the other by religious colonization. Both were founded at the same time and were the result of the Westward impulse in combination with the travelling conditions of the time: one route to California led through Utah and was used extensively. The gold rush had passed over the interior colonization of America at a time when the prairies had for the most part not yet been settled. But Mormon leadership participated by dispatching a Mormon battalion to join the great adventure of establishing an extensive Pacific empire for America. The Mormons expected that this participation would secure their own empire, being established by colonizing the Intermountain Basin. Members of the Mormon Battalion, who had found and acquired gold in California brought it with them to Utah. Others giving in to the temptations of gold, remained in California. Soon these temptations endangered Mormon migration to Utah. Instead of settling in Utah, immigrants could go on to California, thus repudiating their original intention of working within the Mormon community. This danger had to be overcome and the Biblical story of the golden calf served to do so on a religious basis by comparing the attitude of the Israelites in the desert with the Mormons who deviated on their trek:

"There are some persons who for a consideration will supply what we want—I say for a consideration—the Mormon people brethren in this respect resembling the Jews of old, who while effecting to despise the Gentiles, were at the same time strongly enamored of Gentile gold."[30]

Love of gold and lust for it as exemplified by carrying away the gold of Egypt—a favorite theme of American popular humor—and adoration of gold which caused people to desert the religious community and to seek fortunes in California now became the theme of the Mormon leaders' religious admonitions. But the realities and temptations of the situation were calmly taken into consideration by the Mormon leaders. It was expected that such an overflow to California, would carry with it mainly the bad elements who had come to Utah. In the speeches of the church leaders we find the resounding note of "Zion no Refuge for the Wicked."[31] Aside from bankrupts and persons who had come into conflict with the Law in other parts of America, it was hoped that those elements who were not strong enough in their faith would also leave Utah for California. In time the words, "go to California and prosper if you can" were uttered not in derision, but rather in the hope that the Mormon community might benefit from the departure of many such individuals from Utah. The theological question of whether a Saint who, instead of being gathered into Zion, had gone to California to acquire riches might go to Heaven, was afterwards treated with some indulgence.

But later when the gold rush was over and enough merchants —including some who had returned from California—had acquired wealth in Utah, the Mormon Country was praised for its treasures in images based on the Biblical comparison: "Their land is far richer than was the Canaan of the Israelites, and they get from it all they want."[32]

Although the Bible comparisons between Jew and Mormon included many different aspects, the comparison with the post-Biblical Jew was mainly restricted to the persecutions suffered by both. In time this comparison gained importance not only among the Mormons but also among outside observers, as, for instance, in the report of a German traveler:

"There we are led through a water-poor region and over rocky mountains to the seat of the much-maligned Mormons, whose assiduity and righteousness made them an object of hatred to the crooked Yankee rascals until they were twice driven from their settlements with cruelties unparalleled even in the Middle Ages during the persecutions of the Jews—an eternal shame for the United States."[33]

In the self-comparison among the Mormons, the feelings of having suffered injustice rose to full self-identification with the classical figure of the wronged Jew, Shylock: "Has not a 'Mormon' eyes? Hath not a 'Mormon' hands, organs, dimensions, senses, affections, passions? . . . These paraphrased interrogations from Shakespeare, have just as much significance from the lips of a 'Mormon' as from a Jew."[34]

Much later we again read a call by the Mormons to the whole of America, to put an end to the fight against them, and again the comparison with Shylock is the backbone of this appeal: "When the 'Merchant of Venice' was presented, the gentry of London saw no injustice in the spoiling of Shylock. . . . They hated the Jews so cordially that they refused to rebuke the patent cruelty involved in Portia's sentence. But England waked up one day, and recognized that the Jew was a man or not a man, depending on the individual, and not on the race, or the religion. They quit quarreling. And has England been any worse for it? Was England as the British Empire ever greater than when a Jew occupied—and filled, good sirs— the chair of premier?"[35]

136

In time the comparison had its effect on non-Mormons as well:

"It made me think that some people have the impression that 'Mormons' are people with horns—a conception that formerly ignorantly prevailed concerning the Jew." . . . As has been often the case with the Jew the 'Mormons' have frequently been misrepresented and maliciously maligned."[36]

CHAPTER 15

School of Prophets and Bible Language

Puritanism brought with it to America a deep respect for the Biblical way of life and an appreciation of Hebrew as the language of the Bible. Indeed, in "the confusion of tongues" Hebrew was for a long time considered the unifying bond of all cultures. Even a hundred years later a post- revolutionary reminiscence bore witness to a time when "some arguing that the Americans are the chosen people of the New World desired that we should adopt the Hebrew."[1] Religious enthusiasm for the Hebrew language was unlimited as, for instance, in the case of John Eliot, Apostle to the Indians: "He was so fond of the Hebrew language that he used to say that it was better fitted than any other language to be the universal language."[2] And in an "Address to American Critics," they were reproached for accusing American literati of looting Hebrew literature:

"From Hebrew gather many a luscious plot,
To patch up plays, new sermons and romance."[3]

It has been convincingly shown that the theory of the descendance of the Indians from the lost tribes of Israel strengthened the study of the Hebrew language everywhere.[4]

The relationship of the Mormons to the language of the Bible, which took shape so much later, involved several elements which could have brought about a "confusion of tongues." The definitive attitude of the Mormons to Hebrew was based on the fact that in addition to the holy writings created by Mormonism, the Bible was always held to be holy. Since proper access to the Bible was possible only through the Hebrew language its study was required. But at the same time the Hebrew of the Bible and the Prophets was not the only language of revelation, if one accepted the modern renewal. The new revelation was not given in the language of the Bible although its peculiar form of English was influenced by the authoritative English translation of the Hebrew Bible. In this way a situation had arisen where the Prophet spoke "in tongues" as the inner impulse to prophetic language had generally been called. Yet this new language of prophecy could not approach Hebrew, the language of the Bible. In addition, not all the holy writings of Mormonism were direct inspirations in the new prophetic language. For instance, the Book of Mormon describes itself as a translation from old records in another language dictated by a voice from Heaven. According to Mormon theory, this other language was the tongue designated as "Hebrew" three times in one verse of the Book of Mormon. "The language to which this name was applied in the days of Mormon and Moroni was greatly changed from the Hebrew spoken by the Israelites at the time Lehi left Jerusalem, nearly a thousand years before."[5]

The Mormons escaped the danger of a "confusion of tongues" at least spiritually by the realistic recognition of the fact that the only road to deeper penetration into the world of the Bible was the study of the Hebrew language. They required this study of themselves at the same time that they recognized a new language for revelation in our days. They declared that the study of Hebrew was obligatory in the School of Prophets which was instituted by revelation. The way to the Bible was thus open.

With the dissemination of the new Mormon faith there must also have been a practical necessity to follow the example of other religious denominations which had in one way or another organized Hebrew language study in their pedagogical institutions. But this situation in no way diminished the merit of the Mormon's resolution to Hebrew language study. In any case, it was the inner motivation which was primary, no matter how much outer circumstances also pointed in the same direction.

An important element in the historic group relations between Jew and Mormon in this area is the fact that for the Mormons Hebrew studies were only possible if a Jew were employed as the Hebrew language teacher. In fact, this immediate need led to the first meeting between Jews and Mormons within the framework of American life rather than in the imaginary Biblical or historic situations of the Jewish past. In the course of efforts to find a qualified Hebrew teacher, the Mormons made contact with two Jews. Later association with these two resulted in the many notes made by the Prophet about his personal Hebrew studies and those of other Mormons within the School of Prophets and outside of the institution.

The beginnings of Hebrew studies among the Mormons may be traced to the early interest of the Prophet in this language and his personal efforts to establish an institution of higher learning. Although all the exact details in this area have not come down to us such endeavors were already in evidence during the Kirtland period of Mormonism. The essential facts about this were set down by the Prophet himself during this period. In the following Nauvoo period, a remark made during the last days of his life stated that he had studied Hebrew with the earliest important Jewish convert to Mormonism who had followed the Prophet to Nauvoo: "Read Hebrew with Neibaur."[6]

Although there is little possibility today to judge the Hebrew scholarship of Alexander Neibaur, it is certain that he had received a traditionally thorough Jewish education in Germany.

The Prophet's interest in Hebrew study started after he and Sidney Rigdon had completed the work of the "inspired Translation."[7] We learn that on November 20, 1835, Oliver Cowdery returned from New York to Kirtland with Hebrew books, a Bible, a dictionary and a grammar, which he had apparently bought on the order of the Prophet. Joseph Smith spent the next day in his house studying the Hebrew alphabet, and that evening the Elders assembled to make the final arrangements to engage a Hebrew teacher. At that time, a certain Dr. Piexotto, professor of physics and obstetrics in Willoughby, had already been engaged for that purpose.[8] Apparently this was the well known Daniel Maduro Peixotto.[9]

Dr. Piexotto must have disappointed the Saints because even before he had begun to teach, the Saints resolved to send to New York for a Hebrew teacher if "they could get released from the engagement they had made with him, having ascertained that he was not qualified to give them the knowledge they wished to require [sic] of the Hebrew."[10]

140

The opportunity to cancel the contract with Peixotto arrived on January 4, 1836, and we read about it in the journal of the Prophet: "Monday morning, 4th, met and organized our Hebrew school according to the arrangements that were made on Saturday last, as we had engaged Dr. Piexotto to teach us the Hebrew language, when we had our room prepared. We informed him that we were ready, and our room prepared, and he agreed to wait on us this day, and deliver his introductory lecture. Yesterday he sent us word that he could not come until Wednesday next; a vote was then called to know whether we should submit to such treatment or not, and carried in the negative; and Elder Sylvester Smith appointed clerk to write him on the subject, and inform him that his services were not wanted; and Elders Wm. F. McLellin and Orson Hyde dispatched to Hudson Seminary to hire a teacher."[11]

The choice of the committee fell on Dr. Joshua Seixas. Dr. Seixas was already known as a Hebrew scholar among his contemporaries: "I have lately seen a Manual Hebrew Grammar by J. Seixas . . . whose admirable method of instructing (so far as I can learn it from his pupils) is likely entirely to refit the old, rusty, creaking door to oriental learning."[12]

Dr. Seixas had offered the Mormons a term of 7 weeks for 40 pupils for a salary of 320 dollars. "He is a highly celebrated Hebrew scholar and proposes to give them sufficient knowledge to read and translate in the seven weeks."[13] On January 26, 1836, Dr. Seixas arrived in Kirtland from Hudson and began his teaching twice daily, from 10 to 11.A.M. and from 2 to 3 P.M. The salary of 320 dollars for 84 hours of instruction during the whole term was a good one when compared with the yearly income of an Ohio Supreme Judge which amounted to 1200 dollars.[14]

The choice of the new teacher was highly satiscfactory to the Prophet: "At evening visited Mr. Seixas. . . . He conversed . . . is an interesting man. . . ."[15] Smith registered his lessons: "received a lecture from Professor Seixas upon the Hebrew language . . . a lecture upon the Hebrew grammar. . . ."[16] He paid him diligent courtesy. . . . At noon I prepared a horse and sleigh for Professor Seixas to go to Hudson and see his family. . . .[17]

Seixas had divided his pupils into two classes. Rigdon and Smith were in the advanced class.[18]

The Prophet had boundless enthusiasm for Hebrew study: "My soul delights in reading the word of the Lord in the original, and I am determined to pursue the study of the languages until I shall become master of them, if I am permitted to live long enough. At any rate, so long as I do live, I am determined to make this my object; and with the blessing of God I will succeed to my satisfaction."[19]

This enthusiasm was undoubtedly also due to the personality of the teacher, Seixas, who seems to have been engaged for at least another term. According to the Prophet's notes in his journal, dated March 12, 1836, he had ordered a team to go to Hudson to bring up Professor Seixas' property and family and in addition, had engaged a horse and wagon for the professor and his wife.[20]

Seixas achieved fame in the scholarly world of his time and was finally called to Oberlin College as a Hebrew teacher. Letters of his students giving information about him are in existence.[21] In the general catalogue of Oberlin College he is designated as "a Jew from New York . . . hired as a teacher of Hebrew at Oberlin."[22]

Other Mormons were also caught up by this enthusiasm for Hebrew study and we have reports about some who later rose to leadership in the church. For instance, Lorenzo Snow was invited by his sister Eliza to her home in Kirtland to be able to enjoy the Hebrew education he longed for in the School of the Prophets.[23]

While the Kirtland school served mainly for Hebrew study,[24] (Eliza Snow speaks of a school planned "for the sole study of that language")[25] there was, in fact, a little Greek study there too.[26] In the later temple city, Nauvoo, Hebrew was only a part of an already diversified study of old and new languages: "In their college, they teach all the sciences, with Latin, Greek, Hebrew, French, Italian and Spanish."[27]

How much was achieved by the Mormons in their Hebrew studies during the first two decades after their introduction, cannot be established with any degree of certainty. Single Hebrew words or phrases are found scattered through Mormon writings. The Prophet himself inserted several Hebrew words into a polyglot language sample.[28] A poem "Lamentation" ends with the words

נקום דם עבדך השפוך

the traditional invocation to God when the blood of an innocent

142

martyr has been shed.[29] Such poems as "Lamentation of a Jew among the afflicted and mourning Sons and Daughters of Zion, at the assassination of the two Chieftains in Israel, Joseph and Hyrum Smith"[30] were written in imitation of Biblical mourning songs. In this particular case it is reasonable to suppose that its author was really a Jew, i.e., Alexander Neibaur, the only convert from Judaism to Mormonism who would have been able to produce a literary creation on that level.

Other Hebrew words appear in English transcription as, for instance, "Shaumahyeem" for Heaven, [30a] or in Hebrew letters as צדקה for justice.[30b] In any case the difficulties of Hebrew study were for a long time regarded as overwhelming. They served as a paradigm of difficult undertakings in general:

"It is like a man that studies the Hebrew language; he has to drink deep before he can do much with it."[31]

Occasionally, an article treating the Hebrew language in a general way is found in the Mormon press.[32]

The Mormons' unhappy love of Hebrew study was transformed into a pointed reproach by contemporaries who derided the name "Nauvoo" for the temple city in Illinois. In defense of this name, Mormons answered: "Some brasswood editors think the Mormons distorted Hebrew and made Nauvoo. . . ."[33] The scoffers were enlightened by being given the derivation of the word from Isaiah 52, 7 proving that it is used according to its meaning: "Nauvoo . . . fills the definition of the Hebrew word Nauvoo, a delightful plantation."[34]

This explanation was generally accepted by the unprejudiced: "Nauvoo is a Hebrew word, and signifies a beautiful habitation for a man, carrying with it the idea of rest."[35]

It may be well to point out that at that time not one of the Christian denomiations being organized in America had much success with Hebrew studies, in so far as their educational institutions in the West were concerned. For this very reason, Hebrew knowledge was paraded in religious tournaments there as it was once done in Salt Lake City.[36] Nevertheless the merit of the Mormons' efforts to make Hebrew studies an essential part of their program of higher religious instruction cannot be denied. Mormon encouragement of Hebrew under such difficult circumstances reemphasizes the dy-

143

namic power of the new faith which eagerly initiated the seemingly impossible, a new Hebraic tradition. This resolution was certainly strengthened by the consciousness that it was necessary in the competition with other Christian denominations in order to prove the legitimacy of their own faith. However, in its spiritual foundations, the will to study Hebrew was independent of any outside complex of causes. It was essentially a pure expression of love of the Bible.

A few general observations are likely to throw more light on the Hebrew study of the Mormons. Hebrew, as the ideal of education, had already been declining in America of the 19th century. The basis for it among the intellectuals became narrower and narrower until among the literati only a few were familiar with Hebrew literature in the original. Characteristic of this situation were Thoreau's words that to know slang is more important than Hebrew, an opinion which would certainly have been classified as heretical by the standards of the previous century.

This narrowing down of the basis of Hebrew was not really changed by the fact that more and more theological schools introduced Hebrew teachings. Its earlier role as an obligatory part of the curriculum of higher learning was discarded once and for all.

Thus, the turn to Hebrew of the first higher school of the Mormons expressed an independent enthusiasm which was no longer part of the general trend of the time. Accordingly it could not have been elicited by general American developments, a fact which must be taken into account in evaluating the Mormon attitude to Hebrew studies.

Chapter 16

Jewish Converts to Mormonism

Opinion as to the possibility of converting the Jews to Christianity was already divided in early 19th-century America. In New England, for instance, the sermons of the missionaries expressed the conviction that their conversion would take place in the near future.[1] In religious magazines from other parts of the country, the road to conversion was described as a stony one requiring great financial sacrifices and institutions of all kinds to help the converts.[2] In addition to this, the non-religious press even in those early days treated many cases of conversionist activities among the Jews as a humbug of no importance. For instance we find the following statement in Niles Weekly register:

"It appears by a late magazine, that about five hundred thousand dollars have been assessed on the public in one form or other, for the last five years and expended—with what result?—The conversion—real or supposed—of *five Jews.*—This is at the rate of one hundred thousand dollars per Jew—, a pretty round sum for Christendom to make a purchase of the scattered nation. We grant it: but whether Jews convert Christians or Christians convert Jews, what is it to us in this land of civil and religious liberty?"[3]

Vis-à-vis this kind of conversionist activity stood the already alert defense of the growing Jewish community in America whose first periodical ("The Jew," 1824) declared that it was founded for the purpose of defending the inherited faith against the missionaries.

Mormon conversionist activity among non-Jews was generally deemed dangerous since it was carried out with great enthusiasm. For instance a Swiss observer writes:

"I would not wish a person who does not have a strong faith ... to come near a Mormon. Catholic or Protestant, he would soon

145

become a Mormon; because Mormon talk is full of glowing enthusiasm, convincing power and apostolic loftiness and dignity."[3a]

Even the rationalist Germans were forewarned:

"The Germans and Mormonism. A friend who has lived for a rather long time in the West near Mormon settlements reports that the Mormons there win just as many adherents among the Germans as do the Methodists in other parts of the United States and remarks on this that it is depressing to have such experiences among the Germans . . ."[4]

As for the Jews, it was their inaccessibility to Mormon ideas which stood out from the beginning.

There was a great difference between American Jewry and the Christian denominations within the united front of Americans for the preservation of their historic heritage. American Jews had nothing to fear from the Mormon missionaries themselves. It is clear, especially from the papers of the Mormon mission to Palestine that it is impossible to speak of any tangible success among the Jewish masses, whether in England, Germany, or any other country—least of all, America itself. Even during the economic crisis of the Utah "Gentiles," no Jewish trader purchased his economic existence at the price of conversion to Mormonism.

The danger for the Christian anti-Mormons, however, was quite different. Even if we discount the statements of persons actively participating in the conflict, among whom political personalities and clergymen were equally numerous, there were enough impartial observers, including foreign visitors, who attested to the effectiveness of Mormon conversionist propaganda.

In their view, there was no slight danger that the other Christians might see America go Mormon. Repeatedly these descriptions underscore the dynamic force of the Mormon syncretism and the effect of its ardent preaching upon the masses.

Only in the light of all these surrounding circumstances can the success of Mormon conversionism among a few Jews be properly appraised. These conversions took place on the periphery of Jewish life in America, during economic adjustment to Mormon environment at a great distance from the mass stream of Jewish immigrants. Even later when a Jewish settlement existed in Utah, the Jews there represented were only a small fraction of their number in America. In proportion to the Mormons, all Gentiles together were a minority in Utah and the Jews were important there only as merchants, and did not offer a broad base for conversion. On the contrary, the desire of this small Jewish minority to associate itself with the other Jews in America became as strong as it was in other small Jewish communities in America. In letters written from Jews in Utah to Jewish newspapers it was pointed out that in all Jewish respects Utah was the most remote territory in America. In a sense it was much further than California to which a perpetual stream of Jewish immigrants flowed. The Intermountain Basin was much less accessible and thus less frequently visited by Jews. Overcoming this remoteness by means of Jewish community institutions connected with the totality of Jews in America was the essence of Jewish religious history in Utah.[5] Similar to other pioneer settlements of the Jews in the Far West in most respects, this community nevertheless contained some unique features. These derived from the friendliness of the Mormons to the Jewish religious establishment as such, doubtless as a result of their own religious outlook on Judaism.

The conviction that the number of Jewish converts to Mormonism was infinitesimally small was shared by all contemporaries. "Among their adherents there are very few Catholics, Jews and Indians."[6] No matter how few there might have been of the other two groups, there were even less among the Jews. One author goes so far as to deny altogether the existence of such converts:

"The Jews of Europe and Jerusalem took little interest in the history of their brethren who stole away thirteen centuries ago from their native city in such questionable manner, nor of their Nephite and Lamanite descendants in the promised land. Indeed, we have yet to learn of one of the race having embraced the Mormon faith."[7]

Even in 1908 a German Protestant missionary active for a rather long time in Utah had to concede:

"To my knowledge only one Jew, Mayer, a commercial employee has embraced Mormonism a new proof of how much more firmly the Jews cling to the faith of their fathers than many Christians."[8]

The reports of travelers who became acquainted with Jewish converts to Mormonism in Utah were limited by the fact that they were based on visits to Salt Lake City but not to other cities in the territories where, according to other sources, there were some in-

147

dividual Jewish converts. In any case the Jewish traveler Benjamin who mentioned two Jewish converts in the report of his visit to Utah (1861) referred only to Salt Lake City.[9] In another description of a smaller city in Utah whose name is not given it is said: "I saw there the only man of Hebrew birth who (as it is said) has ever become a communicant of that church."[10] It might have been that only one Jew at a given place was a convert. But there were also a number of Jews in several growing cities and there could occasionally be a convert to Mormonism among them too. One of them has even enriched Utah's "chronique scandaleuse" by his quarrels with a public servant and it is interesting that he was regarded as a Jew by contemporary writers and not as a fellow Mormon.[11]

Another author mentions that he was acquainted with a Jewish convert in Utah who was a polygamist.[11a]

The old question of whether Jewish conversion could be lasting came up in Mormonism too. According to Brigham Young's opinion this could never be, and it was also not desirable:

"Let me here say a word to the Jews. We do not want you to believe our doctrine. If any professing to be Jews should do so, it would prove that they are not Jews. A Jew cannot believe in Jesus Christ. Brother Neibaur who thinks he is a Jew, is a good Latter-day Saint; he has not any of the blood of Judah in his veins. The decree has gone forth from the Almighty that they cannot have the benefit of the atonement until they gather to Jerusalem, for they said let his blood be upon us and upon our children, consequently they cannot believe in him until His second coming. We have a great desire for their welfare, and are looking for the time soon to come when they will gather to Jerusalem, build up the city and the land of Palestine, and prepare for the coming of the Messiah. When he comes again He will not come as He did when the Jews rejected Him neither will He appear first at Jerusalem when He makes His second appearance on the earth; but He will appear first on the land where He commenced His work in the beginning and planted the Garden of Eden, and that was done in the land of America."[12]

Mormon experience certainly confirmed this opinion and reports of non-Mormons mentioned Jewish converts who later deserted their new faith. In any case the archives of the Mormon Church do not list several names of Jewish converts, certain proof that they later apostatized. The same was the case in the Mormon settlement of California, San Bernardino: "Two Jews, wealthy and courted, with large families, residing here, were formerly members of the Mormon Church."[13] A notice in the records of the Mormon stake in San Bernardino of June 23, 1855, refers to one of them.[14]

A number of other cases are mentioned in an article in the Jewish press in the year 1906.[15] It added a few new names to those already known. One additional name was that of a certain Dr. Lederer whose statement we find in the title of a Mormon pamphlet.[16]

The fact that these converts later apostatized to such a great extent makes it reasonable to conclude that they had found no spiritual refuge in the new faith. Their conversions took place as a matter of adjustment to the environment but lost any meaning as soon as they changed their surroundings as was doubtless the case in San Bernardino as soon as the Mormons left.

The Mormons general mistrust of Jewish converts found expression in the response of the Mormon press to the news that the conversion of a Jew costs the missionary societies 16,000 dollars: "So, as in everything else, the Jews relinquish their religion for as much as they can possibly get."[17]

It may be stated with full certainty that at least one of the Jewish converts embraced the Mormon faith while still in Europe. He afterwards followed the call of the Prophet to the new Zion by emigrating to America and then arriving in Nauvoo in 1841. The journey, crossing the ocean on a sailing boat in six weeks to New Orleans, was continued up the Mississippi by boat to Nauvoo.[18]

Alexander Neibaur was and remained the only important Jewish convert to Mormonism. He was not only strong in faith but also in the unwavering confidence of his fellow Mormons in him as proven by the blood-theory of the genuine descendants of Ephraim credited especially for him and stated by Brigham Young (see n. 12). A biographical sketch of this remarkable man has been attempted several times.[19] However, everything said up to now could not do justice to the man without explaining the Jewish cultural conditions in Europe from which he came. Likewise, there has been no further illumination of the spiritual life of this man during the American phases of his life. Such information can be of great importance for possible conclusions about both Jew and Mormon.

Alexander Neibaur, educated in traditional Jewish fashion,

149

was typical of the German-born Jewish intellectual who emigrated further west to England. There he acquired academic training for the old Jewish profession of physician, for centuries the only intellectual profession not denied to the Jew. In this he was driven like so many other Jewish intellectuals by the same spiritual forces of Jewish society which had created the Jewish enlightenment of the 19th century. But with all this similarity to the fate of many others, Neibaur did not become the typical rationalist of the *Haskalah*, the "Daughter of Heaven" of the Jewish enlightenment. Instead, he was lifted to entirely other Heavens and a new religious life. He was attracted by the novel religious idea then being propagandized in England, Mormonism. The same Jewish potential which had created in the *Haskalah* an entirely new concept of Jewish religion and a new classical approach to Bible study in the original Hebrew, took a different turn in the case of this man. It was applied, instead, to a new religion, and new revelation in America. Neibaur did not follow the call of the Jewish enlightenment which envisaged an entirely new role for intellect and reason in Europe but rather the appeal of the new faith in America whose additional holy writings once again led back to the ancient Bible. The latter also restored the old faith in the Bible which to a great degree, had been lost by the exponents of the *Haskalah*. This case demonstrates the kind of tendencies which might have affected the Jewish emigrant masses if they had been aware of religious America, or even if they had a closer acquaintance with all the religious dissenters emigrating from Europe at the same time. Even if the Jewish enlightenment had already captured the great masses of Jewish emigrants, from Bavaria for example, at least part of them might have returned to religious concepts. In time a new religious concept might have gained adherents among them and Alexander Neibaur's way, that of the new American religious concept, could have become the way for many others who were also seeking religious modernism. The danger that all America might go Mormon, reported by some observers, would then have applied to the Jews in America as well.

Actually the Jewish emigrant masses had not been estranged from Jewish tradition and their way was not that of Jewish intellectuals of the time. All we can say is that the immigrant, driven by the demands of his new life declared a moratorium on questions of religious conscience. Once the initial economic adjustment to the new continent was achieved, he began to organize his religious community according to proven historical examples which were adapted to the new world.

Many characteristics of the American phase of Neibaur's life were also typical of the life of other German-Jewish intellectuals in the Far West. He belonged to an intellectual profession and possessing the most diversified knowledge in various fields, he tried in every possible way to take root in the economic life of America and to catapult himself to a higher standard of living. In accordance with the habit of German Jewish merchants, he made use of the medium of newspaper advertising to a great extent. This makes Alexander Neibaur an even more typical representative of the German Jew in America since the latter often used this medium very successfully. A good deal of German-Jewish cultural history in America is revealed to us by Neibaur's advertisements as was also the case with general pioneering western life as reflected in the same type of expression. One would have to go far, even in the Far West, to find a man who had so much to advertise without being a real merchant or without misusing his professional standard as a physician by offering a patent medicine. Neibaur was baptized on April 9, 1838[19a] and was the first Jew in the Mormon Church. He was equal among equals although not designated to higher church office.

As the only Jewish convert of stature, this modest man was certainly the only person among the Mormons who possessed a thorough knowledge of the Hebrew language and of historic Judaism. He was accepted by his fellow-Mormons as an initiate in these things even as was the classical Jew himself. Insofar as he had revealed literary activity in these fields, his creations were taken seriously by his new co-religionists.

Neibaur never concluded a plural marriage although he left many descendants.[20] The present writer is inclined to see in this fact Neibaur's spiritual inheritance from Judaism with its traditionally monogamic family life. This conclusion is strengthened by the fact that Neibaur didn't attain the higher church-offices reserved for those who were bound morally together by fulfillment of the revealed commandment of plural marriage. Jewish marital trad-

151

ition must have been strong indeed in this man if he allowed his monogamic life to close the door to higher church offices.

In the course of his economic adjustment to his pioneer-environment, biographical details were revealed by the aforementioned remarkable advertising. Thus Berlin, Liverpool and Preston in England were the former stations of his life and his medical practice was of fifteen years standing. He had already met Brigham Young in England and Young had given him his house in Nauvoo for use in practicing dentistry. He designated himself as "a German Jew" and offered himself as an instructor in Hebrew and German.[21]

At a later time he added the manufacture of matches to his other professions.

"Nauvoo Match Manufactury. The Merchants and Citizens of Nauvoo and its victinity are respectfully informed that Friction Matches warranted superior to any ever brought to this city may be constantly obtained on reasonable terms by wholesale and retail at the Manufactory, at the corner of Water and Durfee Street.

Alex Neibaur a. Co. N. B. All operations on the Teeth still performed at the above place by Alex Neibaur."[22]

The combination of three such different vocations as bringing spiritual light as well as physical and freeing from tooth-aches in the valleys of Ephraim resulted in a deluge of Neibaur advertisements in the Mormon press. That the match manufacturers applied the advertising psychology of the "firsts" in the field like the other German Jews in America is seen in the following sample:

"Neibaur's Matches. A sample of Nauvoo matches was handed us the other day, which, whether they be called percussion, touch, friction, reaction or locofoco, had lucifer enough in them, to catch fire almost as quick as lightning. We say go ahead with the matches, but beware how you handle them, lest you inflame their *lubrification*."[23]

Like the other Saints we see the Jewish convert, strong in faith, make his way to Salt Lake City and we come across more advertisements in the church newspaper there. New in addition to all his established professions he opened a proper German school, this time without a partner. In the first numbers of the "Deseret News" we already find:

"A. Neibaur. Surgeon Dentist, 3d street east, 2d south of the

152

Council House, will attend to all branches of his profession. The scurvy effectually cured."[24]

And later:

"*A. Neibaur, Surgeon Dentist,* grateful to his patrons and friends for the last eleven years' favors, solicits a continuance of their kindness, and the patronage of the citizens of the valleys of Ephraim in general. His charges are strictly moderate, and satisfaction is warranted to be given in all operations performed by him.

"*A German School* will be opened on the evening of the 24th inst., at the residence of A. Neibaur, 13th Ward, where books will be furnished to pupils.

"*Matches.*

"*A constant supply* of Matches of superior quality kept on hand, for which produce will be taken in exchange by *A. Neibaur.*"[25]

The offer to take the produce of the country as payment was as customary in daily commerce in Utah as it was in the rural settlements of Jews in Germany.

Several months later the German instruction was already organized in a class:

"German Day Class. Deutsche Schule.—The subscriber will commence a day class for teaching the German language in all its branches. . . . A. Neibaur."[26]

From this time on Neibaur's advertisement became a constant companion of the Mormon press in Utah. The German school—apparently unsuccessful—later was omitted. Dentistry and match-manufacture, however, remained united in all future newspaper columns. In the first numbers of the Utah press there existed only two advertisers; one of them was Neibaur.

Many proofs of his intellectual stature do exist. In addition to Hebrew he regularly instructed the Prophet in Nauvoo in German as we learn from notices in the Prophet's journal.[27] But his true merit lay in his representing Jewish traditional learning in an authentic way to his fellow Mormons who saw in him, a substitute for the whole ancient people of the Bible.

Brother Neibaur enlightened his fellow-Mormons about Jewish concepts and added in a letter to the editor accompanying his article that he was prepared to say more about it if required:

153

"If you think it will be of any interest to your readers, I shall take another time to continue the subject and tell you the *means,* as held by my brethren the Jews, whereby the Lord will bring to pass this glorious work." (resurrection).[28]

Some of his poems about Biblical themes are extant.[29] Others must have appeared without his name and we may assume that the beautiful "Lament of a Captive Jew in Babylon By a converted Jew" was written by him."[30]

Brother Neibaur's diary containing notices about family events shows how serious he was in his new faith. Under the date of October 23, 1854 we learn of the baptism of Lea Neibaur.[31] On March 27, 1858 he notes the baptism of his son-in-law:

"Mr. Morris Rosenbaum a Jew from Fordohn Grand Duchy of Posea Prussia was baptized."[32] The efforts of the newly wedded couple to establish an economic existence demonstrate the mobility in Utah territory in those days: "My son-in-Law Rosenbaum went out in Echo Canyon."[33] And only a few days later:". . . Myself and my son Joseph William a son-in-Law Morris Rosenbaum started with a load of flower for Provo city Utah Country. . . ."[34] After three years during which the families of Neibaur's children were in Provo,[35] the Rosenbaum family moved to Brigham City.[36] There children were born to Morris David Rosenbaum from 1869 on.[37] Later in life, Rosenbaum concluded plural marriages.

It is interesting to learn that Neibaur remained in touch with his family in Europe after he was already in Utah (July 20, 1858), . . . got a letter from my Father and Brother from Warmbrunn, Silesia in Germany, also one from my sister Holdeman in England."[38]

In his personal crisis, which resulted from the evil ways of his son Isaac, his fellow Mormons stood by him as we learn from his diary:

"19.1.1862. Bishop Wooley prefert a charge in the Tabernacle against myself saying I countenanced my son Isaacs wicket course and practice. I requested a hearing—spoke, then President Young made remarks made me out that I had Incouraged Isaac in steeling, No action taken but refert to the Bishop went in the afternoon to see the Bishop demanded in the presence of my son Joseph a. Br. Joseph Busby an Investigation a. my accusers to be brought face to face, time for hearing set on the 22 Inst.

154

Accordingly Bishop a. his Council met a number of the Br. present an Examination was gone into but no Accuser present. I vindicated and asserted my Innocence. my son Joseph was called to say whether he heard his father approve or disapprove Is course, my son Isaac confessed to being guilty of many things never stole from a Mormon, if he had listened to the Council of his parents would have been a man, thought he knew the best saw his error, confest his misdoings askt forgivness would do better if his Br. would forgive him but if his blood must atone he is willing to die. Br. Ph. Young spoke the Bishop spoke. a. 2 or 3 more were glad to hear Is. Confession, it was manly hoped would Redeem himself. No charge sustained against Br. Neibaur."[39]

In addition to this illuminating insight into the course of Mormon justice in family matters, the diary later indicated that this affair had happy ending for Neibaur:

"26.1.1862. The Bishop of the 13 Ward stadet in the Tabernacle a. in the evening at the Ward house that Br. Neibaur stood fairer than ever a. he wished he could say as much of ever one in his Ward as he can say of Br. Neibaur a. his family."[40]

We see that his rehabilitation took place in the same manner as the accusations against him. There can be no doubt that as a Mormon he possessed his full rights and was never frustrated by being a Jew.

Three years later we learn of another misdemeanour of the youthful evil-doer:

"Police Report:—Isaac Neibaur was arrested on the 6th inst., charged with drunkenness and disturbing the peace. He laid in the lock-up over night and sobered down, and the next morning appeared before Alderman Clinton an was fined D 10.—."[41]

This time the unhappy father was not involved.

The previously discussed facts indicate that the conversion of a few Jews to Mormonism in no way strengthened Christian missionary activities among the Jews in America.

Chapter 17

Early Meeting of Jew and Mormon

On the way to the West, both Jew and Mormon, whether a newly arrived immigrant or already a citizen of the Union, used the same ways and means of transportation; and were observed together in ports of departure or on ships or railways. For instance the following description of a trip on a Missouri boat mentions "several Mormons, probably on their way through the prairies to Utah, besides this Jews, mostly of German birth, many of whom own stores in the city of Kansas and are busy with commerce."[1]

In fictional travel literature the same meeting of Jew and Mormon occured, as when Herman Melville imagined a Mississippi boat with groups of passengers:

". . . modish young Spanish Creoles, and old-fashioned French Jews; Mormons and Papists. . . ."[2]

In the same way European fiction about the American West mentioned Jew and Mormon together. Even a story in a Jewish newspaper told of the Jewish adventurer who met Indians, fur hunters and Mormons.[3]

But all these casual meetings especially with Jewish peddlers must have also occured during the Nauvoo period of the Mormons and on their Utah trek. However, they did not result in any special relationship, either on a personal or group basis.

The first personal relationship between Jew and Mormon occurred in Kirtland when the Mormons sought a Hebrew teacher. This search produced a whole group of literary notes in Mormon historical church writings on the intellectual qualities of these persons and their behavior. The Kirtland episode was the only direct acquaintance between Mormons and American Jews of Hebrew learning. All future meetings with American Jews had other bases and, if one may say so, other purposes, largely to inform them

156

about Mormonism. Other Jewish personalities as, for instance, Mordecai M. Noah were known to Mormons only as literary enemies and were not met personally. The rare case of citing the writings of an American Jew for confirmation of a Mormon theological viewpoint occurred once:

"Mr. Jackson a Jew by birth, and an excellent Hebrew scholar, and also the editor of a periodical called 'The Jew,' says while discoursing upon his vision of Isaiah [ensign upon the mountains] that the work of God, will commence in America, that will ultimately effect the restoration of the house of Israel, and prepare the way for the appearance of the Messiah."[4]

Information could be given in a quiet tone even about the literary enemy if it was simply news:

"Maj. M. M. Noah of New York, a Jew, and for the last thirty or forty years has edited a number of the ablest and best political papers in this city, last Thanksgiving Day delivered an address."[5]

A) *The Nauvoo Period.*

Although a large number of non-Mormons lived in Nauvoo and many non-Mormon travelers came there for commercial and other reasons, we cannot find any trace of Jews as travelers of any kind or sojourners in Nauvoo. However, exceptional circumstances brought Abraham Jonas, an outstanding Jew in Illinois, Grandmaster of Freemasons there, a well-known politician who was later instrumental in the rise to power of Lincoln and the Republicans to Nauvoo on a public mission. He spent 3 days in closest contact with the Mormons and their leaders. The fruit of this visit was a detailed report on them together with a personal political position taken by Jonas on the Mormon question as it stood then. The importance of this manifestation lay in the fact that Jonas' appearance in Nauvoo was the only public mission, in which a contemporary ever was sent to the Mormons in Nauvoo.

The story began when the Mormons wanted to found a Freemason's lodge in Nauvoo. A Masonic source reported on their initiative and the first steps taken on it in the following way:

[The Mormons]
"conceived the idea of instituting a Lodge at Nauvoo. Accordingly, they applied to the Grandmaster for a dispensation to form

157

and work a Lodge to be called Nauvoo Lodge, U.D. On the 15th day of October 1841, a petition signed by the requisite number of Master Masons at Nauvoo was sent to Grandmaster A. Jonas, residing at Quincy, for a dispensation to form a lodge in Nauvoo. The prayer of the petition was granted."[6]

In due time "Grandmaster Jonas issued a dispensation authorizing a lodge at Nauvoo, and five months later, March 15, 1842, he paid an official visit to that place and set the lodge to work."[7]

Jonas' description of the situation he had found in Nauvoo together with his political statement on the Mormon question was published on March 22nd, 1842 in the *Columbus Advocate* and reprinted in the Mormon *Times and Seasons* on the first of April, 1842.[8] The following passages of the statement are of great historical importance since they express the opinion of an impartial witness:

". . . I saw a people apparently happy, prosperous and intelligent. Every man appeared to be employed in some business or occupation. . . . I protest against the slanders and persecutions that are continually heaped on these people. While at Nauvoo, I had a fine opportunity of seeing the people in a body. There was a Masonic celebration, and the Grandmaster of the State was present for the purpose of publicly installing the officers of a new Lodge. An immense number of persons assembled on the occasion, variously estimated from 5, to 10,000, and never in my life did I witness a better-dressed or a more orderly and well-behaved assemblage; not a drunken or disorderly person to be seen, and the display of taste and beauty among the females, could not well be surpassed anywhere.

During my stay of three days, I became well-acquainted with their principal men and more particularly with their Prophet, the celebrated 'Old Jo Smith.' I found them hospitably polite, well-informed and liberal. With Joseph Smith, the hospitality of whose house I kindly received, I was well-pleased; of course, on the subject of religion, we widely differed, but he appeared to be quite as willing to permit me to enjoy my right of opinion, as I think we all ought to be to let the Mormons to enjoy theirs. . . .

"I hope and trust that the people of Illinois have no disposition to disturb unoffending people who have no disposition but

158

to live peacefully under the laws of the country and to worship God under their own vine and fig tree. An observer."[9]

Post factum treatment of the whole issue of the Mormon lodge in Nauvoo by Masonic historians tends to belittle Grandmaster's Jonas' efforts by pointing out his presumed political motives in setting up the lodge:

". . . The natural desire for increase of numbers may have influenced the action of Grandmaster Jonas in this instance. But there were other considerations. The fact should be remembered that he was a practical politician . . . at this time he appears to have been a candidate for a seat in the lower branch of the Illinois legislature, to which he was elected a few months after he had instituted Nauvoo Lodge. This fact should be borne in mind, too, in connection with the highly laudatory letter concerning Nauvoo and its people which he published in his paper immediately after his return home from this official visitation which covered three days, and during which he was the personal guest of the Mormon Prophet."[10]

However, we may point out that Jonas may have had his political plans for a future but so did every other leading Mason in Illinois. Jonas' letter is remarkable for its all-out democratic constitutional position in regard to the Mormon question. A politician's principles cannot be destroyed by the shallow remarks of other politicians. There were many people in Illinois, even among the adversaries of the Mormons, who took Jonas at his word. We may therefore claim Jonas as the first intellectual Jew who gave his opinion of the Mormons unbiased by the political passions of the times. Others were to follow soon.

As to the motivation of increasing the number of members, it may be noted that the Nauvoo Lodge initiated 286 candidates altogether.[11]

As a result of complaints about irregularities, the Nauvoo Lodge was finally declared irregular and its dispensation annulled.[12]

Nothing definite is known about any other Jew being met by the Mormons in Nauvoo. The Jewish name, Michael Katz, appeared once in a Nauvoo paper.[13] He may have been a peddler. We hear of at least one Jew in connection with the Mormons during the trek to Utah:

159

"It was in Council Bluffs in 1852 that Abe Kuhn met Brigham Young."[14]

B) *San Bernardino.*

The first group relations between Jews and Mormons began in San Bernardino, California. They were unique in every respect when considered against their background and other accompanying circumstances.

Jewish settlement there was a result of a concession from the Mormon city founders in the framework of their planned colonization. At the time when the Jewish merchants were admitted into the fort, there was no provision for any other merchants with the same kind of business. All intercourse between Jew and Mormon was basically fair, with the Mormons demonstrating the full ethos of earnest religionists. Jews never participated in any conflict between the Gentiles and the Mormons and never suffered from any inequity or inequality. They outlived the first Mormon settlement and co-existed side by side with the second Mormon settlement during the years when these Mormons did not belong to the main church in Utah. Jewish settlement in San Bernardino was uninterrupted. One of the old Jewish merchant pioneers there has recorded memorable facts of Mormon history in addition to general historical events in San Bernardino.[15] Extraordinary too, was California's general Jewish background in relation to the Utah Mormons, whose chief merchantile ties with California were with Jews in Los Angeles.[16]

The life of the Jews in San Bernardino thus represented our minority-problem in a nutshell. The Mormons themselves were a splinter group in the Californian population with which the Jews had reached a symbiosis, by virtue of being a much smaller minority. All this took place in a region where the extraordinary circumstances of the gold rush created an entirely new society on the Pacific during a single decade. In this new Californian society the Jews generally found equality, and even greater convenience and courtesy within the Californian Mormon settlement. The Jewish pioneers who witnessed this chapter of history, never tired of stressing the fact that the Mormon settlers were morally superior to the element which arrived after the main body of Mormons had left.

A few additional facts will help to clarify the general situation of the Californian Mormons. The news of the Mormon plight in

160

the American West had already been published in the *Californian* in 1846, at a time when California was not yet American:

"The difficulties in which these people found themselves at Nauvoo, and other parts of the states, have led to the resolution to 'break up' and 'be off' for California. About 25,000 have left Nauvoo."[17] The comparison with the fate of the Jews had also been made:

"The fate of the last immigrants.

. . . It was a most horrid picture of human misery; such as has not been witnessed since the siege of Jerusalem . . ."[18]

The first Mormons came to California as a result of a contract, concluded by Brigham Young with the American Government. The agreement stipulated the formation of a Mormon battalion for the purpose of the conquest of California. Members of this battalion stayed on during the gold-rush and brought certain amounts of gold to Utah. Soon the wildest and most fanciful rumors about the gold-riches of Mormons began to appear especially in the press of neighboring Oregon:

". . . they should have taken away so many wagon loads of the precious stuff before the general discovery."[19] Or:

"On the return [to Utah] of the 'Mormon battalion' sufficient of the dust to make money plenty in this place for all ordinary purposes . . ."[20]

And finally:

"The Mormons boast of having an emigration fund of three and a half tons of California gold. . . ."[21]

Soon the rumor changed so that Utah itself was the goldland and the decision of part of the California Mormons to return to Utah was assumed to be in the hope "to find gold there in the same abundance as they find it presently at the Sacramento."[22]

A popular image of Mormon proximity to gold much like the image of the riches of the Jew developed and stimulated the Biblical comparison of all these imagined riches with the golden calf.

The San Bernardino settlement had been planned by the church leadership as an outlet of the Mormon empire to the Pacific. From the beginning good relations with all neighbors were sought. By the time the ranch of San Bernardino was purchased in 1851, the Mormons had announced their good intentions by way of the "Daily Alta California:"

"Mormon Settlement in the South. Here probably this interesting people will make their first establishment on the shores of the Pacific. They profess the best intentions towards the old settlers of the country, and show no disposition, in the slightest degree, to interfere with the right of others. Thus acting, they deserve a kindly consideration, and every encouragement in their plans of settlement."[23]

Very soon it appeared that Jews were included in this friendly feeling. Louis Glaser's store in the fort already existed in 1851.[24] We read furthermore in the dictation of the German Jewish immigrant, Marcus Katz:

". . . He lived in San Francisco a year and one-half, and from there came down to Los Angeles, and from there to San Bernardino, which was in 1852. Mr. Katz was a merchant here. The Mormons were then in here and Mr. Katz went to the headquarters and got permission from them to go into business here. They treated him very kindly."[25]

Fulfillment of the needs of the Mormons population by Jewish stores was planned by the Mormons:

"Three stores, kept by Jews, supply the community with groceries, dry goods, boots and shoes and hardware."[25a]

At the same time San Bernardino was spared the gold-rush:

"In 1852 the Mormon boys brought little nuggets of gold from the mountains, and the Mormons did not like it, for they were afraid that if their was any rumor got abroad that there was gold out here that the Gentiles would come in and interfere with their arrangements . . ."[26]

San Bernardino remained a quiet community, calmly prospering.

The Mormons preached a friendly attitude to "Brother Jew:"

"Elder Theodor Turley addressed the congregation upon the principles in relation to the children of Israel."[27]

As for the Jews we read in Rabbi Eckman's Californian paper that this spirit of friendship had been praised as the shining example California was giving to the whole of America:

"Catholic Mormon and Jewish Rabbi. We are glad to see the narrow-minded sectarian spirit of former ages yielding to more enlarged and enlightened views as has been manifested in the action taken by some of our State Legislatures. . . . Thus we find our

162

Legislature made choice of a Roman Catholic priest—of the Rev. Father Gallagher, and on a former occasion, even of a Mormon for their Chaplain . . ."[28]

We learn some details about the mercantile life and transactions of San Bernardino Jews. Lewis Jacobs owned a general store in partnership with J. R. Brunn.[29] In 1854 Marks David sold a share of a saw mill situated in the mountains to Louis Jacobs and Louis Glaser.[30] An advertisement by Louis Glaser in the Californian Mormon paper gives us a vivid picture of his commerce in connection with the Mormons:

"Read this!
Persons intending to emigrate from all parts of California to Utah, via San Bernardino, are respectfully informed that the undersigned has constantly at hand a full assortment of Groceries, Provisions, Dry Goods, Hardware, Hats, Boots, Shoes, etc. which he offers at the lowest prices both Wholesale and Retail. Surveying Parties orders received, and filled with dispatch. L. Glaser."[31] An 1856 news report gave a glowing picture of the idyl that existed at San Bernardino as well as the function of the Jewish merchants in the community.

"The Mormons at San Bernardino.
The population of the camp is about 2,000 souls—their occupation of course, strictly agricultural, with such mechanical branches only as are necessary for the construction of dwellings and the manufacture and repair of the required implements. Three stores, kept by Jews, supply the community with groceries, dry goods, boots and shoes and hardware. The retail of spirituous liquor is prohibited by the requirement of a license of D100 per month. No quantity less than a quart can be obtained at either of the stores—only two of which keep the *ardent*."[32]

An incident not without some interest occurred on June 13, 1855. The Mormon elder, David Seely, hit Lewis Jacobs with a stick. Jacobs was seriously hurt. How the case was handled and settled within the community with the wholehearted cooperation of the Mormons is noteworthy, indeed. It is a living monument to the harmonious communal living of the Jews and Mormons, and it is an impressive testimony to the highly developed sense of justice of the latter. According to the account by Seely's daughter[33] Jacobs arrived at their place with his peddler's case, sold some goods and accepted chickens by way of payment. He left the chickens at Seely's. Some time later, he returned to pick up the chickens; and the two men began quarreling as to the eggs which had been laid in the meantime. In the course of the argument Jacobs was hit two or three times.

The Mormon community, *pro foro interno* (Jacobs had embraced Mormonism) disposed of the case by accepting the apologies of the repentant church functionary; at the same time, they took his church offices away from him.[34]

"23.VI.1855. A special conference was held at San Bernardino to transact business pertaining to the branch. The case of David Seely, president of the take, who had been guilty of striking Bro. Lewis Jacobs on the head with a stick that endangered his life, was tried. Bro.Seely confessed his fault and begged the forgiveness of the conference. On motion the conference dropped Bro. Seely from the presidency of the Stake and forgave him."[34]

The settlement of the case outside of court brought Jacob an indemnification of D600.—[35]

The criminal proceeding for the assault and battery was then dropped at the request of Jacobs, with Seely paying the cost incurred.[36]

The sharpening of the Mormon question nationally and the outbreak of the Utah war cast the shadows of future events on California as elsewhere. Thus, the fate of the peaceful settlement of San Bernardino underwent a sudden change. When Marcus Katz returned to San Bernardino from San Diego, he found everything changed; the entire background of civic affairs had been altered:

"Things had changed materially. It appeared that a political party had come in here and the Mormons did not like it. The Mormons were going to settle the entire country from San Diego to Salt Lake City, own their own ships and transport their own merchandise, and settle up the whole country. They were pushing that object right along, but they were called back to Salt Lake City in 1857 by Brigham Young to defend their Utah possessions. There were not many Mormons after that, only about one hundred and twenty-five. San Bernardino was then fenced in with high pickets, as the Mormons were afraid of the Indians and consequently fortified themselves."[37]

164

The retreat of the Mormons to Utah was already in full progress by the end of 1857. A December, 1857 report reads:

"On the 31st several persons came in from San Bernardino. There was a very hostile spirit in California. They were driving out everything that ever smelt of Mormonism. The road from San Bernardino was lined with people on their way to G. S. L. Valley."[38]

A later report in an American Jewish newspaper informs us that among the Mormons who had stayed on in San Bernardino, a defection from the main church in Utah led by A. Potter proved successful:

"Against Brigham Young and the [Utah] Mormons the 'New Church' is very hostile, although they themselves rose from Mormonism. But Brigham Young has every reason to be angry at his competitor because he takes away one after another of the Mormons left in San Bernardino."[39]

After the Utah war, many Mormons returned to San Bernardino. At the outbreak of the Civil War the Federal army sent a reconnaissance troop to the town. Its report reads:

"The population of San Bernardino is about 1500 souls; 1000 of them are Mormons. The rest may be made up of some respectable Americans, of a good many Jewish merchants, who control the business of the town and go with any side that pays best for the time being; and then there follow adroit horse thieves and other unprincipled and desperate men, gathered into that point, as well from other parts of California as from Utah. There is a large sprinkling of this latter class. You can judge of a man whose character is such that he could not be tolerated in Utah. Now, the Mormons, whatever their professions, hate us at heart. . . . The Jews, as a rule, have no love for us. The outlaws hate, because they fear us. . . . All but the few respectable Americans would set us at defiance tomorrow if they dared to do so."[40] Also other military reports mention Jews and Mormons in San Bernardino together.[41]

In 1861 the Jewish traveler, Israel Benjamin, visited San Bernardino and wrote:

"Since that time (1857) the growth of the city proceeded rather slowly. The cause for that was the continuing quarrel between the few remaining Mormons and their opponents who would easily have dammed up the spread of Mormonism. Nevertheless even now a Mormon church exists."[42]

165

We also posses a much later description of 1874, describing the San Bernardino conditions in respect to the Jews and the Mormons:

"The population of San Bernardino is nearly five thousand, of whom one fifth are Mormons. The rest of the population is made up of Americans and Hebrews. Unlike all other Southern California towns, there are few Mexicans and Indians. There is a Mormon tabernacle, a Jewish place of worship, and several Protestant and Catholic churches."[43]

Lewis Jacobs, the Jewish convert to Mormonism, later returned to the Jewish fold. Criticism of his action was voiced even many years later:

". . . Lewis Jacobs, of San Bernardino, a millionaire—bought thousands of acres of land at the time he was a Mormon, at government rates . . . Mr. Jacobs is a Jew now—Judaism has gained nothing by it . . ."[44] Another correspondent defended Jacobs against this criticism because "he is now active as a Jewish philanthropist."[45]

C) *Connections Between Los Angeles Jews and the Mormons of Utah.*

With the development of the road from San Bernardino to Salt Lake City, heavy freighting from Los Angeles to Utah became a lucrative enterprise.[46] At that time, during the decade of 1850 to 1860, Los Angeles was a settlement of mostly Jewish merchants. The special trade with Utah which developed was largely in Jewish hands. The Utah bound caravans of merchandise led by Jewish merchants helped to establish lasting commercial connections with leading Utah Mormons. Harris Newmark speaks of a monopoly of Salt Lake business, the fact that these merchants had given credit to the Mormon leaders as well of being in constant contact with Brigham Young.[47] Leading Mormons also visited Los Angeles with commercial intentions which strengthened the existing bonds and even facilitated some social intercourse between these Mormon visitors and Californian Jews.[48]

It was only natural that most of the commercial news about Utah territory in Los Angeles derived from questioning Jewish merchant pioneers who had returned from there. All such information was of great interest to the Los Angeles press.

166

Bachman & Co. were among the first to ship from Los Angeles to Utah. On November 26th 1853 the Los Angeles Star wrote:

"From Salt Lake.

Mr. B. Bachman returned from Salt Lake City this week. He has been absent about twelve months, and has been most successful in his business affairs. He brought with him 500 head of cattle, and only lost seven on the way—he was about a month on the road."[49]

Subsequent issues gave descripions of conditions in Utah which in all likelihood were obtained from Bachman since the paper maintained that its source of information had been "a gentleman just returned from Utah."

There were also Mormon residents from Utah in California outside of San Bernardino. They were part of a problem which had begun to vex the church leaders long ago. Californian gold had attracted persons who had originally come to Utah as an act of faith. "Hearing of the gold regions many left for California," writes an observer from abroad.[50] (1851). The church leadership had to take a position vis á vis this trend and stated:

"If you want to go to California, go and serve Gladden bishop there, but disturb not this community."[51] In this way the servants of the golden calf were eliminated from Zion's camp. Those immigrants who did not want to work and complained about the low wages in Utah were also asked to leave:

"We wish such to go to California. Work one half as you had in foreign lands, and you shall have good wages; . . ."[52]

Nevertheless Mormonism did have a number of dedicated adherents in California outside of San Bernardino, who supported the Utah Church with tithes paid in California gold.

Mormon polygamy was not reported in California itself but information about its existence in Utah was known there. As in other parts of America, every irregularity in marital life was assumed to be "Mormon." It was also the case in California where the main irregularity in this area was the proportionately larger number of divorces than in the Atlantic states. Our age cannot deny its admiration for a naive concept which saw proof of immorality in the 9 divorces which took place among the Jews in California during a four year period:

"California is a great state, producing more gold than happiness. Nine divorces in four years!—We have only heard of one in

167

this city in twenty years. We have united hundreds, but we have
never been asked to *dispense* a divorce. Dr. Eckman, we advise you
hereafter to be paid in advance, or seriously speaking, do not of-
ficiate on such occasions. It is only the worthless that wish to be
divorced from their marriage contracts; let them join the Mormons."[53]

D) *Intermountain Basin.*

More than a decade passed before the first loose contacts of
individual Jews and Mormons developed into the relationship of
an established group of Jewish merchants with the Mormons in
their permanent region of settlement. In any case this process had
proceeded so far by 1865 that the Jews in Utah territory were regarded as a solid non-Mormon group with a common fate. Although only a cog in a great machine they nevertheless helped
shape the course of events together with all other human factors.

The chief motive for Jews to go to Utah was the mercantile
adventure in the Great Basin. Profits were to be made from furnishing necessities for new settlers and from the trade of the California migrants who came through Salt Lake City in their overland
travel.

Merchandise could be brought into the Great Basin by the
Jewish merchant adventurer in two ways, from East or West. The
first could be a covered wagon transport from one of the wholesale
shipping places from the West along the same route the Mormons
took on their trek to Utah. The latter involved making up a special merchant caravan in California and leading it through San
Bernardino to Utah. In time this road, was used more, as the
teamster profession developed in California.

An additional motive of a very special kind, arose when
American troops were stationed in the settlement region of the
Mormons. Jewish merchants thereupon took on the function of
army-sutlers in the military camps.

The traces of the first Jews entering Utah were lost in the
course of later years. Some of them tried their luck there for a short
time and left the territory for good. Others returned years later.
Among them there were a number of characters who had meanwhile explored other places in the Far West especially the chances

168

in California. Their search ended with the conviction that there was a possibility of founding and developing a solid mercantile establishment in Utah. In any case, the fact that there were Jews in the transports of emigrants to California is certain proof that Jews continuously entered Utah for the route through Salt Lake City was the shortest. Advertising this route and establishing it was advantageous to the interests of various circles, not the least of which were the Mormons who derived substantial economic advantages from the migrants passing through. In the same way, however, the non-Mormon traveling over this route, saw his chance if he decided to stay. He might benefit in the same way from future travelers.

This influx of Jewish emigrants from California continued for the entire decade until 1860. It was therefore no accident that among the victims of the Mountain Meadow Massacre (1857) there was also a Jewess. Of Rebecca, the sister of Isaac Goldstein killed on September 29th, 1873 by Indians we are told:

"Unfortunately, it is said, this girl had joined the emigrant transport from Arkansas which, as we know, was attacked by the Mormons and Indians on the Mountain Meadow whereby all members of this transport were killed."[54]

We may consider the first Jews mentioned in Utah as a residue of such California bound travelers. The proof of their existence was already given in documentary form in the U. S. Census of Utah in 1851 which was carried out by the federal unit there. Several names appear which must have been Jewish according to the recorded date and our knowledge of European conditions. This is true of "Solomon Goldsmith, painter, age 28 . . . born Hungary"[55] as of "Bernard Moutnier, 24, male born Hungary" whose name in European form "Mauthner" was at that time a common Jewish family name in Hungary. Even "Jacob 23 Hungary" must be regarded as Jewish.

At the same time a census of Weber county enumerates additional names of Jews:

"Michael Keller, age 52, male, bookbinder, place of birth, Poland; his wife Elisabeth, 46 years, born in Prussia, son Lewis, 16 years, born in Prussia, daughter, Julia, 4 years, born in Indiana, and son, Solomon, 1 year, born in Illinois; Eugene Blum, 26 Jahre, merchant, born in France; Abraham Lewis, 25 Jahre, merchant, born in Poland."[56] We do not know where most of these persons finally settled but we may safely assume that they went from Utah to California.

In the following years names of Jews show up more and more in the post lists published in the Mormon church newspaper, as for instance *Cohn Henry* (1852).[57]

But much earlier, in fact even before the first Utah Census, there was a report about a mercantile venture of Jews with the sole purpose of starting commerce in Utah territory. On June 13th, 1849, the Mormon *Frontier Guardian* reported the departure of these merchants for Utah:

"For the Salt Lake.

John I. Intfeld, M. F. Tiernan, Wm. C. Brent, David Williamson, Sam'l. Loewi, and Joseph T. Intfeld, left yesterday for the Salt Lake. These gentlemen take with them goods of different kinds, for the purpose of trading with the Mormons at that place. If the good wishes of a whole community can do these gentlemen any good, we feel confident they will meet with abundant success. For ourself we hope to see them return to this place with an ever-lasting fortune."[58]

We possess no further knowledge about these persons either but we do know that there were already attempts by Jews to settle in Utah in the first half of the fifties. In September 1855 a Jewish convert to Mormonism was reported to be living outside of Salt Lake City as an established merchant:

". . . There was living at Fillmore a Jew by the name of Levi Abrams who was e[n]gaged in the mercantile business."[59]

In the following years until 1860 new Jewish names appeared in the mailing lists and including that of the first Gentile paper in the territory, as for instance on November 11, 1858 "N. Ransohoff" and in the "Ladies List. Katz, Lydia A."[60] And a single list of the church paper of April 6th, 1859 contained the names of "Bachman B., Brill Nathan, Schonfeld E."[61]

We must consider the following advertisement as the earliest one by a consolidated Jewish firm of 1856 in the church paper:

"Leather. Leather. . . . the 15th ward tannery is now in operation, . . . The mechanical branch of this business will be carried on under the direction of A. I. Toussig, who having been engaged for years in the manufacturing of leather in Austria, Russia, France,

England and the United States, has thoroughly satisfied himself by trial, that the very best article of leather can be furnished from the material with which this country abounds. . . ."[62]

In 1853 an advertisement appeared stating that "French and German" is taught by "Ursenbach & Schonfeld" and there are also "Artificial flowers on sale" by them.[63] And a special mercantile assignment was certainly the reason for the following advertisement:

"*Wanted*

Ten thousand empty bottles, for which *Cash will be paid by*:
H. Rosenfeld & Co.
Salt Lake House, G. S. L. City."[64]

At that time the impact on Utah of the large mercantile caravans from California and from the East were discernible in the Mormon Press. On February 18th, we read in the *Mountaineer*:
"Attention:

Utah Merchants and Traders.
Bachman & Co.,
(Los Angeles, Cal.)
Wholesale Dealers

in
Groceries,
Provisions,

Liquors, Dry Goods, Clothing, Boots & Shoes, and Grain, offer their large assortment of
Goods,

suitable for the *Utah Market,* at prices which cannot fail to ensure satisfaction."[65]

The same advertisement reappeared during the following weeks.[66]

The return of this daring merchant to Los Angeles was reported in the press which reproduced his assessment of the situation in Utah:
"From Salt Lake City.
By the arrival of Mr. B. Bachman in this city, we have advices from Salt Lake City. The papers, *Deseret News* and *Mountaineer,* contain no local news of interest. Mr. B. reports the road in good or-

der; the Indians peacable. Business was dull in the City, and money scarce. It was supposed the troops would be withdrawn from Camp Floyd—a proceeding which was much depreciated there, as it would leave the Territory unprotected, and give the Indians an opportunity of re-opening their attacks on emigrants. Mr. Bachman brought through with him a number of fine horses."[67]

Soon Bachman's competitor in the Utah Trade, also a Jewish merchant from Los Angeles, showed up with his caravan of merchandise in Salt Lake City. On June 16th, 1860 we read the following detailed and well-composed advertisement in the Utah Press:

"That beats the Pony Express.

The Train

of

I. Calisher & Co.

Having arrived here from California in double quick time, they would announce of the public of G. S. L. City and vicinity that they will open on to-day, June 16th, 1860 a large and

Cheap Variety

of

Dry Goods and
Fancy Goods;

consisting in part of Prints, Silk and Velvet Ribbons, Trimmings, Laces, Braids and Tapes; also School Books, Brass Kettles, Tin Ware, Boots and Shoes, and Clothing; also a lot of the best Hoop Skirts.

To country merchants and peddlers, a liberal discount will be allowed.

I. Calisher & Co., next to Irwin & Young's."[68]

This advertisement had been preceded by an earlier one in which the arrival of the train "The latest and the best" was predicted for June 11th, 1860.[69]

On June 23rd, 1860 a special treat was offered the Salt Lake City reader: he was able to find the advertisements of the wagon trains of the two competing Jewish merchants from Los Angeles on one and the same page of his newspaper.[70]

One month later the Calisher advertisement appears in a new version entirely directed to the psychological motivation of the bargain. It becomes clear that the firm wanted to sell out as quickly as possible. This intention was confirmed by the later commercial news of the continued trip of the train and finally by the large scale sale of the remainder of the merchandise destined for Salt Lake City:

"Great Inducements.

A large amount of *Merchandise* to be sacrificed at unprecedented low prices, having opened our establishment on the 'Low Price' and 'Live and let live' system, the undersigned would call the attention of the people of Utah Territory to their

Choice and Assorted Stock
of

Dry Goods, Staple Goods, and *General Merchandise,* which they are determined to sell cheap for cash. If it is your intention to save money in your purchases, call and examine our Stock and Prices, before buying elsewhere, and you will soon be convinced of the truth of our assertion.

We take pleasure, and consider it no trouble to show you our Goods.

I. Calisher & Co., . . ."[71]

In this "Live and Let Live" (Leben und Leben Lassen) we recognize the slogan used by German Jews in their German language advertisements elsewhere. The slogan was repeated half a year later when receipt of the stock of certain merchandise was advertised:

"I. Calisher & Co.,

beg to inform the public that they are in receipt of a shipment of

New Goods,

per Crisman's last train, and are determined to conduct their business as heretofore on the principle

"Live and Let Live."

. . . Dry Goods,

Staple Goods

and General Merchandise

. . . ready made clothing . . ."[72]

Establishment of a store in Salt Lake City was not planned by leading the wagon transport there. The public learned this through the news of the sale of the stock remainder to a settled Salt Lake City merchant. At this point the name of a business partner of Calisher who was apparently also Jewish was mentioned:

"Sold out! Sold out!

Having sold our entire stock of merchandise to Mr. Thomas Taylor, the undersigned would return thanks to their friends for past patronage, and trust that they will bestow a continuance of the same on their successor in business.

All indebted to our firm will please settle up with Mr. M. M. Tokles, the resident partner of the firm, who will be found at the store of Mr. Taylor.

I. Calisher & Co."[73]

The purchaser of the stock continues advertising as a:

"New Store

. . . has bought the entire stock of goods of I. Calisher & Co., . . . at the old stand of the former firm . . .

Thomas Taylor . . ."[74]

Such wagon trains of Jewish merchants brought about a broad contact between Jews and the Mormon population because with the owner came Jewish partners and employees. In the case of the Calisher train, such contact lasted longer because the voyage was continued to the East through Mormon territory to Denver and finally because persons from Utah had joined the train. In Neibaur's diary we find a note dated May 7th, 1861:

"My son Joseph came home with Mr. Calisher's train from Denver—had a letter from my son Isaac;"[75] this letter apparently was taken home from a meeting of the two sons on the road. And on July 6th, 1861 he wrote again: "My son Joseph started again with the Calisher's train for Denver."[76] Wanderlust and striving for gain abroad was certainly furthered among young people in the territory by these mercantile caravans.

Another time the arrival of Calisher's train from the East was advertised:

"First Eastern Train of the season.

A train of eleven wagons from Pike's Peak for the firm of J. Calisher & Co., of this city arrived yesterday morning."[77] This time too the news of the arrival had been preceded by an advertisement:

"Another Arrival.—Mr. Calisher of the firm J. Calisher & Co., merchants in this city, arrived here on Wednesday evening from Pike's Peak. He came ahead of his goods train, which is expected to arrive here tomorrow, or next day. Mr. Calisher reports over-

174

stocked markets, dull trade and flourishing lawyers at the Peak."
And finally:

"Ahead of Time.
First Arrival of New Goods.
The undersigned take pleasure to inform the public that their
Mule Train is expected to arrive in a few days, loaded with a good
selection of

Staple Groceries,

consisting in part, of Tobacco, carefully selected for this market.
Tea of the best brands, *Coffee, Sugar, Rope, Nails,* and other goods
too numerous to mention will be sold at the

Lowest Figures for Cash

Grain, Butter and Eggs will be taken in Exchange.
J. Calisher."[78]

Newly arrived stock from the East was also advertised by an
established Jewish firm:

"New Arrivals of Goods! !
N. S. Ransohoff & Co. would most respectfully invite the attention of the citizens of Salt Lake City and Territory to their
large and well-selected Stock of New Merchandise, just received
from the East. . . . This stock of goods was purchased before the
recent advance in prices, we, therefore, will offer the same at re-
munerative prices, to satisfy purchasers.

The attention of Country Merchants is respectfully invited.
N. S. Ransohoff & Co.,
At the store formerly occupied by Staines Nedham & Co."[79]

A special chapter in Utah history began with the presence
of the U. S. Army, for the soldiers, as non-Mormons, formed a
separate body within the population. The Army had already been
instrumental in bringing merchants, Jews among them, into the
territory as carriers of goods and sutlers in the camp stores where
soldiers bought merchandise for their wages. Such a person was
Samuel H. Auerbach who furnished goods to Camp Floyd. From
his diary we learn that in this Army camp 250 buildings had been
erected.[80] Later, beef for Camp Douglas was procured by the Salt
Lake City Jewish merchant Charles Popper who was also allowed

175

to erect a soap and candle factory on the grounds of the military reservation.[81]

The presence of the Army brought about the first tensions between Mormons and Gentiles but it was still a far cry from the later Gentile front against the Mormons. There were unfavorable opinions about them and assertions that they cheat the California emigrants by high prices had been made earlier, even before the arrival of the soldiers.[82] All in all there had not been enough non-Mormons in the territory to be anything of a social group. With the arrival of the soldiers all this changed. Commercial ambition of non-Mormon individuals could now be based on the consumption of the military. On the other hand the Mormons' view of their life with Gentiles changed and their resentment against the military was easy to understand. This resentment grew after the so-called Utah war of 1857, when military occupation of the territory had become permanent. Thus the profits of the non-Mormon merchants from the military caused ill feelings among the Mormons. The merchants were even accused of having brought the soldiers to the territory because of their greed for profit. The Mormon press of the time was full of attacks against the profiteers of war on the Atlantic coast who had incited the Utah war and against the merchants who had followed on the heels of the Army to make profit:

". . . To speak more plainly; the war in Utah, and the present location of the Army there, were brought about through the influence of sutlers and contractors, for the purpose of plundering the national treasury. They are all, all guilty. And if not equally so, those assuredly are the most to blame who had in former times fattened, and filled their purses from the hard earnings of the honest citizens. . . ."[83]

Speeches of prominent church leaders stressed the fact that large firms on the Atlantic had drawn $500,000 a year from Utah but nothing had been done to enlighten Washington about true condition in Utah.[84]

The soldiers suffered, to be sure, from the unfriendliness of the Mormons. Sometimes, for instance, they were not sold theater tickets, but in one way or another they lived on among the Mormons with some degree of social intercourse. Some soldiers married Mormon girls and converted to Mormonism:

176

"A letter from Camp Floyd states that quite a number of United States soldiers have joined the Mormon Church for the sake of Mormon crinoline."[85] But the distance between the Mormons and the merchants grew greater. The lure expressed in a Mormon poem at the beginning of the Civil War that the war would result in heightened importance of the Mormon commuity to the Union[86] came true in a negative sense. The government decided that the territory had to be occupied because of its military importance so as not to lose it to the Mormons.) Under the pretext that the overland telegraph line had to be secured against the Indians, a permanent military control over the Mormons was instituted. Camp Floyd was followed by Camp Douglas and Salt Lake City stood directly under the cannons of the Federal Government.

The occupation of 1862 had been accomplished by Californian troops. Thus the soldiers came from a part of the Union where Jews were already numerous. This fact facilitated the later influx of Jews into Utah territory.

However the Jews among the soldiers had their own special story. Among the Californian troops was a regiment of New York volunteers who were transferred to Utah. In the list of members of this regiment was find the names Moritz Cohn, Philipp Kohn, Rosenthal and other Jewish names.[87]

Even more since the beginning of the Civil War, Jews were represented among the soldiers in Utah. The following 23 persons appear in the records of California men serving in Utah 1861–1867:

Second Regiment of Cavalry in Camp

Douglas Company A, K, L, Theodor H. Goodman, 1st Lieutenant, to A; Brown, Benjamin P.; Linoberg Jacob (1865); Komp. K. in C. Dougl. (1863-64); Benjamin Landis, discharged at C. D. 1863; Henry Bick; Brown Jacob (mustered out C. D. 1864); Goldsmith, Gustavus; Illig, Morris, Priv. (Utah); Israel, Abrams; Myers, Charles F., Camp Douglas; Myers, Fidel; Norman, Saul. Company L (1863-66 Camp Douglas) Dyler, James; Mayers, Daniel. *Third Regiment of Infantry under Connor, all companies in Utah* Comp. A.: Esberg Henry, enlisted Stockton, Morris, Isadore; Newman Henry, Stern, Louis, Comp. B. Comp. C. Solomon Cohen, Corporal, enrolled in Mokelumne Hill, 1861, 25 IX, "mustered out at Camp Douglas, U. T., Oct. 4, 1864, expiration term of service." Blum, John, Myers, Leopold. Raphael Morris Schnabel, Gustavus, Comp. D. Myers, Leopold, Comp. E. Comp. F., Isador Morris, Davis, Jacob R., Comp. G. Stern, Louis, Sacramento enl. Camp Douglas., Comp. H., Comp. I, Esberg, Henry, C. Dougl. Comp. K.[88]

Data on the enlistment of Jewish soldiers is to be found in the register of recruits:

"Camp Douglas. Register of Recruits. Sept. to June 1864.

Record of Recruits examined by. . . . 24 Sept. 1861. Chas, F. R. Kahn, born Saxony, age 34, profession, Miner, enlisted by Lieut. J. Ustick.

Sept. 27, 1861. Samuel Cahaen, Prussia, age 22, Farmer, enl. by Capt. Lewis.

Oct. 2, 1861. Louis A. Myers, Prussia, 29, soldier. Oct. 3. Leopold Myer, Germany, 34, Servant, enl. by Capt. Urmy. Nov. 23, 1861. Lewis Stern, b. Altstadt, Germany, age 30, Merchant, enlisted by Capt. Urmy. Feb. 3rd, 1862. Fred Lewis, b. Baden, Germany, age 36, Printer, enlisted by Capt. Potts, 'Served as a soldier 5 years in Germany.' May 15th, 1862. Gustavus Schnabel, b. Rheine, France, age 31, Confectioner, enl. Capt. Lewis. July 31, 1862. Lewis Herman, b. Hesse Cassel, Germany, age 35, Musician, Served 8 years in army."[89]

German Jewish soldiers in Utah participated in organizing German singing societies in the military camps just as German Jews did elsewhere in America as indicated by this letter sent from Camp Floyd to New York:

"To make our rather purposeless presence here tolerable in at least one respect several social associations have been formed; we also have 2 English and one German theater. To the latter preference is due because of its play and the decorum during the performance. There exist also two singing societies, the first named 'Teutonia' and the other 'Germania'; the theater belongs to the latter. It was built by the members themselves and with their own means."[90]

Until the end of the sixth decade of the century the number of settled non-Mormons (except soldiers and Indians) was very small. A competent observer wrote in 1861: "The number of Gentiles was not considerable in Utah at the period of our journey; it could not exceed a hundred."[91] That was surely little enough among the then already 60,000 inhabitants of Utah, with 12,000 in Salt Lake City alone.

Among them were only a few Jewish merchants. The Jewish traveler Benjamin, entering Salt Lake City in 1861, wrote: "5 Israelites live here, 2 of them belong to the sect, the other three are merchants and are doing business here very successfully." These three without doubt were the Ransohoff Brothers and Samuel Kahn. The provenance of the Ransohoff family from Westphalia seems proven by the "Actum in der Canton Mairie Nieheim Holtzhausen, 28, June 1809." There we find as of July 24th, 1809 a Nathan Abraham Ransohoff taking the citizens oath.[92]

E) *The First Literary Evalution.*

In this early period, when there were so few Jews settled in Utah, few literary notes about Mormons were made by American Jews.

The first such comment was made by a well-educated German Jewish peddler (1842–43) who later rose to prominence in the Jewish community in Illinois and even played a minor political role there:

"Millerism seems to be somewhat on the decline, and I don't hear as much of it as formerly. Mormonism is another superstition, which, in this progressive and enlightened nation, seems to make strides. A certain Joe Smith, now living and preaching to the people in the western states, claims to be the true prophet of God, a priest of Melchizedek. He purports to have found the true Bible and rejects Jesus, Moses, and Mohammed alike. He proclaims a new religion to the credulous people and, absurd as it seems to me, it is reported to have more than thirty thousand disciples. Terrible!"[93]

The man who wrote this was a young German Jew with a lifelong literary interest. Like so many of his generation he had been influenced by the school of German enlightenment but had remained in his heart a religious Jew. His opinion was certainly typical of many people of the same origin and education at that time.

179

An American Jewish newspaper published (1850) the first general news about Utah and the Mormons before the Carvalho visit as for instance the following:

Deseret.—The editor of the Frontier Guardian—the Mormon paper in Iowa—says he has a great decided objection to the name of Utah, from a low and diminutive tribe of Indians, who inhabit Salt Lake valley and the surrounding valleys. He hopes that a petition will be sent to have the name changed, and that that body will give the citizens of Salt Lake the one they chose for themselves, 'Deseret,' the signification of virtue and industry."[94]

And in an issue of the same paper published three years later we find the first editorial opinion:

"As the Great Basin is the greatest physical, so the inhabitants may be said to be the greatest moral curiosity of the New World."[95]

This early period also witnessed two exceptional attempts by Jews to give a literary evaluation of Mormon society. They came about because of the unusual circumstances which brought these two individuals to Utah as well as their special position which permitted them to observe the things in which they were interested. One, S. N. Carvalho, was an artist, who during his trips in 1851 and 1854 made sharp observations of Mormon life; the other was the Jewish globetrotter, Israel Benjamin (Benjamin II) who undertook religious discussions with Mormon leadership.

Several features of the Carvalho visit and his resulting book are unique and better than what is contained in other travel books and descriptions of Mormon life. Here was a Jew steeped in Jewish tradition, well equipped by his Jewish learning to compare Mormonism with Judaism. At the same time, this man had contact with the Jewish community on the Atlantic as well as in Los Angeles. This book shows that he was well aware of which aspects of Mormonism would most interest the Jews in America. Also unique was Carvalho's sojourn for a number of weeks in a Mormon polygamic household as well as his opportunity (although he had come on a Government mission) to be the friendly companion of Brigham Young on the Governor's official inspection trip of Southern Utah. In fact we owe the only description of the inspection caravan of 23 wagons to him. Added to this was his personal closeness to Brigham Young of whom he made two paintings. He was invited by him to social events in the Mormon community and was almost

180

the only non-Mormon at that time who had meaningful social intercourse with the Mormons. That Carvalho's book was highly esteemed especially among the Jews, is shown by a review in a Californian Jewish newspaper:

". . . Any production emanating from an ingenious mind, like that of Mr. S. N. C. cannot fail to be highly interesting . . ."[96] Considering this interest among Jews, it is remarkable that no comparable reviews of Carvalho's book are found in the contemporary general press of America.

Friend and defender of the Mormons, his attitude developed from his own conscience—religiously as a Jew, as one human being to his fellows and as an American citizen concerned about the consequences of Mormonism for America.

Brigham Young's attitude that everything honestly observed in Utah might be reported, found its fulfillment in Carvalho's book. At its center he put his basic observation of the people as religionists:

"During a residence of ten weeks in Great Salt Lake City, and my observations in all their various settlements, amongst a homogenous population of over seventy-five thousand inhabitants, it is worthy of record, that I never heard any obscene or improper language; never saw a man drunk; never had my attention called to the exhibition of vice of any sort. There are no gambling houses, grog shops, or buildings of ill fame, in all their settlements. They preach morality in their churches and from their stands, and what is as strange, as it is true, the people practice it, and religiously believe their salvation depends on fulfilling the behests of the religion they have adopted."[97]

The polygamy, he observed, did not bring the author to any discussion of the subject with the Mormons who thought their marriage system right, but it caused the author to contemplate in seclusion. He formulated for himself biblical arguments against it[98] which are essentially the same as the arguments American Jews developed once the subject came into the open. The American public learned from his observation that the practice of the plural wife system depended on immigration, and that the immigrants who arrived without knowledge of its existence in Utah,[99] remained largely antagonistic to it.[100]

181

American Jews who had learned from his report that Mormon leaders preached warmly of the Jews' imminent in-gathering to Palestine[101] were at the same time aware that they would be troubled by the Mormons' Biblical argument for their plural marriage system. Carvalho himself, fully conscious that his report was the first thoroughly reliable report on Mormon polygamy, would give this report only if accompanied by documents of an official character appended to his book. From all this he comes to the melancholy conclusion that the Mormon people will have to suffer greatly from its peculiar institution. Nevertheless he retains some hope:

"I hope to live to see more wholesome feeling in this respect, among the leaders of the Mormon Church. A continuation of their present practice must inevitably lead to confusion."[102]

Carvalho doesn't even try to give us a history of the Mormons. His report is pragmatic, giving only the present facts: "They wear an undergarment with distinctive marks upon it, an imitation of the Jews."[103] There is only one argument of a speculative nature, the situation of men who remain wifeless because the polygamic system takes in all the available women. To this speculation Carvalho even dedicates a statistical table. This same pragmatic sense excels in recounting social scenes observed among the Mormons. It is this which makes Carvalho's report a real contribution to Mormon history.

The other literary Jew, who visited the Mormons was entirely different from the artist Carvalho. Israel Benjamin, as a typical autodidact, a product of Eastern European Jewish city life was more apt to discuss religious questions in detail with the Mormons. The background of his voyage was also unique. He was truly a voyager sponsored by the Jewish people. At the time he desired to become a world traveler, the wishes of European Jews to know more about their brethren in distant countries had become strong enough to support this traveler by gifts and advance payment for his works. We also find in the list of his benefactors Christian well-wishers and contributions from the Jewish communities which he visited. He was, therefore, or, at least felt himself to be, an explorer sent out by the Jewish people. His travel report was in the first instance, directed to the Jews. He gave information about Jews and the Jewish community with such general observations as might make the situation of the Jews better understood.

182

If Israel Joseph Benjamin therefore decided, to give a treatise on the Mormons in his book on America, the only treatise outside the realm of Jewish life, he must have felt that his readers in Europe eagerly expected such a study preferably by a reliable Jewish witness rather than by a personality bound to the Christian world. Benjamin promises this study "sine ira and studio." Everything he then undertakes is in contrast to Carvalho. He saw nothing and informed about nothing which he may have seen of Mormon life with his own eyes but he gives a history of the Mormons and instruction about their theological system from the responsible public relations men of the church. But then, in discussion with Brigham Young and the church leaders he argued against religious points which seemed obviously erroneous to him. Other news he only reports as he heard it:

"It is reported to me from a reliable source that after the temple will be erected the three main Jewish festivals (Pesach, Schabuoth and Sukkoth) as also circumcision shall be introduced."[104]

To learn that the new sect is exceedingly friendly to Hebrews "who are called "Brother Jews" was most welcome news to Jews in Europe and their potential emigrants.

The Jews in the world must have been very much affected by his discussion of Mormon polygamy and his statistical table on their plural marriage, as well as his statement that plural marriage was obligatory for persons in higher church office.[105] This must have been especially amazing to the Jewish reader because as a potential emigrant he had heard of a lack of women in America and had seen so many Jewish men returning to Europe for the sole purpose of choosing a Jewish female as mate for a life in America.

Benjamin's treatise arrived at full conclusions. He saw in the Mormon society not only "one of the most wonderful appearances of our modern world" [106] but regarded its existence also as proof that persecutions cement a religious community even more strongly.[107] He stated with frankness that the persecution of the Mormons puts America to shame.[108]

His historical essay on the Mormons was the first systematic treatment of this subject by a Jew.

CHAPTER 18

The Resident Jewish Merchant Class and the Rise of a Gentile Front, Religious Life and Social Contact with the Mormons

The history of the splinter of the Jewish people in remote Utah embodies the basic elements of Jewish history within the unique framework of American history. The minority problem there was that of a minority of Jews in a territory whose majority, the Mormons, was itself a small and persecuted minority in America. Furthermore the Jewish minority represented only a small part of all non-Mormons there. They were all referred to collectively as Gentiles and were all drawn into a historical conflict which was considered a "Gentile," i.e., religious, conflict. Thus Utah Jewry presented the image of a small gear within a somewhat larger machine. Although it seemed to be moving only itself, it was actually setting the other in motion as well.

The religious and social conflict between the "Saints," who became the founding fathers of Utah, and the Gentiles, the ever advancing general population of an expanding America, included Utah's Jewry with all other non-Mormons. However, religious conflict between Jews and Mormons did not exist because the battle of faith went on exclusively on the grounds of established Christianity. Because the Jewish population stood outside the main conflict in the territory, that of religion, historical evidence emerging from the presence of the Jews is especially valuable for judging the course of events. Judaism as a historic phenomenon and the fate of the Jews in Utah thus became an important source of information for Mormon history as well as the history of America's internal growth.

From the viewpoint of Jewish historiography the situation was also a unique "first." For the two thousand years of Jewish existence there was a united Christian front against them, but here the united Christian front rose against a new religion leaving the Jews entirely aside. Indeed, in America's conflict with the Mormons there is hardly any other religious non-participant besides the Jew. No wonder that to this day the Jew has not found a place in the history of this conflict. A complete survey of the simple Jew-Mormon relationship is therefore an indispensible necessity to an evaluation of American history.

The following statement which considered the Jews as an existing political entity may be regarded as the first recognition of Utah Jewry by an outsider:

National March 16, 1860

To his Excellency James Buchanan, President

In relation to "Marshall" for Utah,—There is no one within my knowledge whose appointment would afford more general satisfaction to *Mormons—Jews*—a. Gentiles than Robert Heresford Esq. He is from Virginia, but has lived in the West —California . . . for five or more years . . . is favorably known to all the business men of Utah. Whilst not a Mormon—would be less obnoxious to them than any other person in Utah. . . . Rest assured that this appointment would be acceptable to all parties in Utah. . . .

J. Forney[1]

For as long as a recognizable and effective Jewish community in Utah existed, it was a resident Jewish merchant class and its problems were part of the economic phase of the Gentile conflict. Their economic fate, however, was so closely woven into their general relations with the Mormons that a description of the economic life of the Jews is incomplete without a description of other relations between Jew and Mormon. Even the spiritual life of the Jewish group as a religious community maintained enough relations with the Mormons to require explanation and the illumination afforded by the Jewish press of the time. Usually the reports about Utah's Jews published in the Jewish press blended all these elements, economic, political and religious, although their position as a merchant class was the most enlightening.

But no matter how much we may learn from the point of view of the Jewish minority the burden of all existing questions in the territory lay with the Mormons. The historian's approach to the

185

Gentile conflict may overlook the fact that for the Mormon this was a fight for life. The weakening of its economic roots within the territory and the consequent loss of the economic leadership would, in that phase of the Gentile conflict, have made Utah a colony of the East, and it would of necessity have lost any inner meaning for the faithful. A constantly growing emigration of Mormons from Utah would have been the unavoidable consequence and whatever had not been accomplished by persecution in three stages of westward migration would have resulted from being economically choked. There would have been no impulse for a new emigration under such circumstances. A splitting up of the Mormon people would have followed and the Mormon Church would have lost its spiritual power over its people.

As against all these grave consequences for the Mormon, for the Jewish merchant class the economic conflict in the territory was only one individual episode in the economic adjustment of the Jewish immigrant in America. It had great meaning as a merchant adventure but it did not play a great role numerically in the dispersion of the Jewish communities over the West. As to the economic function of the Jewish group in Utah it was essentially identical with that of Jews in other parts of America. Here too remarkable adventure was involved—wagon trains and freighting among other things.

The dilemma of the Jewish merchant hampered by an exclusively Mormon economic life could continue only so long as the combined factors of California-bound migrants, soldiers and non-Mormons in the territory did not have sufficient consumer power to secure the Jewish merchant against the loss of the Mormon consumer. Such an economic crisis could be overcome in the long run by means of additional consumer demand from the new influx of mining population together with a partial resumption of trade with Mormons.

Events in the territory which took a violent turn and influenced all later political developments, can be evaluated only if we distinguish between the official policy of the church leaders and other factors which furthered the conflict. A group of extremists who regarded terror as a political instrument was certainly in existence. What the Mormon church did with this group, whether it countenanced their deeds as fitting into its plans or whether it opposed

186

them as entirely contrary to the policy of the church leaders, cannot be determined with any degree of certainty. In any case the church leaders did not publicize the violence of this group in any way and took no official position against them. Only by awakening their religious conscience could the terrorists have been deterred. However, the lessons of history should help us to understand that the position of the Mormon church vis-à-vis such a wave of terror was not simple. As always the Mormon violence at the time was supported by the conviction of the mass of people that they had suffered in the past. In addition they feared new sufferings and the possibility of being driven away from the territory by violence.

American Jews had not taken any part in persecuting the Mormons. Their appearance in the territory could not be regarded as forming a new religious front-line against the Mormons. Their arrival there as elsewhere was part of the search for economic chances to prosper. Only an extraordinary constellation of circumstances could push the Jewish merchant class into a front which was to them anything but religious.

To the Mormon community on the other hand, economic exclusivity as soon as it was declared to be the official policy of the church, was entirely religious. The instrument of the cooperative as the economic monopoly of the church was not only an expedient for the individual Mormon, but the way out of a situation deemed dangerous for the church and a means of survival for the church as a whole. (Mormons not joining the Cooperative but making use of economic exclusivity therefore acted against the interest of the Church as a whole.)

Developments in the territory had their repercussions in California. The first major event, the Utah War of 1857, at the time of the in-gathering of California Mormons to Utah, was carefully observed by Jews in California. Neighboring territories were affected by this event: "The entire Mormon population of Carson Valley are in consequence selling out their farms, improvement and cattle and are moving to the Holy City. Numbers of speculators have gone to Carson City to take advantage of this circumstance."[2]

The Utah War awakened the full interest of the Jewish press in America in the Mormon empire. This Jewish interest became world-wide as a result of the book by Benjamin II. Evidence of this

187

is to be seen in the following words of a learned Jewish magazine in Hungary:

"The third section [of the book] deals with the Northwest of America and is especially interesting because of the story of the Mormons given from their own sources and augmented by very valuable notes on the present conditions of this religious community."[3]

a) *Economic life.*

Even before there was a distinct Jewish merchant class in the territory outside, observers were quick to construct parallels between merchants and business there and the image of the Jew:

"There are some persons who for a consideration will supply what we want—I say for a consideration—the Mormon brethren in this respect resembling the Jews of old, who while affecting to despise the Gentiles, were at the same time strongly enamored of Gentile gold."[4]

And moving to the Jews of the contemporary world this author continues:

"But there are many shops of less pretention, devoted to the sale of second-hand or inferior articles, with clothes, hose, and similar goods of home-made manufacture. You soon discover that the keepers of these establishments possess a peculiar aptitude for trade. In dexterity and cunning they seem even to surpass the Jews."[5]

In contrast to such unfavorable descriptions there already were Jewish businesses with considerable capital invested in Salt Lake City. One of them was Ransohoff and Bros. owned by four partners advertising on November 1863 in the *Union Vedette* published in Camp Douglas that in their store (Main Street, Great Lake City, U. T.) . . . Dry Goods, Groceries . . . Fancy Articles, Dress Goods . . ." are on sale.[6] And two weeks later the same newspaper carried the following advertisment:

"Bodenberg, a. Kahan
. . . New Merchandise . . . Dress Goods . . . Clothing, Boots, Shoes, Hats . . . Cigars . . . At the old stand of Hooper, Eldredge a. Co., East Tempel Street."[7]

188

At the end of 1863 the firm Ransohoff a. Bros. was dissolved for the purpose of establishing new firms with widely extended activities. The announcement of dissolution cited the names of the four partners:

"Dissolution.

"The partnership heretofore existing under the name and firm of A. L. Ransohoff a. Bros., has been dissolved by mutual consent. A. L. Ransohoff, Geo. Bodenburg, S. Kahn, M. Elsbach."[8]

From its inception, this firm had had good relations with the Mormons and with Brigham Young personally. It was later assessed as ". . . prominent firm . . . long the leading Jewish firm, who built the best store house in the city. They had extensive dealings with Brigham Young . . . and when Johnson's Army left camp, and their properties were sold, Brigham borrowed D 30.000 of Ransohoff to invest in army pork."[9]

Ransohoff's big advertisments in the church paper already appeared in 1862:

"*A new store*—N. L. Ransohoff a. Co. have this week opened, for retail business, the store formerly occupied by Staines, Needham a. Co. Ransohoff a. Co. have been favorably known as wholesale merchants in this city for some years back. They have brought in a very large assorted stock of staple goods. . . .[10-11] Another big advertisement of the firm at the same time in this paper deals with clothing, shoes, hardware and groceries.[12]

That the firm, as an example of a leading business, was attractive to young Mormons is seen from the fact that a leading church personality had spent his apprentice years there:

"The twelve Apostles.

"Moses Thatcher—He became second salesman in the firm of A. P. Ransohoff a. Co., at Salt Lake City. Having made himself familiar with the details of a general mercantile business, he returned to Logan and engaged in that line with his father."[13]

The influx of Jews into the territory took place as a result of the German Jewish immigration wave together with Germans. Their connection with Germans remained active in the Intermountain Basin. Fred T. Kiesel, a German and later the first Gentile mayor in Ogden "drove a team across the plains in Henry Lawrence's train"[14] (spring 1863) and arrived in Salt Lake City. Partnership with Jews played an important role in his manifold business undertakings.[15] The census of 1870, when the resident Jewish merchant class in Utah was already conspicuous, included 358 persons born in Germany, a number which could have been reached only because of the considerable contingent of German Jews.[16]

Although a sizable number of Jews did not arrive in Utah until 1864, it is remarkable that by the end of that year they were already considered a representative group in American Jewry. A correspondent in the "American Israelite" describes their conditions at that time as follows:

> "Salt Lake City—A soldier writes us from Camp Douglas, in Utah Territory that quite a number of Hebrews of late settled in Salt Lake City as merchants, butchers etc., some of them having opened quite a nice meat market for the saints and ordinary folks. They are engaged with a plan to erect a synagogue for themselves, and are collecting funds for the purpose. Our correspondent says the development of the mineral wealth of this territory, and the exertions of the commanding General Conner, will soon produce a new order of society and laws in this territory."[17]

The Jews, who appeared as a distinct group in the eyes of the surrounding world, were ready to form a Jewish religious community at a time when the total number of the Gentiles in the territory was exceedingly small. Even at the end of 1865 there were no more than 300 Gentiles.[18] The essence of this report was also reproduced in the German Jewish women's paper in America, the *Deborah*.[19] The latter was widely read in the German homeland by the families of the emigrated Jews, thus spreading the news of the Jewish community in Utah to Europe.

The composition of this resident Jewish merchant class is revealed by the advertisements in the Utah papers of that year. New merchants arrived and founded new businesses or were taken as partners in the existing ones. On March 24th, 1864 we read:

> "New Goods—L. Wormser a. Co., late of California, have just opened a splendid assortment of staple and fancy dry goods, ladies' shoes, trimmings etc. just imported from Cali-

fornia. They offer their entire stock low at wholesale, at their store west side of Main Street, Salt Lake City, next door to Cronin a. Clayton's."[20]

This advertisement is repeated in the paper on the next day with "Yankee notions" on sale added to text.[21]

However, new blood was infused into existing businesses by Ransohoff Bros. An editorial notice of April 6th, 1864 informs us of the following:

> ". . . Ransohoff Bros. have associated with them in business Messrs. Conrad Prag and Abraham Ganz, of San Francisco, and that the firm will hereafter bear the name of Ransohoff a. Co."[22]

And on the next page we find the advertisement of the copartnership:

> "Co-Partnership Notice.
> "We have this day associated with us in business Messrs. Conrad Prag and Abraham Ganz of San Francisco, and the firm will hereafter be styled Ransohoff a. Co., instead of Ransohoff Bro. as heretofore.
> > Ransohoff Bro.
>
> S. L. City, April 4th, 1864."[23-27]

In the growth of all firms, old or new, the erection of fire-proof buildings played the same role as elsewhere in the West. One month later we read:

> "Improvements—Ransohoff a. Co., having purchased the fine lot on the west side of Main Street next to Jennings' new structure, are proceeding rapidly in excavating the cellar preparatory to the erection of a fine building to be used as a store . . . we understand the building will be of a first class character . . ."[28]

In following advertisements the clothing business comes to the fore with new firms:

> ". . . Hellman a. Kuhn . . . Ready made Clothing . . . Yankee Notions, Cigars . . . one door north of the Salt Lake House . . ."[29]

And a few days later a firm which later rose to importance in the territory appeared:

"Gentlemen's Clothing and Furnishing Goods . . . Siegel a. Co."[30]

Since a business directory of Salt Lake City was lacking at this early date, we may best see the state of the Jewish merchant class at the end of 1864 from the advertiseing page of the Daily Union Vedette of December 24th, 1864 which apparently included most of the Jewish firms. It reflects a good deal of the economy in the territory and the part which Jewish merchants controlled, including the auction, which was at that time already a frequently employed form of selling in the Far West.

"T. H. Heller   B. F. Snyder
                       Heller a. Snyder
Auction and Commission Merchants
Second South Temple Street.
Will sell at public as private sale, at Ten o'clock every morning, Horses, Wagons, Merchandise etc. Warehouse for Storage.

"Wanted: Products of all kinds."[31]
Further newsworthy firms were
"M. Berger I. Morris. Provision Market . . ."
"G. Rosenbaum, L. Newmann
Largest Meat Stall in the City . . ."

A new clothing firm had a speculative business as a side line:

"The Highest Price paid for California Bounties at the San Francisco Clothing House.

Aron Newfield."[31]

In earlier editions of this paper, advertisements of the Jewish firm Ellis had appeared.[32]

The beginning of the next year 1865 witnessed intensified business activity by Jewish merchants especially in their relations with Camp Douglas:

"Messrs. Rosenbaum a. Newman have associated with them as a co-partner in the meat business, Mr. Chas. Hopper [sic]. The firm is now Rosenbaum a. Co.

192

The rapid increase in their business has induced them to open a branch market in our Camp. This we pronounce as a capital thought and plan. We need not request that the patronage of our Camp people may be extended, as the name of the firm is already familiar to all, and the choice meats for which they are noted have been long ere this fully appreciated."[33]

Charles Popper later became one of the most successsful merchants in the territory. The growth of the meat firms is attested by the introduction of industries dealing with the by products of meat slaughtering:

Messrs. Rosenbaum a. Co. are anxiously looking for an experienced tanner at their meat market."[34]

Speculative transactions were also in greater demand:

"Isidore Morris, of the firm of Morris a. Berger, S. L. City, is buying Certificates of the California State Bounties.

"To those Soldiers who are *determined* to dispose of their papers, we know of no one to whom they can sell to a better advantage. Aaron Newfield is also purchasing."[35]

We hear occasionally of collection worries:

"Messrs. Morris a. Berger make a kind yet urgent appeal to their delinquent customers to settle their accounts. Butter, eggs etc. are very agreeable on the table, but they require the "greenbacks" to touch them off."[36]

In the year 1865 the total number of the Jews in Utah is reported to have been fifty, most of them unmarried.[37]

The overall picture of the merchant class in Utah, Mormons and non-Mormons, with Jews among them, at the end of 1866 was described as follows:

The principal merchants of Utah are Mr. Jennings, Mr. Godbe, Kimball a. Lawrence, Walker Brothers, Ransohoff, Basset a. Co. There are minor merchants, also, who do considerable amounts of business, and for the last few years Jew merchants from California and the Eastern States have poured into Salt Lake City like locusts. The sons of father Jacob, as

193

if from instinct, always flock to a city just about the time that an extraordinary commercial epoch is coming toward it. The reader, perhaps, will be surprised at the amount of business that these Salt Lake merchants already do . . ."[38]

New advertisements of Jewish firms were in evidence:

"S. W. Joel a. Co., general Auctioneers and Commission Merchants . . . Great Salt Lake City."[39] "Cohn a. Co. have removed their superb stock of Dry Goods and Clothing . . ."[40]

The still existing business of the Auerbach family "the oldest Department Store in the interior West 77 years under one ownership and management"[41] appeared in the same number in its embryonic form:

The People's Store!
F. Auerbach a. Bros.,
Dealers in
"Staple and Fancy Merchandise, Dry Goods, Groceries, Yankee Notions, Boots and Shoes, Clothing . . ."[42]

Among the advertisements were some full page ads which appeared continuously with changes in the text. They used psychological motivations, making special offers according to the market situation and dealing mostly with sellouts of specific kinds of merchandise:

"Bodenburg a. Kahn's column.
Second to None
in this Territory.
". . . We have made a great reduction in prices to close our present stock and make room for more . . . we are now selling at cost, wishing to go out of business (in shoes) and offering them wholesale and retail at a great sacrifice . . ."[43]

b) *Gentile conflict.*

The first collision between the Mormons and the U. S. Government—referred to as the Utah War—but in reality only a police action to secure the new territory, took place at a time (1857) when non-Mormons in the territory were so few in number that they couldn't have caused any greater conflict. The Mountain Meadow

194

Massacre—the cause of the Utah War—was described by the Mormons as the fault of the California emigrants:

> "There were many emigrants on their way to Carson Valley and California. Many of those Gentile emigrants shot the Indians wherever they met with them. The Indians fell to retaliation and, if not watched, would kill innocent people."[44]

The expedition of Federal troops to Utah was considered by the Mormons a religious war:

> "The armies of the Gentiles are making war upon us, because of our religion, and we have to defend ourselves against a nation of twenty-five millions of people, and the war has just commenced; we have to trust in God for the result."[44]

Nevertheless the presence of even a few non-Mormons in the territory portended a future time when the influx of a greater number of Gentiles would be considered unavoidable. The problems which would arise from this situation stood clearly before the eyes of the Mormon leaders. They knew, because California was not far away, that in the beginning of the gold-rush private rights to land were disregarded and they feared the same predicament in an eventual mineral rush to Utah. Furthermore a decision by the Transcontinental Railway which planned to go through Utah was not far off and this would open the territory to all America. These various considerations brought the problem of living together with the Gentiles to the fore long before their numbers seemed menacing.

Actually the first Gentile problem resulted from the U. S. soldiers in the territory being isolated by the Mormons from closer social intercourse. Various incidents with the Mormon population were caused by their presence. At the same time the army's presence also brought to the territory a number of civilians who were strongly criticized by the Mormons:

> "I blame them . . . With the army came a flood of workers of iniquity, of every grade, from the merchant and the gambler in broadcloth to the rowdiest fustioned teamster that ever brawled in our streets. . . ."[44a]

But the headaches of the Mormon leaders had actually begun much earlier, at the very beginning of settlement in Utah. Indeed

195

it must be recognized that it was not easy to find the right policy. The route to California through Utah had to be kept open. In the final analysis, it was in the interest of the Mormons. Yet the attempt of individual Gentiles to settle as merchants in Utah could be frustrated only by means which would have made the Mormons appear to be hostile to the rest of the American population. Furthermore the construction of the railway promised big profits for the Mormons, and the exploitation of the mineral treasures even if no rush was forthcoming could not be delayed for long. During this time Mormon economy had to be strengthened to a point where lasting and increasing income would make it independent. Only then would it no longer be in danger of becoming a colony of the East as a result of the influx of Eastern mining capital. This explains the policy of the Mormons leaders to push colonization and to found settlements at all strategic points of the Intermountain Basin. Everything else was reserved for tactical considerations whenever necessary.

The uncertain stand of the non-Mormon merchants was the result of a continuous search for a position which would answer the needs of the present situation and at the same time be of some value for the future. This wavering finally culminated in a crisis in relations with the merchants at the end of 1866. The young resident Jewish merchant class just then organized as a Jewish community together with the other non-Mormon merchants in the territory were confronted with some of the gravest decisions ever documented.

The tortuous path from the first demonstrations against non-Mormon merchants to the outbreak of full Gentile conflict used several methods of attack, of which the merchants' asserted economic exploitation of the Mormon population was only one.

In its unlimited exaggeration this point was finally formulated in the following words:

> "Perhaps in no country in the world have men engaged in ordinary mercantile trading been able to accumulate fortunes so rapidly, during the past ten or twelve years, as in this Territory."[45]

But these a posteriori statements entirely missed the point of historical truth. Because from the beginning the Mormon leaders advised the non-Mormons to go ahead to California and this advice was ominously emphasized:

"I feel to say to Jew and to Gentile, let this people alone in these valleys of the mountains, or you will find that which you are not looking for . . ."[46]

The argument was naturally part of the criticism of prices in the territory which was directed against the Gentile merchants. It was added to the criticism of the volume of purchases made by Mormons in Gentile stores. This point was often expressed by Mormon leaders and Brigham Young was among the main speakers:

(April 9th, 1852):
"The people go to the Gentile stores, on the Saturday, in crowds, to purchase goods. I think we shall not overrate the amount if we say that D. 500.000 has been paid, in the vallies, to the merchants . . . I find no fault with the merchants, for they came here to gather gold by the hundred weight."[47]

Although there were also Mormon merchants in the territory who set the prices, nevertheless Heber Kimball, himself an important merchant, could pose the oratorial question: "Am I dependent upon this Shylock merchant any longer?"[48]

In the end Brigham Young had to address himself specifically to the Mormon merchants and their prices:

"I will refer to our merchants, I mean our 'Mormon merchants' particularly. What do they say about their goods? They do not ask what their goods are worth, or what they paid for them; but what will the people give for them? That is the price . . ."[49]

As to the prevailing prices, their true nature can be established only by comparison with prices in other parts of the Far West. Independent of this search it must first be stated that the volume of capital earned in the territory to a great extent came from the emigrants to California and not from the "inhabitants of the valleys" and was therefore not the result of Mormon work but of the import of goods. This was therefore a 100 per cent effective factor in Utah's economy, enriching the Mormon merchant as well as the Gentile. Indeed, Mormon consumption of imported goods was partly paid for with rural products only. There was no surplus in rural products in the first years of Mormon colonization and the church paper admonished the faithful not to sell but to store them. But a considerable surplus was soon attained as reported in the American press in 1854. Then the incipient barter was beneficial to the Mormons because there was not enough money in the territory and it was also used generally in the transactions of Mormon with Mormon. We have a good example of this in Neibaur's advertisements:

"Neibaur's old established match factory will exchange matches for produce at the following rates:

45 papers for one bushel of wheat
35   ”   for one bushel of corn
45   ”   for one gallon of molasses
 3   ”   for every 2 lbs of flour
25   ”   for one bushel of potatoes.

Single boxes, 15 cts each, containing from 400 to 500 matches.

Boxes by the gross D 16.

N. B. Each single paper containing 72 matches.

A. Neibaur."[50]

The dearth of cash was also indicated in advertisements:

"The highest price will be paid for gold dust and coin. N. Ransohoff a. Co."[51]

But all the speeches had created a first impression that the Gentile was an outsider in Utah's economy and did not fulfill a meaningful function there at all. It was only necessary to add the element of the great virtue in having commercial dealings with one's own people.

Naturally there were in Utah as elsewhere merchants who charged whatever the traffic would bear. But if prices built up in the continuous process of mercantile competition were extraordinarily high, they mirrored the factors involved in importing goods, cost of transport and risks of various kinds, and were, nevertheless, regulated by free competition.

"Men's double sole stoga boots for D 7" and "Woman's best boots for D 3"[52] advertised in 1853 and Brandy and Whisky D 6—resp. D 5 per gallon[53] were prices surely demanded at other remote places in the Far West.

As to prices for board we find the following advertisement of a Jewish hotel owner:

"Eureka House,

"Greenewald proprietor, informs his friends and the public generally that he still continues this

"First Class Boarding House, on Second Street . . .

"The rates of Board have been reduced to D 13 per week and D 1 per meal."[54]

These prices compare well with other hotel prices in the West.

To combat the widespread notion of high prices for imported goods the new slogan of "Eastern Prices" was added to advertisements.[55] One merchant stated as his business priciple: "treating every one as merchants should, giving every one 100 cents for a dollar"[56] which would indeed be the simplest definition for a just price.

Home production had to respond to the demand for a fair price too:

A. Neibaur, Manufacturer"[57]

"Cheap! Cheaper! Cheapest! Matches,

"At the old and well-established Factory . . .

"Boxes, 15 cents apiece; 100 Bunches D. 2.50.

Rural products of the territory naturally seemed lower in price when compared with other goods but were high enough to the observer from abroad: "Prices are very high . . . But the productions of the territory range at lower figures. Beef, fifteen to twenty cents per pound; mutton, a few cents higher; butter fifty cents."[58] The price of butter rose to 80 cents in 1869, a fact to which an anti-Mormon reacted with the outcry ". . . Holiness-in-a-bull's-eye!"[59] hinting that the Mormon Cooperative was involved in the price rise.

The soldiers had many complaints about unjust prices. They were directed especially against the petty trade conducted in the camp by Mormon traders. The interpretation of related facts again shows prejudice on the part of non-Mormons. A letter reprinted in a newspaper speaks for itself:

"An Item for Camp Peddlers.

Camp Douglas, U. T.

"We have frequently heard of the famous counsel of the archtraitor, Heber C. Kimball, 'Brethren, milk the Gentiles,' but we have a decided objection to its enforcement upon ourselves. If the Mormon fraternity will deal honorably with the soldiers, the soldiers will deal honorably with them; but we would advise them in general, and our peddler friends in particular, to be very careful with their 'milking' operation, for some cows will not only kick the milker, but upset the milking pail and waste its content."[60]

Insofar as prices were concerned, there was apparently no criticism of overly high prices in the territory which could be applied particularly to the Jew. Profit earned from business accrued from the volume of business done in the territory and not from high prices. Reported profits of Utah firms usually referred to the biggest firms and were later derived in the same proportion by the Mormon Cooperative.

The most important economic event of the year 1866 was registered in Mormon annals in a few simple words:

(December 1866) "On the 20th, a number of merchants of G. S. Lake City made a proposition to Brigham Young to sell out to him."[61] But the significance of this step may be seen from the circumstance that its authors published it in the form of a declaration in the Gentile newspapers. How serious were the considerations on which the declaration was based may be understood from the fact that one of the signers withdrew his signature at the last moment. The advertisement appeared with 23 signatures in the *Vedette* but with only 22 in the *Telegraph* with the editor's comment: "By request one name is omitted from the original advertisement."[62]

Not all Jewish merchants of the territory showed up among the signers but they represented approximately half of the names. The proposal made to Brigham Young was short and outspoken. As the only motivation for such a proposal, an incipient economic boycott by the Mormon church against the Gentile merchants is mentioned:

"On the fulfillment of the conditions herein named, first— the payment of our outstanding accounts owing by members of your church. Secondly—all of our goods, merchandise, chattels, houses, improvements, etc. to be taken at a cash valuation, and we to make a deduction of 25% from total amount. To the fulfillment of the above, we hold ourselves ready, at any

200

time, to enter in negotiations, and on final arrangements being made and terms of sale complied with, we shall freely leave the Territory."[63]

One historian believes that the proposal could hardly have been made in earnest.[64] But this conclusion cannot be based on the fact that the proposal was made publicly as this author concludes. Without doubt the signers wanted the attention of all America drawn to the beginning boycott. Both Christians and Jews certainly had to consider the possibility that business could no longer be conducted profitably. For the Jews among the signers, there were other factors involved, and they were without doubt forewarned by dangers experienced by Jews on other occasions. America was big enough as far as they were concerned and other territories too were open for mercantile ventures. An indication of the earnestness of the offer may be seen in the fact that the four signers who later went to the Gentile city of Corinne, were Jews.[65]

The question of whether there was a real chance that this offer might be accepted, has nothing to do with its serious intent. So long as it was not entirely hopeless to those who made it, the offer could have been meant seriously. It is a fact that three years later the Mormon Cooperative did buy out the greatest Jewish business in the territory. Given favorable circumstances, the Mormon church might have considered the offer.

Brigham Young's famous answer[66] was given in the same manner as the advertisement—publicly in the church newspaper. He declared that the American public should not be left in doubt about the attitude of the Mormons. He pointed out to the merchants that nobody had called them to Utah's valleys and that nobody was sending them away. Mormons took no official position toward them. (In the Nauvoo Charter peaceful coexistence of different religions with equal right had been officially proclaimed.)[67]

In view of the already existing economic boycott his answer was somewhat hyporcritical. This double-dealing aspect was made evident by a manoeuver Brigham Young had undertaken nine months before. He had gathered 14 signatures, among them the Jewish firms "N. S. Ranshoff a. Co., merchants, Ellis a. Bro., merchants, Bodenburg a. Kahn, merchants" and sent the following wire to General Sherman on April 12th, 1866:

201

"Citizens of Utah to General Sherman.

". . . Sir: We, the undersigned, residents of Salt Lake City, and not members of the Mormon Church, have read the above telegram of Mr. Young, and certify that we fully believe that citizens of every class, who simply attend to their legitimate business, are as safe from intimidation and as fully respected in their rights in this city as in any part of the United States."[68]

The scornful reaction in Young's answer that the offer meant the most lucrative business for the Gentile merchants was certainly not justified. The offer would have brought the fruits of years of mercantile build-up to any person taking over. For the merchants, Jews included, it would have meant the loss of valuable years in their economic adjustment to the conditions of the Far West. The price demanded for the businesses took into account only real values, with a reduction of their assessment, and nothing to be paid for the value of the established firms as such. If payment of the Mormon debts had been asked, a demand especially scorned by Young, then it would have to be said that this point was the moral basis of the whole offer. If the Mormon community as a corporate body took over everything, even if only through its successful merchants, then at least Mormons would have to pay their debts to non-Mormon merchants, Jews included. Furthermore, it may be stated that Jewish merchants especially were more likely to give credit to the customer of weaker financial standing, a privilege undoubtedly used by the Mormons.

Brigham Young's answer was taken by the non-Mormon merchants as the proof that it was safe for them to stay in the territory. The influx of Jews into the territory during the next few years was an immediate consequence of this evaluation of conditions by Utah's Jews.

The extent of the importance and increase of Jewish merchants in 1867 can be ascertained not only by their newspaper advertisements but also by the place they are given in the first business directory of Salt Lake City (1867). While occasionally businesses which were only transitory appeared in the advertisements, the City Directory listed firms which were as permanent as they could be in a new territory.

First of all the specialized aspects of the businesses were more fully recorded in the business directory than in the newspapers of

202

the preceding years. Some firms already owned several stores. Siegel Bros. "Wholesale and Retail Dealers in Clothing" had two outlets.[69] F. Auerbach a. Bros. announced a "New Store and New Goods at Alex Dafts old Stand Fancy and Staple Dry Goods,"[70] while "Our old Stand, the People's Store . . . [has] Coats, Pants, Vests, Boots . . ."[71] No less than five businesses carried the name of Auerbach all within the framework of a family business.

A separate evaluation of the Jews in this general directory shows such new fields of activity as "variety store," "watch maker," "dealers in cigars and tobacco," and also gives us a collection of names typical of German Jewish emigrants as well as a number of Eastern European Jewish names. Jews of East European descent lived side by side with German Jews in the territory. Some names which could be found at that time in other western Jewish communities as well are: Elgutter Morris and Salomon, Eliasohn John, Gans A., N. S. Ransohoff, S. Goldstein, M. Greenberg, E. Kahn, Michael Katz, Lavan Benjamin, (Reich and Lavan), Levy Solomon, Nathan, S. J., Oberfelder Isaac, Ornstein Jacob (Ornstein and Popper), Louis Reggel,[72] F. Reich, Edward Schönfeld, J. Siegel and S. Siegel.

The fact that among the Utah Jewish pioneers there were many pairs of brothers is true of conditions in other new territories in America. The church paper pointed out this feature of Jewish firms in the whole of America to the Mormon reader:

"Half the Jewish firms in America are brothers, business continues in a family and descends from generation to generation."[73]

Expansion of Jewish businesses brought with it as elsewhere in the West new Jewish categories of employment. This is reflected in the directory: "Levy Solomon, clerk at Auerbach Bros.,"[74] and S. J. Nathan, salesman at Siegel Bros."[75]

Because the Directory divides all existing firms according to their branches of commerce it is possible to state the proportion of Jewish to non-Jewish businesses in any given branch. Of six auctioneers three were Jews (Joel, S. W. and Co., Leventhal, A., Levy, L.),[76] of four special stores "Cigars and Tobacco," three were Jews (Greenberg a. Co., Oberfelder Bros., Whitehill, W. H.). [77] All four of the clothing firms were Jewish (Cohn, L. a. Co., Meyer, M., Glockmann a. Co., Reggel, Louis).[78]

This picture of Jewish firms divided according to branches

shows the same kind of concentration as elsewhere in America and especially in the West. Clothing, Dry Goods and Tobacco were in the lead in wholesale and retail trade in this embryonic Jewish community in the same way as, for instance, in the great commercial centers of the West, San Francisco or St. Louis. The Western pioneer's need for these products was the same in Utah as elsewhere in frontier land, and the Jew as the merchant pioneer was sure to come there with this merchandise. He brought with him special knowledge in merchandising these goods which could not easily be acquired by other frontier merchants. Especially as a clothing dealer, the Jew could not easily be beaten. The Mormon Cooperative had reasons to learn this later.

New firms advertised vigorously in the press:

"New Auction Store—A. Leventhal has opened his new auction store, by particular request near the Salt Lake House. The passers-by will undoubtedly stay and be entertained by the great North-American crier of 'Cheap Goods" for cash. Who takes anunder von?"[79]

Some new arrivals in the territory had rich experience in other areas. For instance [Heiman] Henry Cohen, born April 14th, 1831, had emigrated to America when 21 years old and already had many years of merchant pioneering in the Middle West, on the Pacific and in Atlantic states where he had last peddled: "I bought a basket and some dry goods and peddled in the villages near New York."[80] From there he came directly to Salt Lake City where he started out by clerking. Soon after, he went into a business of his own in the Utah countryside.[81] Later he founded his own important firm in Salt Lake City. He later rose to the office of Grand Master of Grand Lodge of Odd Fellows of the Territory of Utah.[82]

In the next year, 1868, the economic Gentile conflict had already grown greatly and by the end of the year, the Mormon side was already making preparations for the economic church monopoly. All facts reported show that in that year the commerce of the Jewish merchants reached its peak—only to fall steeply as a result of the sudden chess-like movement of the Mormons. Travelers had reported the signs of growth among the Jewish merchants:

"On Main Street . . . Walker Brothers, Ramshoff a. Co., Gilbert a. Sons, are the principle Gentile merchants, but the last named *Gentile* firm are also *Jews.* There is known no distinction between Jew and Christian by the Mormon—they are both Gentiles to him . . ."[83]

We see these signs even more clearly in the press:

(V. I. 1868) "Kahn Brothers,

Commerce Building,

Wholesale and Retail. Always on Hand the largest, most complete and cheapest stock of assorted merchandise in the city. The highest price paid for all kinds of produce . . ."[84]

The same is true of an industrial undertaking using resources of the territory:

"Great Western Soap Factory!
Great Salt Lake City, U. T.
Ornstein and Popper, Manufacturers.

"We have constantly on hand concentrated lye, lard and meats for oil, of our own manufacture. Merchants in this city, as well as those from the country, will benefit themselves and their customers by inspecting our soaps before purchasing elsewhere. Every description of grease bought at our Depot in exchange for our soap, and for money."[85]

The variety of meat offered for sale by this firm appeared in another advertisement:

"Ornstein a. Popper,
"Stall No. 2, City Market

"Liver Pudding, Bologna a. Pork Sausage, Head Cheese, Porkers for Roasting, Smoked Bacon, Turkeys, Geese, Chickens, and every seasonable rarity of the market."[86]

At the same time this firm declared that its industrial output had become great enough to satisfy the needs of the whole territory:

"We have now our factory in running order and guarantee to supply the Territory with *Soaps* and *Concentrated Lye* equal to any ever imported, and at prices that will satisfy all. Importation of soaps and concentrated lye from this time will be among the things that are past . . ."[87]

In the same issue "Auerbach and Bros' store" called itself "People's Emporium" and declared "The Eleven Commandments" of purchasing in this Emporium.[88]

An appeal to refined taste was made by a Jewish jewelry firm:

> "Sign of the two clocks . . .
>
> J. Watters,
>
> also Agents for Bernhard a. Co., Ornamental Hair Jewelry, comprising seven hundred different articles of the most beautiful patterns."[89]

At the end of 1868 the Mormon leaders' intention of founding a self-sufficient territorial system of cooperative commerce serving Mormons only, had become so evident that there was an urgent demand for an evaluation of its consequences for Mormons and non-Mormons. In addition, the situation required a cool-headed business-like assessment of the situation as soon as both sides recognized their respective positions within the territorial economy. The following editorial undertook this essential task. Its opinions also had to include the attitude of the Jewish merchants who were entirely in agreement with the viewpoints expressed:

> "Will it pay?
>
> ". . . You, Mormon friends are urged, as a matter of duty and interest, to cease all intercourse with Gentiles in trade . . . will you not be the loser in the end? How many thousand Mormon mechanics, laborers etc. are employed by the railroad and other Gentile companies, not to mention the Mormons trading and peddling along the roads, reaping a harvest of greenbacks from Gentiles? Suppose all the laborers were discharged and trade refused with the others, would you not consider it a great outrage? . . . you must know from common reason that the Gentiles will sooner or later retaliate and discard all Mormons . . . You do not want to trade with us—all right, suppose from this day we do not trade any more with you, that we buy nothing of the Mormons, turn out of our employment all teamsters, mechanics and laborers, and fill their place with ten thousand Irishmen fresh from the Eastern cities . . . What was the condition of three-fourths of the Mormon people before they began to come into close contact with the Gentiles? . . . They had no boots, no shoes, no money to

206

buy the leather to make them, no clothes, no cloth, no crocke-ry, no tinware, nothing but the bare produce of the land . . ."[90]

The other side, however, saw only that the railway would come and that the flood of merchants to Utah had to be dammed. To what extent mining would constitute an entirely new factor in the territory was not yet clear. But the general feeling was that con-centration of the Mormon's purchasing power on church owned enterprises might weaken and there would be damaging effects from the up to then unknown mining element.

The motivation of the Mormon decision regarding the Mor-mon Cooperative was obscured by the turbulent events and the excitement aroused in the American press about events in Utah. In truth, it was a matter of long standing. Brigham Young had long ago been attracted by the cooperative system after having seen it in operation in Boston and had already preached it to the saints in 1852.[91] It had not met with any success then: "The saints were not ready to enter into the 'Trade Union' which our President *first* proposed."[92] But as the development of Utah progressed, the Saints recognized that Mormon group consciousness had to be transfor-med by means of a new economic action which would preserve for the pioneer Saints and their offspring the fruits of all their past labors. The first step to the plan of the Mormon leaders was the contemplated Zion Cooperative. To buy nothing from the Gentiles but to sell everything to them was the saving device in their eyes. The monopoly of Mormon consumption would then be built up to lasting predominance over the Gentiles.

Like everything new, the introduction of the cooperative plan, even under church discipline, needed time and also the application of special measures to overcome resistance. Such resistance origin-ated among numerous small Mormon proprietors and store owners who feared ruin if forced into the cooperative. But this resistance was broken down and the Cooperative instituted. The Saints brought their capital into their common enterprise as well as their merchandise and salable rural products wholly or partly. In addi-tion to the capital gain which was divided by the Cooperative they also enjoyed their natural monopoly of selling to the Mormons. This monopoly was symbolized and protected by the Zion's Coope-rative Sign of the 'All seeing Eye." A certain loss was incurred by cases in which Mormons who had not joined the Cooperative nevertheless installed its sign over their business establishments.

Retail business in Salt Lake City was opened in the Ransohoff firm's house after this firm had been bought out by the Cooperative for 75,000 dollars.[93]

For the highlights of the build-up of the new institution the best source is the Mormon historian of that period. As an introduction to his representation of the subject he cited Brigham Young as the historical point of departure for this new enterprise:

"A Latter-Day Saint should not trade with an outsider."[94] At the time the Cooperative was formed, half of all merchants in the Territory were non-Mormons.[95]

"To the latter class (outsider) a policy of this kind religiously adhered to meant little less than financial ruin. To the merchants who were not 'outsiders,' it meant a wonderful increase in business, the removal of competition except within prescribed circles, and the consequent improvement in the prospect for early affluence."[96]

How the situation appeared to the outsider, we learn from the case history cited by the Mormon historian.

"Their stores were nearly deserted by customers, who passed them by on their way to Mormon business houses next door. Even where Mormons and Gentiles were in partnership the ban was still maintained. In the list of persons coming within the latter category was Samuel S. Jones of Provo, who having . . . effected a partnership with Ben Bachman, Esq., a Jew, was prepared to contest with Peter Stubbs and Kimball a. Lawrence—whose Provo establishment dates from early in 1868—the honor of being the leading business house of Southern Utah. But the teachings of the October Conference at Salt Lake wrought a great change in affairs. Mr. Jones' orthodoxy was beyond question, but Mr. Bachman, however popular he may have been in other respects, stood outside the pale as was made the unwitting obstacle to turn trade from his own and his partner's door. Noting this effect . . . Mr. Jones' active mind was quickly turned in the direction of the destined system of cooperation. . . ."[97]

208

As a result of the Mormon partner's changed attitude, the Jew was soon removed as a partner.

Continued transaction of business with Gentiles was dealt with by Church disciplinary measures. The Mormon group investigating such offenses bore the significant name "School of Prophets." One of the persons guilty of this transgression was a brother of Brigham Young and another a Mormon who had been accused of buying from a Jew. The accused confessed, asked forgiveness and promised to conform with the church rule in future dealings."[98]

The Mormon historian, too, confirmed irregularities:

". . . there were many Mormon dealers who did not merge their stock and interests with it, they nevertheless hoisted its escucheon. 'Holiness to the Lord,' and the 'All Seeing Eye,' over their doors."[99]

At the same time he stressed the fact that the action to institute the Cooperative continued:

"Co-operation.

"The co-operative principle, which we have beforetime advocated, is spreading through the Territory. Co-operative societies have been and are being formed in various places."[100]

The echo of these measures are to be found in descriptive American literature:

"All their stores and shops have signs over the door indicative of their church membership: 'Holiness to the Lord,' 'Zion Co-operative,' etc."[101]

Explanations of this sign did not omit the Jews either:

"The device is one of the many expedients of Brigham Young for retaining his hold over the Mormons, and for driving away the Gentiles. Among the latter are included the Jews, of whom several are engaged in business here and who are numbered among the Gentiles."[102]

Another author described the genesis of the Cooperative and remarked that with the elimination of the Jews, Brigham Young had succeeded where the Christian world elsewhere had only made unsuccessful attempts:

209

". . . strange as it may appear to the outside Christian
would, the majority of these Gentile merchants were Jews.

"Here Brigham and the Mormon faith had forced the
solution of the problem for which the whole Christian world
had battled without success from the birth of Christ. In the
valley of the Great Salt Lake every 'Jew' became a Gentile."[103]

According to contemporary reports the effect of the crisis on
the non-Mormon merchants was judged to be very grave:

"A few Gentiles in Salt Lake City still find customers
who will not leave the merchants who have treated them so
well, even at the risk of the frown of the rulers. One or two
large houses can still compete with Zion's Store. But the number of Gentile traders is relatively less now, in spite of the
opened communication with Gentile markets, than it was six
years ago."[104]

Of interest, too, is the attitude of another cooperative enterprise widely known in America, the Oneida community. Its paper
wrote with restraint, but nevertheless with sympathy:

"Zion's Cooperative Mercantile Institution . . . The
Jews and Gentiles denounce the scheme as a Mormon trick,
admitting that it is a good thing for the people yet claiming
that it takes away their chances for making money which is
undoubtedly true."[105]

How Utah's Jews themselves saw the dangerous situation may
be derived from the words of Frederick A. Auerbach:

"Our business gradually increased until 1868, when the
Institution known as Zion's Cooperative Mercantile Institution was started, which for a time seemed to threaten our existence here as merchants . . ."[106]

The news from Utah aroused excitement among Jews everywhere in America: The *American Israelite* wrote: "The Gentiles
(Jews included) must leave the Mormon territory within a few
months, if the Government adopts no measures for their protection"[107] and followed up these words with a sharp attack on the

210

Mormons seeking to justify the demand for government intervention in Utah.

Meanwhile the Mormons quietly met all attacks on the Cooperative:

> ". . . we always supposed that every citizen had a constitutional right to trade where and with whom he pleased—in New York, San Francisco or even Austin, and with Jews or Gentiles in all or any of these places to suit his own convenience and taste."[108]

The Salt Lake City Directory of 1869 already lists "Zion's Wholesale Cooperative Mercantile Institution, E. T." among the clothing dealers along with five Jews, a larger number than in the 1867 directory.[109] This may be regarded as an indication that well funded firms had a chance to survive and these clothing firms were, as it proved later, in an advantageous position vis-à-vis the Cooperative in purchasing, assorting and selling their merchandise. Other Jewish firms also appeared in this directory.[110]

The battle of the merchants for survival later became part of the political fight as predicted by the Gentiles when they stepped up the anti-polygamy fight as a kind of special retaliation. At this point we may already anticipate the results the Cooperative had upon the Mormons themselves. Even if we fully accept the success of the capital invested in it, it may nevertheless be said that the ultimate success of other firms, non-Mormon and Jews among them, was proportionately the same. The relevant profit figures—capital of one million dollars with more than 500 stockholders and a dividend of 8% in 1880—even if we calculate augmented gains by dividing new shares among the stockholders[111] was certainly not higher than that of stockholders in private capital of the same size at the same time.

But the picture changes entirely if we consider the ideological side of later developments. While private business undoubtedly succeeded, the Cooperative suffered. For this institution, conceived as the Mormon people's common financial instrument, by concentration of its capital in the hands of a few rich shareholders, fell into a predicament entirely contrary to the intention of its founders.[112] In the end capitalist stood against capitalist, and the public's expectations from the Cooperative were disappointed.

As the Cooperative's decisive influence on the economic life of the Jews in Utah increased, it was described in greater detail in the Jewish press:

"There are a few Gentiles here, but since the Cooperative Association had been formed, it will drive the Gentiles away.

"You must know that all the Mormons must give one tenth of their receipts to Brigham, for the Church. This Cooperative Association is formed with a stock Company of so many hundred thousand dollars. President Young, of course, is the head man. The association sends their purchaser East, to buy what goods are wanted, and the goods go to the stores of the association, and then distributed to different ward stores, they paying ten per cent above cost and freightage. The Mormons, therefore, go to the stores here and buy what stock of goods they want, and the Mormon consumers go to the ward stores to buy, so of course the Gentiles have no trade, and it will clear them away."[113]

Soon, in addition to such descriptions, the future of the Jewish community in Salt Lake City came under consideration:

"Brigham, with all his love for us, has classified us among the 'Gentiles,' against whom he has indiscriminately issued an edict of non-intercourse in business; and, while it has affected trade to an alarming extent, to us it is a double injury—it has blocked our progress in a religious point of view. Business no longer being profitable, it mars our increase, and in fact has quite weakened our numbers."[114]

The European Jewish press which up to then had brought to its readers many reports of the respectful understanding between Jew and Mormon in regard to their different religious life now had to describe the new situation: "To promote the wealth of the Mormons, Brigham has issued an edict which forbids the Mormons to have business deals with Jews or strangers. The business thereby is entirely depressed and becomes worse from day to day and if Brigham's thoughts don't take a turn I fear that our coreligionists will have to leave this city. This is sad news the more so because I had written the last time that the Jews here are held in high esteem. Brigham has become a fanatic in his old days and the only

212

hope of our fellow Jews and all the strangers is that the difference
of opinion between the two presidents will cause a betterment of
the situation."[115]

Among Christian non-Mormons the anger about the Cooperative also produced folk reactions of which the following poem, mix-
ing in the image of Judas, is a sample:

"Zions Huge Co-op
". . . Holiness to God!
Go on ye saintly throng.
Holiness to God!
Sell him right or wrong.
Judas—I, the traitor!
For thirty pieces down,
Sold his Lord and Master,
In old Jerusalem town.
Holiness to God!
The Judas of today
Sells his Lord and Master,
Whenever it will pay;
Invests his 'bribe' in bonds,
In bank, and railroad stock,
In Utah 'silver mines,'
And Zion's huge Co-op."[116]

Folk interpretations of the Cooperative's initials Z. C. M. I.
lived on for many years. A report of 1887 registers: "Zion's Children
must irrigate," "Zion's Collection of Mormon Idiots," "Zion's Corps
of Mercenary Impostors."[117] The popular differentiation between
"Church stores" and "Gentile shops" was still in force at that time:
"Nor do the Mormons change the style of designation when a non-
Mormon store happens to be kept by a Hebrew, which is frequently
the case, there being a good many Hebrew merchants in Salt Lake
City keeping Gentile stores."[118]

c) *Religious life and social contact with the Mormons.*

The facts of religious life of the Jews in Utah as seen by the
Mormons lent themselves to continuous observation and interpretation in a neighborly sense. Social contact between Jew and Mormon, infrequent and indirect as it may have been, nevertheless had

213

as a basis the awareness of a self-contained community with its own religious life which had to be taken into account. It was an exception to the usual classification of all non-Mormons as a separate economic group, called Gentiles. The thoughts of Mormons about the religious life of Jews in the world and in Utah territory have without doubt influenced their attitude in all respects.

It was widely observed in the West that an incipient Jewish community usually started with the organization of a Hebrew Benevolent Society to take care of stranded, sick or deceased emigrants or travelers. This step was undertaken in Salt Lake City at the end of 1865, according to the announcement dispatched by the proponents of the new society to the Jewish press in America:

"Salt Lake City, Utah Ter.

"At the meeting of the Israelites of this city and vicinity held on Sunday the 15th ult. the first Hebrew Benevolent Society of Great Salt Lake City was duly organized, and after the adoption of a Constitution and By-laws, the following resolution was carried:

"Resolved: That the *Hebrew* and *Hebrew Observer* of San Francisco, and the *Israelite* of Cincinnati, be informed of our organization and of the election of the following gentlemen as officers for the ensuing term:

"President, Fred Auerbach, Vice President L. Levy; Treasurer, Solomon Siegel; Secretary, Theodore Auerbarch (sic). Trustees—Messrs. James M. Ellis, Harris Aaron, Jacob Ornstein, L. Reggel, and S. W. Joel.

"One of the sections of the constitution adopted by the Society makes it incumbent upon every member to observe in due manner and form, the two most Sacred Holidays in our calendar, viz: Newyears Day and the Day of Atonement.

Theodore Auerbach, Sec'y.[119]

First news of this society's participation in work for the needs of indigent Jews in Europe appeared in the press in 1869:

for the suffering brethren of Western Russia. All credit to our this city, donated the handsome sum of four hundred dollars, for the suffering brethren of Western Russia. All credit to our Mormon neighbours."[120]

214

To imagine how the true Mormon neighbors may have evaluated these endeavors we need only rely on the numerous sympathetic editorials in the contemporary Mormon press, condemning the persecution of the Jews in Eastern Europe. One of them, entitled: "Wholesale Murder of Jews," stated: "With all the boasting of the civilization of the times, the leaven of barbarism is by no means extinct either on this or the other side of the Atlantic, as wholesale murder and slaughter there, and special legislation for religion's sake here amply, but unfortunately demonstrate."[121]

A Jewish observer who was in Salt Lake City in the summer of 1869 fully described Jewish life and its organizational beginnings. He also told of the incident of a male birth there and the performance of circumcisions:

> "Salt Lake City—Mr. A. Kutner, who lately returned from Salt Lake City, has kindly placed us in possession of the following interesting facts: The Israelites, of that city, number about seventy, and are constantly increasing. They already have a Benevolent Society, and are now about to establish a Bene Berith Lodge. A very interesting incident took place lately. The wife of Mr. H. Ahrens having presented her husband with a son, and there being no regular mohel in the city, Mr. S. Abrams, a private gentleman, offered to perform the ceremony of circumcision, and succeeded. When the fact became known, three Jewish gentlemen also had their children (some of them a year old) circumcised by Mr. Abrams. Although liberal compensation was offered to this gentleman, he declined receiving any remuneration for his services. Several young Israelites have married Mormon ladies, one of whom has embraced Judaism, and the others are soon expected to follow. There is an Odd Fellow, and also a Masonic Lodge there, the members of which are mostly Israelites. Great sociability exists among our co-religionists in that place, and they never tire in works of charity, as every needy Israelite, who passes through Salt Lake City, can testify to. Mr. T. Auerbach especially deserves credit for his zeal in every charitable cause.—
>   S. F. Hebrew."[122]

The picture thus revealed was essentially the same as that in other Jewish pioneer communities of the Far West.

But the most extensive description of Jewish community life in all its aspects appeared in a report to another Jewish newspaper at the same time:

From the Land of the Mormons

"Great Salt Lake City, June 11th, 1869.
Messrs. Editors:

"Since you have expressed a desire to hear from this formerly remote, but now the most noted thoroughfare, it affords me pleasure to give you such items, pertaining to Judaism, as have transpired since my residence here—dating back nearly to the oldest and first Jewish organization here.

"It was not until the year 1864 that more than three Jews resided here: one of them is still here, and though a very clever gent, still he has been away from his God so long that he has almost forgotten to what race he belongs—at least to the extent that he never patronizes our society or meetings, nor participates in any of our religious observances.

"In 1865 our co-religionists numbered about fifty—mostly single unmarried men, engaged in various branches of business. A move was then made, which was successful, to hold service during the holidays of New Year and Atonement. The liberality of our people could certainly not be excelled. Remote as we were from East and West, we accomplished all we desired; purchased a *Sepher Thora, Machsorim, Shofer,* and *Prayerbook,* appointed a committee to wait on Brigham Young who cheerfully placed at our disposal, free of charge, one of the neatest halls in the city, where, for the first time in the history of Utah, Israel's God was worshiped in Hebrew, and—with the exception of two—all the stores of our brethren were closed. Service was held in a very solemn and impressive manner by civilians, who volunteered for the occasion.

"The Mormon authorities regarded our move with much favor, and to their praise be it said that Brigham and his bishops freely gave us all the aid they could.

"After the holidays the first Hebrew Benevolent Society was organized—which is still kept up. The society has done much good, and is in a very flourishing condition pecuniarily, having lately donated about D 200 to the sufferers in Russia.

216

We still have a balance of cash on hand of over D 1000, ready to assist the needy of our faith who are worthy and find their way here.

"I must also mention that we have a cemetery of our own, properly fenced, the ground for which was given to our society by the city authorities, at the suggestion of Brigham Young, who pretends to have much love for the house of Israel. Beyond this no progress, religiously speaking, has been made . . .

"Since the date of which I speak, we have had many changes in Jewish society. Many of the old ones have left, and some new ones come. We have had several Jewish families here; several circumcisions, which were performed by skilled men from abroad, as also three Jewish marriages, performed strictly after our religious style, by civilians of our faith, as the laws of the territory do not confine marriage solely to the hands of the clergy or judges—hence we can all exercise the rabbinical function. As to the last marriage which took place here, myself and several others differ as to its legality, and I respectfully ask your views, through the medium of your paper.

"The gentleman who formerly solemnized the ceremonies here, was asked to marry a Jewish couple on the first day of Shevuous, which he declined, saying marriages cannot be solemnized on holidays, nor on Sabbaths. The party subsequently applied to another worthy Israelite, who performed the ceremony, believing of course that there is no law against it. Many of us are deeply interested in this question, and will look to you for an answer.

"There have been many other mooted points of Jewish law here, which were amicably decided by some of our best learned Jewish students. Peace and harmony prevail. There is no discord in our ranks.

"Our prayers are all conducted in the Orthodox style. We have no radicals here, although we hail from various parts of the world; and, with the chances this city has, there are yet hopes, if a change should come over Brigham's dreams, that we may rear a temple to the worship of our God that will adorn this city, on which nature smiles so beautifully. We

217

would all hail it with delight, and God grant that our hopes and aspirations be realized.

Very truly yours

Pioneer."[123]

The fact that the prayers were said according to orthodox custom was noted with favor in the central journal of Jewish Orthodoxy in Germany.[124]

The favorable personal attitude of Brigham Young to the Jews had already played its part, as in the acquisition of cemetery ground:

"1. II. 1867:

"Salt Lake City, Utah—There are in this city ten families and about thirty young men of our persuasion, doing business there. They have united into a benevolent society. President Young presented them with a piece of land, which they improved and arranged into a burial ground. We are told that the Israelites are doing well in point of business, although the Mormons preached against dealing with Gentiles. There are in the Territory 90.000 souls of the Mormon creed, and about 3000 Jews and Gentiles. There are four English Jews among the Mormons for the last twenty years, who embraced the new creed."[125]

At the end of the same year the Jews received new proof of Brigham Young's personal friendliness, when he allowed them the use of a proper place for their High Holiday services. Resolutions of thanks to him were sent to the Jewish press of the East and at the Pacific. The Jewish Messenger in New York wrote: "The Israelites of Salt Lake City have passed a series of complimentary resolutions to Brigham Young, for allowing them the use of an elegant hall as a place of worship."[126] At the same time the *Hebrew Leader* reprinted this news from the California papers combined with a tactless attack on Brigham Young, whom it called "that apostle of lewdness."[127]

A most colorful event feted in neighborly spirit with widespread participation of non-Jews, was a Jewish wedding extensively described in a Utah paper of January 14th, 1867. The details given proved that the occasion was a social sensation:

218

"Israelite Wedding

"We were permitted to witness yesterday the very inter-esting and solemn marriage rites of a Jewish couple. At the Eureka House the numerous friends and invited guests as-sembled at the hour appointed, and at 3 o'clock the religious Hebrew service was commenced by Mr. Reuben, who per-formed his duties as if he understood them. After the conclu-sion of devout exercises, the bride and groom, attended by their relatives and most intimate friends, entered the room. The happy couple were stationed under a canopy, supported by four young men. Mr. T. M. Ellis, the well known merchant of this city, then proceeded to solemnize the marriage in ac-cordance with the established forms of the Jewish Faith. The contract was read, and at a certain point of the ceremonies, a glass was dropped by the bride, and as it fell upon the floor, broke into a number of pieces. The groom crushed the broken glass with his heel, and the two were declared man and wife. This breaking of glass is in accordance with an ancient Jewish custom. An hour after the ceremonies were finished the entire guests sat down to a sumptuous repast. Wine and wit flowed rapidly, and all seemed happy. At the banquet Mr. M. T. Ellis, being called upon, rose and in a most lucid and eloquent manner explained to the party present, who were composed of our principal merchants, officers and others from Camp Douglas and numerous representatives of various professions in this city, law, physic and the press, the importance of the marriage ceremony among the Jews, as well as the sacredness with which it was viewed in a religious point of view. After the conclusion of his intelligent and impressive remarks he pronounced grace in Hebrew and the party adjourned to reassemble at eight o'clock, when the Goddess fo Terpsechore reigned supreme all night even till the small hours of morn, when after renewed congratulations to the bride and the groom, all separated, wishing worlds of happiness to the newly married couple."[128]

But Purim was the occasion for the greatest merriment. A de-scription of what must have been the first Purim ball in Salt Lake was given by the *Daily Union Vedette* of March 23rd, 1867:

"The Festival of Esther—The Israelites of this city celebrated Purim, or the Festival of Esther, on Thursday evening last, by a grand masquerade ball at the Paris restaurant. There were also in attendance many Gentiles of both sexes. We learn that the affair was conducted to the full satisfaction of all, and that many amusing scenes occurred during the evening. The parties were all masked until twelve o'clock (that is those who were in masquerade dress), at which time their masks were removed, and a denouement ensued that created much merriment. We are told that several of the gentler sex embraced the opportunity by personating characters that enabled them to don the breeches. Dancing was kept up until a late hour, and everybody retired to their homes highly delighted with their observance of Purim."[129]

The newspaper followed this report with an explanation of the meaning of Purim taken from the Hebrew Observer.

Parallel to such observations about Jewish festivals in the Gentile press, numerous explanations of Jewish festivals and customs also appeared in the Mormon press.

Mormon comments on the actual religious life of the Jews in the territory and elsewhere in America were important because they were made despite the Mormons' self-imposed seclusion from the outside world in spiritual and social matters. This very seclusion, on the other hand, was the subject of extensive observation and conclusions on the part of the Gentiles, Jews included.

Even during the earlier stages of Mormon persecution there had been some publicly expressed understanding that their feelings must lead to lasting estrangement, even thought of revenge. In one utterance of this kind, this feeling was compared with the situation of the Jews of old:

"... the Mormons 'have been more sinned against than sinning,' and should the latter, in the event of another attack, turn upon their persecutors as did the Jews in the days of Ahasuerus, and inflict upon them condign punishment, no one would interfere to prevent it."[130]

In the remoteness of Utah, the consciousness of having escaped contact with the rest of America by an Exodus was prevalent during

220

the first few years. However, this feeling was shattered by military occupation. Before this occupation, hope sprang from the vision of political unity of the Mormons in the territory which would in time give them a voice in the issues of the American nation. In those days, a song writer expressed the naive hope that if the Mormons were to vote as a block, the problem would be solved.

"The Mormon vote will cast the die,
When they shall vote again.
. . . For Mormons always vote one way,
And soon a voice they'll get."[131]

Although such a poem was called a "Comic Political Song," the deeper meaning underlying it could not remain hidden. No wonder, therefore, that satirical allusions to the "Hebrew vote" produced tension among American Jews, especially if the comparison with the Mormons was added. The soundness of such a comparison was earnestly denied by a Jewish paper:

> *"Israelites as Citizens*
> ". . . The three hundred thousand Israelites dwelling in the United States, from the Atlantic to the Pacific, the St. Lawrence to the Gulf, are simply a body of residents professing a peculiar faith. They do not constitute a nation within the nation, either because of diverse race, as the Indians, or because of essentially distinct religion and manners, as the Mormons. There is no special love of section; nor are the Israelites animated by different political views, as a class, from their neighbors who profess to be Christians. Jews dwelling in the South have identified themselves, by force of circumstances, with the rebellion; . . . Nor are they identified with any *political* organization . . . There were Israelites engaged in speaking in behalf of both party organizations; there were Jewish candidates on either side."[132]

In an attempt to insure spiritual isolation, Mormons undertook to create their own alphabet:

> "February 1856 . . . Prest. Young, for some time had his mind deeply exercised upon the getting up the 'Deseret Alphabet' and carrying it into practical use. The committee were now making books under his direction . . ."[133]

221

The final preparations for the introduction of this alphabet were reported by the American press:

"The Mormon Alphabet—The new 'Deseret Alphabet' is completed, and a font of pica type are published in the St. Louis Democrat, that are of course unintelligible to Gentiles. The type founders have supplied the Mormons with moulds and other apparatus for recasting their old metal, so that the Deseret News will probably hereafter be a profound mystery, at least in part, to all but the initiated. The new characters are forty-one in number, and bear a striking resemblance to those of the Ethiopic alphabet."[134]

The only non-Mormon voice in the territory opposing the alphabet was the Gentile paper *Valley Tan*. It pointed out in its polemic the severe damage it was doing to the education of the children:

". . . We again repeat, educate the children of Utah not in Dutch or Deseret dialect, but in one that will enable them to read and understand other matters beside the precepts and dictates of the Church—but this would prove fatal in the end to the Hierarchy."[135]

The attempt to introduce this new alphabet did not succeed. This was the only case in which the Mormon people revolted against a spiritual undertaking of their leaders. The resulting frustration caused the Mormon leaders to devise other plans to isolate the Mormon people and the economic approach finally won out. In progressive phases of the Gentile conflict, Brigham Young deemed it useful to justify the economic monopoly of the Mormon Church by the motive of religious separateness. He also gave precedents for such an attitude from other religions and thereby involved the Jews:

"You take the Catholics in London and they would go by a thousand doors to find one of their own faith to spend three halfpence. Do not the Jews do it? Yes, they do it all over the world. They say we are obliged to trade with them, but we are not. We would just as soon trade with them as anybody else outside the Church. But do they build up the kingdom of God? No, they hold the name of Jesus in derision and yet they are as full of religion as any sect there is. You may take the Mother Church, and the whole family of Protestants, and the House of Judah is as full of religion as any of them. But are they correct? No, they are not. We offer life and salvation to the whole human family in the gospel of the Son of God, and if they are not disposed to receive it they will suffer the consequence. It is for the Latter-day Saints to live their religion."[136]

From another point of view, the non-Mormons isolated themselves by not understanding Mormon motives and sentiments and by an amoral relationship to the past Mormon persecutions. In addition to this, the fear that satisfactory social intercourse with the Mormons would always be unattainable helped to shape their attitude.

Superficial comparison of the Mormons with the Jews served to bolster this incapacity to do justice to the painful events in Mormon history. First of all, the Gentiles drew a parallel between the materialism embodied in the Mormon theological system and the love of gold of the Jew. Certain features in Joseph Smith's youthful biography were cited in connection with this to explain certain details in the Book of Mormon:

". . . apology for Joseph Smith's early habits in searching after hidden treasures, he being a remnant of the Nephites. The love of gold among the Jews is proverbial, and it is a far more laudable method of obtaining it by digging after the deposits of pirates than by over reaching in commercial, or in other business transactions."[137]

Later the pun Mormon-Mammon arose and Mormonism was reproached for its ostentation as illustrated by the detail that Moses had accomplished his task with tables of stone whereas Joseph Smith needed golden plates. The Book of Mormon was a Golden Bible before it became the Mormon Bible. Untrained Mormon neophytes were confronted with jesting thoughts, jokes and speculations by adversaries in their discussions especially concerning the whereabouts of the pieces from the golden calf.[138] Even critics of our day who see the economic success of Mormonism as the victory of Yankee-thriftiness are also essentially under the influence of

223

that image and with it the historic Jew-Yankee comparison.[139] At the very time that the Jew was seen in this light, a German-Jewish peddler, just at the beginning of his economic adjustment to the new country, wrote in his diary:

> "No, gold shall not drive me to misery. May the devil have the banknotes and let me have a book to read that I may be of good cheer."[140]

That there were such characters in the German-Jewish mass immigration was unthinkable to these critics who sought to beat the Jew with their anti-Mormon literary weapon.

As in the nation at large, the separateness of the Mormons was regarded as complete by the non-Mormon press in the territory:

> "The Mormons call everybody *gentiles,* except themselves. That is, they are separatical in the completest sense."[141]

But outside sensitivity was transformed into aggression and nativist categories of thought were applied to the image of Mormon isolation. A characteristic example is to be found in criticism of the Memorial Day of the Mormons, which marked the day when the first Mormon group entered Salt Lake Valley. It had become the center of their historical consciousness, remembered as the children of Israel remembered the day when they departed from Egypt. The critics, however, compared the celebration of this day with Independence Day to denigrate the Mormons unisono with another group of immigrants also hated by the nativists:

> "Like the Irishman who thought 'St. Patrick a greater man than the Fourth of July', the Mormons regard the 26th of July, the day on which they reached the valley, as altogether a more important anniversary than our Independence Day."[142]

It may have been acceptable to the nativist that the Exodus comparison had served for a century to unite America against its mother country England. But he took offense when the same comparison forced itself anno 1847 on a group of persecuted people because of their common personal fate.

The accusation of Mormon separatism soon joined the other nativist argument that it was foreigners, subjects of foreign nations who want to keep up separatism of a political kind in Utah:

224

"What they say in the States. . . . Three-quarters of the Mormon inhabitants of Utah are subjects of Great Britain. The fact is that Utah, nominally a Territory of the United States, is, in reality, much more an English colony. Worse than that: It is an English colony within the demensne (sic) of the United States, having not the slightest fraternal feeling with the States—the majority of the Mormons not being citizens of the United States, and without any desire to become citizens. The Mormon emigrants came to Utah, not to the United States. If Utah were in Timbuctoo, they would go where Utah was, in the belief that there, for the present, the gates of the Mormon Paradise are opened unto them."[143]

But from the other side of the ocean the wind was blowing in the opposite direction. There the potential Mormon emigrant had to be shown his continuing lack of influence in the new church in America. American nativism had to be used in this case for a hitherto unknown purpose, i.e., to deter the religious dissenter from actually undertaking Mormon group emigration:

"The Welsh furnish a large proportion of these immigrant geese; while, strange as it may sound, there is but one Irish goose, named Sutherland, in the whole Mormon flock! There are but few of these 'birds' of native American breed, the great intelligence, supplied by a proper school system, prevents much proselytism in America; but it does not hinder the cute Yankee from playing the part of the fox; for in reality this is his role in the social system of Mormondom. The president, or high priest and prophet, the twelves and seventies, the elders, deacons, and other dignitaries, are all or nearly all of true Yankee growth; and to call these 'fanatics' would be a misapplication of the term. Call them conspirators, scharlatans, hypocrites, and impostors, if you will, but no fanatics. The Mormon is no fanatic: he is a professor in the most emphatic sense of the word, but not a believer."[144]

Soon inter-group tensions in America had their effect on the Mormons as, for example, the tension between them and the Irish, despite the fact that in other aspects the Irish were compared with the Mormons:

"The Irish and the Mormons.

"The Irish are in for it now, at the hands of the Saints.

"The 'turbulent Irish' and the latter day polygamists don't work well together, for some reason. We fear that the 'Green Isle' has not contributed its proper quota of proselytes to swell the population of Zion, and the few who are here do not belong to the 'rale ould shtock.' We are rather pleased that the *Telegraph* man and Heber have unbottled their disgust at the Milesians."[145]

Other groups in America too were proud of not having lost people to the Mormons:

"It is my special pleasure to assure you that I didn't meet in the whole territory more than three Germans who had entered the community of the Saints of the Latter Days and of one of them I may assert that his faith was not built on a rock."[146] The religious Christian united front against the Mormons certainly contained an element of the American super-patriotism of new immigrant groups. On the other hand it was again a German who reported that in crucial situations German unbelievers could rank together with the Jew and the Mormons, for instance, in the exchange of prisoners in the Civil War in the separate "category which could hope to be exchanged as the last . . . the Jews, the unbelievers and the Mormons."[147]

Tensions among ethnic and national groups and qualities ascribed to certain of those could be utilized by schisms which developed them as theological doctrines. For instance, for the purposes of a Mormon splinter group which found satisfaction in the new name "New Zion Movement" it was argued:

"The Welsh a prophetic race. . . . The Hebrews, Welsh and English are not the only inspired races though they are the best of the prophetic types. The Scotch, of course, are akin to them . . . Joseph Smith is a type of nature derived from the Welsh or Ancient Briton, Brigham Young of the pure Saxon. . . . Out of one grew a divine church and a priesthood, out of the other a Utah and a commercial scheme. Out of the Brigham Youngs grew, also, in England, a nation of shop-keepers and merchant princes. . . . The Mormonism of Joseph Smith, therefore, is more adapted to the Welsh than

226

the commercial religion of that remarkable man who has moulded the people of Utah."[148]

Despite all these divergent opinions which immigrant groups held regarding their relationship to the Mormons, there was one which they shared with the rest of America: Mormonism as a way of life in a new society embodied an old Jewish system of life. One impartial observer after having been among Mormons a long time stated:

"They delight to call their system a 'Theo-Democracy,' and that, in a civil capacity, they stand as the Israelites of old."[149]

The outspoken enemies of the Mormons defined this system in addition in its civilian terms:

"The system of government under which the Mormon lives is a 'Theo-democracy.' They are organized into a state. The president of the church is the civil governor, and rules in right over the community. They profess to stand, in a civil capacity, like the Israelites of old under their leader Moses."[150]

In tracing the development of public opinion about the Mormons, it is clear that only during the first years of Mormon Utah was the old Jewish character of their way of life not pointed out. The peculiarities of the Mormons were spoken of only in the framework of the Exodus comparison:

"This enterprising sect of fanatics having been expatriated from the States, had travelled, like the people of Israel, over deserts and through the wilderness, the pale of civilization; here, unmolested, this large community founded a city, and farmed a state, where they could observe their peculiar religious customs far from persecution, and frame laws suitable to their habits and creeds."[151]

It did not take long for the stigma of the old Jewish social system to be attached to the Mormon community where it remained in the course of American history and during all the decisive years ahead.

Observations concerning the difficulty of making social contact with the Mormons were sometimes made by the uninformed traveler:

"On our way back to Ogden, a gentleman on the cars told me that he had gone to Salt Lake City with letters of introduction to some of the chief men, and, though he had been well received, and shown everything to be seen, he had not received the customary invitations to visit the houses of those to whom he had been introduced."[152] What the traveler could not see was the fact that there was no visiting or open house between Mormon and Gentile in the territory. All the Mormon saw of the Gentile (the Jew included) was his attitude in public, or in certain areas of life which were of interest to the Mormon. As a general class the Gentile was judged severely because of his past behavior: "The spirit of murder is as plainly manifest in the present-day carpet-baggers as in the guilty, brutal, blood-stained mobocrats of Haun's mill and Carthage, or the clamoring Jews before Pilate."[153] To the gallery of American Judases the Mormons made a significant addition with the name of the man who ordered the Utah War. They embarked on a war against his portrait: "While Buchanan was President, the Pottstown bank came into existence . . . the notes contained his portrait. But of late the Bank has received so many mutilated notes, with the words 'traitor,' 'Judas Ischarioth,' etc. inscribed under of the portrait, that it has resolved to call in all the notes bearing the likeness . . ."[154]

Political actions of the Gentiles, Jews among them, met the same scorn, as for instance Jewish participation in non-Mormon juries selected by federal agents in the territory:

"That jury . . . names of the petit jury in the Hawkins case . . . Some . . . are apostate Mormons, and they especially should be held in everlasting remembrance; they have as much right to a niche in the temple of scorn and contempt as their brother Judas, and his name and theirs will henceforth be inseparable."[155] The Jews Jacob Ornstein and Sol Siegel were members of the jury and also" . . . A Jew named J. Baumgarten, who in this case was looking after a government beef contract, and who was formerly a deputy U. S. marshall,"[156] was mentioned in connection with judge Hawley's Court. Other Jewish names appeared among the signers of the "Memorial of citizens of Utah, against the admission of that

228

Territory as a state, May 6, 1872.—Referred to the Committe on Territories and ordered to be printed" and reprinted in the Church paper.[157]

As to the position of the Jews in the world outside Utah, the Church paper was willing to give every cheerful item about them: ". . . it agrees with us to say the best we can of any people especially of the house of Israel, and again especially of a branch of it which has passed through such a persecutive experience as the Hebrews have for many ages passed and, as many of them are still passing . . ."[158] The important success stories of the Jews were given extensive coverage. The Rothschild legend in America was mirrored repeatedly in the church paper.[159] In applying the legend to America, the paper was in accord with the statement of "a fact . . . highly complimentary to the Jewish people, that amid all the financial disturbance, not one Jewish bank or banker suspended. This is attributed to the fact that they never lose their self-poise, so essential to financial transactions. They never venture all. One of their great maxims is to keep a good reserve . . . "[160]

When observed closely in their own territory, the Mormons tended to be rather indulgent concerning the Jewish position in life: ". . . The Jews, like other people, have their faults, but if the Gentiles look well to their own unpleasant ways they will have enough to do without interfering with the Jews."[161]

The Mormons never aspired to completely take the functions of the merchant pioneer in society. Their image of an agricultural pioneer class was so deeply ingrained that the whole class structure in the United States appeared to be topsy turvy: ". . . in these governing classes of society the world . . . completely reversed the relative estimate which should be placed upon them, and hold in greater honor that class which in reality is not essential, and which in the nature of things, events, progress, will probably be dispensed with, for it is written that 'the merchandise of Babylon will fail' and 'her merchants will cry alas.' "[162]

Therefore the Jewish merchants in Utah were also evaluated according to the same principles, as Brigham Young actually did in a speech:

"For instance, look at the Jewish nation. Here are the tribe of Judah in our midst. Do you ever recollect any of them building a house? Think of it, look around now and try if you can find any of the sons of Judah so lost to themselves as to be guilty of making any improvements. I speak ironically. They will bring something to you and get your money if they can, for they are every one of them merchants; but can you find one of them that tills an acre of ground? Search the world over and you will find but few Jewish agriculturists, although there are millions of Jews scattered through the earth, and many of them occupying important positions in the learned world; but they are not producers, they are all consumers. The land of Judea has fallen into disrepute, and it has become a desert just through the apostacy of those who once inhabited it who had the oracles of God among them. This is the fact. Let the Latter-day Saints neglect their labor and they will soon find that they are declining in their feelings, tastes and judgment for improving the elements of the earth; hence we say, improve . . ."[163]

Trivial daily happenings concerning Jews of questionable character were dispassionately reported in the church paper:

"Two Israelites, half brothers, supposed to be of the kingly tribe of Judah, merchants or dealers in ready made clothing, on the West side East Temple street, got into a sort of family quarrel on Monday afternoon and finally from words to blows . . . One was fined D 15 and the other D 10."[164]

Most revealing were Mormon opinions about Jews resulting from actual observation of the religious scene among American Jews. The most startling discovery in this area was secular Judaism. "Many of the Jews—a very large portion of them are infidels . . . Singular it is that the very Jews who deny all the prophets are pertinacious of the peculiar institutions that prophets have given them."[165]

Also astonishing to them was the fact that American Jews founded institutions but did not devote themselves to the hope of restoration to their homeland:

". . . convention . . . Cincinnati . . . to establish a theological seminary . . . Upon the return to Jerusalem, the coming of the Messiah, or Jewish nationalization, nothing was indulged in."[166]

As to the idea of the Jewish Sabbath the church paper reprinted in full an article from a religious Jewish paper and added: "There is a vast amount of good practical sense in the above—without looking at its piety. We commend it to our readers."[167]

The observance of Jewish holy days by Salt Lake City's Jews

230

was occasionally reported in the church paper as for instance services on the day of Atonement in room 17 of the City Hall.[168] A notice on Passover of 1874 made a general statement about Jews in Salt Lake City:

"*Jewish Passover*—the Jewish feast of Passover commences tomorrow evening and lasts six days. It will be strictly observed in every part of the globe by orthodox Jews, of whom there is perhaps a few in this city. It is probable, however, that their numbers hereabout are not excessive, considering the number in Salt Lake belonging to the Jewish race, for were it otherwise, it is probable they would make a move in the direction of erecting a synagogue in which to conduct their religious exercises. . . ."[169]

There were also articles on Jewish customs like "A Jew's marriage"[170] in the church paper.

General opinions of the times regarding the Jews were carefully considered and brought before the Mormon readers when the editors of the church paper found them valid. This was true of a lecture titled "The Jews a Temperate People" of which an extract was given.[171] This lecture followed the general thought of the American temperance movement finding the advantages of temperate life in the example set by the Jews.

But the editors demanded direct application of Jewish laws of hygiene to the life of the Mormon people. The painful facts of infant mortality in the territory could be combatted by such means:

"The lesson which these facts [of Jewish hygienic law] teach should not be disregarded by us. If the Jewish race is distinguished from other races in this manner, there are reasons for this distinction. We presume that this race is more strict in observing the laws of Moses in Europe than it is in the United States; and though this observance may in many respects be far from correct, still, as far as it goes, it is undoubtedly attended with excellent effects. To no people in the world should this subject possess greater interest than to the residents of this Territory. Efforts have been, and still are being, made to enforce upon the attention of the people here the observance of hygienic laws. Should these efforts be as successful as it is hoped they will be, a marked change will take place in the health of the community, and a lower death-rate be reached than prevails in other places where injurious and unhealthy habits exist among the people. We have already a lower rate of mortality among adults than any other country with which we are acquainted; but our death rate among children under two years of age, during the months of August and September, is higher than it should be. Children in our climate during those months are liable to disease; but a more extensive knowledge and practice of those laws which pertain to the preservation of life and health would do much towards alleviating and checking such diseases. Diet, ventilation and correct habits should be studied by parents, mothers especially, and a thorough knowledge of these subjects would have a remarkable effect upon the health and lives of the young in our community."[172]

Aside from actual observations, there were also some folklore reactions regarding the appearance of the Jew. For instance the image of the German Jewish peddler was combined with the wandering Jew or Jewish folkloristic features of the prophet Elijah were attached to the three Nephites.[173] A folkloristic reflection of the fact that Joseph Smith studied Hebrew was contained in the story of the ancient manuscript brought to the Prophet by an American Jew because no one could translate it. The Prophet revealed its contents and the writings became an important part of the creed of Jews in America.[174]

Mormon interest in the religious and social aspects of American Jewry continued to find expression in the Mormon press and in public statements of Mormon leaders. Even the economic problems precipitated by the Zion Cooperative and Mormon exclusiveness could not sever the emotional and spiritual ties between Mormons and the Jewish people—past and present.

CHAPTER 19

From Outright Gentile Conflict to the Achievement of Utah Statehood and Peace

A) *Economic Developments.*

With the creation of the church monopoly, the economic conflict with the Gentile reached its peak.[1] The crisis began for most Jewish firms immediately after the founding of the Zion Cooperative. Extraordinary efforts were required to save the situation. There were new mercantile ventures, the most important among them being the founding of the Gentile city of Corinne. In addition there were individual firms in Salt Lake City itself which held out stubbornly. How the merchants themselves assessed their situation may be seen from the steps they took, and the success of their efforts over a 5 year period may be judged from the business directory of 1874.

But the account of the situation as seen by the merchant in the early days was not complete. The effects of the now finished transcontinental railroad had not yet been fully calculated. Besides this, another up to then unknown factor had to be taken into account, the effect of the beginnings of mining in Utah.

According to persons who later became successful merchants in the territory, Jews and other non-Mormons, the saving factor in this situation was the start of mining. For instance Frederick H. Auerbach and Fred J. Kiesel stated this in nearly identical appraisals of the situation. The latter formulated it in the following words:

"It was the despotism of Brigham Young that drove nearly all the Gentile firms out of the territory or broke them up in business. That was the case until 1871, when the mining commenced, and of course it was the salvation of all of us out here."[2]

The opening of the mines brought about an influx of new workers from the Atlantic and the mining regions of the West. New opportunities to open businesses in mining camps arose and Jewish merchants immediately saw their chances:

"The further strange thing was that most of these adventuring Gentiles were Jews. The Hebrew is an enterprising shopman and into these new valley communities and freshly organized mining camps he had pushed his way to sell his goods,—and he was making good at his trade as he always does on the frontier."[3]

What, in retrospect, seemed to have been a simple event came about with great difficulty. The first shock lasted for some time. But the choice between liquidating business and taking on the challenge of a new fight for economic survival after years of extraordinary effort in founding a firm in a new territory, did not permit any delay. One might conclude that a decisive factor could have been the loyalty of the Mormon population to their accustomed merchant class. But contemporary reports in this area were not very encouraging.[4]

Under these circumstances it was certainly very discouraging to fellow-merchants when one of the solid Jewish firms sold out to the Zion-Cooperative. This event was widely discussed in the Utah press. It caused mixed feelings especially because this sell-out had come about as a result of the personal relationship between Brigham Young and the owner of the firm. Other firms had no such opportunity to sell out to the Mormon Cooperative:

"*Sold out.*—Messrs. N. S. Ransohoff & Co., one of the largest firms in the city, have sold out their large and commodious store building and mammoth stock of goods to 'Zion's Co-operative Mercantile Institution,' Brigham Young being the purchaser. Messrs. N. S. Ransohoff & Co., have been among the leading merchants of this city for a number of years, we believe twelve, and have always done a large and thriving business with the Mormon people. Their fair and just dealings won for them a patronage from every part of the Territory. Their stocks always found favor and purchasers, being selected by experienced men in the East expressly for the Utah market. The establishment here has always been conducted upon strict business principles, and was universally popular."[5]

But together with discouraging signs, a star of new hope had risen with the founding of the new Gentile city of Corinne. The chief importance of the new city was as a freighting point to Montana. Yet it awakened irrepressible hopes not only among the hard pressed Gentile merchants of Utah but also in Montana itself:

"Corinne.

The sale of town lots in this new railroad town commenced yesterday and continued all day. The lots were sold at prices ranging from D 400— to 800— . . . The bidding was very lively, the sale being attended by all the Salt Lake merchants, particularly those who have been tabooed by reason of being Gentile . . . The principal business street has been named Montana . . . when once peopled with a thorough energetic, and, enterprising class of business men, good bye to Salt Lake, her monopolies and her business restrictions and commercial gags."[6]

The result of all these hopes and the rush of merchants we learn from contemporary reports:

"Cheering from Corinne—we had the pleasure of a call yesterday from Messrs. Theo H. Auerbach and S. Rieggel, who left the new city of Corinne on Sunday morning. They purchased lots and a ranch for each near the city. Their ranches lie side by side and contain a hundred and sixty acres of land each . . . Mr. Auerbach has opened with a new stock of clothing and dry goods in a tent, and Mr. Rieggel will open his stand next week . . . The population is as yet rather floating, but there are already something near 800 residents. Our friends expressed themselves as so charmed by the beauty of the location that they hated to leave, and think there is not a spot in Utah so clearly marked by nature as the site of a great city."[7]

In the style of genuine American promoting, the coming and going of personalities to and from Corinne was reported with the intention of encouraging other people to participate in the new venture of founding a city:

"*Arrived.*—Fred Auerbach of the firm of Auerbach & Bro., has returned from the East, where he has been purchasing a large stock of goods for this market and Corinne. Fred looks as smiling as a May-morning—is in fine spirits and is welcomed home by all who know him. This firm is one of the largest in this city and—long may they wave."[8]

The manner in which this news was given indicated that at first, merchants thought that Corinne would help them to hold their ground in the territory and in Salt Lake City too. In the beginning many considered establishing branches of their businesses in the new city until the storm against their main establishments in Salt Lake City quieted down.

Meantime the reports about the arrival of prospective merchants to the new Gentile City and the related promotion continued:

"Another Gone.—The popular Mr. Rheinhauer, well and favorable known among us from his long stay in the house of Ransohoff & Co., started yesterday morning for the 'new dispensation' at Bear River. He has a stock of goods on the road and takes with him a frame tent, in which he will open his establishment until a more substantial edifice can be erected. Success attend him in Corinne."[9] To be sure, the report of new stores of merchandise received by other Jewish firms in Salt Lake City like "Cohn & Co." are proof[10] of the will not to give up without a fight and consideration of plans of various kinds by the firms.

On April 21st, 1863 the "Salt Lake Daily Reporter" changed its name and place of publication to *The Utah Daily Reporter. Corinne*. Open promoting of the new city now became its main purpose and there was no end to items urging others to come:

"Come out of Her.—On Monday evening we had the pleasure of greeting our old friend, Mr. L. Cohn, of the old firm of Cohn & Co., Salt Lake City, who had just arrived from that place in company with several other gentlemen. Every coach out of Salt Lake City is loaded with passengers, while few or none return. It looks like Brigham would soon have his wish, and Salt Lake City be a mere 'Cathedral town.' "[11] Even special stores like "J. Kupfer . . . Jewelry . . . Watches . . ." were established at this early date.[12] Such signs of confidence in a new city on the part of Gentiles must make us wonder what the Mormons had to say of this new venture. These pioneers, experienced in religious colonization, were firmly convinced that the whole enterprise would fail because the conditions of the Intermountain Basin requires the devotion inspired by a religious movement. Although this last thought was not always openly expressed, it lay behind D. H. Wells' remarks about the theme of the new city on April 4th, 1863:

236

"I heard recently of a city that the outsiders are endeavouring to start, called Corinne, which it is said is to be the great city of the interior West. Who are going there to expend their labor? Can cities be built without labor? I think not. I have no idea that a great city will be built in the location designated, unless a different class of people go their than is to be found in such places generally. I have no doubt that the soil is rich and that by industry the elements necessary for the building up of a great city could be developed. But any person who expects that a large city is going to be reared without industry and hard labor reckons without his host. There may be a rush there, for a short time, of speculators, loafers, and rowdies; but if these are the only classes of people who go there —as there is good reason to believe—this great city that is to be, like others of the same class, will soon die out, and the people be scattered to some other places."[13]

That was sober talk, but there was no lack of religious prophecies about the ultimate downfall of the new miniature-Babylon in the midst of the Saints' territory.

In time the appearance of the new city became similar to that of other permanent merchants' settlements at central points of productive regions. However in the case of Corinne there was no ring of rural settlements whose population could have provided a permanent market. Nevertheless substantial stores had already been erected in 1871, and a picture of "Corinne . . . 1871" showed a store with the firm sign "F. Auerbach & Bro."[14] All in all there were so many merchants in Corinne by that year that the columns of the newspaper now called "Corinne Daily Journal" reported the same disturbances which occurred in other cities:

"Police Court.
The people vs. J. Cohn, charged with disturbing the peace; found guilty and fined D 100 and cost."

"Civil Cases.
J. Greenwald vs. J. Kupfer; action to recover personal property . . ."[15]

Advertisements in the paper revealed "Ransohoff & Co. . . . Segars . . ."[16] and "L. Lebenbaum, J. Goldberg. L. Lebenbaum & Co. . . . Groceries . . . Cigars, Tobacco . . ."[17] furthermore "Henry Leiwes . . . Liquor, Cigars . . ."[18] i. e. three special stores for tobacco in a settlement whose highest population figure amounted to 700 souls. There was also a clothing firm:

"L. Strauss & Co., keep the best and largest stock of Boots and Shoes, Gent's Furnishing goods, Hats, etc., that can be found in the West. Store on Montana Street, between Fourth and Fifth."[19] And furthermore a "Metropolital Hotel, Walsh & Greenwald, Proprietors."[20]

So much of the assurance and pride of new citizens was expressed in the editorial of the first number of the "Corinne Daily Journal," that we are tempted to believe that there was much serious hope for the future of the city and that not everything was an attempt to attract people:

"Shall we have a new city! The Americans in Salt Lake City are beginning to feel the want of elbow room. The *Tribune* asks, 'Shall we have a new city?'. . .

They now present to the Gentiles of Utah the 'new city,' they are calling for, well organized, provided with an able, honest, economical city government, responsible to the people and not to a theocrat. . . ."[21] And in time the new city would not only provide economic liberty for the Gentile—merchant but would also have a goal; i. e., to drain off the commerce of Salt Lake City. People had to be made to believe that this goal was attainable.

"The Salt Lake *Tribune* thinks that the grasping policy of the church will in the future as in the past tend to divert trade from Zion to the capital of Heathendom, Corinne; so mote it be."[22]

In retrospect it may be that Corinne—whatever its final fate—fulfilled its historical mission of allowing a breathing space for the hard-pressed Gentile merchants. During its first year freighting together with concentrated produce—commerce at one point reached the huge sum of four million dollars. The decline of Corinne as a result of changed transportation conditions was drawn out long enough to enable the participating merchants to enjoy new experiences which they later put to use at such new places as Ogden. There Fred Kiesel achieved lasting success and was finally elected the first Gentile mayor in Utah.

It took a number of years for the "capital of Heathendom" to become a near-ghost town. A "Wholesale Market Report, corrected by Ransohoff & Co.," in a "Daily Corinne Reporter" of May 13,

1873 indicates the interest of the merchant class there in the great commercial transactions of the time.[23] Later when the failure of the new venture became apparent, Jewish merchants made quick decisions and began to move away shortly thereafter. Yet we find Jewish names there not only in an 1874 Utah directory,[24] but in even greater numbers in 1878 in a Directory of the Far West:

"Cohn Julius, tailor,
Cohn Marcus, Clothing, boots, shoes, hats and caps,
Eisler Philip, Liquors,
Kassman M. F., Liquors,
Kupfer Mrs. Lena, Watches and jewelry,
Kuhn, A. & Bro., Drygoods and clothing,
Lachman Benj., Hotel, bakeries and groceries,
Liewes Henry & Co., Groceries and liquors".[25]

The population of the place in the directory was still given as 700 souls. There were late greetings from this lonely city in 1888, when a lonely Jewish child, Hanna Keller wrote to the editor of a Jewish youth journal:

". . . I can't write much about the town of Corinne, as it is a small town. It used to be a large business place, though at present it is somewhat dilapidated . . ."[26]

In any case, by 1872 it had already become clear to the majority of the Jewish merchant class in Utah that the idea of founding a Gentile city to compete with the Mormons, rather than from economic necessity or as the conesquence of opening mines had miscarried. Those who remained in Corinne after that time could only exploit smaller opportunities as was the case with Jewish merchants later also at other localities. This made possible economic existence for individual Jews dispersed over the territory but the main question remained: whether Jews could maintain themselves in Salt Lake City.

Not all the facts of how they succeeded in conquering the crises of these decisive years have become known to us. However, the coming of the railroad which carried new people seeking their fortune in mining into the Territory, enabled the Jewish merchants also to attract the custom of this new element and to complete successfully with the Zion-Cooperative in certain regions. In any case the low point had already been passed in 1874. At the same time

239

the general American crisis of 1873 resulted in three serious crisis years for the Cooperative which even had to suspend paying dividens during this period.

Salt Lake City's Directory for that year, 1874, shows us the astonishing fact that compared to the number of Jewish firms prior to the establishment of the church monopoly new Jewish firms had been added. This was particularly true in the clothing branch, clearly demonstrating that in the end the Cooperative could not compete with the superior experience of the Jewish clothing-dealers. There were already nine Jews among the 12 clothing firms in Salt Lake City. Thus in comparison with 1867 when there were only 4 clothing firms there, all Jewish, the number of clothing firms had tripled while the number of Jewish firms had more than doubled.[26a] In Drygoods there were four Jews among 11 firms,[27] in fancy goods three out of five stores were Jewish.[28] Some figures prove that besides healthy competition the influx of people of different religions had brought about a change and the Mormon Cooperative was not the same deterrent any more.

The most important role in the successful maintenance of Jewish firms was played by the Jews who had remained there during the years of crisis, such as Kahn Bros. and J. Watters and Bros. whose business advertisement had appeared without interruption.[29] In 1873, when the illusion of the future of the Gentile City had already evaporated a single number of a Salt Lake City paper printed 10 advertisements of Jewish merchants.[30] And in 1874 a number of new Jewish names appeared; the list of Jewish names in Salt Lake City commerce included 1 Cohen, 4 Cohn, 2 Levi, 3 Levy, as well as a number of German-Jewish and Eastern European Jewish names.[31] In addition to Corinne, we find in Logan "Bergman & Goldman, General Dealers,"[32] in Alta, B. D. Abe Cohen, owner of a saloon,[33] and in Bingham, B. D. the following: Blumenthal Bros., Boots and Shoes, Clothing, Hoffman L., Clothing, Klopenstein & Miller, Clothing and Drugs, and H. Robitschek.[34] In the mining camp Ophir, B. D. Joseph Selig, General Merchandise,[35] and in Provo "Benjamin Bachman, Dealer in dry goods, groceries, boots and shoes, hats and caps."[36] The latter was an early victim of the church monopoly.

The importance of Ogden as the center of early mining interests is evidenced by the list of Jewish merchants there: "Plousky

240

S., boots and shoes. Clothing: Levy Samuel, Mendelssohn Julius, Plousky S. Drygoods. Levy F."[37]

Indeed, the statement in regard to California mining camps, viz: that the arrival of new Jewish merchants at a place was proof that the mining there had been successful, may also be applied to Utah.

Another business directory for the year 1878 contains data not only for Salt Lake City, Corinne and Ogden where new names of Jewish merchants were listed, but for a whole series of new locations. Merchants recognizable as Jews were living in Adamsville, American Fork, Minersville, Monroe, Morgan City, Sandy and Scipio. The names of Joseph J. H. Chipman J., Watterman, J. G. Lessing, Louis, Seigal & Marks, Behrman J., and others appeared as owners of general stores, as well as special stores for liquors and boots and shoes.[38]

The expansion of the commercial activities of Jewish merchants throughout the territory of Utah was thus considerable in scope and mirrored the rising productivity of the whole territory, in many areas, including mining. For Salt Lake City, which already numbered 20,000 inhabitants, this directory listed besides a number of new Jewish specialty stores in clothing, tobacco, liquor and jewelry, a cigar manufacturer, a boot manufacturer and the firm of Bamberger, J, E. & S., which was designated as interested in mining.[39] The Jewish-owned stores dealing in special goods, especially clothing, were reported to be large.[40]

It was taken for granted that the simple Mormon people would obey the economic directives of the church. Nevertheless, commerce of the Gentiles with the Cooperative itself was not prohibited and cash-customers could under certain circumstances obtain even better conditions than credit-seeking Mormons:

"About this time I was buying a bill of goods at the Co-op Store of which Snow was manager, and I noticed that I got five packages of coffee for a dollar but the Brigham City people got only four.

I joked with Snow about it. He said: 'It is like this, Alex, you Gentiles over there in Corinne don't have to trade with us and these people here can't very well get out of it. Besides, you pay cash and our Mormon people, so many of them, want time, so we are bidding for your trade.' "[41]

241

Concerning Brigham Young's personal attitude even more was said:

"From the first to last I found Brigham Young the squarest man to do business with in Utah, barring none, Mormon, Jew or Gentile."[42]

During this decade economic events in the territory in relation to the Jews were naturally mirrored in the American Jewish press of the day which also received detailed correspondence of Jewish trans-continental travelers. A report of 1870 reflected the mood of crisis which followed the introduction of the economic church monopoly:

"In our visit to some Israelites, we found about eight Jews keeping stores in the places (Salt Lake City), five of them having families. . . . Several Jewish families have lately left on account of bad business, the railway having drawn away many teamsters. Business was also much damaged by Brigham Young's co-operative stores; all Mormons being 'marked' who trade anywhere but in them."[43]

But by 1872 reports from Utah sounded calmer:

"There are quite a number of Israelites there, who, so far as I could judge, and from general report, are an orderly and respectable class, adhering conscientiously to the old faith, and mostly engaged in the cigar and clothing business. I tried to distinguish the difference in appearance between the Mormons and the Gentiles, which generic term is applied to all who are not Mormons, but could find none."[44]

Four years later a detailed description of the impression the firm-sign of the Cooperative made on the unbiased visitor to Utah, was printed in a Jewish youth journal. The description ended with a fair assessment of the good credit-standing of the Mormons with the merchants of the Pacific coast who were mainly regarded as fellow-Jews:

"Clusters of thrifty farms and little villages are found all along the road, and nearly everywhere we find a store whose shingle contains a painting of a big eye and the mysterious letters Z. C. M. I. You may bet your bottom dollar that the visitor did not see it twice without asking for an explanation, and our kind Cicerone replied: Zion's Co-operative Mercantile Institution. This 'bullseye' shows the believers where they can sell for the highest price and buy at a fair bargain, without being cheated by a wayfaring Gentile, and hundreds of country stores are supplied from the large one in Salt Lake City, and buying in immense quantities, they can afford to sell cheaper than their Gentile neighbors.

It must certainly be set down to the credit of the Mormons, that their credit stands very high all over the Pacific coast, and even in the East, and many a merchant of San Francisco has assured me that he never lost a cent by a Mormon, a thing which ought to be followed by other professing Christians and Jews."[45] Another report of the same year already emphasized the big news:

"The great interest of Utah—one which overshadows all others — is her mineral treasures. In that respect she is fast becoming a formidable competitor with California."[46]

A year later an editor in a correspondence from Salt Lake City, July 7th, 1877, presented economic facts and already mentioned one Jewish firm with mining interests:

"There are in this Territory, about 140,000 Mormons and 10,000 Gentiles, including 200 Israelites, most of them in Salt Lake City. The valley is well cultivated by the Mormons, and the mines are worked by the Gentiles, who are also the principal merchants. The Mormons have their co-operative stores, marked 'Z. C. M. I.,' i.e., Zion Co-operative Mercantile Institution, one of which, in Salt Lake City, is very extensive. The Mormons do not deal much with the Gentiles, althoug they do some.

There are some very extensive business houses here. Among Israelites I saw several houses like Auerbach Bros., Seigel Bros., Kahn Bros., which are very large firms. Others, like Bamberger Bros., are engaged in mining, Charles Popper in wholesale butchery, and other business."[47]

What was still news to the Jewish world, had been treated extensively in the American mining press from 1869 on. First of all the changed attitude of the Mormon church to mining had been reported:

". . . Mormon Church edicts, or 'divine revelations' to Brigham Young are fast giving way, however, before Eastern capital and enterprise."[48]

This is followed by descriptions of the arrivals of prospectors at the beginning of the mining boom:

"Utah. The new mines.

. . . The streets of the city are full of the same old bummers, who for twenty years have earned a very precarious livelihood, by trading and trafficing in the gullibility of the pilgrims who came from the states with well-filled purses . . ."[49]

And in 1871 came the first news of mining investments by Mormon capitalists:

"Salt Lake City, Utah, at the present time, presents a scene of busy life, and *bullion* seems to be the crowning feature of the city and country at present. . . . Mine selling seems also to be a good business . . . *Church Dignitaries going into Mining.—*The *Tribune* says that a new mining company is being formed to operate in Provo Valley, comprised of Church Dignitaries amongst whom the name of A. Milton Musser appears prominently. This appears to be a 'New departure' on the part of Mormon church dignitaries, who have heretofore refused to have anything to do with the development of mines."[50]

With the Mormon's appearance as a miner, a new element was added to the labor market:

". . . Utah labor is plenty and cheap as skilled Mormon miners from Wales, England, Sweden, Norway and other sections of the globe are ready and willing to work, and board themselves, at D 3 per day, and the leaders of the Church of Latter — day Saints advise and instruct their followers to accept situations in the mines at that price. . . ."[51] It was a far cry from the first efforts of Jewish merchants in Utah mining to the full fledged flow of Jewish capital from the East. This capital created the greatest mining adventures in the world of their kind, and at the same time represented the greatest industry in the state of Utah. In 1895 the Jewish paper in St. Louis printed a report which indicated this great change:

". . . The copper works erected here which have cost half a million of dollars already and will need as much more before completion, have passed entirely into the control of our Jewish brethren; Mr. Dave May, the clothing king of Denver is president, and will push the work in his well-known activity; Mr. Sachs and Messrs. Schoenberger Bros., of New York, are the other associates in this great enterprise."[52]

Even when the great mining interests of Jews still lay in the future, there was an increased number of Jewish merchants in the Utah Territory mainly along the intercontinental railway. We have a travel report which declared that on the way from Utah to Cali-

244

fornia every railway stop displayed business signs of Jewish merchants:

"For two long days we steamed through Nebraska, Wyoming and Utah, till we reached Ogden, the terminus of the Union Pacific Railroad. In all the little places wherever we stopped, we found our Jewish brethren. Wherever there is a row of those wooden country stores, we read on the signs the names of our co-religionists. They can not be mistaken.—Cohn, Levy and a lot of names for the 'Israel' are displayed everywhere."[53]

A second report of the same period stated:

"On the road from Omaha to Ogden in Utah, you will find in every little snug town some Jews, who keep all kinds of stores. Whenever the train stopped, and the conductor called out 'twenty-five minutes for breakfast or dinner,' we who had to eat our meal in the car, ran around to look at the place and found there written on the signs of the stores: S. Cohen or A. Levy, or some other names which indicated that our brethren are on hand."[54]

B) *The Course of the Political Conflict.*

The Jews in Utah had to work only for economic freedom because their existence as a separate religious group was never questioned and there was no religious battle-ground between Jew and Mormon. Christian denominations, however, were not mere onlookers insofar as the religious movement in Mormon colonization was concerned. They were concerned partly because they had already lost souls to the Mormon faith in the old homeland and partly because they felt the success of Mormon colonization might weaken their own position in America. The urge to win back lost religious terrain was recognizable as part of the Gentile-strategy in Utah even when it was disguised as a "manifest destiny" to win the mineral treasures of Utah for the whole nation. Such economic conquest could bestow political power whereby the Mormons would also be weakened religiously. One of the weapons of political strife, the polygamy issue, gave the Gentiles of Utah the feeling that they were also pioneers on behalf of their respective Christian denominations.

This aspect of the struggle did not affect Utah's Jews. They had come to the territory "as merchants and not as missionaries"[55] and they always remained aware of this fact. Whenever and where-ever they were forced by circumstances into the Gentile camp and were consequently numbered among the Gentiles, it was the result of factors entirely outside their Jewishly religious consciousness. When they suffered from the general Gentile conflict in the terri-tory they were not religious victims. But where on the other hand the general outlines of the Gentile conflict were given for the Chris-tian denominations[56] the historic group relations between Jew and Mormon were not given at all.

The alignment of Jew and Gentile was most complete in the area of social intercourse represented by the all American organiza-tions of fraternal orders, at that time, Masons and Odd Fellows. The Mormons were not represented in these orders. Jews, according to one observer, were thought to give preference to the Odd Fel-lows:

"It was observed that the Hebrew Gentiles as a rule belong to the Odd Fellows more than to the Masons."[57]

Nevertheless Jews played an important role in Utah Masonry from the beginning not only in Salt Lake City lodges, but also in the Provo[58] and Corinne[59] Lodges.

The two orders were in existence in Utah much earlier than the Jewish order of B'nai B'rith and the Jewish congregations which were founded much later, and had attracted many Jewish males:

"Some of them, like Louis Cohn and Colonel Kahn, are high and zealous free Masons, Odd Fellows, etc. No Bnai Berith lodge and no Jewish congregation yet in the Mormon land."[60] (1879). Some of these personalities like Colonel Kahn at the time were also especially active in Gentile political activity and in the found-ing of periodicals which might serve to counter the Mormon press in the territory.

The fact that Jews participated in such organizations gave them a voice in all matters common to the non-Mormons in the ter-ritory. The weight of their opinion was added to the Gentile camp. Occasional discord between Jew and Gentile in their common cause arose in rare cases as in the following quarrel in Bear River city (Corinne):

"He ('Horatio Vattel' alias the 'lightning scout') was denounc-ing the Jews in particular, and every one in general, when one

246

gentleman of the Jewish persuasion took exception to what 'Horatio' was saying, and an altercation ensued, in which the unterrified 'scout' came off second best."[61]

General antipathy to Jewish merchants was also expressed occasionally. Thus Bishop Talbot tells of a Salt Lake City stage driver who had played a foolish trick on Jewish merchants and for this reason lost his job:

". . . Hank lost his place as driver, and the company had to pay a good round sum for damaged samples and outraged feelings. The news quickly reached Salt Lake and spread through the city. Public sympathy was at once enlisted in behalf of Hank and subscription started. A fine team and express-wagon were presented to him, and he was set up in the delivery business in the Mormon city. Popular sentiment brought him a large patronage, and the old-stage driver's road to a good living was made sure and easy."[62]

With the exception of such rare incidents, there was great respect for the Jewish merchant in Utah and regard for certain personalities who held a special position in public life was correspondingly high in the Gentile world:

"Colonel Kahn.

In this gentleman we have the very singular example of the Jew-Gentile, which illustrates how much our Mormon-brethren have confounded distinctions. The Colonel has long been a resident of Utah—we believe over fifteen years,—and is one of the most influential merchants of Salt Lake City. He has gone shoulder to shoulder with Walker Brothers, and has entered into every movement of a revolutionary and political nature with 'full purpose of heart.' He donated liberally to start the first magazine of Utah, and has for years continued his liberality for the support of a free press. He is a United States man rather than a Jew or a Christian."[63]

During these same years of active social intercourse between Jew and Gentile in Utah, a corresponding relationship between Jew and Mormon was not established. The old Mormon concept of seclusion in the valleys of Ephraim included the notion that the Gentiles were unwilling to think that the Mormons were happy there:

"And though they perceive it, they'll hate to believe it; How mightly and merry the Mormons will be."[64]

Later the Mormons defended themselves against the charge of unsociability:

"Against the Latter-Day Saints, there is a stereotyped charge of unsociability . . . says the stranger . . . we are deprived of social intercourse with your families. That is really so; but that is not the result of exclusive teaching . . . We need not point to the high regard the community has shown for moral men of other faiths to free us from the charge of bigotry, exclusiveness and unsociability. We have an aim in life, we steadily pursue it . . . For good men we have nothing than the kindest feelings: for the others, we have nothing but supreme indifference . . ."[65]

It was a long way to the first manifestations of social rapprochement between Gentiles and Mormons. It was given practical expression by participation in Mormon public events such as the parade celebrating the day of the Mormon's entry into Salt Lake City. A report of the parade on July 24th, 1880 mentioned that: "Cohn and Company's car followed, upon which was exhibited loose wool and wool in bales."[66] This picture of peaceful commerce appears to be a symbol of a change which in the end affected social intercourse as well.

But during the decade after Utah was opened by the railway, the political fight superseded all other social phenomena. Its foundation, the extraordinary stratagem of the anti-polygamy fight was imbued with real religious zeal among non-Mormon Christians. It is significant that a Methodist found no better comparison for this zeal than the passion of the Jew—although his was in worldly matters:

"They have as keen and unerring a scent in missionary labors as the Jews have for the direction of commerce, and it led them to Utah to find proselytes among the Mormons at a time when society there was in its upheavings."[67]

In addition the Christian adversary of the Mormon never lost his conviction that it had been old Jewish ideas which had provoked this political struggle:

"The conflict of ideas.

. . . Eighty to hundred thousand people believing in the religion—political form of government, all of whom recognize a supreme head or ruler, have been gathered from various European nations, thoroughly imbued with the idea of divine head-ship, and, as an outgrowth of this idea, we have polygamy and the practical

248

endeavor to establish a kingdom in all essential features the same as the old Theocracies of the Jews."[68]

And he continuously used the argument that the world had outgrown these ideas:

"What sense is there in going back to the age of Israel and quoting his example as a model for us moderns to pattern after? . . . The slave-holders thought they had just as sure a thing with the Bible. . . . We have improved upon the social system of those old wandering Israelites. . . . The fact of Israel having four wives does not prove that the business man or the mechanic should weight himself with a similar burden."[69]

Under such circumstances the mental attitude of the Jews in Utah was complicated and it was not easy to come to the decision to side with the Christian non-Mormons in the political fight in the territory. On the one hand they were powerless to combat the false picture of ancient Jewish life which would be in the best interest of American Jewry; on the other hand the church's economic monopoly had brought the fight for survival to a decisive phase and Jews understood that without a political fight there could be no survival. That this political fight was fed by an inaccurate image of Judaism was in this case the lesser evil. They therefore decided to fight it although the religious aspect was contrary to their feelings. Esteem for law and order was their main reason for the fight and a contemporary saw this as their essential attitude:

"The Hebrew citizens of Utah are generally respected for their integrity. They are friends of law and order, and are always ready to assist both with money and personal effort, in every good work. . . . Our Hebrew fellow citizens were among the earliest non-Mormon settlers, and in the dark days previous to 1870 were among the foremost of the trusty few on whom the representatives of the Government could rely for aid."[70]

To love law and order was not easy however when the bearers of law and order, the representatives of the Federal government, were considered enemies and opposed by the overwhelming majority of the population. Any help given to these federal representatives, any help given by them was necessarily regarded by the Mormons as directed against them. As a result the Jews lost any sympathy they might have won from the Mormons or had, at least, partly already won. Therefore, if they joined the fight it was be-

249

cause they deemed it unavoidable. Outsiders might easily overestimate the situation and believe that the Jews would have come through the crisis in any case because they had some advantage over the Christian non-Mormons:

"But for the mines no outsider could find anything whereby he could earn a living in Utah. From this rule, perhaps, the Israelites might be excepted—the old-time polygamists."[71] But the actual situation was better understood by Utah's Jews who had experienced the crisis than by those people who seemed to enjoy the slogan of the Jewish polygamy so much.

The change in Mormon sympathy for the Jews was already indicated in reports concerning the beginnings of the "Gentile City" which was destined to become the hub of the anti-Mormon political front:

"Cape Cod Nantucket" and all along the R. R. Line, April 27, 1869.

. . . Corinne is "on the fence." Gen. Stanford could give the consulting committee no assurance of Central Pacific patronage in founding upon Bear River the "hope and sheet anchor of Christian civilization for Utah" . . . "God Almighty, have mercy on the people of Ogden, if the carcasse of Corinne is to be disembowled in their streets." . . . Manners and customs that prevail in the mushroom bourg . . . A species of biped known in the Corinne tongue as a "Capper," (a numerous race indigenous to that locality.) . . ." This somewhat disguised description of the Jewish merchants is further identified by his speaking "in somewhat broken English."[72] It is followed by a real life story of a "little Jew" in the style of contemporary American humor:

"Correspondence.

Hot Spring Siding, M. P. R. R. May 27, 1869. . . . A Jew in this region recently let a Gentile have goods on time. Gentile sold the goods and was making his way to California with the proceeds when he was overtaken at the Promontory, brought back and incarcerated in the cotton calaboose of Ba-ar-town. On Monday night last, some 40 persons took him from the calaboose and turned him loose. The Jew arrested and shipped him to Brigham city, where he was arrested on a charge of felony; when after a week in court, the prosecution failed to sustain the charges, Gentile

250

was discharged, the heavy costs falling upon the unfortunate little Jew, and losing his goods into the bargain. Technicalities are something in law. He will probably be arrested again tonight on a charge of fraud, on which, possibly he may be convicted again."[73]

Estrangement turned into embitterment from the moment Utah's Jews participated in the political elections on the side of the Gentiles. A correspondent reported from his visit to Salt Lake City, in 1870, to his American Jewish newspaper:

"I was informed that the Mormons had been rather favorable to the Jews until the last election, when the Jews voted with the Gentiles."[74]

Election events by their nature, tend to be forgotten if consequent politics can transform them and make them workable by compromise. But in this case the opposite occurred. The interests in the territory were lined up for a long fight monolithically shaped by politics. The Mormons were striving for statehood for the territory which could have brought them, as the overwhelming majority, self-government. But all their adversaries were battling for one single goal—to obstruct statehood by delaying the decision for the time when, as a result of expected influx of new population, the Mormons would no longer have a workable majority in the new state. The permanent expression of this desire, on the part of Gentile politics was presented in a memorandum of the non-Mormons in the territory to the American Congress dated May 6th, 1872. It is important to single out the names of the Jewish signatories to this memorandum for the purpose of showing how far reaching support of the political Gentile front was among the Jews in Utah:

"Ishel Watters, Jeweler, Salt Lake City
T. Woolf, Cigar manufacturer, Salt Lake City
Sam'l Levy, Cigar maker, Salt Lake City
Abraham Watters, Jeweler, Salt Lake City
Fred Reich jun., Miner, Salt Lake City
Samuel J. Nathan, Merchant, Salt Lake City
A. Blumenthal, Merchant, Salt Lake City
B. Blumenthal, Merchant, Salt Lake City
Michael Katz, Builder, Salt Lake City
C. Reich, Miner, Salt Lake City
Louis Reich, Clerk, Salt Lake City

251

Henry Heilbrouner, Merchant, Salt Lake City
Sam'l Schoen, Saloon-keeper, Salt Lake City
M. Woolf, Merchant, Salt Lake City
Jacob Ornstein, Butcher, Salt Lake City
Alfred Abraham, Clothier, Salt Lake City
B. M. Pearlman, Liquors, Salt Lake City
Solomon Oppenheimer, Merchant, Salt Lake City
A. Oppenheimer, Merchant, Salt Lake City
David S. Reinberg, Merchant, Salt Lake City
Louis Boukofsky, Merchant, Salt Lake City
N. & E. Boukofsky, Merchant, Salt Lake City
D. Abrams, Merchant, Salt Lake City
Chs. Meyerfeld, Merchant, Salt Lake City
A. Leventhal, Auctioneer, Salt Lake City
H. A. Van Praag & Co., Merchants, Salt Lake City
Elie Siegel, Merchant, Salt Lake City
Eman. Kahn, Merchant, Salt Lake City
Sam'l Kahn, Merchant, Salt Lake City
Joseph Silver, Merchant, Salt Lake City
Jacob Behrman, Merchant, Salt Lake City
Moses Hirschman, Miner, Salt Lake City
A. Greenewald, Hotel Corinne."[75]

Even if some important names were missing from the memorandum, because some Jewish merchants feared the complete disruption of their connection with the Mormons and had declined to sign, the meaning of the memorandum was clear: the majority of the Jews had decided.

In their answer, the Mormons now separated the Jews from the general political Gentile front:

". . . memorial addressed to Congress by a number of people styling themselves non-Mormon voters of Salt Lake City. . . . Sol Siegel, Boukofsky, Watters, Rehmke, Cohn, Kahn, Adler and Sholes are Jews, who care neither for Mormons nor Gentiles so long as they can make money. As the Mormons generally patronize the cooperative stores, they have but little to hope from them. If they refused to join in the measures of the 'Ring,' they would make the town unpleasantly warm for them."[76]

The political step of 1872 signified the end of that phase of the

Gentile conflict during which terror against individuals could be used. The new phase began with the mutual conviction that only political facts established by the American nation could decide the fate of the territory. Even earlier acts of violence in Utah had been an exception in frontier life; it had not been the Indian who was feared: "I would have trusted myself with the Indians in those days quicker than with the Mormons,"[77] stated a well-known Gentile merchant pioneer. The official version of the Mormons denied acts of violence and especially the existence of an organized terror group the "Danites," reported by the general American press.

The Mormons, too, recognized the importance of public opinion in their political fight for statehood and therefore tried at the time to create good will on the part of the American public. Visitors and through travelers should see the facts of life in the territory and bring back their favorable impressions to the Atlantic so that the whole world might know them. Travel literature and reportage in the press demonstrated that the Mormon Church cooperated with the qualified visitor and observer and let him come to his own conclusions. Such a report in the Jewish press nevertheless showed that the non-Mormons made their own comments on this situation:

"I had conversation with a party who had resided there some years (never mind if he be Jew or Gentile), and I was praising highly the manner in which strangers were everywhere treated. My newly-made friend pointed significantly up the street to the "bench," where were visible a few white tents and remarked, 'That's what's the matter. They are on their best behavior, those few soldiers are monitors, and remind them, that Uncle Sam is in no humor to be trifled with. Had you come here a few years ago, you would have seen the difference. It is all deceit, all put on, they are anxious to make a favorable impression upon strangers, but even now, let Brigham Young but give the hint that your life should be taken, and I would not insure you for three cents."[78] Nevertheless this Jewish visitor reached his own conclusions in full fairness to the Mormons:

"I left Utah in full sympathy with the Mormons, so far as hoping that hostile legislation will not force them, for the third time, to quit their pleasant homes to undergo the miseries of another pilgrimage. Such action would be, as some one observed worse than a crime: it would be a mistake. Coercion has never yet eradicated heresy, and all religions have suffered far more from prosperity, than they ever did from adversity."[79] There was to be sure, no other way of thinking for the moral observer.

This political situation kept the threat of war alive through decades. The fighting spirit of the Gentiles was not even broken by the very thorough election defeats of the first years of this fight. Our reporter says of his informant: "He also spoke of politics, was not discouraged at the result of the last election, and was sanguine of a final triumph."[80]

The fight concentrated mainly on the election of the delegate of the territory to the American Congress. Together with the national agitation concerning Mormon polygamy it was aggravated by reports from the territory until the government determined to destroy the plural marriage system of the Mormons. The immigration argument against polygamy was used more and more in this fight because the efforts of the Mormon Church to create new colonies by means of immigration were also considered from the viewpoint of the political ends of the Gentiles in the territory. The following editorial opinion of a Jewish newspaper of November 1881 is remarkable because it combined the two viewpoints at a time where full enforcement of later anti-polygamy measures was not yet envisaged:

"Among the records of immigration for the past months appears the statement that large numbers of Mormons have landed and proceeded to Utah. It is also known that a party of Mormons styling themselves 'missionaries' passed through this city recently to preach their immoral doctrines in the Southern States and in Europe. The object of these missions is twofold. The Mormon authorities are anxious to secure money and voters. The tenant farmers of Europe are induced to emigrate that they may own the soil they till while the Church is enriched with the proceeds. Then the arrival of new men enables the Mormon Church to send out parties of devoted Mormons to found new settlements in the adjacent states and territories, and so extend Mormon influence and power. How rapidly this policy is being pushed the public is not aware, but some day, when a question of vital interest to Mormonism arises, there will be a rude awakening. It will then be found that not in Utah alone, but in large sections of the West, the whole local power is held by Mormon hands, and that the authority of

254

the Prophet is superior to that of the President of the United States. The apathy of the government, of Congress, and of the people is permitting the nation to drift on this question to the brink of a precipice, where blood and treasure will have to be sacrificed."[81]

Even if these opinions only partly mirrored the moods and arguments current in the nation, they undoubtedly stemmed from an awareness of dangers for Jewish immigration. Evil consequences of the admission of one immigrant group could not but affect the admission of other groups. This was already sensed by Jews at a time when there could not have been any conception of the scope of the coming Jewish immigration from Eastern Europe.

The more this political phase of the fight progressed, the more the purely economic tensions diminished. The church monopoly had been met by adjustment to the new times and the Cooperative was no longer the object of a fight against it. In time it was used more and more by non-Mormons, although the special bond of the Mormon population to it was not weakened. A description of the Cooperative in an American Jewish newspaper of 1884 dealt with this institution with all the lore and local gossip surrounding it as is possible only when an institution is no longer a fighting issue:

"The Great Cooperative Store is in the vicinity with its all-seeing eye emblazoned over the entrance, and the initials Z. C. M. I., meaning Zion's Co-operative Mercantile Institution, and not as the irreverent interpret it—"Zion's children must increase.' This is certainly a magnificent store, nearly equal in size to Stewart's in its palmy days. Every conceivable object that can be needed in a civilized household is for sale, and both Mormons and Gentiles patronize it. It has branches in the city and throughout the territory, and its credit is good in the East despite the peculiar character of its stockholders and the difficulty of enforcing legal process in the local courts. Between the Co-op, as it is familiarly called, and the large Gentile house of Walker Bros., there is considerable rivalry, and the local doggerel supposed to be sung by Mormons has some point: 'Mother, may I go out to shop. Yes, my darling daughter. Be sure you buy at the nice Co-op and don't go near the Walker.' "[82]

During the most trying years for the Mormons, when enforcement of anti-polygamy laws brought sorrow to thousands of Mormon families, the attitude of their Jewish neighbors was divided.

255

Rank and file members of the Liberal party, the political organization of the Gentiles in the territory stood for an all-out battle on the polygamy question. But there were others who stuck to their old position of not participating in any political demonstration against their neighbors. Their viewpoint was best represented by a statement of Frederic H. Auerbach:

"A petition was circulated prior to the passage of the Edmunds Bill, intended by those who circulated and got up the petition to prevent the passage by Congress of that or any similar bill, it being a petition to investigate here. They went around with the petition and asked us to sign it, but we refused on the ground that we never interfered with political affairs. That was used by Mormon merchants against us, and for a time made inroads into our Mormon Jobbing Trade. . . ."[83]

But there were also a few steadfast and proven friends of the Mormons who for the sake of their own consciences condemned every public interference in family life, helped Mormon families and intervened for the Mormons even on the high level of national politics. The most worthy of them was Fred Simon, whose merits were recorded by the official historian of the Mormon Church as follows:

"The schism in the ranks of the Liberal party, inaugurated by him and his associates at that time, and the influence exerted by them at the seat of government, did as much as anything to give the disfranchisement schemes their death blow; and the changed conditions that followed culminating in Statehood for the once distracted territory, were due in no small degree to the individual labors of this staunch friend of Utah."[84] The three groups among the Jews, representing different basic attitudes to the Mormons continued until the Liberal party dissolved after some of its members had entered the two national parties of America. With the dissolution of the People's (Church) party as well the two national parties achieved the same position in Utah as in all other states.

The Jewish press reported this memorable turn of events in the following from Salt Lake City:

"Utah is at present on the eve of a great political revolution. The old Liberal party, which by its herculanean efforts has sounded the dead knell at Mormonism in the Territory, is undoubtedly splitting up and preparing to join hands with the People's or

Church party and to divide on national party lines. The movement was inaugurated by the purchase of the Mormon mainstay, the Salt Lake *Herald,* by a syndicate of prominent Gentile citizens, among whom we may mention our popular Jewish townsman, Mr. Simon Bamberger, who was also honored by a place on the directory of the company. The journal will in future devote itself to the promulgation of Democratic principles."[85]

That many Jews rallied early to the Democratic party was indicated by the fact that at the Democratic Convention of 1892 Jos. M. Cohen was the alternate from Utah.[86] When peace in the territory was restored the first non-Mormon elected governor of Utah was the Jew Simon Bamberger, who was also the only Democrat in this office for a long period. Bamberger's election evoked lively interest among American Jews and the sympathy for the Mormons expressed itself by the creation of a Utah club in New York.[87]

A by-product of the final phase of the Gentile conflict and the anti-polygamy fight on the national scene was the increased interest in women's life in Utah. The American Jewish press catering largely to the immigrant reader enlightened him with an introduction to all the intricacies of American politics connected with this question:

"General Nathan Kimball, of Ogden, Utah, a member of the Utah Commission, said recently that the work of the commission was a fair beginning of the fight against Mormonism, though he believed the coming elections would result in returning a Mormon delegate. He said the effect of the commission's work was already apparent in various actions of the Mormons. Many of them were beginning to separate their families, with a view of avoiding the cohabitation clause of the law, and large numbers of them are taking out naturalization papers. The effect of registration and elections held under the strict surveillance of officers acting under the law will be a largely increased Gentile vote. Heretofore the election machinery was so entirely in the hands of the Mormons that the Gentiles had fallen into a practice of staying away from the polls. The activity of the Mormon officials is shown also in the orders issued to Mormons settled in other states to oppose the re-election of every congressman who voted to declare Cannon's seat vacant, and it is expected that in several cases they are sufficiently numer-

257

ous to effect this purpose. The Liberal convention which closed its sessions on October 12th, nominated Philip T. Vanzile, United States District Attorney for Utah, for delegate to Congress. The platform adopted arraigns the Mormon Church for making Utah disloyal to the Government, retarding its growth, and setting its people at variance with the people of the United States, and declares there can be no fair and impartial civil Government in Utah while the Mormon Church is permitted to control the law-making power. It repeats the demand of the last Territorial Convention for a Legislative Commission and indorses Governor Murray and the Edmunds Election Commission. To the latter it tenders its thanks for their judicious conduct of the registration of the voters under great and peculiar difficulties."[88]

At the same time the Jewish press deserved credit for not joining the wave of anti-Mormon satire and caricaturing of their family life which then flooded America. The Jewish press restricted itself to only those aspects of women's life in Utah which had a meaning for Jews: mixed marriages between Jew and Mormon. This problem appears here only in its beginnings:

"Several also, who still professed to be Jews, had married Mormon women; and a daughter of Orson Hyde, one of the 'twelve' had 'cleared out' with a Jew."[89]

In any case, with the advent of statehood peace was restored among the warring factions in Utah and Gentiles and Mormons alike were able to devote themselves to the advancement of economic growth and the restoration of political stability.

CHAPTER 20

Polygamy and Political Strife

At the peak of the Gentile conflict which had resulted from
the economic church monopoly, a new strategical element against
the Mormons was added, Mormon polygamy, which up to then had
been subject only to legal restriction. At this point it was built up
to be the basis for a political fight. Due to the nature of this institution, a political fight dressed-up as an anti-polygamy crusade
could appeal to the whole of America. It could thereby carry the
territorial Gentile conflict to the rest of the country, thereby making America a united anti-polygamy front, which was actually an
anti-Mormon front.

The following state of affairs emerged from this turn of events.
A tug of war ensued on the part of the Mormons, for speedy at-
tainment of statehood; on the part of the Gentiles, for postpone-
ment of statehood until the complete opening-up of the Territory.
An ideological slogan asseptable to America at large, even to the
Atlantic states, so far removed from the Mountain Empire, but still
concerned with all economic advantages, could be of great value to
the Utah Gentiles. Polygamy was a godsend to the opponents of the
Mormons in their campaign to postpone the granting of statehood
to the Territory until their wishes were realized.

Opinions of historians about the course and the result of this
fight are varied but the majority regard it as the great political
mistake of the Mormon leaders. They foresaw the coming catas-
trophe and did not change course at the right time. How ever justified this view may be it has nothing to do with the establishment of
the facts and the sequence of events.

It is a confusion of effects with causes if it is asserted that the
anti-Mormon campaign ended with the abolition of polygamy. Actually, the Gentiles had won the complete opening of the Territory

259

just at that time, so that there was no longer any purpose in the Mormons' continuing the fight. Their only hope now lay in Utah's achieving statehood, and towards this end it was necessary to liquidate that symbol which was visible to all America, polygamy, in order to save whatever still could be saved of "Zion."

It is a peculiarity of the history of ideas that powerful popular notions which may spring from them can determine the general course of history. The anti-polygamy fight contained at least one point assumed by contemporaries to be Jewish. It was argued that the origin of polygamy was to be traced to the historic beginnings of the Jewish people. This retracing touched a sensitive point for Jews. But actually it could mean much more. The historical experience of the Jewish poeple had shown that mere imponderabilia in the general history of ideas became effective historical factors once people began to believe that the Jews were the carriers of such imponderabilia. Therefore it was not mere sensitivity but rather an admirable sense of reality on the part of American Jews to see in the "Biblical" argument for polygamy a real danger for American Jews. Indeed to the extent that emigration was necessary for Jews in other countries, it was also a danger for the Jews in the whole world. Because even then—one hundred years before the "Protocols of the Elders of Zion" it was clear to them that there was no nonsense about the Jews which could not find adherents even in the new world if it were firmly based upon a political fight. Thus even a fight against "Jewish polygamy" semed likely to result in great damage to the American Jews. Mainly it would effect Jewish immigration, but in its wake dignity of the whole Jewish community would suffer. The scope of this problem and its concomitant danger will become slowly apparent as we trace the anti-polygamy front. It must be stated at the beginning that this point involved not only the religious difference between the Mormon concept and the monogamic life of the Jews in America but also the fact that the perception of this danger for the Jews resulted in a special conflict between Jew and Mormon. It was, in fact, the only one outside Jewish participation in the general Gentile front. Consequently it was unavoidable that the American Jews should be more sensitive to the anti-polygamy fight than they might have been otherwise. A number of thoughtless utterances about the Mormons in the Jewish press can be explained as a result of the discomfort of

260

being entangled in an entirely unwanted and above all unmerited situation. And if the Mormons deserved to be reproached by the American Jews of that period, it was only because the Mormons showed no understanding of the precarious situation of the Jews in the fact of an entirely ignorant American public excited by a sensational and novel political fight.

America, for which the "sex o'clock" whistle of the new century had not yet sounded, experienced in the picture of Mormon polygamy a stimulation of sexual curiosity which tore down the fences of Puritan inhibitions. Mormon polygamy became the first and only sexual subject to be described and discussed in public, making of this event—at least in the press—a precedent for the entire Anglo-Saxon world. When finally, in 1852, plural marriage in Utah was made public by the Mormons themselves, European interest in this hitherto mystery-shrouded point was also aroused thus making of this peculiar Mormon institution a world wide concern.

The extent of this interest was reflected in part by the descriptive literature about the Mormons, in which considerable space was devoted to their polygamy. There is however a much more informative barometer in the popular humoristic literature of America. The Mormon in wit, humor and caricature was largely seen through the prison of polygamy. In this way, the sexual curiosity of the new world was documented for the future at a time when it could not be demonstrated in any other way. That "Mormon crinoline" contributed to the success of the new faith by causing soldiers from the military camp to convert, had already been asserted by the first Gentile paper in Utah.[1] Especially noteworthy in this area was a news item in the Jewish press which placed this issue in its proper light:

"A Jewish Mormon.
A correspondent at Denmark reports of a Jew . . . In the meeting of the 1st of September, a Jewish peddler, no doubt convinced, was immediately admitted into the bosom of Mormonism, and received the usual consecration . . . obtained the floor, and proposed formally the abolition of polygamy . . . indignation . . . a large number of women of the lowest classes supported the disciple of Moses,]others opposing[you will succeed no longer in making proselytes—
. . . If polygamy will cease in our midst, "said a German tailor, I leave immediately the ranks of the Mormons; for I have adopted it

261

with but the intention of marrying so many times as it will please me." In reporting this scene, we are pleased with the morality and domestic honesty, subsisting in a Jewish hearth, even when it was carried away to dangerous innovations. Dr. Lil."[2]

Reports of Jews don't tell very much about actually observed Mormon polygamy. Carvalho lived for a time in a Mormon polygamic household in Southern Utah and described it extensively.[3] Letters of a Jewish intellectual in California contained observations about this subject as well as general conclusions:

"The man I went to see has five wives, he was born in New York State but removed early to the Far West. He can neither read nor write, is as sunk in ignorance and its concomitant degradation as I would suppose a Russian serf to be. 3 of his wives are from the coal mines, England and I believe have worked in the pits. The other 2 are from Denmark; as near as I could find out none of them can read or write, not a vestige of printed matter did I see about the house. . . .

A Mormon buys a farm and instead of hiring workmen he marries wives, who, labouring in the fields maintain themselves and children and enrich their master. I expect that by next year this state will be flooded with Mormon women who, being strangers to those feminine qualities which civilized men consider indispensably requisite in women of whom they should make wives, will be an immense accession to the lowest of the vilest of our population."[4]

Oral reports were repeated just as eagerly:

"I have been informed by some very intelligent gentlemen who have just arrived from Salt Lake City that they have good reason to believe that fully one half of the Mormon women should be glad to leave, even under the present circumstances, had they any adequate protection, such for instance as the U. S. troops will doubtless afford them, and that if a fair proportion of the 'worlds people' were mixed up with them that none of the women would remain content, for they would then have opportunities of comparing or rather contrasting their servile, degraded condition, with that of women living in monogamy."[5]

The first indication that this picture was at odds with reality came when the Mormons fearlessly introduced women's voting rights. Even an inimical press had to concede:

"The decision of the Mormon leaders to let their numerous

women folk vote . . . proves in any case a remarkable confidence in the firmness of the church-and social structure this peculiar people has erected."[6]

By way of contrast emotional opposition to women's voting lived on for a time among Utah's Gentiles. A witty report of this situation written by a Utah female correspondent appeared in a Jewish newspaper in 1894:

"At the last election I presented myself at the poll of our district as a voter, but the Judges of election watching the purity of the Ballot Box, were all old bachelors, and when they saw me, with a ballot in my hands, one of the Judges fainted, the other went into ecstasy, and the third one shrugged his shoulders and remarked: 'Miss, your dresses are not long enough, and therefore we are forced to refuse your vote. No woman's—right—men in this district.' I told them that I would send 'Miss Mary Walker' and she would snatch them bald-headed . . ."[7]

However, before any serious observations could be made, everyday American humor had so many things to say that sober observation was at first engulfed by the products of a humor which even entered letters written from Europe to American immigrants. For instance a German clergyman wrote to his spiritual daughter on October 11, 1854: "Watch only your husband that he shouldn't go to the Salt Lake of the Mormons."[8]

An inventory of American wit referring to the Mormons will include few items which do not show in words or drawing, directly or indirectly—a relationship to plural marriage. A caricature "a desperate attempt to solve the Mormon question" shows Brigham Young as a Polyp stretching one of its arms over the Atlantic to Ireland.[9] Most spoken themes are only variations, often rather refined ones, of the ubiquitous polygamy theme:

"What," asked the schoolmaster, "is the term applied to the crime of possessing two wives at one time?" "Bigamy," replied the scholar. "And if there be more than two, what should you call it?" The scholar reflected a moment, then, chancing to cast his eyes upon a map of Utah that decorated the wall, he smiled and confidently answered: "Brighamy, sir!"[10]

Even the economic circumstances of a polygamous household were dealt with humorously:

"The Mormons are the only ones in our country given to polygamy; but this relict of barbarity is gradually dying out, for the luxury is too expensive, it does not pay, and it is all a man can do nowadays to keep one in silk dresses, and to let her go for a few weeks to a watering place. Now if the Bible would not have set such a bad example, I think Mr. Young would never have thought of such a thing, and as for me I always considered Solomon a fool and his father no better than anybody else. . . ."[10a]

Nothing was sacred, not even widowhood—that classic example of Biblical protection,—before the sharp sword of satire. Brigham Young's nuptial bed was often a subject of derision in humorous newspapers. "In Memoriam Brigham Young" shows at the center of an endless row of pillows an empty one over which hangs a top-hat.[11]

Even more conspicuous is the extraordinary coverage given to a humorist in representative magazines, even those directed to special readers, as soon as he attacked the "peculiar institution" of the Mormons.[12] This may be regarded as further proof that the press did not easily relinquish such an attraction. On the lower level of general folk-instinct the lure was even greater. A veritable steam-roller of sexual curiosity was a "Grand Exhibition England to Salt Lake, on Life among the Mormons," i.e. an illustrated prospectus of "Jarman's Scenes of Mormon Life. 600 Lovely Views Shown." Prominent among the pictures naturally was "The Family Bed." To do a complete job the prospectus announces special lectures for men under 18 and for women over 18.[13]

Mormon polygamy was employed to frighten girls in an early folk ballad:

"Sweet Betsey from Pike.
. . . They stopped at Salt Lake to inquire the way.
When Brigham declared that sweet Betsey should stay;
But Betsey got frightened and ran like a deer,
While Brigham stood pawing the ground like a steer."[14]
Old material from European humorous journals was worked into the Mormon theme:

"Brigham Young.
For his youngest wives don't like white wool,
And his old ones won't have red;
So with tearing it out,

264

Taking turn and turn about,
They have torn all the hair from his head."[15]

The hurricane of derision is remarkable in that the fact of free sexual promiscuity in other American religious communities, although previously known, had not merited any greater attention in wit or in serious description. This fact further emphasizes the complete isolation of the Mormons in a matter which was the touchstone of all their experiences on American soil.

To counteract this folk-humor the Mormon had very little which might appeal to folk-fantasy. Occasionally there was an attempt to depict their family happiness in a propagandistic manner. The following excerpt from "A Welshman abroad" deals with a disappointed California emigrant:

". . . The Merica country don't suit me so well;
I wish I can fly to old Wales in a moment,
And left this far west for the Yankees to dwell.
Yet Mormons in Utah is doing lots better,
Good wives they keeps many,
But me none at all.". . .[16]

However, the first specimen of anti-polygamous popular humor had been published in 1858 in a Utah Gentile paper:

"Mormon Love Song.
Say Susan, wilt thou come with me,
in sweet community to live?
Of heart and hand, and home to thee,
a sixteenth part I'll freely give.
Sophronia cooks and sweeps the floors,
and Hepzibath makes up the beds,
Jemima answers all the doors,
and Prudence combs the children's heads.

. . . Into thy hands such tasks as take a
dignity, will I consign;
I'll let thee black my boots,
or make the sock and shirt department thine."[17]

From the time that Mormon plural marriage was made public, the Mormon always discussed it in absolute seriousness and only when they were morally forced to do so. Their sensitivity to popular humor was understandably great and a joking remark like the one made by a Mormon and recorded by a Jewish author was very rare.[18]

Any regulation of female life and fashion in Utah was sure of a wide publicity in America. The very fact that fashion items were considered seriously enough to be worth a regulation had a humorous effect. "Brigham Young has fixed the legal length of Mormon ladies' dresses. They may extend to the top of their shoes."[19]

A special aspect of American folk humor in all areas has always been the search for Biblical images of comparison. Innumerable puns and witty tendencies sprang up from the Biblical knowledge of simple men and could be understood only by means of such knowledge. It began with the creation-story:

"Brigham Young is said to be a lean man, but it wouldn't be easy to count his ribs."[20] Mormon polygamy furnished a rich hunting ground for these comparison hunters armed with Bible weapons. Understandably enough, all this could be associated with those Bible stories which mention polygamous life. They had extraordinary luck with the story of Lot's wife who became a pillar of salt. Nothing could be more apt for the Salt Lake and the pillars of Mormon society. It was expressed in epigrammatic brevity in the following way: "Brigham Young is, indeed a pillar of Salt Lake. His idea of a wife is—Lots."[21]

In refined elaboration the "Lot" motif appears in the ballad of the sailor, who collected his girls from the various port-cities to Utah:

"Utah Jack.
. . . And so, to cut his 'true loves not,'
This Mormon harum-scarum
Collected all his wives, and went
To Utah with his harem.
　　Like Lot's one wife, should Utah's lot
Look back and turn to salt,
With such a lot as his, the price
Would make a summersault;
And 'Sal' would then by very dear
　　At any price at all;
Saltpetre could not save the 'saints'

266

Should such a thing befall.

For women, whether salt or flesh,
The 'Church's' pillars are:
And Salt Lake Saints would let it slide
Without more *fresh* ones there."[22]

The Lot Leit-motif also appeared in the other, the commercial meaning of the pun, i. e., to marry several women was the purchase of a "Job-Lot," whereby a good family-head wanted to save money.[23]

The rare products of Jewish folk humor connected with the image of polygamic life dealt with individual behavior as in the following case in a Jewish community: ". . . the reader 'Leopold' was dispensed with on account of reading the history of Brigham Young, and on the supposition of following his footsteps too closely."[24] And the only comparison in Jewish humor remained Solomon: "King Solomon the wise man was, as is known, a Mormon."[25]

It is not necessary to consider the many serious discussions at the time about the polygamy of the ancient Jews and its strong influence on the Jewish people to recognize the situation. Even the humorous use of the Biblical Lot Leitmotif as a characterization of Mormon polygamy could damage the dignity of the American Jews since they were considered the only believers in the unchanged Bible by both friend and foe. An occasional Bible joke, pragmatically regarded, was one thing. But it was entirely different to stray from life values deemed fundamental by contemporary society as a result of staggering about in the old Bible world. Thus concentration on the Hebrew Bible as represented by Judaism was made ridiculous as were its dedicated adherents, the Jews in America.

Symbolic of such a unification of inimical instincts against Jew and Mormon is a cartoon "Morality-Education" in which "Free Love," "Mormonism" and "Judaism" are chased out together from America. Judaism was represented by three Rabbis with Jewish hats cocked on one another in the manner in which, the "old clo'" men of the time carried their merchandise.[26] Anyone, who could not see the imponderabilia of the times, in such a cartoon, could simply not be helped. Fortunately, American Jews understood everything. Although even later no direct battleground between Jew and Mormon on the polygamy-question ever developed, the American Jew was endangered if only indirectly, by this peculiarity of Mormon life. In troubled times when anti-Jewish arguments were sought a resourceful propagandist could reveal the Mormon argument that polygamy originated with the Jews and therefore they should be payed back for this monster.

In any case the Jews had to resort to a public explanation of Jewish marital law. It was necessary to show that the new American religion had seized on occasional facts mentioned in the Bible but had overlooked the spirit of selective development of its marriage system. This was considered most urgent because few Americans would have been willing to discuss any Mormon argument for polygamy other than the Bible one. This also conformed to the will of the Mormons who wanted their "peculiar institution" appraised only as a religious one recommended by God. Thus the attitude of the Mormons was seen by most Americans only as an imitation of Bible life with no relationship to the needs of a modern society and the special demands of living conditions in the pioneer environment of the West. Mormon statements involving non-religious arguments appeared only after plural marriage had already been done away with. They were part of a historical appraisal and a justification of the past.

During the time that the Bible argument was being discussed there were no direct talks between Jew and Mormon. Rather the discussion took place in a triangle. Public opinion in America challenged by the Biblical argument expressed its thoughts about this and about the Jewish people as the bearer of this literature in past and present. Only then was the Jewish public in a position to answer.

The first known facts of the "peculiar institution" of the Mormons were treated by reference to events in Biblical times, for instance in a report on conditions in Nauvoo:

"A Mormon Breeze.

General Bennet, an ex-Mormon, and the prophet Joe Smith, have had a grand flare-up, and each has published his card, in order that all the world and his wife may see into their affairs. General Bennet calls Joe Smith, the great Mormon seducer—one who has seduced not only hundreds of single and married females, but more than the great Solomon attempted to seduce by which it appears that Solomon did not succeed at all—and Joe, denying the allegations of Gen. Bennet, calls him an adulterer. Joe must be a great man, if he has had more wives and concubines than Solomon. We, however, are not inclined to think him so great a personage. If he establishes a Turkish religion, in regard to plurality of wives, we are afraid that many of our young men will turn Mormons, and go to Nauvoo to keep a harem of houris."[27]

The short ironical reflection in the following remark represents the attitude of many contemporaries:

"Why should not the Book of Mormon be as good a thing as the Psalms of David? Was not Joseph Smith also o polygamist?"[28]

The rendering of the Mormon Bible argument was made in good faith. For instance a statement of the Mormon elder Thomas to soldiers was formulated in these words: "that they (Mormons) believe in a plurality of wives as a religious sentiment; not as a dictate of the passions. That they have as precedents in this faith the Jews, and two-thirds of the present inhabitants of the earth."[28a]

A comparison between a Biblical and a contemporary situation, with the thorny problems of the present measured by the Biblical past, is to be found in the following report:

"G. D. Watts, a Mormon from England, brought *his half-sister* to Brigham once, requesting to be married to her, as his second wife. Brigham refused. Mr. Watt urged that Abraham married *his* half-sister, and 'he guessed he had just as much right as Abraham!' The point was knotty, because if Abraham's example justifies polygamy, evidently, his example must justify such a marriage. The girl was rather handsome; and so, to settle the whole matter effectually, and to spare the necessity of George Watt's being still more Abrahamic than his brethren, Brigham *took her himself!* So far, so well. But she was not contented; and so, after a few weeks, Brigham bethought him that, after all, there was much force in Watt's argument and Abraham's example; and he told Watt that he might take her *then,* if he wished. Of course, he wished, and Brigham divorced her in order to effect this convenient compromise."[29]

Folk belief that polygamy originated in Bible times was already wide-spread in America in the 18th Century as evidenced by an early religious discussion between Jew and Christian.[30] Nevertheless the true picture of old Jewish life as monogamous was clearly delineated by learned men in America. In progressive phases of the

269

discussion of the Bible argument, enlightened Christian opinion was based upon the same sources as Jewish public opinion.

At first, by explaining the life of the patriarchs, it was shown that they could not be called polygamists. In a study, "The false claim of Mormonism," the following explanation appeared:

"Only Jacob, in the long history of two thousand five hundred years, is the husband of two wives; and he, against his own wish and convictions, is tricked into the union by the fraud of his idolatrous and selfish father-in-law. Where is the honesty of men in reading this ancient history?"[31]

From the Biblical story of the patriarchs critical consideration broadened to encompass the whole historical picture of the ancient Jewish people. Biblical catastrophes were ascribed to polygamous transgressions:

"Polygamy—Ancient and Modern.

. . . The Bible gives us the earliest accounts of the fruits of polygamy. Of these, feuds in families ending in murder are ever the most prominent. Lamech 'slaying a young man to his hurt,' Abraham turning his concubine with her baby into the desert at the instigation of his wife, Jacob swindling Esau, Joseph's brethren selling him into Egypt, Absalom's rebellion against David, the revolt of the ten tribes from Rehobeam and numberless succeeding revolts, feuds and tribal wars between Judah and Israel are cases in point."[32]

The Lot motif was extended by creating a fighting Biblical slogan from the salt of the earth:

"Sodom and Salt Lake City are synonymous. You can hardly think of the one without thinking of the other. Both rested in the midst of fertile plains, Sodom and Utah. Both were near salt, fishless seas. Both were the capitals of the most accursed wickedness. Both are doomed."[33]

Tus the frequently mentioned similarity between Utah and the Biblical landscape might also lead to unfavorable comparisons.

Significantly an explanation of the polygamy-question from the Jewish viewpoint was given by the rabbinal authorities in American Jewry in the same year, 1869, which was a turning point in the Gentile conflict in Utah. Naturally there was no special reference to Mormonism but it was silently assumed to be the actual American background of this question. A rabbinical conference

270

took place in Philadelphia from November 3rd to 6th, 1869. The opinion of a participant that "it is not necessary that anno 1869 still one has to declare himself as against polygamy" was set aside and the matter was dealt with. The further argument of this participant: "One throws with this a shadow on past Judaism as if polygamy had been permitted"[34] was exactly the viewpoint of the majority of the conference who felt that this very point had to be illuminated. It was stated that the temporal circumstances under which the Bible mentions cases of polygamy must be separated from the spirit of the Bible, God's word, which sanctions only monogamous marital life. This was in opposition to the Mormon argument that in Biblical times polygamy had been according to the will of God. The old wedding formula "after the law of Moses and Israel" should be changed to "after the law of God" so that anyone willing to make a mental reservation of polygamy within the "mores of Moses and Israel" might be restrained by the clear "law of God."[35]

These arguments are not only interesting to us because they formed the basis of all inofficial discussions with the Mormons but also because they express the background of the times. Furthermore their importance is not diminished because of the fact that this rabbinical conference represented only the reform wing of American Jewry.

The change in the wedding formula was accepted at the conference and a formal statement was made to the effect that polygamy was belied by the Jewish concept of marriage.[36] If the new formula was nevertheless not applied by the majority of the Jewish people it was only because the already existing religious laws were considered sufficient to maintain monogamy for all Jews.

However, although clarity vis à vis Mormonism was the real purpose—the deliberations of the conference were also meaningful for the internal Jewish situation in America. Oriental Jews from Mohammedan countries had emigrated to America too,[37] and American Jewry could be confronted with the question of religious and legal acknowledgment of polygamous marital status brought over from there. In respect to the European Jewish immigrants, however, an even greater problem existed. It was expressed by one of the participants of the conference:

"There have been already some cases in which men from Eastern Europe, perhaps also from Western, deserted their women,

271

went to America and remarried there without having dissolved their first marriage in any way."[38] Persecution of Jewish immigrants for polygamy were occasionally mentioned in the Jewish press.[39]

The resolutions of the Philadelphia conference awakened an echo in the European Jewish press on this very point and one paper commented:

"Monogamy was at all times dominant among the Jews, even in countries, where the law did not prescribe it. Nevertheless Jewish law shaped by legal decisions does not demand it because the spirit of Judaism brought it to full confirmation in the mores of the Jews."[40]

Even before the rise of the Mormon Church Mordecai M. Noah in his Ararat-address had precluded polygamy for the Jews in America and had mentioned the marital conditions of the Jews in Africa.[41] Later, during the Civil War era, an attempted discussion of the Biblical arguments, in the slavery and polygamy questions was opposed by an American Jewish newspaper which fought against both together:

"There is a very black mark on the forehead of each institution when it first appears. Polygamy first appears in the family of Lamech, the descendant of Cain; and what kind of a family was his?"[42]

Self-enlightenment among the Jews also played a role in the lecture-program of the Jewish literary society. The statements made there already contained the essentials of subsequent research into Jewish cultural history.[43]

Before the polygamy discussion was made part of the political fight of the Gentiles, the Jewish public attitude to the comparison with Bible times was restrained and its judgment of Mormon life fair and just. This may be illustrated by the polemics of a Jewish newspaper against an article of Fitz Hugh Ludlow in the *Golden Era* of March 2th, 1864. This article had attempted to identify Jews with Mormons in all respects not merely in reference to polygamy, in the following statement:

"The whole secret of their fanaticism is intelligible the moment that you understand one fact—they are saturated through and through with a love for the Old Testament civilization as understood by them. You cannot talk with one of their strongest men

—like Young or Kimball—for an hour without seeing that their national model is the Jewish people. Like the Jews they are grossly sensual and physical in all their ideas of religion and a future state. Like them they have no notion of the pure conjugal relation and consider polygamy its highest form. Like them, they . . . will 'compass heaven and earth to make a proselyte.' Like them they think themselves doing God a service by assassinating such as have made defection from their creed."[44]

The reply was expressed as follows:

"It is not our purpose to defend the Mormon creed; we know nothing of the people, or their customs, save by report. That report, also says that they were most shamefully persecuted in free America for their religious belief; driven out by fire and the sword from their towns and cities, and despoiled by their adversaries, until they were forced to seek a shelter and a habitation. Under a leader they traversed the Rocky Mountains, and in the great basin of the continent, on the shores of a Salt Lake, in a desert country, as uninviting as that surrounding the Dead Sea, they settled, prospered and became a people.

. . . We can see no reason why Mormondom should become the especial mark for Christian malevolence. . . . The Mormons, in making proselytes, do just the same as other Christian denominations. . . . The Jews as a people are polygamists only in the lands where that custom exists. Whenever the Jew dwells in Christian lands, he conforms to its moral laws, and we have yet to meet with a Jew who is a polygamist, or an advocate or defender thereof, in the United States. . . . The millions of 'poor unfortunate females,' who are the victims of the 'social evil,' reflect a far more lasting disgrace on monogamy, than the abuse of polygamy by the Mormons. The Jewish people as a body, are a monument of what Christian intolerance can inflict; and we judge from our past history and persecutions, what the Mormons have in the past, and are yet to endure in the future. Aside from their religion, they are an industrious, united people."[45]

It is noteworthy that this answer pointed out the general "social evil" thereby adhering to the usual Mormon argumentation.

The original article and the answer to it were reprinted in the Mormon Church newspaper. The comment applied to them de-

273

serves our attention because it represents the overall position of the Mormons to the Biblical promises to the Jews:

"*The Hebrew.*—On another page of this issue, we published an editorial from *The Hebrew,* a young paper in San Francisco and edited by an experienced journalist, Philo Jacoby, formerly of the *Gleaner.* The article will repay perusal, not so much for its defence of Mormonism, as for the general facts stated. We are obliged for the liberal disposition of *The Hebrew,* but we are accustomed to so much misrepresentation and tall lying about the Mormons nearer home, that we have got used to that kind of thing, and fear that it would go bad with us if that class of writers found anything about us to praise. There is considerable consolation in the thought that we are at least not under that warning: 'Woe unto you, when all men speak well of you.' Apart from the matters alluded to, we commend *The Hebrew* to our citizens of the 'literal descent'; it is a very interesting, well conducted paper abounding in matters of interest to those who believe in 'the promises made to the Fathers.' "[46]

With the Gentile fight in full swing, the tone of the Jewish press changed, especially when the writers were men of the European enlightenment who based their statements on information from the German-American press. A typical example was Chicago's Dr. Chronik, who took his material from the *New Yorker Staatszeitung*: "In this respect *Moses* was surely a better judge of men and ethical teacher. He forbade such marriages, not only because of incest, but also for the reason that it is not decent to turn the love of sisters into the enmity of competitors driven by jealousy.

. . . The city at the Salt Lake numbers 17,000 inhabitants . . . and in the past October, the healthiest month of the whole year, 60 persons died, among them 44 children . . . A Mormon cemetery is a cruel sight due to the many fresh small graves. Many Mormon fathers have buried 20 to 30 of their children. The last year was a relatively healthy one but mortality in Utah was this time too greater than in the other states and territories west of the Mississippi . . ."[47]

The approach chosen by the Mormons to defend their "peculiar institution" involved not only the relationship of revelation to the majority public opinion as a matter of principle, but it also presented actual examples of a clash between religious institutions

274

and majority public opinion. For both, the chosen sample was again taken from Judaism:

"It seems that what the world called 'Mormonism' is about to be weighed in the balance of Congressional legislation. The revelation on polygamy or 'celestial marriage' is termed by a portion of that body 'a pretended revelation,' and therefore it must be suppressed by the strong arm of legislative prohibition and by military power. The Jews said that Jesus pretended that God was his father, and because of this reputed pretension they crucified him and brought ruin and death upon their nation and a lasting disgrace upon their fugitive and scattered remnants.

I do not suppose that the unbelief of the Jews had any more to do with the truth of the revelations of Christianity than the unbelief of Mr. Cullom has with the truth of the revelation to the Latter-day Saints upon the subject of plural marriages. The unbelief of the Jews did certainly not render fallacious and void the great system of redemption through the atonement of the Son of God, neither extracted its sting from those who rejected it. . . .

But who shall determine whether this revelation is a real or pretended one? The unbelievers therein claim the right to judge. . . . The Jews claimed the sole right to judge of the merits of our Saviour's mission into the world. . . . The Jews, His bitterest and most inveterate enemies, claimed it as their right alone to say whether Jesus and His Revelations were real or pretended. They pronounced them the latter, just as the House Committee on Territories pronounced the revelation on polygamy 'a pretended revelation. . . .' If they say that the Jews had no right to condemn the Saviour's mission and revelation they must also say that Mr. Cullom and his co-workers have no right to sit in judgment upon or to pass laws against the mission of Joseph Smith and his revelations. Orson Hyde."[48]

Polygamy was compared to circumcision, which was handled as a question of judicial judgment. An imaginary law case posited "two uncircumcised Jewish aliens who" apply for naturalization. . . . "The Judge asks him if he believes it right and in accordance with the laws of God for a man to be circumcised." This question provides the point of departure for drawing a parallel to the situation of the Mormons:

"The Ruling of Chief Justice McKean.

275

. . . The Israelites, it is wellknown, believe in and practice circumcision. It is a part of their religion. They observe it conscientiously. But suppose Congress were to pass a law as in the case of polygamy, declaring it a penal offence. Must the Jew, therefore, foresake this practice of his religion, and be excluded from the covenant which he firmly believes God made with his forefather Abraham? . . . A Legislative body might say; such a law is disgusting . . . cruelty to children. . . . The alternative would thus be presented to the Israelites of disobeying the laws of man and risking the penalty of that or, on the other hand, of disobeying what they as a nation, believe to be the law of God. . . . This is precisely the position of the Latter-day Saints respecting polygyny, with this exception, that its practice among them is not universal as circumcision is among the Israelites."[49]

The didactic treatment of this theme closes with the exclamation:

"Men of Israel, Citizens of the United States . . . what think ye of the Chief Justice of a Territory who renders such decisions?"

In simpler propaganda, the Mormons used the example of contemporary monstrosities such as the first advertisements by "matrimonial offices: Oh, poor Utah! You land of many wives! You are much behind the times!. . ."[50] Thus they added another instance to their slogan of white slavery, among the Gentiles.

In this connection it is of interest to note that the Oneida community which lived in promiscuity took great pains to show that its "No wife system" was remote from Mormon polygamy. To explain this the Oneida community also chose a Biblical example, drawn this time entirely in contrast by the gospels:

"One system represents the civilization of the Old Testament; the other that of the New; war and polygamy appear on one side; non-resistance and freedom for women on the other."[51, 52]

Insofar as argumentation was concerned the Mormon Biblical argument at first met no response, but it elicited negative sentiment by the time the Christian controversy reached its peak. In the frame of Judaism meeting Mormonism, the purely Christian discussions between Mormons and Christian denominations regarding this question have no place. But it may be taken for granted that such discussions did not cause the Christian world to consider the Jewish people in ancient or modern times as the exponent of

276

polygamy. Rather, the Bible argument as formulated from the Jewish point of view was accepted by enlightened Christians. The Mormon's argument that what seemed pleasing to God in Abraham's times must also be valid for America, was in no case regarded as a Jewish concept. Thus, Mormonism was separated from Judaism even by enlightened Christian judgment. The Jews of Utah sharply denied all rumors of a connection with the Mormon marriage system:

"I know he errs as to the position of the Hebrew race in Utah, whom he mentions as belonging to an old nation of polygamists. I am convinced from personal observation that there are in that Territory no citizens who comply more strictly with the letter and spirit of the national laws, who more consistently and unflinchingly oppose the doctrines of the Mormon faith than the descendants of Israel."[53]

The Mormons were thus entirely alone in their Bible concept of plural marriage. This already was an indication of the hopelessness of their "peculiar institution" from the viewpoint of the history of ideas, which had not often encountered such a case of ideological isolation. There is an analogy to the immanent connection between idea and fate in that the attempt to preserve plural marriage brought the historical conflict between Mormon society and the rest of America to a climax even if we take into account the role of Gentile political manoeuvers in using it as an instrument of retaliation. Without the complete spiritual isolation of the Mormons in this matter this weapon too could not have been so effective in the political field.

But the polygamy struggle had another aspect which extended to the immediate interest of American Jewry. This was the repeated argument that the "peculiar institution" of the Mormons could be preserved only by immigation. This argument was especially disturbing to American Jews who not only had an interest in free emigration but also in the quiet growth of their communities which were the outcome of immigration. This process could surely be disturbed by any general argument against immigration. Such opposition could only give weapons to nativism and encourage it to search for arguments in other directions possibly against Jewish immigration.

The immigrationist argument against the Mormons in its

shortest form stated simply: "Polygamy is kept up by foreign immigration."[54] But in its exploitation by nativism, the argument was expanded and broadened:

"The strength of this people (Mormon) would be materially lessened if our immigration laws were so amended as to cut off this great influx of the ignorant, almost pauper, emigrants of the old world. Let 'America be henceforth for Americans.' The struggle for bread, for life is becoming too severe here, since the country has become so filled with adult aliens from abroad. We need the room—shut down the gates!"[55]

In time it became known that the American government had undertaken steps abroad in connection with Mormon immigration. The logic as well as the adequacy of such steps was discussed in public:

"It seems rather strange that the United States Government should address a circular to foreign Governments at all; still more strange that they should go to length of protesting against further Mormon emigration from England, Germany, Norway, Sweden and Denmark. . . . But the right place to put a stop to it is in Utah. . . ."[56]

This statement issued in 1879, sounded ominous for the approaching mass immigration of Eastern European Jews. A discussion of the measures to be taken—either in Europe or later in Utah could lead to general difficulties for immigrants—Jews included —and certainly did not make the situation of the Jews in Utah any easier. A watchful American Jewry therefore began to feel special discomfort in every discussion which connected Mormon plural marriage with immigration. This discomfort was only partly relieved by the existence of other religious communities in America with odd relationships between the sexes. These were mentioned occasionally in the Jewish press:

"The Oneida saints have brought more misery into private families and are covered with more disgrace than the Mormons dreamt of and still they are, unmolested and unnoticed, practicing in fact what everybody condemns in theory."[57]

The reason for this apparent disregard of their odd sexual practice was without doubt the secluded existence of such an experimental community which did not seek recruits from continuous immigration from Europe. The attempt of this Jewish paper to do more justice to the Mormons by talking of the "Oneida Saints" therefore had little chance of success.

In its concern for its immigrants the *Reorganized Church* as representatives of the "non-polygamous Mormons" had demanded to be except from any governmental steps abroad.[58]

Primitive instincts against the Mormons could even be awakened by images of the time when the Indian was enemy No. 1, if only a relationship to polygamy could be reaffirmed:

"The Indians were, however, easily reconciled to Mormonism, being already polygamists, and believing in the slavery of women; all they had to do was to be baptized, and they were better Mormons than can ever be made of the Anglo-Saxon race. . . ."[59]

Occasionally one is also reminded that polygamous African tribes allow every wife a separate place of habitation thus making "arrangements like those of our respected fellow citizens, Brigham Young and the other magnates of Utah."[60]

But such small irritations were nothing in comparison with figures for plural marriage which might come up in any immigrationist polygamy argument. In the first place the first census in 1850 in Utah revealed an excess of men over women. This surplus grew from census to census. Polygamy therefore could not be supported by an eventual surplus of women in the territory. It could be realized only by artful manipulation within the population or by immigration.

There were no reliable statistics to the number of plural marriages and the number of wives in any given polygamous household. Early rumors of Mormon polygamy which also mentioned the number of wives were ridiculed by the Mormon "Frontier Guardian" of December 1849. The tone of the article was that of a vague concession and in a rudimentary fashion it pointed the way to the later Bible argument as well as the argument of the "social evil."

"Some of our exchanges say that the Mormon men at Salt Lake Valley have from five to twenty-five wives. If this is so, they are certainly ahead of us, and if they keep on, they will be as bad as King David and Solomon, and some others of whom we read in olden time; or as righteous as some modern lawgivers who practise what their laws condemn."[61]

In time some figures emerged. They were naturally only estimates by more or less competent observers, mostly newspaper cor-

279

respondents. Such figures were adapted by others, among them for instance the Jewish traveler, Israel Benjamin. He reported "married men with 7 or more wives 387, . . . with 5 and more 730, . . . with 4 and more, 1100 and with 2 and more 1400. Summa 3617."[62] Benjamin took his figures from the "New York Herald" but this newspaper had obtained them, at least in part, from the Utah Gentile paper which referred to notes taken by the Utah correspondent of the Chicago *Tribune*.[63] The number of unmarried men in Utah did not appear anywhere.

Benjamin contributed to the understanding of the Mormon system of plural marriages by his statement that all incumbents of higher church offices were obligated to conclude plural marriages and that without having fulfilled this obligation no Mormon could rise to higher church office.[64]

There were individual cases of plural marriage which took place as an act of charity. One such case was reported of a man who was a Jewish convert:

"Kimball, calling on a Prussian immigrant named Taussig one day, asked him how he was doing and how many wives he had, and on being told he had two, replied, 'That is not enough. You must take a couple more. I'll send them to you.' "[65]

It took a time until the question of polygamy in Utah attained its national character. Before the Civil War, sectional deliberations in the interest of the South delayed a congressional decision in the case of the proposed expulsion of the Utah delegate, Dr. Bernhisel: "If a man is to be expelled because he owns a dozen of wives, why may not another be expelled some of these days for owning a dozen slaves."[66] However even befor the Civil War the "settlement of the Mormon question, that is, whether polygamy shall be a national institution" was demanded in impulsive words.[67]

Before the issue entered its final phase, a voice could be heard from time to time, expressing the hope of all well meaning people that Mormon life would "ultimately result in their renunciation of polygamy, and their restoration to the confidence of the government . . ."[68]

Enlightened Jews certainly thought along these lines. Jewish public opinion was even more impressed by the success of Mormon colonization than the rest of America. Certainly, there are occasional reports of obstacles facing Jewish merchants in Utah accompanied by attacks on the Mormons. However, there was no active will to fight Mormon polygamy as a matter of principle and thereby to contribute to the national polygamy battle. This is especially remarkable since the Jewish press of these years could in no sense be called unwilling to plunge into a fight.

The picture changed around 1880. Jewish public opinion felt that the issue was reaching its final stage. It no longer exercised restraint in strongly expressing its opinion. Nevertheless, compared with the rising excitement engendered by this question in all of America, the attitude of the Jewish press was generally informative. It did not urge that any further steps be taken. Besides this it gave little space to its declaration of principles in comparison with its report of the events:

"The President's Message.

. . . Polygamy occupies the next place in the message and Mr. Hayes having recently visited the headquarters of this national scandal, his righteous soul was vexed by what he witnessed. The evil is denounced in unmeasured terms, and prompt and vigorous steps are recommended for its suppression. The President acquits the United States authorities of complicity or connivance in the matter, and states his conviction that while the juries are under the control of the Mormons there is no hope of obtaining convictions and no use in instituting legal proceedings. He advises Congress to make exceptional provision for governing the State, and to exclude from the privileges of citizens any person known to be living in polygamy. . . ."[69]

Indeed the Jewish press was generally moderate in tone considering the times and the exciting nature of the subject matter:

"Polygamy is one of the many subjects urgently demanding the attention of Congress. As at present practiced in Utah it is a standing defiance to the government, as well as an outrage on morality and civilization. There are several features of the crime which render it one difficult to deal with, and these difficulties interpose to prevent detection, as well as punishment. It is gratifying to learn that the Judiciary Committee of the Senate has framed a bill designed to deal with the offence in respect to both these issues. Its aim is to render detection more easy and to inflict such punishment as will destroy the political and social power of the offender. The bill is understood to be a combination of the two bills prepared

281

respectively by Senators Edmunds and Logan, and it covers the ground mapped out in the President's message. To facilitate detection and conviction it provides that the fact of bigamous relations subsisting between the parties shall be deemed a sufficient evidence of marriage having taken place, without actual proof of such marriage; a provision designed to overcome the difficulty arising out of the secrecy with which Mormons enshroud the disgusting ceremonies of the Endowment House. Among the penalties to follow conviction are disfranchisement and exclusion from office. There is evident wisdom in the selection of both penalties, for at present the power of the Mormon Church is largely based on the fact that all the offices in Utah which are filled by the votes of the people are occupied by polygamists who have been elected by the votes of polygamists. It is well known that the non-Mormon population of Utah constitute but an insignificant proportion of the voters, and that not one of them could in the present condition of affairs hope to gain office. It is by securing to polygamists all the executive offices within the vote of the people that the Mormon lawbreakers have been able to evade punishment, and it is this power which the new bill is designed to destroy. The progress of the bill through Congress will be watched with considerable interest by all friends of morality and social decency."[70]

The progress of all the political manoeuvering was reported by the same newspaper:

"Mormonism is not disposed to surrender its peculiar institution without a stubborn fight. Arrangements have been made to obstruct and render as harmless as possible the operation of the Edmunds bill in the approaching elections, and in addition to this effort an attempt is to be made to overthrow the bill altogether. Judge Jeremiah Black has been retained by the Mormon leaders as their champion. The Judge is stated to have prepared an argument for submission to the Secretary of the Interior, attacking the legality of the acts of the Utah Commission and of Governor Morgan, and testing the legality of the law."[71]

In this way the upheaval of those years was kept before the Jewish public until at last the day came the Jewish press could also report the final solution:

"Polygamy banished.

282

At the general conference of the Mormon Church, held in Salt Lake City last Monday, the official declaration of President Wilford Woodruff, forbidding in future any marriages in violation of the laws of the land, was read, and the congregation numbering nearly 10,000 persons, including the apostles, bishops and leading elders of the Mormon Church, by unanimous vote recognized the authority of the President to issue the manifesto, and accepted it as authoritative and binding."[72]

The future path to an entirely new constellation of society in Utah lay open from that day on. The actual situation in the territory had changed decisively during the previous decade. Mining had become Utah's greatest economic factor. The former economic factors which were important in the Gentile conflict had largely ceased to exist. The new relationships among all groups also meant that there would be an end to the extraordinary position of the Jews in the Gentile conflict of the past, and they would assume a different role in the future of the new state.

Chapter 21

Jews and Jewish Matters in the Mormon Press

The press as the foremost cultural agency of the Mormon people not only registered actual events in the meeting of Jew and Mormons, it also expressed the entire concept of the Jew's existence to the Mormon people. In this task it proved to be the foremost religious instrument of the church since this concept of the Jew is primarily a religious one. It fulfilled this task as does any other press, by bringing news from the whole world. Since direct correspondence from the world theater to the Mormon press was meager, it carefully selected world news from all possible sources. This function of selecting news made the Mormon press not only a purveyor of news but a creator of public opinion for the Mormon people. Actual relations between Jew and Mormon in Utah were to a great extent based on this attitude of the press and to the extent that Mormon public opinion became known in America all of American Jewry was influenced by this attitude. In the end the general American image of the relationship between Jew and Mormon was formed by these references in the Mormon press.

The news about Jews in the Mormon press may be divided into purely religious items concerning Mormon creed and doctrine, world news about Jewish life usually religiously colored and reports about the Jews in America.

On the religious scene, the Mormon press cultivated the image of the Jew as the divinely ordained companion of European peoples in the course of their history. This situation created a unique religious relationship between the Jew and the surrounding world. It was followed by depicting all conditions of religious and social Jewish life which could be related to the position of the Jew in Mormon creed and doctrine. Thus the Jew existed not only in a religious landscape created by the Mormons but also in an actual life situation. Aside from this there were also lessons to be learned from the fate of the Jews and wisdom to be preached from it. The peoples of the earth were confronted with the injustice done to the Jews and this example was then applied to the experiences of the Mormons.

No other instrument could have been more apt for this purpose than the Mormon press which was missionary to the outside world and pioneering within Utah and other parts of the Far West. The fact that the press served all the needs of the pioneer gave the "Deseret News," circulation 4,000, an outstanding position out of proportion to its numbers. In addition, the Mormon press outside of Utah served the interests of a group completely concentrated on a religious task, which was the essence of life for many contemporaries. Consequently, the image of the Jew and his world community handled in uniform fashion by the whole Mormon press, pioneer—or strictly missionary, made an indestructible and harmonious impression on the hearts of the faithful.

As to the substance of Mormon news about Jews, there was a preference for all reports from or about Palestine because of the implied confirmation of Mormon religious truths by such Palestine news. This category included messages from Palestine to the Jews, stressing the promise that the land would be given to them.

However, reportage about the Jewish people all over the world held its own and gave a realistic picture which, wherever possible, was introduced by religious interpretation according to Mormon creed. Finally and most important for us are the Mormon press reports about their contemporaries, the American Jews and of special significance are its views of the religious future of American Jewry.

The purely technical side of this news service did not differ greatly from other American newspapers and magazines. Contemporary material about the Jews was assembled from wherever it could be found, from Jewish, non-Jewish, American or European press. There was no differentiation in this respect between friend and foe. Even active adversaries of the Mormons enjoyed hospitality in the Mormon press when their utterances were widely reprinted, provided that their statements had something relevant to say about the Jews. This is true even of the active Jewish opponent of the Mormons, M. M. Noah.[1]

In addition to factual information, the Mormon press was

eager to keep alive its readers' continuing interest in the Jews by printing artistic forms of poetry and prose to bring the feelings and hopes of the Jews to the attention of its readers. A sample of this kind is the "Lament of a Captive Jew in Babylon. By a converted Jew."[2]

Among the themes based on serious information, the most important was the universality of Jewish peoplehood. This universality, it was stressed, was at the same time part of the Jewish people's religious character. No opportunity was missed to demonstrate that Jewish wanderings were directed by God and would ultimately lead to a goal. For instance an article on "Immigration" stated: "The God of Israel, who in the disposal of events, has made all these things redound to the spread of his cause; and we trust to the good of his people."[3]

Leadership by Providence was seen even in the statistical conditions of the Jews:

"The statistics of the Jewish population are among the most singular circumstances of this most singular of all people. Under all their calamities and dispersions, they seem to have remained at nearly the same amount as in the days of David and Solomon— never much more in prosperity, never much less after ages of suffering. Nothing like this has occurred in the history of any other race. . . ."[4]

A glorification of Jewish history followed.[5] And after this came the demonstration of the omnipresence of the Jews in all countries:

"I have seen them in San Francisco, in Chile, in Scotland, in England and in every part of the United States and Canada; and wherever my brethren, the Elders of this Church, have been; I can assure them of one thing, if they have looked about them they have seen a Jew or Jews. Wherever there is a nation to be found, or a people of commerce, ships, camels, or any other means of conveyance, there will be found Jews; that we know."[6]

At the same time, the empirical picture of vocational distribution of the Jews as seen in America was also given:

"At the present time the employment of the Jews is generally that of merchants, brokers, bankers, jewelers, dealers in clothing, watches, gold and silver, ornaments, peddling, etc . . ."[7]

Many general articles which shed light on the living conditions of the Jews of the world appeared in the Mormon press. Some were

286

independent treatises, but others were only gleanings of the most readable matter printed about Jews. All this was enthusiastically reprinted, whether it was a general Palestine report from the "Orient"[8] or a description from "Frazer's Magazine'[9] or even an article "Restoration of the Jews" from the "Mercantile Journal."[10] The decisive factor in the choice was always the fact that something otherwise inaccessible was brought to the Mormon reader. Even the efforts of the Christian missionary societies among the Jews were not overlooked although the Mormons had their own ideas about it.[11] On the other hand the dedication of the Jews to their faith was treated just as objectively. A reprint from the "Jewish Intelligencer" about a work treating the Shulchan Aruch is prefaced with the following words: "The Jews. It will be seen by the following that the Jews are as zealous in the propagation of what they consider true principles as any of the sects of modern date. . . ."[12]

The basic features of the Jewish story of sufferings—the persecutions in past and present, were explained to the reader and their significance for him as an adherent of a persecuted faith was pointed out. A look at their neighbors in America showed that basically humanity was desecrated by the Jewish persecutions:

"What would the Irish Catholics have thought had the British government dealt with them as their great Pontificate has dealt with the poor Jews."[13] Even more stress was placed on injustice against the Jews in present times:

"Persecution of the Jews in Turkey. The Jews in Smyrna are exposed to the most wanton outrages on account of their religion. One of them was recently thrown into prison because a cat was missing! and no crime is committed of which they are not supposed to be guilty by the bigoted inhabitants."[14] It seems clear that such words were to be applied to the tendency of their neighbors to ascribe crimes of all kinds to the Mormons.

Generally news of the Jewish situation in all countries was reprinted. Even "Jewish officers in the French Army"[15] seemed worth reading. Nevertheless there was considerable concentration on news from Russia. It was the site of the main sufferings, and one could escape by emigration. The Orient was sifted just as thoroughly for news which on the other hand were regarded in the light of the hope for the future.

The attitude of England, which according to contemporary

opinion, was friendly to the Jews, was compared with their oppression by the Czar.[16] But if once in a while there was good news to report from Russia, it was given with the same eagerness:

"Russia. 'The emperor' of Russia, by a recent ukase, enacts the Jews who may undertake to colonize the Steppes, shall each receive 150 roubles, a certain quantity of land, and the permission to employ Christian laborers; also that they and their laborers shall be exempt for twenty years from military service."[17]

The widespread opinion expressed by the press of the entire world that the House of Rothschild had the capacity to better the situation of the Jews also appeared in the Mormon press:

"The Rothschilds possess great influence in many European courts. Can it not be used at the present time in behalf of their oppressed brethren?"[18]

Events in the Orient concerning the Jews were separated from other Jewish items in the Mormon press by two special viewpoints which took into account the religious angle of the Mormons: First of all, they were an empirical broadening and continuation of what the two missions to Palestine had reported to the faithful and, secondly, they served as a direct appeal to the Jews everywhere, especially in America, to rebuild their ancient home in Palestine. The latter effort reached a peak when an appeal for Palestine—proclaimed by the Jews themselves—was reported.

Detailed news of Palestine and even of the whole Near East received special treatment in the Mormon press as a result of its assumed importance for the mass of its readers. "The Jews of Damascus"[19] were stuff for a separate article due to their special martyr-story. Notices about Jewish immigrants in Palestine appeared repeatedly in one and the same newspaper.[20] In occasional lesser items the achievements of the Jewish population in Palestine were pointed out:

"Sir Moses Montefiore has presented his coreligionists at Jerusalem with two presses, and the necessary types, for printing Jewish tracts. The office consists of twenty-two people of the Jewish persuasion."[21]

Special attention was given the political aspects of the Palestine question:

"Sir Montefiore has convenanted with Mehemet Ali for a

288

tribute equal to present receipts, on the condition of re-colonizing the whole of Palestine with Jews.

"Memorials have been sent to all the Protestant Princes, soliciting their interference in the present dispute between the Sultan and Mehemet Ali, about Palestine, to secure that country for the speedy return of the Jews."[22]

General Jewish appeals for help to Palestine insofar, as they were directed to Jews in all countries formed a separate category. Such appeals were reproduced not only in their press, but also in the general writings of the Mormons. For instance in 1841 the appeal of the "Congregation of the German Jews" in Jerusalem, copied from the "Morning Herald," was reproduced in full in a book.[23] This trend reached its peak, however, years later when the pioneer organ in Utah printed its introduction to the complete reprint of the appeal of the Chief rabbi of England, Dr. Adler: These words may stand as the essence of all the good wishes the Mormon people had for the Jews:

"The deplorable condition of the remnant of Israelites, the ancient people of God, now resident in the Holy Land, has called forth the sympathies of their brethren resident in England and America, at the head of which charitable movement stands Sir Moses Montefiore. An appeal has been made by the latter gentleman in a pamphlet directed to his brethren throughout this Union, in language which it is impossible to read without a thrill of mingled sympathy and horror. The Israelites in the East have nobly united with their English brethren in their benevolent exertions, and we feel assured that those residents of the Pacific shores will not need incentive to prompt their hearty cooperation in so charitable a deed. Their brethren in the Holy Land, a band of faithful watchers near the homes of their forefathers, are perishing from absolute want. The Israelites of this country are famous for their disinterested charity, probity and high moral worth—and we have every reason to believe they will not pass so worthy and touching an appeal without taking prompt action thereon."[24]

The Jewish messengers from Palestine who came to America to solicit help during the early years of Mormonism, gave the Mormon press an opportunity to write about these personalities and their mission. A detailed report of this kind stemming from the Kirtland period of Mormonism was titled "The Rabbi from the

Holy City."[25] And in 1849, the Mormon paper in Iowa, from the way-station of the exodus to Utah reported to the faithful: ". . . The honored messenger, now here, the Rabbi Echiel Cohen, who is to convey the fruits of our bounty to the Holy Land. . . . Send him not away to the banks of the Jordan without purse . . ."[26] The readiness of the American Jews to help in this as in any other charity was taken for granted: ". . . when was an appeal made to the charitable feelings of the Jew to aid his brethren, that is was not cheerfully, liberally responded to?"[27]

It goes without saying that in 1870 when Salt Lake City had an opportunity to hear the lecture of such a messenger, the church paper harangued the public to go to this lecture and published a report of this event:

"The Holy Land.—We remind the public of the lecture by Rabbi Sneersohn, which will commence at seven o'clock this evening, (Wedn. 16.XI.1870) in the Tabernacle. The doors will be opened at half past six. The literal gathering of the Jews to the Holy Land is firmly believed in by the Latter-day Saints, being part of their faith. The subject, as it will be treated upon to-night, cannot fail to be interesting and instructive to them. We hope to see a large attendance on the occasion. The price of admission is within the reach of all, being only twenty-five cents.

"The Holy Land.—The lecture in the Tabernacle last evening was listened to by an audience of about three hundred persons. The subject, the Holy Land, was handled in an interesting manner by Rabbi Sneerston [sic]. . . . The Rabbi concluded by expressing his firm hope and belief that the time would come when Israel would inherit their own country and the smile and the glory of God would yet rest upon it."[28]

The tendency to do justice to the Jew was also effective in the spiritual food furnished by the Mormons to their children in *The Juvenile Instructor*. General knowledge was transmitted first:

"Every child who reads this has no doubt heard of the Jews. They are to be met in many countries, and though they live like other people they are different from them in a great many things."[29] Following this Biblical history, events, wisdom and morale of the ancient Jewish people was dealt with in numerous pedagogic articles throughout the volumes of this magazine. Occasionally even folkloristic stories were told.[30] Whenever something good was said

290

about the children of Jewish immigrants, the magazine transmitted it, to its young readers.[31]

The same friendliness to the Jews was shown in a typical Mormon home journal.[32]

In contrast to the highly emotional Palestine news, the reports of the Mormon press about American Jewish affairs were more empirical. Nevertheless they retained something of the ideal viewpoints of reportage. The prosperity of the Jews in America was seen as a good omen for the restoration hope, as was their rise in other countries as for instance in England. It was pointed out that the American Jews would increase further by immigration: "In this country they are greatly on the increase, and it is supposed that the Bremen, Hamburg and English vessels will bring out twenty thousand emigrants the current year . . ."[33]

There were reports about the general situation of the Jews in America[34] as well as their endeavors to create organizations, like the Board of Delegates.[35] In addition, a great number of smaller news items were printed to acquaint the reader with the religious life of the Jews in the country as for instance: "The Jewish Passover commences on the evening of the 3d of April (1844). Several Bakers are actively engaged in baking the Passover bread for 10,000 people of that persuasion in New York."[36] An interesting item is the reprint of a notice in the San Francisco *Hebrew*: "A generous gift. The following letter, inclosing a draft of D400— from the First Hebrew Benevolent Society in Salt Lake City, was received by Mr. C. Meyer, President of the First Hebrew Benevolent Society of this city:

Salt Lake City, Sept. 28th, 1869. Mr. C. Meyers; Dear Sir—At a meeting of the First Hebrew Benevolent Society, held on the 26th instant, the motion was unanimously carried to send to you four hundred (400) dollars of our funds. for our suffering co-religionists in Western Russia, which I take pleasure in sending you herewith. Please accept the same, and oblige by acknowledging the draft. Yours respectfully.

Sol Levy.

In the name of our suffering brethren far away, we express to the members of the First Hebrew Benevolent Society of Salt Lake City our best thanks. To which we add our hearty amen."[37]

Of special interest to us are some cases in which the Mormon

291

press revealed its attitude toward internal religious questions within American Jewry, such as the following statement on Jewish Reform:

". . . it has been reserved for these last days to witness what is called Jewish reform, or in other words, to witness Jews forsaking or apostatizing from the traditions of their fathers, and accommodating themselves in some respects to the tendencies of modern thought and civilization.

This singular movement has been gradually developing itself in this country for the past few years, and now we hear of orthodox and heterodox Jews, and of congregations of the house of Israel dividing because of their differences in religious views and sentiments."[38]

In taking a position in the Sabath question of the Jews, the Mormon press leaned toward the extreme Jewish reform and supported the shift of the Sabbath to Sunday:

"We judge our Israelites in this country would have no difficulty in adopting his suggestion. [of a radical reformer]. Instead of its being an inconvenience to some of them to have a different sabbath it is rather the contrary. They all, we believe, keep their stores open on Saturday, and some of them, we are told, on Sunday too. If they had any qualms of conscience about dealing on Saturday, they do not visibly affect them. Probably the longitude of this city may have something to do with their disrespect of this time—honored day among The Israelites."[39]

A picturesque description of the Jewish services in San Francisco was given to the youth by a report of Geo. A. Smith, Wilford Woodruff, A. M. Musser and the Editor Cannon:

"Saturday being the Jewish Sabbath—for Jews observe the seventh day which they claim to be Saturday—we repaired on that day to the synagogue El Emanuel, said to be the finest in the city. It is a brick structure of an architectural appearance strikingly oriental. By the kindness of the gentleman in charge who proved to be an old acquaintance of the editor when he was on a mission in California fifteen years ago, we were shown to a seat where we could witness the services and command a view of the congregation to the best advantage. . . . Though we could not understand anything that was said in these portions of the service we appreciated the singing which was very fine."[40] (The mixed choir consisted of 2 men and 2 women).

An important reaction to new education trends within American Jewry appeared in the Following 'Editorial Thoughts": "Miss Emma Lazarus, a Jewess of prominence, has been giving expression to her views respecting the best means to adopt to kill the taints of intolerance and remedy the evils from which the Jews suffer. Her plan is to teach trades to the young Israelites. This will have the effect, she thinks, to make them more like the people among whom they dwell, and less noticeable than at present. This she regards as more important than the observance of the Jewish religion. She regards the present time as of such difficulty and danger that the primary consideration of Jews 'should not be the teachings of *Thora,* not the inculcation of the Talmud, not the preservation of the Hebrew tongue, not the maintenance of synagogue worship, not even the circumcision of the flesh. . . .' As Latter Day Saints we can form some idea of their nature. . . . We know how the Saints feel when they are advised to give up their religion and become like other people . . . now . . . they are told to yield the belief in and practice of celestial, or patriarchal marriage. 'If you will only give up this obnoxious practice,' they say, 'all trouble will be ended.' . . . But would such a denial of faith have such an effect? Certainly not. . . . This is true of the Jews. Had they yielded their religion or sought to avoid persecution by making themselves as near as possible like those who surrounded them, they would have disappeared as a race . . ."[41]

This survey of Jewish items in the Mormon press clearly indicates that the tendencies discovered were common and imminent in Mormonism and were not altered by any splits within the Mormon church.

CHAPTER 22

The Jewish Press on Mormons and Mormonism

Early meetings between Jew and Mormon were sporadic and unlikely to bring about a reaction to the new community of faith on the part of the Jewish public. As to Europe, although Jewish and Mormon immigration to America up to 1880 took place simultaneously, most of the Jews came from countries far from the places of origin of the Mormon waves of immigration. This was true for the Scandinavian Mormons as well as for the English Mormons. There was no Jewish emigration from Scandinavian countries and the one from England was not in touch with any religious dissenters, of whom the Mormons were only one special group. Significantly, there is an absence of any news about the early phase of Mormon emigration in the Jewish press in Europe.

In America too, Jews were the only ones entirely uninterested in the current Christian debate about tenets of the new faith. They therefore did not participate in the flood of early discussions about the origin of the new religion. For the most part, they did not live in the vicinity of the various Mormon settlements before the Utah trek. Little wonder, therefore, that the Mormon persecutions were not mirrored in the Jewish press of that time, European or American, especially since direct correspondence usually came from places with an established Jewish community. The existence of the Mormons and their fate was known to the Jews only through reading or indirect reports, although they were certainly aware that the rest of America had formed a front against them.

During all these years it could scarcely have been felt that any tenet or religious practice of the Mormons had an immediate relationship to the religious life of the Jews, among the nations in general, and in America in particular. The Biblical connotations of the new faith were regarded in the same light as the utterances of Biblicism among European sects. The Mormon system of plural celestial marriage and the Bible argument for it had not yet been publicly pronounced and the reaction of the American public was not yet very intense because information about the existence and scope of Mormon plural marriage was lacking. There was no expressed Jewish public opinion about this point at that time either.

Consequently the slowly developing attitude of the Jewish press to the Mormons and Mormonism was entirely empirical— very much in contrast to the position Jews and Judaism held in the Mormon press from the beginning due to their religious tenets. This fact helps to explain the weak and strong points of this attitude. Credulity could lead as easily to a caricature of the real situation as personal, penetrating observation could result in material valuable for the documentation of cultural history. The subsequent need to discuss the Biblical argument of polygamy was likely to furnish an opportunity to expound Judaism to the whole of America. Other subjects of explanation could be the situation of the Jews in Utah, aspects of Jewish immigration in view of the question of Mormon immigration and the participation of American Jews in all the general political questions connected with the admission of Utah as a state to the Union.

The interest of the Jewish press in such things grew with the founding of a Jewish community in Utah, and it was world-wide. There were numerous reports about the Mormon community in Utah together with the life of the Jews there in the Jewish press in all parts of the world: England, Germany, France, Italy and also in the Hebrew press of Eastern Europe. American correspondents of Jewish newspapers often visited Utah on the way to California, as a result of which long reports appeared in the Jewish press. Some of them are of enduring value because of their factual accuracy. However, the same press also carried enough trash, unproven material and frivolous news, indiscriminately taken from other papers, to indicate the problem created in those days by the dearth of sensational news.

Occasionally a resident Jew in Utah volunteered as correspondent for a Jewish newspaper in America, but the chief connection between the Utah Jews and the American Jewish press lay in their eagerness as readers. They were among the most highly regarded subscribers to Jewish newspapers from the Far West:

"Salt Lake City, Utah, Nov. 12, 1869.

"Dear Sir: Appreciating the good work of the *American Israelite* in the cause of Judaism and confident of its long life and usefulness, we inclose twenty-five dollars as our subscription for the American Israelite and Deborah, for five years, from Oct. 1879 to Oct. 1884. With assurance of high regard, we remain,

Yours very truly,

F. Auerbach a. Bro.

"In all our years of editorial labor we have had no similar experience."[2]

The special contact between the California Jewish newspapers and the Jews in Utah was seen in the announcements by the latter in the newspapers.

The task of sifting the Mormon news in the Jewish press requires the elimination of the products of sheer ignorance: For instance "in Utah at the Salt Lake there live among the Mormons also Jews who according to the custom of the country and following the habit of the patriarchs live in polygamy."[3]

The Jewish Teachers' Journal in Germany which gave this report was unaware that the above statement applied only to individual Jewish converts to Mormonism. In omitting this fact the impression was created that the Jews in Utah, by then (1870) already a sizable community, lived in polygamy.

Or mere gossip was repeated uncritically:

"Brigham Young is also eager to convert Jews, especially women. Up to now he succeeded to convert *one* Jew who now has four wives."[4]

On the other hand rumors current in America were amplified by the correspondent and transmitted to Europe:

"The Mormon People on the Way to Palestine.

"From the midst of the Mormons at Salt Lake there is a report of a movement which is wholeheartedly wished the best of success, one which should be supported in every way by the American people and its government. A German American newspaper, the well edited 'New Yorker Demokrat' reports the following: The Prophet Brigham Young reached the wise conclusion that it would be of no use to continue to oppose the westward flow of the stream of world

296

history. The only way to save himself and the church, he thinks now, is to leave the front line at which he has stood up to now and move to the rear of the immigration wave and modern civilization. Brigham, so it is said, has worked out a plan for settlement of the Mormons in Palestine. Already a company of dignitaries of the Latter Saints is preparing to voyage to the Holy Land, to find out a fitting location for building a new city of the Saints."[5]

This was written in 1873 and it is clear that the second mission of the Mormons to Palestine had brought about this rumor.

Furthermore there were imitations of American popular humor in the matter of Mormon polygamy:

"Brigham Young says he would be willing to give up half of his wives, if he were certain they would get husbands who could lead them to eternal salvation. . . . Barbe Bleue, with frolicsome Irma as the seventh wife of that rascally old Mormon Blue Beard."[6]

Or a comparison was drawn with the classical representative of polygamy who was now already awakening to reason:

"The Turk bethinks himself and says: 'To marry once will do for me,' He had his own peculiar ways Like Mormons, roosters, marrow ape."[7]

Imitation of American folk humor brought the figure of the Mormon to the ballroom in mask and costume. This occurred at masked balls arranged by various groups as for example the German "Arion" mask festival. A similar representation at a New York Jewish Charity Fair was written up as follows in the humorous journal of this Fair:

". . . Here we have not only the Jews and the Christians, the Germans, Americans and the French, but even the Gentiles were represented, for here could be seen the 'Heathen Chinee,' in the person of Ling-Wang Lau . . . And here I also saw 'Saint' Joseph Young, the three hundred and sixty-fifth son of the modern Prophet, Brigham Young, from among the 'Latter Day Saints . . .' "[8]

In contrast to this tendency to satirize or even vulgarize the notion of the Mormon, there were also serious news items in American Jewish newspapers about the life and activities of the Mormons. The following items selected from the same newspaper at short intervals during the year 1869 serve to illustrate this point.

"The Mormons have eighteen Sunday Schools with 2500 attendants in Salt Lake City."[9]

And immediately following:

"Brigham Young is making an extended tour through Southern Utah, and his journey is said to be a perfect ovation."[10]

Furthermore:

"Last year the Mormons of Utah artifically irrigated and made fruitful nearly 94.000 acres of land."[11] And: "One hundred and ten Mormon missionaries have just been sent by Brigham Young to the various cities of the United States."[12]

To be sure anything newsworthy was printed and the Jewish newspaper succumbed to sensational reports from outside as did the other American newspapers. In any case it was recognized fully that the Jewish public in America, like the general public, had a lively interest in news of any kind about Utah and the Mormons.

At that time more inclusive reports written by travellers through Utah began to appear in the American Jewish press. These reports, to be sure, sometimes contained self-satisfied and rash judgments. However, on the whole they were supported by sharp and accurate observation and may be considered typical of what the traveller saw or heard when he stopped at the way station, Salt Lake City. The following rather self-conscious report may have been rendered more so because of the notion that the writer was being watched by 500 secret police:

"Among the Mormons

"Mormondom—The Theatre—Brigham and his Wives—Mormon Laws and Business—Unique Preaching

"Dear Messenger:

"Here am I, in the city of the Mormons, and having an hour or so to spare before leaving here will write you particulars of this infamous place and infamous people. I arrived at Ogden Friday morning, and a stage brought us to this city in about five hours. We are forty miles away from the Railroad and Brigham is building a road, but will not complete it for some months yet. After dinner our party went to the Theatre. There were about 50 people, in an immense house, lighted by lamps. After theatre I talked with the landlord, a Mormon, having three wives. I asked him many questions, and although he said he was willing to answer any question I might put to him I could get but little knowledge from him.

"Saturday we called on President Young. He seemed glad to see us, and asked us many questions about the R. R. etc. He said he was glad the road was finished, as it would bring many people to Salt Lake, who could see for themselves what an elegant institution Mormonism was, and destroy the prejudices now existing with us Gentiles. He is 67 years of age, and medium size and build. He has 3 cotton factories and 2 woolen mills here. He introduced us to his council—all prophets. Brother Smith, Brother Jones, etc., etc. He himself is a fine intelligent looking man but as for the rest I cannot write in the highest terms. The women are miserable looking specimens of femininity. They are complete slaves, and I have not seen a smile on the countenance of one of them since I have been here. I cannot learn how many wives Brigham has: they are estimated from 25 to 72. No one seems to know. The Mormons have two kinds of wives, one kind for this and the next world; the other kind for this world only.

"Yesterday we went to the Tabernacle, a building 130 ft. wide by 250 ft. long. It will seat 10.000 people. It is full but twice a year when conferences are held. There are but 20,000 Mormons here but it is estimated there are about 100.000 in the Territory, and Brigham Young is the leader. He is called President. Some say he is the richest man in the United States, others say not. . . .

"They have no form of prayers, but the congregation is addressed by anyone that chooses to say anything. The President speaks in the church very seldom: we heard Brother Smith speak. He is the son of the Prophet Joe Smith, and is one of the twelve Apostles. He said the Railroad was going to do good as it would 'bring a large number of Gentiles, who would immediately adopt the faith and go to Heaven; and if they didn't, they might go to H—l.'

"We were told that we should go to a certain ward meeting in the evening, where a Brother was in the habit of using strong language: we went there, and the room was crowded. A big, fat Dutchman, who is one of the prophets, was speaking. He did speak rather plainly, and said all the Gentile women were deep dyed sinners, and we Gentiles were all going to the bad. He wanted everybody to bring money to the President, that the poor people could be sent for. They wanted no fine ladies, but poor people, who would work, clean shirts and make themselves useful. He wanted such women here, 'none of your band-box humbugs. Bring the women here, marry them, as many as you like, get as many young ones as you can, and then you will go to heaven sure.' This is the style of preaching that is going on every Sunday.

"The Gentiles are very closely watched, there being about 500 secret police always about. Every now and then, some Gentile (for good cause no doubt) is missing. So, I need not tell you, we are very careful of ourselves.

Yehudah.

Salt Lake, July 1st, 1869."[13]

Only a quarter of a century had passed since the Mormons entered the Salt Lake Valley and it had become clear to an amazed America that the greatest colonizing success of the time, an unanticipated victory over the desert, had been achieved by this new community of faith. World-wide praise was heaped upon this successful venture. American and the world press vied with one another in poetical descriptions of the beauty of this well executed labor of human hands. This work was set in extraordinary natural surroundings whose very description fascinated the reader. The American Jewish press was no less moved by this combination of natural beauty and human effort. Their correspondents, personalities of varied backgrounds travelling through Utah submitted a number of fine articles about nature and human beings in the spirit of unbounded admiration for the successful colonization effort. Other feelings were involved in these expressions of appreciation. A half century had already passed since various literary schemes for the collective settlement of Jews in America had appeared with no practical results. This sympathetic recognition of what had been accomplished by the Mormon community contained an element of awareness of limitations. This realistic attitude of American Jewry,

300

retained despite their failures in colonization (one of them in Utah), must be appreciated. It is characteristic that the same feeling of inability to accomplish such a wonder was also prevalent in another urban group in America, the Irish:

> "Or shall we admit that the Mormons, with their miscreed, are able to do a work for which we have neither heart nor strength? They have made the desert bloom by peopling it with the very poorest emigrants who could be found in Wales or Denmark, bearing often the expense of the voyage from Europe and the journey across the continent. I have heard one of their leaders proclaim, as he pointed to the homes of his people surrounded by orchards and wheatfields, that there was the miracle of faith; that there God's garden had blossomed in the midst of a desert that stretched a thousand miles on every side. Whoever among us should propose an enterprise of so difficult a character would be set down as a madman. The project would be declared impossible, even while it unrolled itself beneath our eyes."[14]

The Jewish press offered both a picturesque description of Utah's transformed lands and a moral evaluation of the success of the colonization. The following description which makes no reference at all to the life of the Utah Jewish community gave a visually graphic picture:

> "Salt Lake City (Special to the Independent Hebrew)— Salt Lake City is located in a beautiful valley or basin, on a dead level, surrounded on three sides by high ranges of mountains, on the other bordered by the lake. It is laid out in regular squares with streets eight rodes wide, each square an area of ten acres. The streets are lined with cottonwood and locust trees, giving abundance of shade and beautiful foliage. The locust trees are now in full blossom, the fragrance from which perfumes the whole city. It is a very garden of Eden in the luxuriousness of the production of fruits and flowers. Apricots, nectarines, cherries, peaches, apples and pears are produced in great abundance. At this time the apricot trees are loaded with the young fruit which has already attained the size of pigeon eggs, cherries are more than half their full size,

and apples and pears give equal promise, though the fruit is somewhat smaller. All vegetation is somewhat ahead of Connecticut. No doubt this extraordinary fertility is owing in great measure to the system of irrigation which has been so successfully instituted. The early settlers saw that the long periods of drouth would cut all their crops, and without some artificial means of irrigation they must starve. The mountain streams were dammed and diverted from their accustomed channels and today on each side of every street there is a running rivulet, which in time of need supplies every yard and garden in the city, which makes what would otherwide be a desert 'to bloom like the rose.' The water is also used for drinking purposes, and there is none better . . ."[15]

A leading Jewish personality of the time, Dr. Lilienthal, paid tribute to the physical landscape and then evaluated the transformation as the moral achievement of Mormon Society:

". . . But all this monotony passes away as if by a magic wand as soon as you enter Utah. The Mormons, guided by Brigham Young, have changed this wilderness into a Paradise.

"We had made up our mind to go to Salt Lake City instead of continuing our journey on the Central Pacific Railroad to San Francisco. And we shall never regret this trip. How beautiful is the Salt Lake! how splendidly cultivated the land all along the road! One seems to be in Belgium, where neat, clean houses greet you from all sides, where the husbandman works on his fine fields, where orchards and blooming gardens adorn the neighborhood of the farmer's house.

"I will not dilate on all we have seen in the country and the city. I will only mention that we visited Brigham Young, the Tabernacle, that mighty and splendid building in which 15,000 people can congregate, the Zion's Cooperative Institute, the Mormon's store, larger than any in the West and the Pacific Coast, the theater, the baths, the museum and so on. Think what you may of Brigham Young and his queer doctrines of polygamy, but he is a mighty organizer, and one of the remarkable men of the age. . . .

"We had witnessed another striking proof of the adage, 'union is strength.' No matter what we may think of Brigham Young and his polygamy, he has changed the sagebrush wilderness into a paradise; the people under his administration have been taught to work and to prosper by their labors; they live under the principle that they must produce what they consume, and idlers, drones, and loafers are banished from the State, at least so far as the Mormons themselves are concerned."[16]

All this was even more impressive when addressed to the Jewish youth in America as a moral instruction by a Jewish juvenile journal. It was presented as an imaginary talk with Brigham Young:

". . . you made laws by which idleness is considered a crime and thus obeisance to paternal laws is the rule, and it has been vouchsafed to you to enjoy the fruit of your labors, and may for many a year yet a kind Providence watch over you! . . ."

And to lead this youth to a correct judgment, the following was added:

"Let Mormonism be right or wrong, they have made the law in their territory that idleness is a crime, and beggary is therefore unknown. We must not teach our Indians bad infernal whiskey drinking. . . ."[17]

Several such descriptions, which do not reflect on general political or special Jewish conditions in America, are to be found in the American Jewish press.[18] There is even a description of Utah mining in the mining town of Park City.[19]

The Jew-Mormon comparison imposed by world opinion and the connection in thought between Judaism as an old Biblical system and Mormonism was often expressed in public in America. It evoked a feeling among the Jews that a self-evaluation of Judaism as against Mormonism was required. Jews the world over seemed to accept the fact that Mormonism was concerned with a phenomenon of extraordinary importance in religious and contemporary history, as evidenced by the following article from the London Jewish Chronicle, reprinted in America:

". . . We know that singular sects, like the Shakers and the Armenian brethren established their communities. And perhaps the most singular religionist that our age or any age in modern history has ever witnessed—the Mormons or Latter Day Saints—have consolidated their power and obtained not only a standpoint but even a citadel, for their community in which they can practice their eccentric observances and promulgate their monstrous doctrines. . . ."[20]

Jewish self-evaluation vis-à-vis the Mormons took the position that even under equal conditions, a territorial concentration of the Jews in America should not have resulted in the same difficulties for the American government as the Mormon settlement did:

"Although the idea of Judge Noah, who promoted the establishment of a Jewish colony in America many years ago, was not practically successful, still we think that under suitable organization and judicious management there might be formed a State in which Jews might establish themselves with advantage to their own interests and to the country at large. The Jews are not Mormons; Jewish morality is not the morality of Utah, and we are quite certain that no Jewish state would give any trouble to the Central Government at Washington."[21]

The temptation to begin such a self-evaluation with an a priori statement and to end with it was great. Such a statement could have been based on the fact that the mores of the Jews, including their monogamy, were known to the nations. Nevertheless, there were enough representatives of spiritual Jewish life in America who wanted to see with their own eyes the actual living difference between Jew and Mormon. The outcome of such investigations was printed in Jewish newspapers in various forms from factual reports and commentary on them to apparently complacent, systematic, theological condemnation of the whole Mormon system.

The following conventional newspaper interview with a Mormon by a correspondent in Salt Lake City is informative in every respect in that it expressed the essential opinions of the simple Mormon people:

". . . I told him I should be pleased to hear his opinion

on that subject, that I looked upon polygamy as a remnant
of Eastern customs, the Christian boast of bettering the condition of woman was untenable that monogamy was a Western custom, and though divorces were as easy as in Indiana,
no more than one wife was allowed in Rome a thousand years
before there ever was heard the name of Christianity, and
that this improvement on Jewish civilization, like all Roman
improvement, had acted unfairly, bettering some, but degrad-
ing many. 'Yes, answered he, stopping me short, 'only I think
of the misery and degradation of so many thousands of women
in New York and Boston, think of the curses which monogamy
has entailed upon humanity, to go down to unborn generations, and tell me if polygamy is all wrong. I have been a
monogamist and a polygamist, I know both systems well, and
I know polygamy is the better. Our wives have every confidence in us, and are never jealous.' I could not help thinking, though I did not say so, little room for jealousy, if you
can bring each 'flame' home as soon as 'kindled.' I asked him
if he remembered the denunciation of old, 'Your king will
multiply to himself many wives,' and if there was not danger
of rich men doing the same in modern times. 'No,' he answered, 'we must be virtuous, we must overcome our evil pro-
pensities, we must fear God.' I told him that where men acted
like that, all things would be right; but it was the abuse in
most systems where the danger lies. He said, 'You talk like all
people from the outside world; but here we are different; we
do not act as they do.' He went on to say that he never took
a new wife without feeling a deep responsibility, and that he
was undertaking a difficult and onerous task, but it was his
duty, and he did it. 'Why,' said he, 'are we the only
polygamists? Congressman —— was here some time ago, and,
after he went home, poured out on us the vilest abuse, and I
know that that man has more wives than I have, the only difference being, all my wives take my name, and I acknowledge
all my children, which he does not.' He further told me, that
the wives generally live separate from each other, 'though
some men,' he sneeringly remarked, 'kept all their wives in
one house.' He asked me if they looked like a debauched peo-

305

ple. I answered, if he was a fair sample, they certainly did not. I was going on to offer some further objections, when he told me that God had expressly commanded them to practice polygamy, and they had no choice but to obey. This, of course, stopped further argument on that subject.

"We next turned to politics; he told me that the last election had been an exciting one, that the apostates had joined the gentiles and nominated a ticket, but they had polled but a few votes. I did not wonder at that when he informed me of their manner of voting, every ticket being numbered, tantamount to open voting. I think this is a matter in which Congress should legislate; in no country can there be so much need of secret voting. I remarked to Mr. Groo that I was disappointed in seeing bar-rooms. 'Yes,' he said, 'I suppose so, but we have so many gentiles here now, that we find we can regulate the sale of liquors better by licenses than by prohibition.' I parted from him with many sincere thanks for his kindness and condescension to an unknown and travel-stained wayfarer.

"As I turned from the doors of the City Hall, I pondered at the mystery of such a man believing in such a religion. He was too enthusiastic for me to think him insincere, he was too intelligent for me to believe him a dupe, but when I remember what religious fanaticism has sometimes done, I no longer wonder that even Mormonism finds a votary in Isaac Groo. I was afterwards informed that Mr. Groo was a bishop as well as alderman, and the husband of four wives."[22]

The same correspondent was fortunate enough to receive information also at the highest levels of Mormon leadership. In a talk with Brigham Young immediately following his interview with the plain people, he learned something about the religious convictions of the Mormon leader:

"A conversation then ensued between Mr. Young and the Western man about the second coming of Christ; the Western man seemed in doubt, and Mr. Young told him he was not posted, and then slyly glancing at me, said: 'Here is a gentleman, who does not believe he has come once.' This so astounded the Indianian that it fortunately closed his mouth, and I had an opportunity to talk to Mr. Young. We first conversed about the size of the tabernacle and Westminster Hall, and then I asked if the Mormon church believed in universal salvation. He answered, 'All can be saved,' but he put such a stress on the word 'can' that I presumed him to mean that the great majority would undoubtedly be damned. I understood Mr. Young to say that this earth was to be the future Paradise. I asked him if it would hold all. 'Yes,' he said, 'there will be room enough.' 'Room enough,' I observed: 'no doubt there will if the doctrine of many churches be correct.' To this he made no response. . . . He next asked me where I was staying, and when I told him at the Revere House, such a shade of displeasure passed over his face that I presumed he thought my staying at a gentile house evinced unfriendliness to the Mormons, so I explained that my staying there was the effect of a chance that, at the depot, I had stepped into the first carriage that offered."[23]

But there were also investigators who were anxious to supplement word of mouth with printed material which would give a dependable picture of the Mormon way of life:

"The catechism in use among the Mormons of Utah has the following queries and answers: Q. What does the first paragraph of verse of this Word of Wisdom teach us? A. That it is not good to drink wine or strong drinks excepting in the sacrament of the Lord's Supper, and that it should be home-made grape wine; that it is not good to drink hot drinks, or chew or smoke tobacco; that strong drinks are for the washing of the body, and that tobacco is a herb for bruises and sick cattle. Q. Why is it not good to drink wine or strong drink. A. Because they excite men unnaturally, inflame their stomachs, vitiate their appetites, and disorder their whole systems. Q. Why are not hot drinks good for man? A. Because they relax and weaken the stomach and indeed the whole body. Q. Why is it not good to smoke or chew tobacco? A. Because these habits are very filthy, and tobacco is of poisonous nature, and the use of it debases men. If such doctrines do not make angels of the Mormon youth, it will be no fault of the Latter Day Saints."[24]

Some visitors to Salt Lake City rounded out their observation by reading. In some cases they arrived at on the spot conclusive judgments about everything: Life and teachings of the Mormons and especially the elements in Mormonism that were in their opinion Jewish. Isaac M. Wise was one of these:

' I spent my Sabbath in this Zion of the Mormons, bought a Mormon catechism and studied that last feature of human observation. We all know that all follies are committed by man, hence we ought not to be surprised by any. Yet we are. It is with folly as with women's fashions. It is all a change in the arrangement, the material remains the same. Mormonism is Protestantism with the hierarchy of Catholicism and a portion of the ancient Levitical laws fantastically mixed. The colors, artificial flowers, ribbons, etc., are differently arranged. In principle there is certainly no difference between faith in Peter and Paul, or in Mr. Smith and Mr. Young, and obedience to the Pope or to Brigham Young. It is a new edition of the old thing. . . .

"Mormonism is a social-political religious organization on a small scale, as popery was in the Middle Ages on a large scale. The Mormon must believe that Brigham Young is a veritable prophet, and his aids are all divinely inspired. Consequently his will is law and his command is God's command. Some Mormons actually believe Brigham Young after his death will be a god, as they believe in a plurality of deities. There the danger lies. It is all one man's will. This one man is almighty and infallible. A good many men are better than their religion; so it is also among the Mormons. They are not half as bad as they might be under their religion. There are a good many good men and women among them, although most of them are bigoted, deluded and ignorant. They have no free schools, and want none. They learn little and believe much. They need little and work much. They are a sort of simple pastoral people, who verily believe themselves to be chosen ones of God and the heirs of the civilized world, the saints. There is less spiritual than materialistic life among the leaders. There is a million in it. The Mormon pays a tithe of everything and the leaders take and distribute it among themselves. The Mormon pays more besides his tithes than any other class of people and the leaders are responsible to none. There is a good deal of money and bigotry involved in the Mormon question."[25]

In a later report he discussed the contrast between the Mormon attitude to marriage and the Biblical conception:

". . . I met all sorts of Jews. Two of them have turned Mormons, one living in Salt Lake City gave three of his daughters in marriage to a brother Jew Mormon in the country, who, according to the laws of Moses, ought to be burned together with his three wives."[26]

A travel report years afterward commented on the manner in which the church-tax was borne by the Mormon people:

"Tithing House. . . . But while the poor give ungrudgingly one-tenth of their entire income, the wealthy limit their obligation to their net revenue, and as no one questions their arithmetic the amount is generally insignificant."[27]

This criticism of the rich in the church was followed by a general criticism of the riches collected in religious societies, a point on which the Mormons stood on a part with other religious communities, including the Jews:

". . . If the Mormon Church is growing rich, and, in view of the law that inhibits a religious corporation from owning more than so many thousands of property, subdivides itself into a score or more of branches, each duly incorporated and each owning less than the maximum limit—can wealthy members of Trinity Church, St. Patrick's Cathedral, or Temple Emanuel complain."[27]

The same correspondent furthermore compared the religious enthusiasm of the Mormons and other denominations with the relatively lax religious and educational practices of the Jews in Utah:

". . . the one lonely synagogue that is only opened twice a year when the spirit moves the fifty Hebrew families to do their duty religiously. . . . The schools are now sectarian, every church has its school-house in which the elements of secular education are taught with such coloring as the clergyman or his aids impart—all but the fifty Hebrew families, who seem so engrossed in business affairs as to care little for the moral and religious training of their children, and are satisfied to leave them to the ministrations of Catholics and Episcopalians."[27]

No matter how many half-truths, superficialities, inaccuracies or even outright mistakes might have been included in all these descriptions they contained one common element of truth. They all expressed a genuine interest and attempted to obtain a coherent image of the new community of faith. They made an effort to discover the relationship of this faith to the general values of American life and to Judaism and the life of the Jewish community in America. Therefore it may not come as a surprise that the overwhelming majority of contemporary American Jewish opinion rejected precisely that position of the Jew in Mormon creed and doctrine which proposed the gathering-in of the Jews to Palestine. The polemics of the Jewish press against this point was particularly sharp. The Mormons were instructed concerning the extraordinary situation of the American Jews and their sensitivity on this point was explained. In addition these responses to the Mormons expressed the Jewish attitude to all the unsolicited current theological speculations about the Jews:

"The Mormon Prophet, Barnet Moses Giles, in behalf of the Prophet Joseph Smith, addresses a harangue of seventy inches closely printed nonpareil type to this unbelieving world concerning the restoration of Israel to Palestine by Indian hunters. The idea is certainly odd enough for any sensational sheet. He wants first the Jews converted to Mormonism, and then his prophecy is to be fulfilled. It is strange that all the American prophets, saints, missionaries, tract peddlers, revival preachers, the whole host of heaven's voluntary police force on this continent have their chief troubles about the Jews, who do not interfere with any of them, and are quite willing to let them go to heaven in their own way. Why do they not get up some scheme, prophecy, some *modus operandi*, to convert the politicians to tell the truth and the party organs to publish it? Why not take care of all the gamblers, prostitutes, ruffians, confidence men, swindlers, liars, hypocrites and impostors, who evade the law and dodge the police? Why do they not make the attempt to feed the hungry, to house the stranger, to give raiment and fuel to the needy? Why do they go by the indigent widow and orphan, and stop before the door of the Jew, who tells them a thousand times we have no need of you? The Jews will not go to Palestine, that is settled. There is no such a thing as the lost ten tribes of Israel, that is also settled. The world is not going backward, hence the Jew cannot go back to Christianity or Mormonism, both of which are dead in philosophy, science and common sense. What do they want of us? If the Holy Ghost can do no better than craze such prophets, he is done for; and if St. Peter and Joseph Smith can find no better agents to do their business they better close up the shop."[28]

The same right to be left unmolested also had to be conceded to the Mormons, and in that connection the following conjecture was made:

"If the Latter Day Saints be left alone, schism will continue to pour in thousands of strangers, Mormon young ladies will continue to 'clear out' with gentile gentlemen, and when the leaders have gone to their graves, the whole system will languish, and, in a few years, Mormonism will be a thing of the past, and the surviving twin relict of barbarism will join his defunct brother in the bourne whence no traveller returns."[29]

The problem of religious freedom entangled in the political fight against Mormon polygamy was given space in the Jewish press which presented an honest exposition of the Mormon viewpoint.[30] In this, to be sure, the danger of the political consequences of religious bigotry for American Jews was not overlooked:

"You appear to be shocked that in what you call a Christian country like this, an Israelite should be permitted to pray at the opening of Congress. . . . You dread the Mormons coming; but he has been there already; he has sat, at least, and spoken in Congress, and if he be invited to pray perhaps it will be found that this, too, would do no injury to any one. It is, after all, the boast of America that all his inhabitants are equal, that no one has a superior legal claim; . . ."[31]

One special kind of report in the Jewish press referred to an alleged meeting with the wandering Jew in Utah:

> "*Salt Lake City*—The *Deseret News* brings the astounding information that '*Ahasverus, the wandering Jew*' in his wanderings all over the globe, has by the way of Siberia and the Behrings strait, arrived on the American continent. Michael O'Grady, a farmer, who received him hospitably, obtained from him as a mark of gratitude an old folio volume bound in hogskin, containing extracts from the Babylonian Talmud, and a testimonial that the former owner was the veritable Ahasverus—not a Polish Jew, as surmised by one."[32]

Even before the political phase of the fight against polygamy had begun in 1870, the Biblical argument used by the Mormons in its support "which even preaches polygamy as the fulfillment of a divine commandment"[33] was also opposed in the Jewish press of Europe. The hotter this political fight became the more outspoken was the Jewish press in America about this point. It treated it entirely apart from the political argument of the time, purely as a matter of opinion about the right interpretation of the Bible and its times. However this did not obviate the fact that the same press was also to a certain extent a participant in this political fight. The struggle to find the true meaning of the old Bible was strengthened by demonstrating the old monogamic tradition of the Jew which, so the argument went, made the Jews themselves immune to Mormonism:

> "At a recent Methodist meeting, wherein the mission among the Mormons was under discussion, a speaker declared that the Mormons were of all creeds and nationalities except two—he had never seen an Irish or a Jew Mormon. We cannot vouch for the truth of this statement as to the Irish, but we are willing to stake our veracity as to the rest of the speaker's statement. There are Jews living in Utah, but they are all Gentiles. Jews understand too well the value of good

wives to attempt to improve on the monogamic system that
bears the approval of centuries. Solomon was a great Mormon
in one respect; but, with all their appreciation of his wisdom,
his people never credited him with any remarkable sense for
his passion for wives innumerable, and he has never been
held up as an example of domestic virtue, a model of a husband. True marital happiness can only be found in one wife;
and, as we Jews are strongly domestic in our tastes, we want
to preserve peace in our homes, and rear children who shall
always think of their parents with deep regard, and this cannot be said of a Mormon household."[34]

But if the above dealt only with Jewish tradition combined
with the psychological facts of Jewish life, there was also another
view of polygamy based on historical analysis and a deep penetrating knowledge of the Bible. Ultimately, such an analysis could be
decisive for Jewry as a spiritual entity:

"In his sermon on Saturday at the Lloyd Street synagogue,
Rev. Maurice Fluegel spoke of Mormonism. He said that in
his recent Thanksgiving Sermon Rev. Henry Ward Beecher
had said that 'Mormonism was the literal acceptance of the
Old Testament. Who believed in the inspiration of the Bible
could fling no stones at Mormonism. It had polygamy. So
did all the saints. Mormonism was the reintroduction of
Mosaic institutions.' Mr. Fluegel showed that polygamy was
a deep-rooted institution from hoary antiquity, which the
Bible could not help tolerating, but did not teach. No, it
stigmatized it. The actual doctrine of the Pentateuch is clearly
and distinctly monogamy. In Genesis II we read that 'God
created but one wife for Adam. She is part of himself. She
is to work and to rule conjointly with him.' Concluding with:
'Therefore shall man leave father and mother and cling to
his wife and form but one person.' Mr. Fluegel showed furthermore that the Patriarchs originally married only one wife,
but the barbarous pride and pomp of the times forced polygamy upon them. So it was with Hagar and Sarah, so with
Lea and Rachel, so with David and Solomon. The consequences were direful. The Bible takes everywhere great

care to show polygamy with its baneful hydra-head and its thousands ills and misfortunes. At the rise of Christianity monogamy was the firmly-established rule in Palestine. There woman was highly respected. She was the first in the household. The Bible gave woman her honorable position. 'Whoever wronged his wife, makes the altar shed tears over it,' is a rabbinical saying. 'A poor father selling his minor daughter, her master shall marry or free her. A warrior bringing home a fair captive has but the same choice.' Divorce is allowed but for immoral behavior. Explicitly or implicitly the Bible takes great care to show the baleful results of polygamy, and teaches monogamy as the only rule of God and nature."[35]

To what extent Jewish learned circles regarded the Mormon concept of marriage as a caricature of the genuine Biblical approach may be seen from the tendency to characterize any seemingly disparaging treatment of the Jewish marital law as "Mormon." This was the case in a literary controversy with Rabbi Isaac M. Wise's practice of sanctioning certain marriages which were regarded by other rabbis as contrary to Jewish law. A literary satire called "An Address on Polygamy" transferred horrors perpetrated by "Rev. Dr. T. M. Smart" to the Utah scene. "Such were the events of that day in Salt Lake City."[36] These sensational events put together in a "Mormon Story" were given even more extensive coverage by the European Jewish press, which gave its own commentary on the American scene:

"In order to mock the practice of Dr. Wise, his sermons and marriage ceremonies and to condemn his writings and conduct, whose only goal is humbug and making money, the Jewish Times invented a story from Salt Lake City (the Mormon city!). In this story a Rabbi Dr. Smart, meaning 'artful dodger' (Schlaukopf) has in a single day sanctioned the following marriages: 1) a man with a second wife—bigamy, 2) a man with the widow of his uncle, 3) a brother-in-law with his sister-in-law and afterwards forced a man to give a Haliza. The speeches and Biblical quotations of Dr. Smart are cited according to their contents and the dollars earned and bottles of wine drunk with the choir boys during the intermissions in these functions are enumerated."[37] (Significantly a case like No. 2 appears in Mormon literature on the advice of

314

Brigham Young who quoted the Mosaic institution of Haliza to Franklin D. Richards in 1854.)[38]

Finally the literary quarrels reached a point at which participants proposed to transfer the whole scene to Utah should arguments no longer be of any use:

"Then there is nothing left but the proposal to unite with the Mormons. In their country the *Cherem of Rabenu Gerschom* (the rabbinical ban on polygamy) doesn't exist . . . and people who believe in the Book of Mormon will easily understand which day of the week is the right, unfalsified Sabbath of the logs vulgo of the decalogue. There also is an employment for prophets . . . Therefore, on! l'schanah haba l'Utah Territory-" (The coming year in Utah Territory!)[39]

At all times the thought of free immigration to America remained the key to understanding the attitude of the Jewish press to the political question of Mormonism, directly or indirectly. Therefore the infrequent descriptions of Mormon immigration in the American Jewish press are of special importance to us. The fact that the emigration of Mormon converts from Europe represented the only privately organized successful group-emigration during the period of the "old immigration" was clearly recognized in the following detailed description (1872):

". . . Six hundred Mormon converts, single men and women, were landed at this port during the week. They were composed of English from the mining districts, Welsh from the mountains, and Germans from the Rhine Valley. In appearance, writes a contemporary, they are a seedy, ignorant lot. The men have evidently been chosen with a view to the development of the mining resources of Utah or for the defense of the place, and the women to become the help-meets of the men and mothers of future generations of Mormons. The men were mostly large, powerful fellows, with brawny bodies, and coarse, unintelligent features, just the men to embrace the faith of the Latter Day Saints, and maintain it against all opposition, whether it came in the shape of reasoning or physical force. The women were nearly all under twentyfive, and had evidently been selected by some aged saint who had an eye for souls in fresh, young bodies.

315

There was a noticeable lack of the gaunt, elderly females who are supposed to form the staple for conversion, and this fact, it is said, was frequently remarked during the voyage. That considerable foresight had been displayed in the gathering of the 200 men and 300 young women is evidenced by the fact that during the voyage no sickness occurred, though of course the ship's officers contributed to the happy result. The men did not care to speak of the faith they had embraced, and when a coy maiden was asked if she knew that she was liable to be the consort of a man with a dozen other wives, she maintained her modesty in the diplomatic reply: 'It's na propper to ax me, an I shall na tell ye.' She was a blushing girl of twenty-one, and there being some anxiety to know how these young females reconciled purity with polygamy, the question was pressed: 'You would surely rather be the one wife of a man in your own country?' 'I'm me ain mistress, an it's nobody's beesness.' The reply was discouragingly independent. and, moreover, as the Mormon girl moved away a knot of her brawny countrymen had gathered with lowering looks, and prudence counselled silence. It was evident that they had all been cautioned against intruders before the arrival in New York, in order that they might not be ashamed of their new-found faith or disenchanted with their promised land. They all seemed to know that there was something awkward in the condition they were about to bring upon themselves, and were disinclined to speak of it."[40]

Even in the Eighteen-eighties, the decade of horror for the Mormons—at the time of the new immigration of Eastern European Jews, such a description of a group of Mormon immigrants appeared. It was written as part of the political fight to the finish to liquidate polygamy in Utah. It was, furthermore, influenced by the generally held conviction, supported by America's diplomacy, that by stopping Mormon immigration the peculiar marriage-system in Utah could be destroyed:

"The latest batch of Mormon-emigrants from abroad— five hundred in number—again calls attention to the deplorable fact that America continues to be made the dumping-

316

ground for Europe's least desirable population, who are 'sent on to the next parish,' across the Atlantic."[41]

Occasionally reports of these diplomatic steps by the American government appear:

"The Mormon question. The active measures taken by this pseudo-religious people to propagate their peculiar practices, one of which is in direct contravention of the law of the United States, have been for years the subject of diplomatic action.

"The Salt Lake people are continually sending elders of their church abroad to entice foreigners into the field of polygamy. The fields of their work have been closely watched by our foreign agents. . . ."[42]

The Jewish press like the general American press stressed the fact that in addition to stopping new Mormon immigrants, measures had to be devised to carry out American law in Utah:

"Undoubtedly the intentions of the Government are good in discouraging the increase of Mormonism through immigration, and the great majority of editors will applaud Mr. Evart's circular to the various powers in treaty with Washington. But does no one trace any similarity, however slight, between the Secretary's action and the attempted Chinese proscription of the last Congress? There would be no question as to the duty of the Government did it rigidly enforce the laws as to polygamy; but we quietly sanction the rites and usages of the Mormons in a Territory under the direct control of Congress and the Executive, and see a prosperous community growing in our midst openly defying all efforts to suppress what is universally deemed by the non-Mormons as an iniquity, and our Secretary would forbid foreigners to approach our shores if their expressed intention is to settle in Utah as members of the 'law breaking' community. If the government would direct all its powers to uproot Mormonism, it would have the support of good citizens, but the Secretary's circular is not a strong instrument for the needed work."[43]

The comparison between the Mormons and the Chinese was

later treated in a similarly thoughtless manner. No consideration was given to the fact that the attitude of Californian Jewry to the Chinese was highly objectionable to the Jews outside California.[44]

But thoughtless repetitions of slogans from the general American press were exceptions. In the responsible publication of Jewish opinion the two elements—law on the one hand and the rights of the Mormons on the other—were equally stressed:

"Mormonism and polygamy are by no means synonymous, yet most people when talking of one subject always include the other. If our government proposes to suppress the religion of the majority of the settlers in Utah and of a formidable minority in Idaho, it will soon find it to be an impossible enterprise, and the Mormons as other persecuted tribes will rally more closely than ever around their standard. This country cannot legislate for or against religion of any kind—it must protect all so long as public decency and the prescribed statutes are not violated. But polygamy is a terrible evil that the government is justified in crushing at any cost. Respectable Mormons understand the issue, and are willing to submit if their civil and religious rights that they ought to enjoy in common with other citizens are respected. Polygamy must go, but Mormonism will stay—if Congressmen adopt more of their anti-Chinese style of legislation."[45]

Other statements in the style of the time were entirely political. However, the dominant feeling was that a basic question of American society was involved, not a remote territory question:

". . . Within recent years the Mormon question has become, and in the near future it will be in a greater degree, the burning social question. We say advisedly 'social question.' The extirpation of this flagrant blot from our land, is not a religious problem; would not be religious intolerance. The question for the people of this country to decide is whether such an organized flouting of the sacredness of marriage, such a retrograde movement to barbarism, such a pestiferous plague whose baleful influence extends beyond the territory within whose borders its practice is legally confined, shall be permitted to live and grow in a country not yet entirely alienated from ethical principles."[46]

The public conscience was burdened with the peculiar institution of the Mormons in the same way as it had been with Negro slavery. Both institutions were compared with one another and a warning of consequences as grave as those of slavery had been issued:

"The campaign against the Mormons is making headway, despite the counter-arguments of Elder Cannon. The spectacle of legalized polygamy in Utah is a blot on Republican America, which, like slavery in decades past, will produce as bloody a nemesis, unless it be summarily abolished. Undoubtedly the Mormons have rights, which are to be respected with all due deference; but the moral conscience of America has too long been violated by the blustering and braggart Mormons, who are widening their influence in the Far West."[47]

Yet in the midst of all the noise of political strife, contemplation was not entirely absent. Deeper thought could not miss the point that laws alone cannot remedy the weaknesses of human societies and that the struggle against one weakness so often means the concealment of other weaknesses. In the case of the anti-polygamy battle, criticism was leveled against the Mormons, but not against the rest of a society whose morals were so doubtful that they could be preserved only by hypocrisy. A fight against all moral evils rather than against one, selected as a cover for the others not being considered, was preached by the following thoughtful voice. This spokesman tried to do full justice to the arguments of the Mormons who answered the polygamy accusation by confronting American Society with its public amorality:

"There was quite a breeze in the political world about the Anti-Mormon bill, and the clergy and laymen of the Republican creed were quite demonstrative in their denouncements of polygamy. This may be right as far as it goes for political reasons, and no moralist will say ought against the suppression of a vice which is passed off as a religious creed and which turns family life into an antiquated fable . . . But it would not be amiss to remind our devout politicians and moralists that there is a good deal of sweeping to be done before our own door in that regard, and if morality can triumph when it becomes a principle on the "platform' of a political party, let such parties try to take charge of social morality altogether. Let all husbands who betray their wives and are careless of the training of their children be disfranchised; let some punishment be devised for ladies who forget their duties. It may be that a revision of our divorce laws would be beneficial; legislation regulating the contents of 'Journals of fashion,' the conduct of the gay at balls and party-gatherings, the indulgence of wealthy young citizens, etc., may help us on the road to morality. For let it be honestly said the example of the rich sinners is by far more damaging to social morality than the excesses of the poor. . . . The Mormons, it is said, recruit their forces from the poorest and most benighted classes of the 'Gentile' world; they hold women almost in a state of slavery and by their labors they live; on their degradation they thrive. This is indeed a stain on the civilization of the time; may it be wiped out. But we can find numerous examples of this kind in civilized communities, and in churches living on the contributions of poor working men and servant maids anxious for the salvation of their souls, which only the priest can secure. Should they be ignored?"[48]

A two-faced morality as opposed to its absolute form was a problem even in America, the continent of incomplete Puritanism —and was so regarded by this moralist of the ancient Jewish people in the light of the times.

CHAPTER 23

The Jew-Mormon Relationship in American Public Opinion

The utter amazement of the American Christian world concerning the new American revealed religion risen so inopportunely was matched only by the bitterness aroused. The Christian churches were fully occupied, busy, at the time, in organizing their own communities on American soil. They regarded the new American church's claim to revelation as treason against the unified Christian civilization of Europe and as an actual frustration of their effort to give America the ultimate perfection, hereditary religion. Since every Christian denomination was liable to lose to Mormonism, in the same fashion, a united Christian front comprising all denominations grew out of this fight against the Mormons. It took time for the bitterness in which the battles were fought to dissipate into a quieter consideration of this new phenomenon. However in the background of all the rationalization about the origin and the inner meaning of the new religion there was at all times a degree of resentment against what it had done to universal Christianity. A prime element in this feeling was that of surprise that the new "monster" could have been born from the womb of Christianity. This bewilderment was expressed in a series of statements which still did not draw any direct relationship to Judaism nor any comparison with it nor any remark about the derivation of Mormonism from Judaism. At first the feeling of strangeness vis à vis this new apparition was so strong that it was considered wholly incompatible with America, and as such it could only have originated outside of this continent. In consonance with the widespread American feeling about the inferiority and backwardness of Asia and the Asiatic element, it was the simplest thing to regard Mormonism as an intellectual product of Asia:

". . . Mormonism bears on its face the impress of an Oriental rather than of a Western system."[1]

Furthermore, as a product of the bitterness engendered, the accusation of syncretism was made and used against Mormonism. According to this argument its tenets and religious notions rose out of a deliberate mixture of different religions. The circle of the religions used for this explanation included all old religions "in this gross compound of Buddhism, Brahmism, Manicheism, Judaism and Christianity, which is called Mormonism."[2] According to another opinion which specified the elements of the reprehensible syncretism, the circle of religions employed was narrower:

"This is an amalgamation of sects, denominations and superstitions. Zoroaster, Mahomet, the Christ of India and of Palestine, have done this, and Joseph Smith will do it. We predicted this long ago, and affirm it still. We predicted it when it was under deep persecution. We rested our prediction not on preternatural foresight, but on the fact that the plan covered all the ground, and combined principles and motives exactly calculated to do it. The Jewish account; the Christian religion; a revelation, latter day saints; all gifts and graces; ecclesiastical honors; an armed, peaceful neutrality, well disciplined and springing up in the midst of a free people; points taking in all our large cities and from the world a grand concentration in America . . ."[3]

Finally the circle of these religions became even more narrow and included essentially only the religions of the Near East originating in Judaism. A Christian missionary in Utah identified Mormonism as "a strange compound of Christianity, Judaism and Mohammedanism; of saintliness, sensuality and superstition: of the devout and the diabolical."[4]

It is of as deep significance for the mental state of the American Christian world as for that of the American Jew, that finally, of all the religions used to explain the origin of the phenomenon of Mormonism, only Judaism remained. This direct derivation from Judaism became identified with the continued existence of Mormonism whose destruction was at first hoped for by the Christian world. The connecting link with Christianity insofar as it

322

was still asserted, became ever looser and the connection with Judaism was stressed more and more:

> ". . . It is a mixture of Judaism and Christianity with a sprinkling of new revelations . . . There is no use in trying to discuss the religious aspects of polygamy with the Mormons unless those who venture to do so are willing to throw the Old Testament out of the court."[5]

Finally only Judaism was left as the asserted origin and basis of Mormonism according to an overwhelming majority of American opinion. It was also partly true of world opinion of this new religion's system which offered a great variety of religious thoughts to the world, and fruit for discussion by the American public.

There were still some lonely voices which pointed out a special Christian aspect in Mormonism: "It aped the system of primitive Christianity."[6] Or they saw Christianity as at least an equal dynamic element in the origin of Mormonism:

". . . nevertheless they need Judaism and Christianity, to inflate their religion with them."[7] However, the preponderance of the element of Judaism over that of Christianity was pointed out early: "That Judaizing spirit which would supersede the New Testament by the Old; which imposes Mosaic ordinances as Christian laws; . . . prepares the mind for the corresponding dogmas of Mormonism."[8]

In a word, the continuing centuries old search for Judaizers in Europe had now found its American variation. A detailed description of this predominance of Judaism over Christianity was also offered:

> "While, however, Salt Lake may with propriety be deemed a city founded on a religious creed, it is based more upon the Old Testament ideas and formulas than upon the New. The Master, whose kingdom was not of this world, but in the inmost hearts of men, here gives place, and Moses comes forth as the interpreter of the will of God. As in the days of the Hebraic theocracy, religion permeates and governs in all the concerns of life. Nothing is above its dictation—nothing too trivial for its watchful care. The laws of Moses were far more minute, both as regards questions of morals

and matters of commercial law and the every-day affairs of life, than the statutes of any of our States; and all this legislation was a portion of the Jewish religious faith."[9]

According to one statement Mormon religion was "Judaic rather than Christian" and was "much like the Pharisee's prayer . . ."[10] This led directly to the traditional concept of Christians about Jewish conditions of old.

Where the kingdom, "not of this world," is opposed by a dominion on earth it might, according to American public opinion, not be the democratic system of America: "The Mormon polity claims to be theocratic, i.e., as was the old Jewish government, and is, therefore, in its very nature, opposed to democracy."[11] The Mormons had to meet this accusation early by asserting that they had succeeded in creating a synthesis between the two systems.[12] But their enemies saw only theocracy in their faith which, they said, was basic to the whole theology:

"He stated that 'Mormonism was a theocracy which incorporated the features and the forms of the Jehovah theology of Moses.' This included a dictated and controlled system of tithing and various ceremonies in the temple. . . ."[13]

But even when there was no inimical intent but simply an exploration of the true motivations of the religious life of the Mormons, the same picture was presented: A people directly led by God referring expressly to ancient Israel led by God to prove that this was possible:

"Deriving their rules of action from sources believed to be directly inspired by the Almighty, they justified themselves by the example of the Israelites and respected no laws —natural, social, or municipal—which came in conflict with these heavenly commands."[14]

From the general statement that a revived Jewish theocracy was here involved, a special study of the form of religious organization extant in Mormonism developed. It reached the unavoidable conclusion that here as in Bible times an old Jewish priesthood was involved:

"From this glance at the outward form of the Mormon

Church, it will be seen that in its organization it is an attempt to reproduce, in part, the form of the Jewish Church, as, in its general spirit and practices it seeks to revive many of the ideas and customs of Judaism."[15]

Even European opinion, far from the American background of Mormonism, assumed that this example of Judaizing in the new world, was extraordinary:

"Nowhere is the parallel with the foundation of Judaism drawn so clearly—and so intentionally. By combining spiritually related masses into one religious mixture perhaps *at no time* was so much intention and so much reflection on historical cases of precedence at play."[16]

What meaning this assumed transformation of Mosaism into Mormonism might have within the frame of a rising American culture and material civilization was a hotly debated subject of the day. Rough voices talked of "The Mormon Monsters . . . On the shores of Salt Lake—in that city, so suggestive of Sodom and Gomorrha, with the Dead Sea by their side—"[17] without seeking any further relationship to religious developments in the country or to the colonizing success of the Mormons. But other voices tried to evaluate all this and to deal justly with this new society held together by firm spiritual bonds in newly settled areas. Nevertheless, even they saw certain dangers for all America from such a transformation from Judaism:

"We look with astonishment at the progress of this wonderful people. Transplanting the institutions of the mystic East into the practical and active West, reviving the old Hebrew theocracy among the backwoodsmen of the Mississippi, uniting the voluptuous sensuality of the Oriental harem with the stern virtue and far-seeing shrewdness of the American republican, these, we confess, are anomalies of which we cannot determine the result. Shall our boasted institutions be overturned from an obscure quarter, whence we now dread no harm? Shall we witness the rise of a new system of religion more energetic than Islam, and more potent than Rome, spreading through our Western continent, . . . introducing theocracy in place of republicanism, and polygamy in place of marriage."[18]

It may have entered the mind of more than one American

325

that his personal freedom of movement in the Far West might be hampered by colonizing decisions of the Mormon leadership. For instance a resident of St. Thomas, a Mormon settlement given up by the Mormon leadership when it became part of Nevada, wrote:

> "I must come to Los Angeles, and seek a chance there or in San Diego county (the best grape climate known to me) a place where I can make another home, such as shall be secure from the rule of a nomadic Judaism and its blighting influence upon all energies, from which no priestly edict may at any moment send me forth, a homeless wanderer upon the desert earth . . ."[19]

The way chosen by the letter-writer pointed only in one direction—voluntary flight before the Mosaism assumed to have been revived in Mormonism. In contradistinction to such an individual decision there were innumerable other possibilities: i.e., rather to force the revived "monster" into flight than to turn the back to it.

It was left to the German American "New Yorker Demokrat," a voice from an immigrant group in which political persecution had played a more important role than religious, to express a naive opinion about how America could be freed from Mormonism, one of its most characteristic phenomena. When at the time of the second Mormon mission to Palestine there were rumors that this was a preparation for a Mormon emigration there, this paper saw it as the only meaningful solution for the continuing existence of this group:

> "One has to wish sincerely that this plan may ripen and succeed to be executed. On the side of the Mormons there would hardly arise any difficulty because the prudent Prophet has certainly not neglected to demonstrate the plan as a direct divine revelation to his faithful. One may be tempted to consider the plan divine because it cannot be neglected that if there is any inhabited spot on earth where the Mormon could fit in and belong it is this old homeland of the Israelites. This is meant not jokingly but in earnest because persons more closely acquainted with Mormonism assure us that its main thoughts and forms are nothing but an attempt to revive old Jewish theocracy. In all parts of the earth dominated by Christianity, Mormonism must remain a hysteron proteron. Even in this country that should be based on the most

unconditional religious toleration it has proved itself as an anomaly incompatible with the general folk-spirit.

Its real origin is in Asia, the very ancient homeland of the positive revelations, of theocracies and realms of priests. Even in our days, Asia is the cradle of polygamy, which even in our country of personal independence and freedom of faith made this innocent sect into an unassimilable element, a "state in the state" which cannot be tolerated. If Mormonism really carries in it the seed of longer life it can clearly find a fruitful soil for its growth only in Asia. That grave injustice was done to this sect as a whole as well as its individual adherents in this free and tolerant country and that the sect was several times the victim of unjustifiable violence cannot be denied. Now because it is simply impossible for such injustice to be repeated, the complete removal of a continuing source of fanaticism and the lust to persecute, would be a highly welcome event in the interest of the honor of the American nation. What the Mormons desire to do could also be done by Persian and Rumanian Jews. They could go to Palestine and labor there or, supported by European capital, engage in commerce or in crafts." To this the German Jewish newspaper, which brought this American editorial opinion to the attention of their European readers hurriedly stated for the Jews: "They would rather go to America, they are not the ferment of demoralization which the Mormons rather seem to be to us, and America's *free* earth offers more guarantees for the development of the Jews and of Judaism than the genuine orientally emasculated Turkish Palestine."[20]

No matter how much agreement there was in American public opinion that Mormonism was a transformation of Judaism, there was disagreement as to exactly what were the Judaistic features of the Mormon system. Furthermore there was no uniform opinion about the specific American situation which had brought about the adaptation of a specific feature believed to be Judaistic. According to one opinion the Mormons had been very much impressed by the Biblical Sabbath:

"In their ambition to reproduce ancient Judaism (and this ambition is the key to their whole puzzle) the Mormons are Sabbatarians of a strictness which would delight Lord Shaftesbury. Accordingly, in order that their festivities might not encroach on

327

the early hours of the Sabbath, they had the hall on Fourth of July eve, instead of the night of the Fourth."[21]

But this referred only to formal solemnity in observing the Sabbath rest. The thought of holding the seventh day of the week holy appeared only later in certain groups which split from the main church.[22]

Others spoke for the close resemblance between the organization of the Mormon priestly orders with the old Biblical idea of priesthood, and even saw them as an aid to gaining Jewish converts:

> "The 'Aaronic' division of the priesthood comprises Bishops, Priests, Teachers, and Deacons. It seems to have been devised for the purpose of infusing a Jewish element into the new church, and to make provision for such Jewish Priests and Rabbis as should be converted to the Mormon faith; for the Bishops belonging to this branch of the priesthood must be literal descendants of Aaron."[23]

In view of the position the Jew holds in Mormon creed and doctrine, this theory was especially wrong.

Consequently all attempts to explain Mormon receptiveness to an assumed Judaism remained rather general and vague: According to another theory, the general glorification of Judaism in Western culture had brought this about:

> "Judaism has been praised, honored, imitated, kept alive in the Christian teaching of the age, until it has at last found disciples to reconstruct it as a living institution."[24]

But in the end, it was asserted, it had been the idea of the "Chosen People" which evoked Mormonism and made it so strong that there was no danger from syncretism:

> ". . . their creed embraces features belonging to almost every religion. Mormonism is the antithesis of Judaism in this respect. Its alien elements, however, are cemented together by the institution of polygamy, which renders them more like one another than any one of them is like the surrounding elements of American civilization. The Jews were polygamists for economic and sociologic reasons quite in

328

keeping with the evolutionary exigencies of their early days. The Mormons, of course, justify polygamy among themselves on the ground that it was practiced by the 'favorites' of Jehovah. But, evolutionary conditions having changed, the economic and other reasons of the Jews no longer exist. The Jews themselves are not now polygamists. A people in the midst of a progressive Western civilization, deliberately committing itself to a reactionary doctrine like that of 'plural marriage,' must have done so with the distinct purpose to 'come out and be separate.' No other barrier could have been half so complete or permanent."[25]

Indeed, everything is included here: the "peculiar people," which introduced its "peculiar institution" only to be different from other peoples and equal to the old "peculiar" Jewish people in its chosenness, hoping to maintain its extraordinary position by means of polygamy. In any case it was not stated that the chosenness of ancient Israel had been based on polygamy—which was widespread among their neighbors.

American observers had their own, highly individual reactions to seeing Jew and Mormon side by side, as shown in this 1871 description of Salt Lake City:

"I saw in the court a Jew, lineal descendant of the old Patriarchs whom these Mormons like to exemplify. His dark, shining eyes, aquiline beak, and wavy coarseness of hair made a strong contrast with those Saxon and Scandinavian races, fair-haired and highly colored around him. He had marched down through two thousand years of wandering to accord with the century and Europe. And these Europeans had marched back six thousands years to resume the civilization the Jew had abandoned. What a feast for skepticism is this."[26]

In the course of time, the real differences between the two living communities of Jew and Mormon in America made an impression upon the mind of the American public. This difference was considered in keeping with the peaceful co-existence of various religious denominations in America:

". . . We permit Judaism, we have even allowed Buddhism to raise its unclean temple at San Francisco; but as we say, to tolerate

329

a minority is one thing—to allow a small and insignificant local minority to affect the manners and morals of a whole nation is a very different matter. . . ."[27]

The clarification of the Jewish view of its own past, which was a reaction to the Biblical argument of polygamy and was actually encouraged by it, had already borne fruit. Because of it, the Jewish community of faith stood straight and strong before the eyes of the American public:

> "A few years ago the Jewish Church in this country would have been classed with the Quakers, or the Moravians, with the sects that are falling away from their former integrity and strength, or perhaps with such imposture as the Mormon sect. Now, it stands fairly with the leading denominations of Christians, in the attention given to its utterances, to its festivals, and to its progress in art and knowledge."[28]

Looking back at history there can be no deeper significance for the Biblical ideas of Israel of old, than the fact that one single misinterpretation of it could throw a new religious community into conflict with the whole world. On the other hand the discarding of this concept could bring peace and dignity to this community. Indeed, discarding an unreal conception of the marriage system of the ancient Jews actually opened the way for many fruitful Biblical ideas to become an effective part of Mormon creed and community.

330

Conclusions

Group relations of American Jews developed with immigrant peoples as well as with groups newly formed on native soil. With the Germans it was largely a continuation of a cultural milieu that had already existed in Europe, with the Irish, another immigrant people, situations peculiar to America developed. With the Mormons, a newly formed group on native soil, the relationship developed in an environment shaped by religious ideas.

Strong religious notions and conceptions about the Jews existed in all social groups in America, immigrant or native. These were the ideas inherent in Christianity concerning the relationship of the Jews to its founder. Such concepts were steeped in European historical tradition and the newer religious current in British Christendom which had announced the coming restoration of the Jews to their old homeland had little influence. Ideas of this kind had come to America in diluted form, representing only a weak echo of the British voice rather than an original religious creation in America. They were embedded in an emotional layer of the European crucifixion story.

Therefore, it was a real American miracle that things were so different in a newly formed native religious group composed of dissidents from various Christian denominations. Furthermore, the role of historic Judaism was assessed anew in respect to all basic facts in the life of this new group. It is also remarkable that, in addition to the historic Jewish-Christian struggle finding only weak reverberations in the new religion, the Biblical period of the Jewish people was regarded as essentially meaningful. On the basis of the Bible, images of personalities were formed, models of behavior were established, and the structure of this new religious society was derived. Revelation, Prophecy and Priesthood, as the pillars of the new religious experience, were traced to their Biblical origin, and on this basis a new religious world scene was formed, once again the vision of the millennium. This vision and the trials connected with it in the course of fateful events in the life of this new American community raised other elements of historic, even post-Biblical Judaism, to importance for the new Saints.

In all this Mormonism appears as the conqueror of old Christian-European inhibitions vis-à-vis Judaism and as the creator of a new relationship to the old Bible people and its religious world.

To be sure, all this happened under circumstances very far from the life of the masses of the Jews transplanted from Europe to America, and with only a weak connection with their spiritual life at that time. Nevertheless, a unique situation originated, first, as regards the religious position of the Jew in the new Mormon faith. Later, when the Mormons entered American history by creating their own territory, a minority problem of a unique nature arose—the American Jew as part of a newly formed religious community in America.

Although very limited in extent, this complex of problems gains importance by the course it took and by the solutions to which it led. It is true that just as for the philosopher, the smallest abyss is the deepest, for the social historian the solution of smallest dimension is the most meaningful. The fact that the new religious establishment of the new group known as Mormons could contribute to the consolidation, socially and spiritually, of the oldest European religious community in the New World represents one of the most astonishing phenomena in the history of ideas.

NOTES

CHAPTER 2

1. Herbert Schöffler, *Abendland und Altes Testament.* . . . Bochum 1937. (Kölner Anglistische Arbeiten . . . No. 30.).

2. M. Hamlin Cannon, "The English Mormons in America," *American Historical Review,* vol. LVII (1952), pp. 892–908, 899.

3. Schöffler, pp. 46–80.

4. *Sons of Utah Pioneers. Centennial Caravan* . . . Salt Lake City 1948, pp. 8–46.

5. Compared with this the freely chosen monastical names of the Ephrata Community in Pennsylvania (18th century) are overwhelmingly Biblical. *(Chronicon Ephratense; a history of the community of the Seventh-Day Baptists* . . . Lancaster, Pa., 1889, pp. 120/121).

6. "History of Las Vegas Mission compiled by Andrew Jenson," *Nevada State Historical Papers,* vol. V (1925/26), pp. 119–284. Biblical images show up in relations with Indian converts. They come to the Mormon mission "as soon as it is known that there is corn in Egypt."

7. *Utah since Statehood. Historical and Biographical,* Chicago 1919, vol. II.

8. Andrew Jenson, *Latter Day Saint Biographical Encyclopedia,* vol. I, Salt Lake City 1901, index.

9. Jenson, Enc.

10. *Round Table,* vol. IV (1866), p. 170.

11. William P. Johnston, *The Life of Gen. Albert Sidney Johnston* . . . New York 1878, p. 198.

12. *Western Humanities Review,* vol. II (1948), p. 79, "Utah Place Names." The Beaver Island's Mormon sect had a Jordan, Lake of Galilee, a Mount Pisgah and a city of Enoch. (Henry Ed-

ward Legler, *Moses of the Mormons; Strang's city of refuge and island kingdom* [Milwaukee 1897], p. 154).

13. *Guide to the Second Year's Course of Study in the Young Ladies Mutual Improvement Association. . . . Sanctioned by the First Presidency of the Church,* Salt Lake City, (no date), p. 52, "Home Management. Lesson VIII. Cookery in the home. Meat."

14. *Deseret News,* vol. VIII (1858), p. 76, "Plain and Simple Food."

15. *Chronicon Ephratense,* Lancaster 1889, p. 32

16. *Chronicon Ephratense . . .* von Br. Lamech u. Agrippa, Ephrata 1786, p. 17.

16a. *Doctrine and Covenants of the Church of the Latter Day Saints: . . .* Kirtland, Ohio, 1835, p. 202.

17. *Deseret News,* v. IX (1859), p. 80, "Tabernacle."

18. *Salt Lake Leader,* vol. IV. No. 38, 27.IX. 1873, p. 5, "A Word for Modern Israel."

19. [J. Strang] *Ancient and Modern Michillimackinac . . . ,* 1854, p. 25.

20. *Manual of the Seventh Day Baptists . . . ,* New York 1858, p. 53.

21. Israel Joseph Benjamin, *Drei Jahre in Amerika,* Hanover 1862, 3. Teil, p. 49.

22. *Atlantic Monthly,* vol. XIII (I–VI 1864), pp. 479–495, "Among the Mormons," p. 485, "In their ambition to reproduce ancient Judaism (and this ambition is the key to their whole puzzle) the Mormons are Sabbatarians. . . .'"

23. F. R. A. Glover, *Israel or the ten tribes, . . .* London (1874), p. 69.

24. Edward Hine is the author of many Anglo-Israelitish pamphlets.

25. Jewish tradition did everything to meet the christological challenge of the Melchisedek concept and its inherent idea of "the order of the son of God." Not only does the Midrasch extol Aaron as a priest over Melchisedek, but every word is said to represent Melchisedek as a human being subjected to the same divine judgment as other people. He was saved from the deluge because of his meritorious deed of feeding the animals in Noah's ark. (Braude, William G., *The Midrasch on Psalms,* New Haven 1959, vol. I, p. 423, vol. II, p. 235).

CHAPTER 3

1. *A series of pamphlets by Orson Pratt*, . . . Liverpool 1851, p. 12.

2. Geo. Alfred Townsend, *The Mormon Trials of Salt Lake City*, New York 1871, p. 47.

3. *New York Herald*, Jan. 19th, 1842, quoted by Fawn M. Brodie, *No man knows my history. The Life of Joseph Smith . . .* , New York 1945, p. 270.

4. *University of California Chronicle*, vol. XXVII (1925), pp. 153–165, Merrit V. Hughes, A neglected document in American Frontier History.

5. T. W. P. Taylder, *The Mormon's own book*, London 1855, p. 86.

6. *Harper's Magazine*, vol. III (1851), pp. 700–702, "Editors Table."

7. *Yankee Doodle*, Portland, vol. I, No. 8, 7.VIII. 1844, p. 3, "Mormonism."

8. Thomas Ford, *A history of Illinois, from . . . 1818 to 1847*, Chicago 1854, p. 269.

9. Thomas Tyson, *Joseph Smith, the Great American Impostor*, . . . London 1852, p. 35.

10. *Harper's Magazine*, vol. III (1851), p. 66.

11. Edward W. Tullidge, *The Women of Mormondom*, New York 1877, p. 5.

CHAPTER 4

1. Abraham Berger, "The Ten Lost Tribes," *Universal Jewish Encyclopedia*, vol. X, pp. 304–5.

2. Mordecai M. Noah's, "Proclamation to the Jews." (Sept. 1825), *Publications of the American Jewish Historical Society*, No. 8, pp. 11–15.

3. *Sabbath-Blatt . . .* red. v. Ad. Jellinek, IV. Jhg (1845), p. 134.

4. Alan Heimert, "Puritanism, the Wilderness and the Frontier," *New England Quarterly*, Sept. 1953, pp. 361–382, p. 376.

5. *Das Nord-Amerika. Historisch und Geographisch beschrieben*, Hamburg 1777, 1, Teil, p. 1.

6. *Overland Monthly,* v. X (1873), pp. 230/31.

7. This hoax led Dr. Felsenthal to consult Abraham Geiger and the fraud was revealed as "the bungling work of an unskilled stone mason." (David Philipson, "Are there traces of the lost tribes in Ohio?", *Publ. Am. Jew. Hist. Soc.* No. 13, pp. 37–46).

8. Noah, Proclamation. *(Publ. Am. Jew. Hist. Soc.)*

9. Albert James Pickett, *History of Alabama,* Charleston 1851, p. 113, quoted by Mildred M. Nelson, "Folk Etymology of Alabama Place-Names," *Southern Folklore Quarterly,* December 1950, pp. 193–214.

10. A survey of the oldest books containing the American Indian Israel theory is made in: William L. Clements, *The William L. Clements Library of Americana at the University of Michigan,* Ann Arbor 1923, p. 168.

11. Elder George Reynolds, *Are we of Israel?,* Salt Lake City 1883, p. 23.

12. *Zion's Reveille,* vol. II, No. 24, 2. IX. 1847, p. 98.

13. Maurice O'Connor Morris, *Rambles in the Rocky Mountains . . . ,* London 1864, p. 71.

14. *Puck,* vol. XXXVII (1895), p. 395.

15. Livingston Hopkins, *A comic history of the United States,* New York 1876, p. 210.

16. Carl Meyer, *Nach dem Sacramento,* Aarau 1855, p. 252.

17. J. G. Kohl, *Reisen in Canada . . . New York und Pennsylvania,* Stuttgart 1856, p. 425.

18. Hilda Doyle Merriam, *North of the Mohawk.* [Chicago], 1950, p. 3. In Jewish folk humor of the time too we occasionally find a trace of "Looking for the lost ten tribes." *(Purim. New Fashioned Annual for an Old Fashioned Feast,* London 1883, pp. 62–69).

19. James F. Cooper, *Works,* New York 1857–60, vol. XXXI, The Oak Openings, p. 270.

20. Ibid., p. 327.

21. Ibid., p. 356.

22. Ibid., p. 252.

23. Ibid., p. 365.

24. *The Jewish Times,* Vol. IV (1872/73), p. 771.

CHAPTER 5

1. *The Book of Mormon.* Translated by Joseph Smith, Jr., Independence, Mo., 1948, p. 147, "Second Book of Nephi," verses
53–55, 64.

2. *The Truth Teller,* Bloomington, Illinois, vol. I–II (1864/
65), p. 8.

3. *Book of Commandments . . .,* Zion 1833, p. 9.

4. "Discourse . . . Brigham Young," *Deseret News,* vol. XIX
(1870), p. 212.

5. *Deseret News,* vol. XX (1871), p. 559.

6. *The Corsair,* New York, vol. I (1839), p. 120.

7. *The Book of Mormon,* 1948, p. 15.

8. Ibid., pp. 41, 42.

9. *Biblioteca Scallawagiana. Catalogue . . . Charles L. Wood-
ward,* New York (1880), p. 4.

10. *North American Review,* vol. XCV (1862), pp. 190/191.

11. "Die Mormonen Bibel," *New Yorker Staatszeitung,* Jhg. VII
(1840–1841), No. 2, p. 1.

12. *Harper's Magazine,* vol. III (1851), pp. 701/702, "Editors
Table."

13. *The Life and Adventures of Henry Smith, the celebrated
Razor Strop Man . . .,* Boston 1848, p. 67, "If any think me too
severe, Or call my yarn a wicked libel, I'll take, to prove myself
sincere, My "davy"—on a Mormon Bible." (James F. Meline, *Two
thousand miles on horseback, Santa Fe and back,* London 1868,
p. 263).

14. *Harper's Magazine,* vol. III (1851), p. 64.

15. Rudolf Glanz, Jew and Yankee: A Historic Comparison,
Jewish Social Studies, vol. VI, No. 1, 1944.

16. *New Yorker Staatszeitung,* Jhg. VII, No. 9, 10. II. 1841,
p. 1, "Transatlantische Sternbilder." Von Professor Alfred Schück-
ing.

17. Henry Brown, *The History of Illinois,* New York 1844,
p. 490.

18. Ibid,, p. 394.

19. *New Yorker Staatszeitung,* Jhg. VII, No. 2, 23. XII. 1840,
p. 1.

20. Harper's Magazine, vol. III (1851), p. 701.

21. Ibid.

22. Ibid.

23. *The Book of Mormon. . . .* 1948, p. 157 (Second Book of Nephi, verses 53, 54, 55, 64).

24. *Book of Commandments for the Government of the Church of Christ, organized to Law, on the 6th of April 1830,* Zion 1833, p. 19 (Revelation to Cliver, April 18th, 1829).

25. *Jewish Messenger,* vol. XLVIII (1880), No. 16, p. 1.

CHAPTER 6

1. *The Book of Mormon . . .* 1948, p. 37.

2. *Doctrine and Covenants . . .,* Kirtland, O. 1935, Revelation January 1831, pp. 119/20, Revelation February 1831, p. 131.

3. Correspondence of Reverend Ezra Fisher, ed. by Sarah Fisher Henderson, letter of June 14, 1853, *Oregon Hist. Quart.* vol. XIX (1918), p. 237.

4. William Warren Sweet, *Religion on the American Frontier,* vol. III, *The Congregationalists,* Chicago [1939], p. 147 (Church Records April 17, 1839).

5. Sweet, vol. II, *The Presbyterians.* 1783–1840, New York 1936, p. 859 (Synod of North Carolina, Sept. 1837).

6. Reverend Ezra Fisher's Correspondence, letter of August 1st, 1849, *The Oregon Historical Quarterly,* vol. XVII (1916), p. 279.

7. Charles Thompson, *Evidences in proof of the book of Mormon . . . ,* Batavia, N. Y. 1841, p. 39.

8. *Journal of Discourses,* vol. V, p. 4 (July 5, 1857).

9. Edward W. Tullidge, *The Women of Mormondom,* New York 1877, p 78.

10. *History of all the religious denominations in the United States . . .,* Harrisburg, Pa., 1853, p. 348.

11. Douglas C. MacMurtrie, *The General Epistle of the Latter Day Saints . . .,* Chicago 1937, p. 7.

12. [Joseph Smith] *Doctrine and Covenants of the Church of the Latter Day Saints . . .,* Kirtland, Ohio. 1835, p. 154 Revelation of 1831).

13. *Deseret News,* vol. III (1852/53), No. 7, p. 2.

14. [William Elkanah Water] *Life Among the Mormons* . . ., New York 1868, p. 165.

15. *The Truth Teller*, Bloomington, Illinois, vol. I–II (1864/1865), p. 124.

16. *The Olive Branch*, Kirtland, Ohio, vol. I (1848), p. 25 (VIII 1848), "The Word of the Lord to His People."

17. Ibid., Vol. II (1849), pp. 116/117, "Our belief—California, or the country beyond the wilderness of Deluca," pp. 117–120, "A description of Bashan or California."

18. Ibid., vol. II (1849), p. 179, "The Sabbath."

19. Ibid., vol. II (1849), p. 115, "Public Meeting in Voree."

20. Ibid., vol. II (April 1850), p. 152/153.

21. Ibid., vol. II (April 1850), p. 152.

22. Ibid., vol. II (IV 1850), p. 153.

23. Ibid., vol. II (1849/50), (February 1850), p. 117.

24. *Journal of Discourses*, vol. XIII (1871), p. 138 (Orson Pratt, 10. IV. 1870).

25. [Stamp, J. S.] *A lecture on the conversion of the Jews* . . ., New York 1846, p. 18.

26. *Gospel Herald*, vol. IV (1850), No. 47, 7. II. 1850), p. 275.

27. Ibid., vol. IV (1850), p. 275.

28. *Journal of Discourses*, vol. XII (1869), p. 38 (Brigham Young 14. IV. 1867).

29. Ibid., vol. XII (1869), p. 113 (Brigham Young, 8. XII. 1867).

30. Ibid., vol. IV, p. 232 (Wilford Woodruff, 22. II. 1857).

31. Ibid., vol. XVIII (1877), p. 64 (Orson Pratt, 25. VII. 1877).

32. Ibid., vol. IV (1850), p. 232 (Wilford Woodruff, 22. II. 1857).

33. Ibid., vol. XXI (1881), p. 271 (Geo. Qu. Cannon, 2. XI. 1879).

34. Ibid., vol. XXIV (1884), p. 23 (Orson Pratt, 26. X. 1879).

35. Ibid., vol. XVIII (1877), pp. 67, 68 (Orson Pratt, 25. VII. 1877).

36. M. H. Cannon, The Mormon Declaration of Right, *Harvard Theological Review*, vol. XXXV, p. 187 (Given on the 6th of April 1845).

37. Ibid.

38. Ibid., pp. 189–190.

39. *The Doctrine and Covenants of the Church of Jesus Christ of Latter-Day Saints* . . . Salt Lake City 1925, p. 156.

40. James E. Talmage, *The articles of faith,* Salt Lake City 1899, p. 348.

41. *The Alton Telegraph,* vol. V, (1840), No. 46, p. 2 (quoted from Snider, C. A., *"The attitude toward Mormonism in Illinois" (1838–1840).* In New York Public Library.

42. *Journal of Discourses,* vol. III (1856), (P. P. Pratt, Oct. 7, 1855), pp. 127–139, "Literal Fulfillment of Prophecy—Restoration of Israel—The Coming of Christ."

43. *Evening and Morning Star,* Kirtland, vol. I (1832/33), pp. 134–136, The Jews: Again.

44. *The Frontier Guardian,* 5. IX. 1849, p. 1, "California Song" by Lucius N. Scovil.

45. *Bee-Hive Songster,* . . . By "Jeuan" . . , Salt Lake City 1868, p. 23.

46. *The Seer,* Washington, D.C., vol. I (1853), No. 1, p. 4.

47. [Russel F. Ralston] *Fundamental Differences between the Reorganized Church and the Church in Utah,* Independence, Mo., 1960, pp. 185–208, "Mountain of the Lord's House."

48. *Deseret News,* vol. XVIII (1869), p. 359, "Correspondence."

49. *Oneida Circular,* vol. IX (1872), p. 20.

50. Douglas C. MacMurtrie, *The General Epistle of the Latter Day Saints* . . . , Chicago 1937, p. 7.

51. Woodruff C. Thomson, "Mormon Word Creation and Specialization," *Western Humanities Review,* vol. III (1949), p. 67.

CHAPTER 7

1. *Journal of Rev. Francis Asbury, Bishop of the Methodist Episcopal Church,* vol. I (1771–1786), New York [1901], p. 215.

2. *Deseret News,* vol. III (1852/53), No. 5, p. 3.

3. *Journal of Discourses,* vol. VII, p. 294 (Brigham Young at Willow Creek, 12. VI. 1860).

4. *History of all the religious denominations* . . . , Harrisburg, Pa. 1853, p. 348.

5. Geo. T. M. Davis, *An Authentic Account of the Massacre of Joseph Smith,* St. Louis 1844, p. 7.

6. *The Mormon Tribune,* vol. I (1870), No. 11, p. 84, "Mormon and Gentile."

7. *Utah Monthly Magazine,* vol. IV (1887/88), p. 5, "President John Taylor."

8. *The Mormon Tribune,* vol. I (1870), No. 10, p. 74, "Democracy, the Government of the World's Future."

9. *Salt Lake Leader,* vol. IV, No. 38, 27. IX. 1873, p. 4.

10. Edward W. Tullidge, *The Women of Mormondom,* New York 1877, p. 78.

11. Sergeant Daniel Tyler, *A concise history of the Mormon Battalion in the Mexican War,* 1881, p. 230.

12. Rollin J. Britton, Early days on Grand River and Mormon War, *Missouri Historical Review,* vol. XIII, (1918/19), p. 297.

13. *Proclamation of the Twelve Apostles . . . ,* New York, April 6th, 1845, p. 4.

14. Elder George Reynolds, *A dictionary of the Book of Mormon . . . ,* Salt Lake City 1891, p. 156, "Israelites. The people of Israel called by that name once in the Book of Mormon. (Helaman, 8:11)."

15. Charles Thompson, *Evidences in proof of the book of Mormon . . . ,* Batavia, N. Y., 1841, p. 7.

16. *One hundredth Annual Conference . . . 1930 . . .* Salt Lake City, p. 15.

17. Edward W. Tullidge, *The Women of Mormondom,* New York 1877, p. 1.

18. Ibid., p. 5.

19. *Deseret News,* v. XIII (1863), No. 3, p. 1, "Instruction by President Brigham Young, in April and May, 1863 to the Latter Day Saints in the Settlements South of Great Salt Lake."

20. Ibid., v. XVII (1868), p. 4.

21. S. N. Carvalho, *Incidents of Travel and Adventure in the Far West . . . ,* New York 1857, p. 189.

CHAPTER 8

1. Leo Spitzer, *Essays in Historical Semantics,* New York 1948, pp. 171–178, "The Gentiles."

2. [Th. Ch. Haliburton] *Nature and Human Nature,* New York, 1855, p. 19.

3. Sidney Roberts, *To Emigrants to the Gold Region* . . . , New Haven, January 1, 1849, p. 10.

4. Alfred Kreymborg, *Our singing strength*, New York 1929, p. 183 (Ambrose Bierce).

5. *The American Israelite*, vol. XVI (1869/70), No. 21, p. 11.

6. John W. Clampitt, *Echoes from the Rocky Mountains*, Chicago 1889, p. 285.

7. *Illinois Monthly Magazine*, vol. I (Vandalia 1831), p. 441.

8. [Joseph Smith] *Book of Commandments, for the Government of the Church of Christ, organized to Law, on the 6th of April, 1830*, Zion 1833, p. 37.

9. [Joseph Smith] *Doctrine and Covenants of the Church of the Latter Day Saints*: . . . , Kirtland, Ohio, 1835, p. 84.

10. *The Book of Mormon* . . . , Independence 1948, p. 35 (I. Book of Nephi.)

11. S. N. Carvalho, p. 150.

12. *Boadicea; The Mormon Wife. Life Scenes in Utah*. Edited by Alreda Eva Bell, Baltimore . . . [1855], p. 16, "A Mormon Hymn."

13. *The Truth Teller*. Bloomington, Illinois, vol. I-II (1864/1865), p. 124.

14. Daniel T. Kidder, *Mormonism and the Mormons* . . . , New York 1842, p. 235, "Hymn 265. P. U."

15. *Times and Seasons*, vol. IV (1843), p. 18.

16. Ibid., vol. III (1842), p. 304.

17. *Deseret News*, vol. XVI (1867), No. 13, p. 104.

18. *The Prophet*, New York, vol. II (1844), No. 8, p. 2, "Our Situation."

19. *Deseret News*, vol. III (1852/1853), No. 9, p. 2.

20. *Journal of Discourses*, vol. XII (1869), p. 159 (Brigham Young, Feb. 8th, 1868).

21. Discourse Brigham Young of Dec. 23rd 1866 quoted by Milton R. Hunter, *Brigham Young the Colonizer*, Salt Lake City 1941, p. 181.

22. John C. Bennet, *The history of the Saints*, Boston 1842, p. 278.

23. *Plu-ri-Bus-Tah* . . . , [Thomas Mortimer] New York 1856, pp. XXII, XXIV.

24. Fred E. Bennet, *A Detective's Experience among the Mormons* . . . , Chicago 1887, p. 97.

25. Humphrey J. Desmond, *The A. P A. Movement,* Washington 1912, p. 40.

26. *Valley Tan,* vol. I (1858/1859), No. 38, p. 3, "Mass Convention."

27. Ibid., No. 5, p. 3.

28. *Daily Union Vedette, August 20, 1864,* quoted by Robert Joseph Dwyer, *The Gentile comes to Utah . . . ,* Washington 1941, p. 27, note 67.

29. *The Peep o'day,* vol. I (1864), p. 40.

30. *Times and Seasons,* vol. V (1844), p. 453.

31. E. K. Tullidge, *The lost tribes of Israel in England and America,* New York 1881, p. 314, "The joke . . . has the merit of a fine old age." (J. H. Beadle, *The undeveloped West . . . ,* Philadelphia 1873, p. 112).

32. *Sporting Times and Theatrical News,* vol. VI (1869/1870), No. 131., p. 13, "Everybody's Column."

33. *The Mormons Tribune,* vol. I (1870), No. 11, p. 84, "Mormon and Gentile."

34. Robert von Schlagintweit, *Die Mormonen . . . ,* Cöln 1878, p. 134.

35. Israel Joseph Benjamin, Teil 3, p. 47.

36. *Daily Union Vedette,* August 17, 1865, quoted by Robert Joseph Dwyer, *The Gentile comes to Utah . . . ,* Washington 1941, p. 7, note 12.

37. [William Elkanah Water] *Life among the Mormons . . . ,* New York 1868, p. 95.

38. G. A. Zimmer von Ulbersdorf, *Unter den Mormonen in Utah,* Gütersloh 1908, p. 59.

39. *The Peep o'day,* vol. I (1864), p. 43, "Notes of the Week. By Quiz."

40. *Journal of Discourses,* vol. II, p. 200 (Wilford Woodruff, Febr. 25th 1855).

41. Ibid., p. 64 (Orson Pratt, July 25th, 1877).

42. Ibid., vol. II, p. 200 (Wilford Woodruff, Feb. 25th, 1855).

43. Ibid., vol. XXI, p. 271 (Geo. Qu. Cannon, Nov. 2nd 1879).

44. *The Mormon Tribune. Organ of the liberal cause in Utah,* vol. I (1870), No. 1, p. 4, "Platform of the Movement."

45. *The Mormon Tribune,* Salt Lake City, 15. I. 1870, p. 21, "Record of the Movement."

46. *The Peep o'Day. A Salt Lake City Magazine of Science, Literature and Art,* vol. I (1864), No. 2, p. 40, "Mormon and Gentile."

47. *Deseret News,* vol. XVII (1868), p. 251, "Remarks . . . Br. Young . . ."

48. Woodruff C. Thomson, Mormon Word Creation and Specialization, *Western Humanities Review,* v. III (1949), p. 67.

CHAPTER 9

1. H. L. Goudge, *The British Israel Theory,* London [1933], p. 35. For the Mormon version see chapter VI, n. 30.

2. *Journal by Francis Anne Butler,* Philadelphia 1835. vol. II, p. 49.

3. *Overland Monthly,* vol. XIII (VII-XII 1874), pp. 264–267, "Lair Gawain."

4. *Jewish Messenger,* vol. XLVI (1879), No. 3, p. 3.

5. *The Standard of Israel . . . ,* London, vol. I (1875), p. 10.

6. J. H. Titcomb, *The Anglo-Israel Post Bag . . . ,* London 1876, p. 111.

7. *The Standard of Israel . . . ,* London, vol. I (1875), p. 27.

8. *Deseret News,* vol. XXIII (1874), p. 549.

9. *Gospel Herald,* Voree, vol. IV (1849), p. 1.

10. Geo. M. Davis, *An Authentic Account of the Massacre of Joseph Smith,* St. Louis 1844, p. 7.

11. Charles Thompson, *Evidences in proof of the Book of Mormon . . . ,* Batavia, N. Y. 1841, p. 139.

12. Lorenzo Snow, "Mormonism. By its Head . . . ", *The Land of Sunshine . . . ,* October 1901, p. 252.

13. *A selection of Sacred Hymns . . .* Selected by Emma Smith, Nauvoo, Ill., 1841, p. 140.

14. *Journal of Discourses,* vol. XII (1869), p. 38 (Brigham Young Apr. 14th 1867).

15. Ibid., vol. IV, p. 232 (Wilford Woodruff, Nov. 16th, 1856).

16. Ibid., vol. II, p. 269 (Brigham Young, April 8th 1855).

17. *Deseret News,* vol. XIX (1870), p. 212, "Discourse . . . Brigham Young."

18. *Journal of Discourses,* vol. II, p. 268 (Brigham Young, April 8th, 1855).

19. Israel J. Benjamin, vol. II, Teil 3, p. 47.

20. Journal of George Washington Bean in the Library of Congress, p. 7 (Oct. 18th, 1857), p. 8 (Oct. 18th, 1851).

21. Georgia Metcalf Stewart, *How the Church Grew,* Independence 1959, p. 220.

CHAPTER 10

1. *Niles Weekly Register,* vol. XLV (VIII 1833–II 1834), p. 48.

2. *The Nation,* vol. CLXXIV, May 24th, 1952, Lowry Nelson, Mormons and the Negro; Ibid., vol. CLXXV, August 6th, 1952, Roy W. Doxey, The Mormons and the Negro.

3. Russel F. Ralston, *Fundamental Differences . . .,* Independence, Mo., 1960, p. 232.

4. *Deseret News,* vol. XXII (1873), p. 84, "Discourse . . . Orson Pratt."

5. N. Slater, *Fruits of Mormonism . . .,* Coloma, Cal. 1851, p. 64.

6. [William Elkanah Water] *Life among the Mormons . . .,* New York 1868, p. 165.

7. B. H. Roberts, *The Rise and Fall of Nauvoo,* Salt Lake City 1900, p. 60.

8. *The Latter Day Saints Millennial Star,* Manchester, vol. I [1840/1841], No. 3, p. 89, "Late from America." Details of the first Mormon Mission to Palestine are given in: Karl E. Ettinger and Abraham G. Duker, A Christian Zionist's Centenary, *The New Palestine,* Oct. 17th, 1941), pp. 15–16.

9. *The Weekly Picayune,* vol. III, No. 13, 18. V. 1840, p. 51.

10. *History of the religious denominations in the United States . . .,,* Harrisburg, Pa., 1853, p. 347.

11. *Deseret News,* vol. V (1855), p. 33.

12. *Correspondence of Palestine Tourists; comprising a series of letters by George A. Smith, Lorenzo Snow . . ., Salt Lake City . . .* 1875.

13. *Deseret News,* vol. XXI (1872), p. 589, "Bound for Palestine." A description of the travel in: Eliza R. Snow Smith, *Biography . . . Lorenzo Snow,* Salt Lake City, 1884, pp. 496–581.

14. Ibid., vol. XXII (1873), p. 179. "Correspondence. Camp near Jaffa Gate, Jerusalem, March 4th, 1873."

15. "We have had a short account from Brother George A. Smith about the land of their fathers; we can draw our own conclusions as to the causes which have brought about the present condition of that land and of the descendants of the ancient worthies to whom it was given . . ." (*Deseret News,* vol. XXII (873), p. 356, "Discourse . . . Brigham Young.")

16. *Deseret News,* vol. XXII (1873), p. 420, "Discourse . . . George A. Smith."

17. B. H. Roberts, *The Rise and Fall of Nauvoo,* Salt Lake City 1900, pp. 62/63.

18. Robert von Schlagintweit, *Die Mormonen . . .,* Cöln 1878, p. 173.

19. Ibid., p. 275.

20. *Times and Seasons,* Nauvoo, vol. IV (1843), p. 8.

21. Ibid.

22. Ibid., vol II (1840/41), No. 1, p. 232.

23. *Correspondence of Palestine Tourists . . . ,* Salt Lake City 1875, p. 224.

24. *Times and Seasons,* vol. IV (1843), No. 20, p. 509.

25. Ibid.

26. *Deseret News,* vol. VI (1856), p. 63, "Gibraltar Mission. By Elder Edward Stevenson. Letter No. 7. April . . . 1853 . . . 16th. . . ."

27. *Times and Seasons,* Nauvoo, vol. III (1841/42), p. 805.

28. *Journal of Discourses,* vol. XVI (1874), p. 96, George A. Smith, "An account of his journey to Palestine."

29. Ibid., vol. XVI (1874), p. 96.

30. See note 14.

31. *The Book of Mormon . . .,* Palmyra 1830, title page.

32. *Times and Seasons,* vol. III (1841/42), p. 304.

33. Ibid., p. 305.

34. Ibid., p. 304.

35. *Journal of Discourses,* vol. XVI (1874), p. 96, George A. Smith, "An account of his journey to Palestine."

36. Ibid., vol. XVIII (1877), p. 199 (Elder John Taylor, June 6th, 1876).

37. *The Prussian Mission of the Church of Jesus Christ of Latter-Day Saints . . .*, Liverpool 1853, p. 5.

38. Ibid., p. 3.

39. *Journal of Discourses,* vol. XVIII (1877), p. 65 (Orson Pratt, July 25th, 1877).

40. *The Prophet,* New York, vol. II (1844), No. 3, p. 3.

41. *Document containing the Correspondence, Orders a. C. in relation to the disturbances with the Mormons . . . ,* Fayette, Missouri: 1841, p. 112.

42. *Journal of Discourses,* vol. IV, p. 219–220, quoted by M. R. Werner, *Brigham Young,* New York [1925], p. 404.

43. *Times and Seasons,* Nauvoo, vol. II (1840/41), No. 1, p. 232.

44. J. W. Gunnison, *The Mormons . . .,* Philadelphia 1857, p. 99.

45. Theodor Olshausen, *Geschichte der Mormonen . . .,* Göttingen 1856, p. 4.

46. Phil Robinson, *Sinners and Saints,* Boston 1883, p. 119.

47. *The Weekly Oregonian,* vol. IV, 26. IV. 1873, p. 3.

48. Henry Caswall, *The prophet of the nineteenth century . . .,* London 1843, p. 195.

49. Joseph B. Felt, *The ecclesiastical history of New England . . .,* Boston 1855, vol. I, p. 433 (Massachusetts 1641).

50. A. Wetmore, *Gazetteer of the State of Missouri,* St. Louis 1837, p. 93(Jackson County).

51. *Journal of Discourses,* vol. II, p. 189 (Brigham Young, February 18th, 1855).

52. Dr. Moriz Busch, *Die Mormonen,* Leipzig 1855, p. 87.

53. Robert von Schlagintweit, *Die Mormonen . . .,* Cöln 1878, p. 135.

54. Dr. Moriz Busch, *Die Mormonen,* Leipzig 1855, p. 87.

55. *Voice of Warning to the Church of Jesus Christ of Latter-Day Saints. Composed by Barnet Moses Giles, a literal descendant of the House of Israel,* Salt Lake City, Utah 1874–5634, p. 16.

56. Ibid., p. 15.

57. The Jews in Jerusalem and the Jews in Utah. . . . From the *Monthly Companion,* Boston, Mass., Oct. 1877, vol. VI, pp. 1, 475.

58. Ibid., p. 2.

59. Ibid., p. 3.

347

60. *Voice of Warning . . .*, p. 23.

61. James Fenimore Cooper, *The travelling bachelor; or Notions of the Americans,* New York 1859, p. 584.

62. *American Israelite,* vol. XVI, (1869/70), No. 26, p. 3.

CHAPTER 11

* The British phase of the Restoration idea is dealt with by Franz Kobler, *The Vision Was There. A history of the British movement for the restoration of the Jews to Palestine,* London 1956.

1. [Thomas Greene Fessenden] *The modern philosopher . . .,* Philadelphia 1806, p. 26.

2. *The Cincinnati Miscellany,* vol. II (1845), p. 196.

3. *Letters from John Pintard to his daughter . . . 1816–1833,* New York 1940, vol. III ,p. 49 (Collect. N. Y. Hist. Soc., vol. LXX).

4. *The Nation,* vol. II (1866), p. 172, "The South as it is."

5. *The Western Cincinnati Journal,* Cincinnati 1836, p. 365, "On Judahs Hill."

6. John Reynolds, *Sketches of the Country,* Belleville 1854, p. 136.

7. *Niles Weekly Register,* vol. XI (1820), p. 168, "Gathering of the Jews."

8. *Los Angeles Star,* 6. VIII 1853, p. 1.

9. Elhan Winchester, *An Oration on the Discovery of America . . .,* London [1792], p. 7.

10. Walter March, *Shoepac Recollections: A way-side glimpse of American life,* New York 1856, p. 171.

11. *The American Israelite,* vol. XIII (1866/67), No. 49, p. 6.

12. *The Signet and Mirror,* St. Louis, vol. III (1850), p. 285.

13. *The Edinburgh Review,* American Edition, April 1854, No. 202, p. 178.

14. Le Grand Richards, *Israel! Do You Know?* Salt Lake City, 1954.

15. *The Truth Teller,* Bloomington, Illinois, vol. I–II (1864/1865), p. 97.

16. *Sword of Laban.* The American Anti-Mormon Association Leaflet No. 5, p. 2.

17. *Deseret News,* vol. XX (1871), p. 101, "Discourse . . . Orson Pratt. . . ."

18. *Times and Seasons,* Nauvoo, vol. I (1839/40), No. 6, Commerce, Illinois, April 1840, p. 86.

19. *Proclamation of the Twelve Apostles . . .,* New York, April 6th, 1845), p. 3.

20. *Journal of Discourses,* vol. V, p. 4 (Brigham Young, July 5, 1857).

21. *Proclamation of the Twelve Apostles . . .,* New York, April 6th, 1845, p. 7.

22. *Journal of Discourses,* vol. XVII, p. 64 (Orson Pratt, 25. VII. 1877).

23. *Western Standard,* vol. I (1856), p. 122, "The Jews—Their Destiny?"

24. *Deseret News,* vol. XXI (1872), p. 78, Discourse . . . Orson Pratt."

25. See Chapter X, Note 31.

26. *Journal of Discourses,* vol. II, p. 245 (Wilford Woodruff, Oct. 22nd, 1865).

27. *Book of Commandments, for the Government of the Church of Christ, organized to Law on the 6th of April, 1830,* Zion 1833, p. 130 (Revelation March 7th, 1831).

28. *Times and Seasons,* vol. IV (1842/43), p. 109, "The Jews."

29. Ibid., vol. V (1844), p. 475, "The Jews.

30. Ibid., vol. III (1841/42), p. 805.

31. *Journal of Discourses,* vol. XVI, p. 341 (Orson Pratt, January 1st, 1874).

32. *Deseret News,* vol. XVIII (1869), p. 85.

33. *Journal of Discourses,* vol. XVI, p. 342 (Orson Pratt, January 25th, 1874).

34. *The Prophet,* New York, vol. II (1844), No. 6, p. 1.

35. *Deseret News,* vol. II (1851/52), No. 19, 24, VII, 1852.

36. William Chandless, *A Visit to Salt Lake,* London 1857, p. 352.

37. *Daily State Tribune,* Sacramento, vol. II, No. 56, 11th Sept. 1855, p. 2, "Return of the Jews."

CHAPTER 12

1. *Deseret News,* vol. XXIV (1874), p. 42, "Tithing."

2. Ibid., vol. XX (1871), p. 478, "What Will the Mormons Do?"

3. Edward W. Tullidge, *The Women of Mormondom,* New York 1877, p. 79.

4. S. N. Carvalho, New York 1860, p. 185. The spelling of Melchi(s) (z) edek (c) is inconsistent in the sources.

5. The *Deseret News,* vol. XIV (1865), p. 355, "Summary of Instructions."

6. B. Winchester, *A History of the Priesthood,* Philadelphia 1843, p. 69.

7. Paul A. W. Wallace, *Conrad Weiser.* Philadelphia 1945, p. 106 *(Chronicon Ephratense.* Lancaster 1889, p. 120).

8. S. N. Carvalho, New York 1860, p. 185.

9. J. W. Gunnison, *The Mormons . . .,* Philadelphia 1857, p. 23.

10. Edward W. Tullidge, *The Women of Mormondom,* New York 1877, p. 78.

11. *The Private Papers and Diary of Thomas Leiper Kane, a friend of the Mormons,* San Francisco 1937, p. 5.

12. *Deseret News,* vol. III (1852/1853), No. 12, p. 4.

13. *Journal of Rev. Francis Asbury, Bishop of the Methodist Episcopal Church,* vol. I (1771–1786), New York [1901], p. 215.

14. Jules Remy, *A Journey to Great Salt Lake City,* London 1861, vol. II, p. 55.

15. *Jewish Messenger,* vol. XLVIII (1880), No. 10, p. 6.

16. Fitz Hugh Ludlow, *The Heart of the Continent,* New York 1870, p. 529.

17. *The Mormon Tribune,* vol. I (1870), No. 2, 8. I. 1870, p. 10, "Saved from a collision with the United States." By Edward W. Tullidge.

CHAPTER 13

1. *Deseret News,* vol. XX (1871), p. 344, "Editorials."

2. *Juvenile Instructor,* vol. XVIII (1884), p. 88, "Editorial Thoughts."

3. *Evening and Morning Star,* vol. I–II (1832–1834), p. 37, "Restoration of the Jews."

4. *Deseret News,* vol. II (1851/52), No. 24, p. 4.

5. *Deseret News Extra, containing a revelation on Celestial Marriage . . .* , Salt Lake City, August 28th, 1852, p. 34.

6. *Deseret News,* vol. IV (1853/54), No. 3, p. 2.

7. *Journal of Discourses,* vol. XVI, p. 108. (Brigham Young, June 27th, 1873).

8. Ibid., vol. XVI, p. 104 (George A. Smith, June 27th, 1873).

9. Ibid., vol. II (1855), p. 8.

10. [W. M. Blane] *An Excursion through the United States and Canada during the years 1822–1823,* London 1824, p. 487.

11. *Journal of Discourses,* vol. II (1855), p. 142 (Brigham Young, Dec. 3rd, 1854).

12. Ibid.

13. A Journal of Alexander Neibaur, p. 41. (In the archives of the Church of Jesus Christ of Latter-Day Saints, Salt Lake City).

CHAPTER 14

1. Rudolf Glanz, Jew and Yankee: A Historic Comparison, *Jewish Social Studies,* vol. VI, No. 1, 1944.

2. Fitz Hugh Ludlow, *The Hearth of the Continent,* New York 1870, p. 529.

3. *Deseret News,* vol. XVIII (1869), p. 457, "Apostasy and its Causes."

4. Henry Brown, *The History of Illinois,* New York 1844, p. 400.

5. John Codman, Mormonism, *International Review,* Sept. 1881, p. 227.

6. *The Galaxy,* vol. IV (1867), pp. 541–549, "Brigham Young and Mormonism," p. 544.

7. *The Private Papers and Diary of Thomas Leiper Kane, a friend of the Mormons,* San Francisco 1937, p. 71.

8. *Evening and Morning Star,* vol. I–II, Kirtland (1832–1834), p. 71.

9. Ibid., p. 118.

10. *Niles Weekly Register,* vol. XL (III 1831–IX 1831), p. 353.

11. Charles H. Brigham, The Mormon Problem, *Old and New*, vol. I (1870), pp. 628–641, p. 632.

12. *Niles Weekly Register,* vol. LXXIV (VII 1848– I 1849), p. 336.

13. *De Bow's Review,* vol. XVI (1854), pp. 368–382, "The Mormonism in the United States," p. 377.

14. *The Literary World,* New York, vol. VII (VII–XII 1850), p. 328, "The Mormons A. Discourse . . . by Thomas L. Kane." (Reviewed).

15. *Niles Weekly Register,* vol. LXXIII (IX 1847–II 1848), p. 174.

16. Charles H. Brigham, "The Mormon Problem," *Old and New,* vol. I (1870), pp. 628–641, p. 630.

17. *Journal of Discourses,* vol .XIII (1871), p. 256 (Lorenzo Snow, Oct. 9th, 1869).

18. Walter Colton, *Three Years in California,* New York 1850, p. 83.

19. Dr. W. A. Zimmermann, *Californien und das Goldfieber* . . . Berlin 1864, p. 191.

20. *The Daily Graphic,* New York, vol. I (1. III–30. VI, 1873), No. 38, p. 1.

21. John Udell, *Incidents or Travel to California . . . ,* Jefferson, Ohio, 1856, p. 301.

22. *The Mormon Tribune,* vol. I (1870), No. 5, p. 37.

23. *The Hebrew Sabbath School Visitor,* vol. III (1876), p. 309, "My second trip to California."

24. John Ross Dix, Esqu., *Amusing and thrilling adventures of a California artist,* Boston 1854, p. 65.

25. *Deseret News,* vol. XXI (1872), p. 67, "The Mormon Muss."

26. "John Codman, Mormonism," *International Review,* September 1881, p. 227.

27. M. Hamlin Cannon, English Mormons in America, *American Historical Review,* vol. LVII (1952), pp. 892–908, p. 899.

28. Thomas Ford, *A History of Illinois,* 1818 to 1847, Chicago 1854, p. 269.

29. *New Yorker Staatszeitung,* Jahrgang VII (1841), No. 31, p. 2.

30. Austin N. Ward, *Male Life Among the Mormons . . . ,* Philadelphia 1863, p. 18.

31. *The Frontier Guardian,* Kanesville, Iowa, vol. I (1849), 8. VIII. 1849, p. 4.

32. *Old and New,* vol. I (1870), p. 631.

33. Dr. W. A. Zimmermann, *Californien und das Goldfieber . . . ,* Berlin 1864, "Prospektus."

34. *Philadelphia, May, 1877.* "To the press of the United States." (Signed) A. Milton Musser, "Mormon" Elder.

35. *A forcible appeal to true Americans,* Salt Lake City [1906], p. 7.

36. *Truth for Truth-Seekers on Utah and the Mormons. By Non-Mormons,* Salt Lake City [1913]. (Harvard Library, Perkins Collection).

CHAPTER 15

1. *The Galaxy,* vol. II ((1866), p. 442, "The confusion of the tongues."

2. Ezra H. Byington, *The Puritan as a colonist and reformer,* Boston 1899, p. 217.

3. Peter Quince, "Address to American Critics," *The New England Quarterly Magazine,* Boston, No. 3, 1802, p. 286.

4. David De Sola Pool, Hebrew Learning among the Puritans of New England prior to 1700, *Publ. Am. Jew. Hist. Society,* No. 20, pp. 31–83, p. 81.

5. Elder George Reynolds, *A dictionary of the Book of Mormon . . . ,* Salt Lake City 1891, p. 137.

6. B. H. Roberts, *History of the Church,* vol. VI, p. 402 (written by the prophet on May 23rd, 1844).

7. Daryl Chase, Sidney Rigdon—Early Mormon, Chicago 1931 (M. A. Thesis, University of Chicago), p. 105, footnote No. 1.

8. Eva L. Pancoast, Mormons at Kirtland (M. A. Thesis, Western Reserve University), May 1, 1929, p. 116. Quoted: Smith, Hist. Church, vol. I, p. 606 and Cleveland Daily Advertiser, August 17, 1836.

9. *Jewish Encyclopedia* vol. IX, p. 583, "Daniel Levi Maduro Peixotto".

10. Pancoast, p. 116 (quoted: Smith, Hist. Church, vol. I, p. 596, 606, vol. II, p. 4.).

11. *Deseret News,* vol. II (1851/52), No. 19, p. 1, "Life of Joseph Smith."

12. *New England Magazine,* vol. V (1833), p. 423, "Peritissimorum."

13. Pancoast, p. 117.

14. Ibid., pp. 116/17 (quoted: Ohio City Argus, January 19, 1837).

15. *Deseret News,* vol. II (1851/52), No. 23, p. 1.

16. Ibid.

17. Ibid., No. 24, p. 1.

18. Daryl Chase, Sidney Rigdon, p. 109.

19. Inez Smith Davis, *The Story of the Church,* Independence, Mo., 1943, p. 39 (quoted: Smith, Hist. Church, vol. II, p. 26).

20. Pancoast, p. 117.

21. Robert S. Fletcher, *A History of Oberlin College,* Oberlin 1943, vol. I, pp. 368, 369, 370.

22. Pancoast, p. 117 (quoted: Oberlin College, General Catalogue, 1909, pp. 72, 73).

23. Ibid. (quoted: Eliza Snow, Biography and Family Record of Lorenzo Snow, *Historical Record,* February 1887, pp. 140–141).

24. Dr. Moritz Busch, *Geschichte der Mormonen,* Leipzig 1870, p. 115; *Historical Record* . . . by Andrew Jenson, vol. V, Salt Lake City, 1886, index: Hebrew School in Kirtland, pp. 18, 25, 39, 43, 50, 54, 64.

25. Pancoast, p. 117.

26. W. J. MacNiff, The Kirtland Phase of Mormonism, *Ohio arch. a. hist. soc. Quart.,* vol. L (1941), pp. 261–268, p. 267.

27. C. B. Marryat, *Narrative of the Travels and Adventures of Monsieur Violet* . . . , Paris 1844, p. 369.

28. *General Joseph Smith's Appeal to the Green Mountain Boys, December, 1843,* Nauvoo 1843, p. 4.

29. *Times and Seasons,* vol. V (1844), p. 591, "Lamentation."

30. *Nauvoo Neighbour,* vol. II (1844), No. 14, p. 1.

30a. *Times and Seasons,* vol. III (1842), p. 703.

30b. Ibid., p. 726.

31. *Journal of Discourses,* vol. V, p. 103 (George A. Smith, Aug. 2nd, 1857).

32. *Deseret News,* vol. VI (1856/57), p. 131, "Hebrew Idiom."

33. *Nauvoo Neighbour,* vol. II (1844), No. 32, p. 2.

34. *Times and Seasons,* v. I, No. 8 (June 1840), p. 123.

35. Marryat, *Narrative,* p. 391.

36. Robert Joseph Dwyer, *The Gentile comes to Utah,* Washington 1941, p. 162, n. 39.

CHAPTER 16

1. Oliver Wendell Elsbree, The Rise of the Missionary Spirit in New England, 1790–1815, *New England Quarterly,* vol. I (1928), pp. 295–322.

2. *The Western Luminary,* Lexington, Ky., vol. I (July 1824–July 1825), p. 24, "Dr. Griffin's Speech."

3. *Niles Weekly Register,* vol. XI (1820), p. 260, "The Jews."

3a. *Anschauungen und Erfahrungen in Nordamerika. Eine Monatsschrift.* Herausgegeben von Heinrich Boßhard, Zurich 1853, vol. I, p. 246.

4. *New Yorker Staats-Zeitung,* Jhg. VII (1841), No. 48.

5. This religious history is treated by Leon Watters, *The Pioneer Jews in Utah,* New York 1952.

6. Robert von Schlagintweit, *Die Mormonen . . . ,* Cöln 1878, p. 133.

7. Thomas Gregg, *The Prophet of Palmyra . . . ,* New York 1890, p. 161.

8. G. A. Zimmer von Ulbersdorf, *Unter den Mormonen in Utah,* Gütersloh 1908, p. 59.

9. Benjamin, Teil III, p. 83.

10. *The Continent,* Philadelphia, vol. I (Febr. to June 1882), p. 261, "The Homes in Utah."

11. William Chandless, *A visit to Salt Lake,* London 1857, p. 278, "Abraham the only Jew in Utah." An assessment of city lots registers: Abrams Levi 13 and 19 Ward D7.60 (Deseret News, Vol. VI (1856/7), p. 328).

11a. Fred E. Bennet, *A Detective's Experience among the Mormons . . . ,* Chicago 1887, p. 170.

12. *Montana Post,* v. III, No. 21, 19. I. 1867, p. 1, "Affairs in Utah."

13. *American Israelite*, vol. XXVIII, No. 3, 15. XII. 1881, p. 17, "Wayside Etchings."

14. Church Archives, San Bernardino Stake. Court File quoted by Rudolf Glanz, *The Jews of California*, New York 1960. See Ch. XVII n. 33–36 for details.

15. *American Hebrew*, vol. LXXVIII (1905/6), p. 292. An even earlier case, in 1888, ". . . that fraud Dr. (?) Joseph, is now in Salt Lake City, where, with his cheek, he proposes to buy up Mormondom. I should not be at all surprised if Mr. Joseph would soon become a Mormon elder and spread the light of Joseph Smith among the Roumanians . . ." (*American Israelite*, v. XXXIV (1887/88), No. 51, p. 8, "Maftir").

16. *"Visions of Joseph Smith the Seer, with the statements of Dr. Lederer (Converted Jew) and others,"* Plano, Illinois.

17. *Deseret News*, v. XXI (1872), p. 223.

18. *Improvement Era*, v. XXII (1918), 782. (Charles W. Nibley on the Neibaur family).

19. *Utah Genealogical and Historical Magazine*, vol. V (1914), pp. 53–63, "Alexander Neibaur." *Utah Historical Quarterly*, v. XV (1942), p. 32. *Improvement Era*, v. XXII (1918), p. 782 (Charles W. Nibley) "In 1841, the Neibaur family emigrated to Nauvoo, spending some six weeks on a sailing vessel, on the ocean from England to New Orleans, thence up the Mississippi river by boat to Nauvoo."

19a. Blanche E. Rose, "Pioneer Dentistry. Alexander Neibaur," *Utah Historical Quarterly*, vol. XV (1942), p. 32.

20. *Utah Genealogical and Historical Magazine*, vol. V (1914), p. 53–63.

21. E. Cecil MacGavin, *Nauvoo, the Beautiful*, Salt Lake City, 1946, p. 60.

22. *Nauvoo Neighbour*, vol. II (1844), No. 38, p. 3.

23. Ibid., vol. II (1844), No. 40, p. 2.

24. *Deseret News*, vol. I (1850/51), 15. VI. 1850, p. 8.

25. Ibid., vol. II (1851/52), No. 3, p. 4.

26. Ibid., vol. II (1851/52), No. 25, p. 3.

27. B. H. Roberts, *History of the Church*, vol. VI, pp. 267, 426.

28. *Times and Seasons*, vol. IV (1842/43), p. 233, "The Jews."

29. *Utah Genealogical and Historical Magazine,* vol. V (1914), pp. 53–63.

30. *Times and Seasons,* vol. III (1842), p. 592.

31. Journal of Alexander Neibaur, in Church Archiv., Salt Lake City, p. 41.

32. Ibid., p. 49.

33. Ibid., p. 50.

34. Ibid.

35. Ibid., pp. 50, 51.

36. Ibid., p. 57.

37. Eliza R. Snow Smith, *Biography and Family Record of Lorenzo Snow* . . . , Salt Lake City, 1884, p. 491 (He was born July 11th 1831 in Fordam, Prussia).

38. Journal Neibaur, p. 51.

39. Ibid., p. 59.

40. Ibid.

41. *Deseret News,* 14. IX. 1864, p. 400.

CHAPTER 17

1. Thomas H. Gladstone, *Bilder und Skizzen aus Kansas* . . . , Leipzig 1857, p. 138.

2. Hermann Melville, *The Confidence Man. His Masquerade.* (The works of Hermann Melville, vol. XII). London 1923, p. 8.

3. *Jüdisches Volksblatt,* vol. I (1854), p. 12.

4. B. Winchester, *A history of the Priesthood,* Philadelphia 1843, p. 122.

5. *Gospel Herald,* vol. III (1849), No. 44, (No. 3), p. 242.

6. Albert C. Stevens, *The Cyclopedia of Fraternities* . . . , New York 1899, pp. 70–72, "Freemasonry among the Mormons," p. 71.

7. S. H. Goodwin, *Mormonism and Masonry,* Washington, D.C., [1924], p. 4.

8. *Times and Seasons,* vol. III (1842), pp. 749–50.

9. Ibid.

10. S. H. Goodwin, *Mormonism and Masonry,* Washington, D.C., [1924], pp. 6, 7.

11. *Reprint of the Proceedings of the Grand Lodge of Illinois*

from its organization in 1840 to 1850 inclusive, Freeport, Ill. 1892, p. 59.

12. Stevens, p. 71, *Reprint . . . Proceedings . . . ,* pp. 52, 58, 70, 71, 85, 95, 130.

John C. Reynolds, *History of the M. W. Grand Lodge of Illinois . . . ,* Springfield 1869, pp. 140, 166, 193, 255.

13. *Nauvoo Neighbour,* vol. I (1843), No. 49.

14. *American Hebrew,* vol. CXXIII (1927), p. 689, "He followed Brigham Young to Utah. Abe Kuhn, first Jew in the Deseret State, at ninety-one tells of his pioneering adventures. By R. L. Olson."

15. "Reminiscences Marcus Katz" in *Ingersolls Century Annals of San Bernardino County . . . ,* Los Angeles 1904, pp. 348–352.

16. Harris Newmark, *Sixty Years in Southern California,* New York 1930, p. 345.

17. *The Californian, Monterey,* vol. I, No. 2, 22. VIII. 1846, p. 4, "The Mormons."

18. Ibid., vol. I (1846), No. 36, p. 2.

19. *Oregon Free Press,* vol. I (19. VIII. 1848), No. 20, p. 2.

20. *Oregon Spectator,* No. 7, 27. XII. 1843, p. 4.

21. Ibid., vol. V, No. 13, (4. XII. 1850), p. 3, "The Mormons in England."

22. Johann Weik, *Californien wie es ist . . . ,* Philadelphia 1849, p. 47.

23. *Daily Alta California,* 14. VII. 1851, p. 2.

24. *The Pinkos . . . Commemorating Seventy-Five years of Jewish activities in San Bernardino and Riverside Counties. 1860–1935,* San Bernardino, Cal., p. 16.

25. Dictation of Marcus Katz, Bancroft Library.

25a. H. F. Raup, *San Bernardino, California Settlement and Growth of a pass-site city,* Berkeley 1940, p. 26, "from unpublished manuscript journal of Amasa M. Lyman, in church archives, Salt Lake City. The date was September 21, 1852."

26. Dictation of Marcus Katz.

27. *The Western Standard,* vol. I (1856), p. 38, "Minutes of a special conference of the San Bernardino Branch of the Church."

28. *Weekly Gleaner,* vol. I (1857), p. 6.

29. E. P. R. Crafts, *Pioneer Days in the San Bernardino Valley,* Redlands, Cal., 1906, p. 45.

30. George William Beattie and Helen Pruit Beattie, *Heritage of the Valley* . . . , Pasadena, 1909, p. 211.

31. *The Western Standard*, v. I (1856), p. 58.

32. *San Francisco Daily Evening Bulletin*, 29. IV. 1856, p. 1.

33. Kind information of Mr. Harry Allison, County Clerk of the Superior Court of San Bernardino, given to the present writer.

34. Records of the San Bernardino Stake in Church Archives, Salt Lake City, see Ch. XVI, n. 14.

35. Account by Seely's daughter given to Mr. Allison.

36. Rudolf Glanz, *The Jews of California* . . . , New York 1960, p. 88/89.
County Clerk's Office of Superior Court of County of San Bernardino, Court of Sessions 1855, p. 23.

37. Dictation of Marcus Katz.

38. "Incident 1855–1867" (Manuscript in Bancroft Library).

39. *Sinai*, vol. III (1859), p. 950/951.

40. *United States War Department. War of the Rebellion. Official Records* . . . , Washington 1897. Series 1, vol. L, James H. Carleton, Report (Dated) "Headquarters Camp Fitzgerald, near Los Angeles, Cal. July 31, 1861," p. 548.

41. George William Beattie and Helen Pruit Beattie, *Heritage of the Valley* . . . , Pasadena 1939, pp. 359/360.

42. Benjamin, 2. Teil, p. 146.

43. Ben C. Truman, *Semi-Tropical California*, San Francisco 1874, p. 199.

44. *American Israelite*, vol. XXXIV (1887/88), No. 28, p. 9, "Maftir."

45. Ibid., No. 38, p. 3, "San Bernardino, Cal."

46. 1. *Pacific Historical Review*, vol. XI, pp. 73–75, Early Freighting on the Salt Lake-San Bernardino Trail;

2. *Southern California Historical Society Quarterly*, vol. XIV (1935), p. 334 "By Ox Team from Salt Lake to Los Angeles."

47. Harris Newmark, *Sixty Years in Southern California, p.* 345.

48. Ibid.

49. *Los Angeles Star*, 26. XI. 1859, p. 2.

50. William Shaw, *Golden Dreams and Waking Realities* . . . , London 1851, p. 187.

51. *Journal of Discourses,* vol. I, Liverpool 1854, p. 84 (Brigham Young, March 27th, 1853).

52. *Deseret News,* vol. III (1852/1853), No. 20, p. 2.

53. *Jewish Messenger,* v. IV (1858), p. 93.

54. *Der Zeitgeist,* vol. I (Milwaukee 1880), p. 55.

55. *Utah Genealogical and Historical Magazine,* vol. XXVIII (1927), p. 174, "U. S. Census of Utah, 1851, Davis Co.," No. 147.

56. Census of Weber County (excluding Green River Precinct) Provisional State of Deseret 1850 . . . , Ogden, Utah, *The Historic Records Survey,* October 1937, p. 20, No. 201, No. 202, p. 21, No. 210. With this first census the vivid interest of America for population figures in Utah started. For the later decades the number of the Mormons is often compared with the numbers of the Jews in America. (*Deutch-Amerikanisches Konversations-Lexikon,* New York, vol. XI (1874), pp. 195/196; G. Brückner, *Amerikas Geography und Naturgeschichte,* St. Louis, [1858], p. 75).

57. *Deseret News,* vol. III (1852/1853), No. 18, p. 3.

58. *The Frontier Guardian,* Kanesville, Iowa, vol. I, 13. VI. 1849, p. 4, reprinted from St. Joseph Gazette.

59. *Western Humanities Review,* v. I (1947), p. 160, from "Volney King, Millard County, 1851–1875." A letter for "Abram the Jew" appears in the post list of March 31st, 1856, *Deseret News,* vol. VI, p. 32.

60. *Valley Tan,* vol. I, Salt Lake City 1858/1859, No. 2, p. 3.

61. *Deseret News,* vol. IX (1859), No. 5, p. 40.

62. Ibid., v. VI (July 12th, 1856), p. 7.

63. Ibid., vol. IX (1859), No. 1, p. 2.

64. *The Mountaineer,* Salt Lake City, vol. I (1859/1860), 10. IX. 1859, p. 11.

65. Ibid., 18. II. 1860, p. 3.

66. Ibid., 25. II. and 3. III. 1860.

67. *Los Angeles Star,* 13. IV. 1861, p. 2.

68. *The Mountaineer,* 16. VI. 1860, p. 3.

69. Ibid., 9. VI. 1860, p. 3.

70. Ibid., 23. VI. 1860, p. 4.

71. Ibid., 21. VII. 1860, p. 4.

72. Ibid., 2. II. 1861, p. 72.

73. *The Deseret News,* vol. XI (1861/62), No. 24, 23. X. 1861, p. 191.

74. Ibid., vol. XI, No. 32, 5. II. 1862, p. 255.

75. Journal Alexander Neibaur, p. 57.

76. Ibid.

77. *Deseret News,* vol. XI (1861), p. 76.

78. Ibid., pp. 68, 72.

79. Ibid., vol. XII, No. 14, 1. X. 1862, p. 110.

80. *Utah Historical Quarterly,* vol. XIII (1940), "Journal of Captain Albert Tracy," p. 52, note 85.

81. Fred. B. Rogers, *Soldiers of the Overland,* San Francisco 1938, p. 122.

82. N. Slater, *Fruits of Mormonism,* Coloma, Cal., 1851, p. 10.

83. *The Mountaineer,* vol. I, 24. IX. 1859, p. 2, "Causes of War."

84. *Journal of Discourses,* v. I, p. 55 (speech of Brigham Young, April 9th, 1852).

85. *Valley Tan,* vol. I (1858/59), No. 32, p. 2.

86. *The Mountaineer,* vol. II, No. 18, 2. II. 1861.

87. Guy J. Giffen, *Californian Expedition. Stevenson's Regiment of first New York volunteers,* Oakland 1951, pp. 36. 109.

88. *Records of Californian Men in the War of Rebellion, 1861–1867.* Compiled by Brig.-Gen. Richard H. Orton . . . Sacramento 1890, pp. 197, 513, 544.

89. National Archives, Department of War, Camp Douglas.

90. *New Yorker Criminal-Zeitung,* v. IX (1860), p. 28, "Aus dem Lager in Utah, Camp Floyd."

91. Jules Remy, *A journey to Great Salt Lake City . . . ,* London 1861, vol. I, p. 214.

92. File "Nieheim" in the Yivo Institute for Jewish Research.

93. *American Jewish Archives,* June 1951, pp. 81–111. "A Jewish peddler's diary 1842–1843." Abraham Vossen Goodman, p. 109.

94. *The Asmonean,* vol. III (1850/51), p. 46.

95. Ibid., vol. X (1854), p. 103.

96. *Weekly Gleaner,* vol. I (1857), p. 4.

97. S. N. Carvalho, p. 143.

98. Ibid., p. 151.

99. Ibid., p. 144.

100. Ibid., p. 151.

101. Ibid., p. 185.

102. Ibid., p. 146.

103. Ibid., p. 148.

104. Benjamin, 3. Teil, p. 49.

105. Ibid., pp. 48, 79.

106. Ibid., VIII.

107. Ibid., p. 46.

108. Ibid.

CHAPTER 18

1. National Archives, Attorney General Papers. Letters received. Utah 1853–1869.

2. Solis Cohen, Jr., A California Pioneer. The Letters of Bernhard Marks to Jacob Solis-Cohen (1853–1857), *Publ. A. J. H. Soc.*, vol. XLIV, No. 1, pp. 12–57, p .56, d. Placerville, Sept. 18, 1857.

3. *Ben Chananja,* Szegedin, vol. VI (1863), p. 235.

4. Austin N. Ward, *Male life among the Mormons . . . ,* Philadelphia 1863, p. 18.

5. Ibid., p. 257.

6. *The Union Vedette,* 27. XI. 1863, p. 3.

7. Ibid., 11. XII. 1863, p. 2.

8. Ibid., 25. XII. 1863, p. 3.

9. *Z. C. M. I. Advocate,* vol. V, p. 247, vol. IX, No. 9, p. 130.

10. *Deseret News,* v. XII (1862), p. 92.

11. Ibid.

12. Ibid., p. 96.

13. *The Historical Record . . . ,* ed. by Andrew Jenson.

14. Statement Fred J. Kiesel, Ogden, Utah. Mss. in Bancroft Library.

15. Ibid.

16. *Deutsch-Amerikanisches Konversations-Lexikon,* vol. XI, p. 287.

17. *The American Israelite,* vol. XI (1864–65), p. 213.

18. Robert Joseph Dwyer, *The Gentile comes to Utah,* Washington 1941, p. 32, quoted from Vedette of Aug. 17th, 1865.

19. *Die Deborah,* Jahrgang X (1864/65), p. 107.

20. *Daily Union Vedette,* 24. III. 1864, p. 2.

21. Ibid., 25. III, 1864, p. 3.

22. Ibid., 6. IV. 1864, p. 2.

23.–27. Ibid., p. 3.

28. Ibid., 13. V. 1864, p. 2.

29. Ibid., 2. VII. 1864, p. 3.

30. Ibid., 16. VII. 1864, p. 2.

31. Ibid., 22 Dez., 1864, pp. 1, 3.

32. Ibid., 12 Oct. 1864, 14 November 1864.

33. Ibid., 11. I. 1865, p. 3.

34. Ibid., 1, II. 1865, p. 3.

35. Ibid., 3, II. 1865, p. 3.

36. Ibid., 28. I. 1865, p. 3.

37. *Monatsschrift für Geschichte und Wissenschaft des Judentums,* vol. XVIII (1869), p. 480.

38. *The Galaxy,* New York, vol. II (1866), p. 351–364, "The Mormon Commonwealth. By a Mormon Elder," p. 362.

39 .*The Daily Union Vedette,* 1, VIII. 1866, p. 1.

40. Ibid., 1, VIII. 1866, p. 2.

41. *Utah Historical Quarterly,* vol. IX (1936), p. 140.

42. *The Daily Union Vedette,* 1, VIII. 1866, p. 2.

43. Ibid.

44. Ms. Incident 1855–1867, "August 1857," "Sept. 1857," in Bancroft Library.

44a. *The Mountaineer,* 12. XI, 1859, p. 2.

45. *Deseret News,* vol. XIV (1864), p. 164.

46. *Journal of Discourses,* vol. I, p. 84 (Brigham Young, March 27th, 1853).

47. Ibid., vol. I (1854), p. 55, (Brigham Young, April 9th, 1852).

48. Valley Tan, vol. I, (1858/59), No. 41, p. 3.

49. *Deseret News,* vol. XIV (1864), p. 99, "Remarks."

50. Ibid., vol. XIII (1863), p. 82.

51. Ibid. vol. XIII (May 4th, 1864), p. 252.

52. Ibid., vol. IV (1853/1854), No. 1, p. 3.

53. Ibid., No. 22, p. 4.

54. *Daily Union Vedette,* April 30th, 1867, p. 1.

55. Ibid., 19th July 1864, p. 3.

56. Mss. "Statement Frederick H. Auerbach, Salt Lake City, U." in Bancroft Library.

57. *Deseret News,* vol. IV (1853/54), No. 22.

57a. Ibid., vol. XII, 11. XII. 1862, p. 112.

58. [William Elkana Water] *Life among the Mormons . . .,* New York 1868, p. 95.

59. *Salt Lake City Reporter,* January 8th, 1869, p. 3.

60. *Daily Union Vedette,* 6. II. 1865, p. 2.

61. Mss. Incidents 1855–1867, in Bancroft Library.

62. Andrew Love Neff, *History of Utah, 1847–1869,* Salt Lake City 1940, p. 817.

63. The Montana press had followed the developing Gentile conflict with great interest. Articles titled "Utah" and "The Troubles in Utah" (*Montana Post,* vol. III (1866/67), No. 20, p. 4 and No. 21, p. 1) reprint the letter of the merchants and the answer to it in full. Reprinted also in Orson F. Whitney, *History of Utah,* Salt Lake City 1892–1904, vol. II, pp. 164/65.

64. Dwyer, p. 52.

65. Jesse Harold Jameson, Corinne: A study of a Freight Transfer Point in the Montana Trade 1869–1878. Master's Thesis, University of Utah, 1951, p. 306. Auerbach and Brother, Louis Cohn, Kahn Brothers, Ransohoff and Company.

66. Reprinted in Whitney, vol. II, pp. 165/66.

67. *Times and Seasons,* vol. III, No. 15, 1, VI. 1842. p. 807.

68. *The demoralizing doctrines and disloyal teachings of the Mormon Hierarchy . . .,* New York 1866, p. 15.

69. *Salt Lake City Directory . . .* By G. Owens, 1867, p. 17.

70. Ibid., p. 10.

71. Ibid.

72. In the course of a law suit against Louis Reggel his attorney reported an appraisal of Reggel's properties by R. G. Dunn and Co., amounting to 26,000 dollars. (National Archives, Department of Justice, received Aug. 8th ,1882.)

73. *Deseret News,* vol. XXI (1872), p. 396.

74. *Salt L. C. Dir.* 1867, p. 71.

75. Ibid., p. 79.

76. Ibid., p. 208.

77. Ibid., p. 211.

78. Ibid.

79. *Daily Union Vedette,* 27. V. 1867, p. 3.

80. *California Historical Quarterly,* vol. XIX, pp. 289–298. "Saint Louis and Poker Flat in the Fifties and Sixties." *From the*

Jugenderinnerungen of Henry Cohn. Translated and edited by Fritz Ludwig Cohn, Stettin 1914, p. 290.

81. Cohn, Henry . . . Statement . . . Salt Lake, in Bancroft Library.

82. Ibid.

83. [William Elkanah Water] *Life among the Mormons . . .,* New York 1868, p. 95.

84. *Deseret News,* 7, I. 1868, p. 3.

85. *Ibid.,* 7. I. 1868, p. 8.

86. *Salt Lake Daily Telegraph,* vol. IV, No. 304, 25, VI. 1868, p. 1.

87. Ibid., p. 3.

88. Ibid.

89. *Salt Lake Daily Reporter,* 16. XII. 1868, p. 1.

90. Ibid., 22. XII. 1868, p. 2.

91. *Deseret News,* vol. II (1851/52), No. 18, p. 3.

92. Ibid.

93. Leonard J. Arrington, *Great Basin Kingdom. Economic History of the Latter Day Saints,* Cambridge 1958, pp. 301, 302.

94. Orson F. Whitney, *History of Utah,* Salt Lake City 1892–1904, vol. II, p. 279.

95. Ibid., p. 278.

96. Ibid., p. 279.

97. Ibid., p. 283.

98. Arrington, p. 494, n. 15.

99. Whitney, vol. II, p. 294.

100. *Deseret News,* vol. XVII (1868), p. 276.

101. *The Cincinnati Excursion to California . . .,* Cincinnati 1870, p. 129.

102. W. F. Rae, *Westward by Rail,* London 1870, p. 105.

103. John W. Clampitt, *Echoes from the Rocky Mountains,* Chicago 1889, p. 285.

104. *Old and New,* vol. I (1870), p. 634.

105. *The Circular,* vol. V (1868), p. 171, "A Visit to Salt Lake City."

106. Statement Frederick H. Auerbach in Bancroft Library.

107. *The American Israelite,* vol. XVI (1869/1870), No. 24, p. 11.

108. *Deseret News,* vol. XVII (1868), p. 322, "The Mormon Question."

109. *Salt Lake City Directory and Business Guide 1869,* p. 157.

110. Ibid., pp. 97, 131, 157, 158.

111. Zion's Co-operative Mercantile Institution, Salt Lake City, 1880. Mss. Utah Miscellany in Bancroft Library.

112. Andrew Love Neff, *History of Utah,* 1847–1869, Salt Lake City 1940, p. 833.

113. *Jewish Messenger,* vol. XXVI (1869), No. 3, p. 4.

14. Ibid., vol. XXV (1869), No. 25, p. 5.

115. *Der Israelit,* Mainz, Jhg. X (1869), p. 779.

116. *Rattling Roaring Rhymes on Mormon Utah and Her Institutions.* By "Will Cooper," Chicago 1874, p. 57.

117. K. D. Forgerson, Unwritten Utah, *Woman's Magazine,* Brattleboro, Vt., vol. X (1886/87), pp. 326–330, p. 328.

118. Ibid., p. 326.

119. *The American Israelite,* vol. XI (1864/65), p. 165.

120. Ibid., vol. XVI (1869/1870), No. 17, p. 6.

121. *Deseret News,* vol XIX (1870), p. 210.

122. *The American Israelite,* vol. XIII, No. 5, (3. VIII. 1866), p. 6.

123. *The Jewish Messenger,* vol. XXV (1869), No. 25, p. 5.

124. *Der Israelit,* Mainz, vol X (1869), p. 662.

125. *The Israelite,* vol .XIII, No. 30, 1, II. 1867, p. 6.

126. *Jewish Messenger,* vol. XXII, 6. XII. 1867, No. 22, p. 3.

127. *Hebrew Leader,* vol. XI, No. 9, 6. XII. 1867, p. 4.

128. *Daily Union Vedette,* 14. I. 1867, p. 3.

129. Ibid., March 23rd, 1867, p. 3.

130. *The Alton Telegraph,* vol. IX (1844), No. 31, p. 2. (C. A. Snyder Collection in New York Public Library).

131. *Deseret News,* vol. II (1851/52), No. 21, p. 4.

132. *The Jewish Messenger,* vol. XVI (1864), p. 172.

133. Pac. Mss. Utah. Historical Incidents. 1855–67, p. 6 (in Bancroft Library).

134. *New Orleans Weekly Picayune,* 7. IX. 1857, p. 6.

135. *Valley Tan* ,vol. I (1858/59), No. 17, p. 2.

136. *Deseret News,* vol. XVII (1868), p. 346, "Discourse" (Brigham Young).

137. E. D. Howe, *Mormonism unveiled,* Painsville 1834, p. 55.

138. Alexander Toponce, *Reminiscences* . . ., [Ogden, 1923], p. 173.

139. Bernard de Voto, The Centennial of Mormonism, *The American Mercury*, Jan. 1930, p. 1–13.

140. *American Jewish Archives,* June, 1951, p. 109, "A Jewish peddlers diary 1842–1843." Abram Vossen Goodman.

141. *Valley Tan,* vol. I (1858/59), No. 2, p. 3.

142. [William E. Waters] *Life among the Mormons* . . ., New York, 1868, p. 178.

143. *Valley Tan,* vol. I (1858/59), No. 38, p. 3.

144. J. B. Franklin, *The Mysteries and the Crimes of Mormonism* . . ., London [1855–56], p. 6.

145. *Daily Union Vedette,* 5. VI. 1867, p. 2.

146. J. Schiel, *Reise durch die Felsengebirge und die Humboldtgebirge nach dem stillen Ocean,* Schaffhausen 1859, p. 124.

147. Bernard Domschke, *Zwanzig Monate in Kriegsgefangenschaft* . . ., Milwaukee 1865, p. 54.

148. *The Mormon Tribune,* vol. I (1870), No. 14, p. 108.

149. J. W. Gunnison, *The Mormons* . . ., Philadelphia 1857, p. 23.

150. J. B. Franklin, *The Mysteries and the Crimes of Mormonism* . . ., London [1855–56], p. 6.

151. William Shaw, *Golden Dreams and Waking Realities* . . ., London 1851, p. 187.

152. *The Jewish Messenger,* vol. XXVIII (1870), No. 3, p. 1.

153. *Deseret News,* vol. XXIII (1874), p. 503, "The Cloven Foot—it cannot hide."

154. Ibid., vol. XII (1862), p. 107.

155. Ibid., vol. XX (1871), p. 448.

156. Ibid., vol. XXI (1872), p. 256, "Judge Hawley's Court."

157. Ibid., p. 266.

158. Ibid., p. 396.

159. Ibid., p. 209, "The Rothschilds."
  " vol. XIII (1864/65), p. 46, "Stray Thoughts on Our Career Through Life."
  " vol. V (1855/56), p. 322/23, "The Rothschilds."
  " vol. XII (1863/64), p. 211, "War between Money Kings."

160. Ibid., vol. XXII (1873), p. 600, "Jewish Bankers."

161. Ibid., p. 376, "The Hebrews."

162. Ibid., vol. XIV (1865), p. 324, "Classes."

163. Ibid., vol. XXII (1873), p. 356, "Discourse . . . Brigham Young."

164. Ibid., vol. XIII (1864), p. 384, "Police Report."

165. *Gospel Herald*, vol. II (1847), No. 42, p. 3, "The Jews."

166. *Deseret News*, vol. XXII (1873), p. 456, "The Hebrews."

167. Ibid., vol. XIII (1864), p. 233, "[From the Jeshurun]. The Jewish Sabbath."

168. Ibid., vol. XX (1871), p. 395, "Jewish religious exercises."

169. Ibid., vol. XXIV (1875), p. 150.

170. Ibid., vol XII (1863), p. 131.

171. Ibid., vol. XX (1871), p. 415.

172. Ibid., vol. XVIII (1869), p. 436, "Immunities of the Jewish race."

173. Hector Lee, *The Three Nephites* . . . ,Albuquerque 1949, pp. 77/78.

174. Austin and Alta Fife, *Saints of Sage and Saddle, Folklore among the Mormons*, Bloomington 1956, p. 37.

CHAPTER 19

1. Some years later, even an act of physical violence against a Jewish merchant was perpetrated by a Mormon dignitary. (Watters, pp. 35, 70).

2. Statement Fred J. Kiesel in Bancroft Library.

3. George Robert Bird, *Tenderfoot days in territorial Utah*, Boston 1918, p. 18.

4. See Chapter XVIII, note 104.

5. *Salt Lake Daily Reporter*, 20. III. 1869, p. 3.

6. Montana Post, vol. V, No. 30, 2. IV. 1869, p. 6.

7. *Salt Lake Daily Reporter*, 31. III. 1869, p. 3.

8. Ibid., 7. IV. 1869, p. 3.

9. Ibid.

10. Ibid., 10. IV. 1869, p. 2.

11. *The Utah Daily Reporter*, Corinne, 21. IV. 1869, p. 3.

12. Ibid., 23. IV, 1869, p. 3.

13. *Journal of Discourses*, vol. XIII, p. 24.

14. *Utah Historical Quarterly*, vol. IX (1936), p. 140.

15. *Corinne Daily Journal*, 5. V. 1871, p. 3.

16. Ibid., 2. V. 1871, p. 2.

17. Ibid., p. 3.

18. Ibid., 9. V. 1871, p. 1.

19. Ibid., 5. V. 1871, p. 3.

20. Ibid., 2. V. 1871, p. 3.

21. Ibid., p. 2.

22. Ibid. 14. V. 1871, p. 3.

23. *Daily Corinne Reporter*, 13. V. 1873, p. 1.

24. Edward L. Sloan, *Gazetteer of Utah, and Salt Lake City Directory 1874*. Salt Lake City, pp. 58, 59, 60.

25. *Business Directory of the Pacific States and Territories, for 1878 . . .*, San Francisco 1878, pp. 252/253.

26. *Sabbath Visitor*, New Series, vol. XVII (1887/88), p. 767, "Letter Box. Hanna Keller, Corinne, Utah."

26a. Edward L. Sloan, p. 309.

27. Ibid., p. 310.

28. Ibid.

29. *The Mormon Tribune*, vol. I (1870), p. 5.

30. *Salt Lake Daily Tribune*, 2. VI. 1873, pp. 2, 3, 4.

31. Sloan.

32. Ibid., p. 63.

33. Ibid., p. 80.

34. Ibid., p. 81.

35. Ibid., p. 93.

36. Ibid.

37. Ibid., p. 108.

38. *Business Directory . . . 1878*, pp. 251–259.

39. Ibid., pp. 261–268.

40. Robert v. Schlagintweit, *Die Mormonen . . .*, p. 118.

41. Toponce, *Reminiscences*, p. 248.

42. Ibid., p. 198.

43. *The Jewish Messenger*, vol. XXVIII (1870), No. 3, p. 1, "Across the Continent."

44. *The Israelite*, vol. XIX (1872), No. 5, p. 10.

45. *Hebrew Sabbath School Visitor*, vol. III (1876), p. 295, "My second trip to California."

46. *Independent Hebrew*, vol. I (1876), No. 9, p. 3, "Salt Lake City."

47. *The American Israelite*, vol. XXIX (1877), No. 3, p. 4.

48. *American Journal of Mining*, vol. VII (1869), p. 132, "Utah."

49. *Engineer and Mining Journal*, vol. X (1870), p. 357.

50. *Mining and Scientific Press*, vol. XXIII (1871), p. 53.

51. *Engineer and Mining Journal*, vol. XI (1871), p. 197.

52. *The Jewish Voice*, vol. XVII (1895), No. 16, p. 7, "Salt Lake City."

53. *The American Israelite*, vol. XXII, No. 22, 2. VI. 1876, p. 4.

54. *Hebrew Sabbath Visitor*, vol. III (1876), p. 178, "From California."

55. Statement Frederick H. Auerbach in Bancroft Library.

56. Dwyer, Chapter VI, "The Torchbearers," pp. 151–189.

57. *Daily Tribune*, July 13, 1875, quoted by Dwyer, p. 156, footnote No. 15.

58. *Utah Grand Lodge Proceedings 1872*, Utah Lodge, U.D. Provo, Officers: Ira M. Swartz, W.M.; Benjamin Bachman, J.M.; Charles F. Swartz, Secr. Entered Apprentices; Hess Jacob; Proceedings 1875, Story Lodge No. 4, New, Gustavus S., Paul, Samuel.

59. *Proceedings Grand Lodge 1873*, p. 53, Corinne Lodge U.D., Master Masons: Cohn, Louis; Frankel, Joseph; Goldberg, Gumpert; Hoffmann, Lazarus.

60. *The American Israelite*, vol. XXIX (1879), No. 3, p. 4.

61. *Salt Lake Daily Reporter*, 8. I. 1869, p. 3.

62. Ethelbert Talbot, *My people of the plains*, New York 1906, p. 79.

63. *Phrenological Journal, May 1871*, p. 343, "The Utah Gentiles." Kahn was commissioned a director of the Penitentiary of Utah Territory on June 28th, 1870. (*Deseret News*, vol. XXI (1872,) p. 5.

64. *The Mountaineer*, 2. II. 1861, p. 1.

65. *Deseret News*, vol. XIII (1863), p. 218, "The unsociability of the Saints."

66. *The Utah Pioneers. Celebration of the Entrance of the Pioneers into Great Salt Lake City*, Salt Lake City 1880, p. 12.

67. *Phrenological Journal, May 1871,* p. 343, "The Utah Gentiles."

68. *Weekly Salt Lake Tribune,* 1. III. 1873, p. 4.

69. *The Salt Lake Leader,* 6. IX. 1873, p. 3, "A false teacher."

70. E. K. Tullidge, *The lost tribes of Israel in England and America,* New York 1881, p. 314.

71. C. C. Goodwin, "The Political Attitude of the Mormons," *The North American Review,* March 1881, pp. 276–286, p. 278.

72. *Deseret News,* vol. XVIII (1869), p. 153.

73. Ibid., p. 205.

74. *The Jewish Messenger,* vol. XXVIII (1870), No. 3, p. 1, "Across the Continent."

75. *42nd Congress, 2nd Session. Mis. Doc. No. 208 . . . Memorial of Citizens of Utah, against the admission of that Territory as a State. May 6, 1872.—Referred to the Committee on Territories and ordered to be printed.*

76. *Deseret News,* vol. XXIV (1874), p. 88, "The Forty-Fife Limned."

77. Statement Fred Kiesel, in Bancroft Library.

78. *The Jewish Messenger,* vol. XXVIII (1870), No. 3, p. 1.

79. Ibid., No. 3, p. 1.

80. Ibid.

81. *The Jewish Advocate,* vol. IV (1881/82), No. 1, p. 1.

82. *Jewish Messenger,* vol. LV (1884), No. 1, p. 4.

83. Statement Frederick H. Auerbach, in Bancroft Library.

84. Whitney ,vol. IV, p. 306.

85. *American Israelite,* vol. XXXVII (1890/91), No. 52, p. 1, "Salt Lake City."

86. *The facts ln the Utah Case,* Salt Lake City 1892.

87. *American Hebrew,* vol. C (1916), p. 236, "The New Governor of Utah."

88. *The Jewish Advocate,* vol. IV, No. 12, p. 1, (X. 1882).

89. *The Jewish Messenger,* vol. XXVIII (1870), No. 3, p. 1.

CHAPTER 20

1. *Valley Tan,* vol. I (1858/59), No. 32, p. 2.

2. *The American Israelite,* vol. III (1856), p. 147.

3. Carvalho, pp. 143–145.

4. J. Solis Cohen, Jr., A California Pioneer. The Letters of Bernard Marks, *Publications A. J. H. S.*, No. 44, p. 57.

5. Ibid.

6. *New Yorker Staatszeitung*, 15. II. 1870, p. 4.

7. *The Jewish Voice*, vol. XVI (1894), No. 3, p. 7, "Salt Lake City."

8. Dr. Louis F. Frank, *Pionierjahre der Deutsch-Amerikanischen Familien Frank-Kerler in Wisconsin und Michigan, 1849–1864 . . .*, Milwaukee 1911, p. 288.

9. *Puck. Illustriertes Humoristisches Wochenblatt*, Jhg. VIII (1884), pp. 344/345.

10. *Spirit of the Times*, vol. X (1864), p. 23.

10a. *The Hebrew Sabbath Visitor*, vol. III (1876), p. 309.

11. *Puck. Illustriertes Humoristisches Wochenblatt*, Jhg. I (New York 1877), No. 51, p. 16.

12. *Spirit of the Times*, vol. XI (1864/1865), p. 96, "Artemus Ward, p. 128, "Artemus Ward among the Mormons," p. 144, "Artemus Ward."

13. Houghton Library, Cambridge, Mass. Ms. 34789.1.12 (Supplemental), vol. IV, No. 9.

14. [Stone, John A.] *Put's Golden Songster*, San Francisco [1858], pp. 50–52.

15. *The "Brigham Young Songster."* Robert de Witt, Publisher, New York 1871 (in Houghton Library, Ms. 34789.1.12* Mormons [Miscell.], vol. XVI).

16. *Bee Hive Songster . . . By "Jeuan" . . .*, Salt Lake City 1868, p. 26.

17. *Valley Tan*, Salt Lake, vol. I (1858/59), No. 5, p. 1.

18. Newmark, *Sixty years . . .*, p. 345.

19. *Illuminated Western World*, New York, vol. 1 (1869), No. 15, p. 7.

20. *Yankee Notions*, vol. X (1861), p. 281.

21. Ibid., vol. XIV (1865), p. 357.

22. *Harper's Magazine*, vol. XLIV (1871/72), p. 951.

23. *Puck. Ill. hum. Wochenblatt*, Jhg. III (1879), p. 39.

24. A. F. Frankland, Kronikals of the Times. Memphis 1862. Edited by Maxwell Whiteman, *American Jewish Archives*, vol. IX, No. 2 (Oct. 1957), pp. 83–125, p. 120.

25. M. Bergmann, *Herbst-Früchte. Knittel-Verse. Zum Besten des Hebrew Orphan Asylum,* New York 1881, p. 56.

26. *The American Punch,* vol. I (1879), pp. 102/103.

27. *New York Atlas,* vol. V (24. VII, 1842), p. 2.

28. Frederic Law Olmstedt, *Journeys and Explorations in the Cotton Kingdom,* London 1861, vol. II, p. 359.

28a. R. Glison, *Journal of Army Life,* San Francisco 1874, p. 122.

29. *Harper's Weekly,* vol. I (1857), p. 442.

30. *Gentleman's Progress. The Itinerarium of Dr. Alexander Hamilton, 1744;* edited with an introduction by Carl Bridenbaugh, Chapel Hill 1948, p. 34.

31. *Scribners Monthly,* vol. III (1871/72), p. 574.

32. *Anti Polygamy Standard,* vol. I, (1880/81), p. 35.

33. Ibid., vol. I, p. 57.

34. *Protokolle der Rabbiner Conferenz abgehalten zu Philadelphia, vom 3, bis zum 6. November 1869,* New York 1870, p. 25.

35. Ibid.

36. Ibid., p. 24.

37. Ibid. pp. 24, 25.

38. Ibid., p. 25.

39. *American Israelite,* vol. XXX, No. 28 (11. I. 1884), p. 5.

40. *Jüdische Zeitschrift für Wissenschaft und Leben,* Breslau, vol. VIII (1870), pp. 1–17, "Die Versammlung zu Leipzig und die zu Philadelphia," p. 3.

41. "Mordecai Manual Noah" (Address), *Publications Am. Jew. Hist. Soc.,* No. 21, p. 251.

42. *The Occident,* vol. XIX (1861/1862), p. 362, *"The American Crisis."*

43. E. Neufeld, *Ancient Hebrew Marriage Laws,* London [1944], Chapter VII, "Polygamy and Concubinage" reads like a repetition of these arguments.

44. *The Hebrew,* San Francisco, vol. I (1864), No. 16, p. 4, "More slanders refuted."

45. Ibid.

46. *Deseret News,* vol. XIII (1864), p. 232.

47. *Zeichen der Zeit,* Chicago, vol. I (1869), p. 63.

48. *Deseret News,* vol. XIX (1870), p. 84, "Manti City, March 9, 1870. Editor *Deseret News:—* "

49. Ibid., vol. XIV (1870), p. 436.

50. *The Mormon,* vol. I (1855/56), No. 49, p. 2, "Matrimonial."

51, 52. *American Socialist, Oneida,* vol. IV (1879), p. 59 and further articles p. 84, "Wide apart" and p. 284, "Unlike the Mormons."

53. *Eclectic,* December 1881, p. 781 (opposing an article of Judge Goodwin in the March number of the *North American Review.*)

54. William L. Cole, *California . . .,* New York 1871, p. 18.

55. Veronica Petit, *Plural marriage. The heart history of Adele Hersch,* Ithaca, N. Y. 1885, "Preface."

56. *San Francisco News-Letter,* 13. IX. 1879, p. 20.

57. *The American Israelite,* vol. XVII (1870/1871), No. 25, p. 6.

58. Elder R. Etzenhouser, *From Palmyra, New York 1830 to Independence, Missouri, 1894,* Independence, Mo. 1894, pp. 289/90.

59. Caroline M. Churchill, *Over the purple hills . . .,* Denver 1881, p. 246.

60. *Harper's Magazine,* vol. XIII (1857), p. 164, "Negroland and the Negroes."

61. *The Frontier Guardian,* 26, XII, 1849, p. 2.

62. Benjamin, III Teil, p. 79.

63. *Valley Tan,* vol. I (1858), No. 32, p. 3.

64. Benjamin, 3. Teil, p. 48.

65. Benjamin J. Ferris, *Utah and the Mormons,* New York 1854, p. 158.

66. *New Orleans Weekly Picayune,* 4. I. 1858, p. 8, "Washington Letter."

67. *The Century.* New series, vol. I (1860), p. 216.

68. *The Kansas Magazine,* vol. III (1–VI 1873), p. 516.

69. *The Jewish Advocate,* New York, vol. III (1880/1881), No. 2, p. 4.

70. Ibid., vol. IV, No. 4 (II. 1882), p. 4.

71. Ibid., vol. IV, No. 12 (X. 1882), p. 1.

72. *The American Israelite,* vol. XXXVII (1890/91), No. 16, p. 6.

1. *Times and Seasons,* vol. V 1844), pp. 587–589, "Letter of M. M. Noah . . . New York, June 18th, 1844." *Frontier Guardian,* 20. III. 1850, p. 1.

2. *Times and Seasons.* Nauvoo, vol. III (1842), p. 592.

3. Ibid., vol. I (1839/40), p. 123.

4. Ibid., vol. V (1844), p. 475, "The Jews."

5: *Nauvoo Neighbour,* vol. II (1844), No. 1, p. 3, "The Jews," from "Frazers Magazine."

6. *Journal of Discourses,* vol. III (1856), p. 127–139 (P. P. Pratt, October 7th, 1855), p. 134).

7. *Times and Seasons,* vol. IV (1843), pp. 220–232,, "The Jews," p. 231.

8. Ibid., Vol. II (1840/41), p. 436.

9. Ibid., vol. II (1840/41), p. 461.

10. *The Prophet,* New York, vol. II (1844), No. 7, p. 3.

11. Ibid., No. 3, p. 3.

12. *Times and Seasons,* vol. IV (1843), p. 810.

13. Ibid., p. 348, "Persecution of the Jews."

14. Ibid., vol. III (1842), p. 587.

15. *The Mountaineer,* 11, XI, 1859, p. 1.

16. *Times and Seasons,* vol. IV (1843), p. 365, "The Jews."

17. *Deseret News,* vol. II (1852), No. 22, p. 4.

18. *Times and Seasons,* vol. IV (1843), p. 349.

19. Ibid., vol. II (1840/41), No. 9, p. 341.

20. Ibid., vol. IV (1843), pp. 8, 64.

21. *The Prophet,* New York, vol. II, (1844), No. 10, p. 2.

22. *The Latter Day Saints Millennial Star,* vol. I, No. 1, May 1840, p. 18, "Restoration of the Jews."

23. Charles Thompson, *Evidences in proof of the Book of Mormon . . .,* Batavia, N. Y. 1841, pp. 114–120.

24. *Deseret News,* vol. IV (1853/54), No. 43, p. 1, "The Jews at Jerusalem."

25. *Evening and Morning Star,* Kirtland, vol. I (1832), pp. 134–136.

26. *The Frontier Guardian,* Kanesville, Iowa, vol. I, 13. VI. 1849, p. 1, "Building of the Temple at Jerusalem by a Jew."

27. Ibid., vol. I, 13. VI. 1849, p. 1.

28. *Deseret News,* vol. XIX (1870), pp. 463, 477.

29. *The Juvenile Instructor,* Salt Lake City, vol. I (1866), p. 2, "The Jews."

30. Ibid., vol. XXIII (1888), p. 383, "The Wandering Jew. by J. J. W."

31. Ibid., vol. XXVII (1892), pp. 442/43, "The Children of the Hebrews," p. 611.

32. *Zion's Home Monthly,* Salt Lake City, Vol. II (1893/94), p. 336, "Speak kindly of the Jews."

33. *The Prophet,* New York, vol. II (1844), No. 19, p. 1, "Restoration of the Jews."

34. *Deseret News,* vol. IV (1853/1854), No. 7, p. 1, "The Jews."

35. *The Mountaineer,* 10. XII 1859, p. 1.

36. *Nauvoo Neighbour,* vol. I (1843), No. 50, p. 2.

37. *Deseret News,* vol. XVIII (1869), p. 433.

38. Ibid., vol. XX (1871), p. 344, "Editorials."

39. Ibid., vol. XVII (1868), p. 354, "A Common Sabbath."

40. *Juvenile Instructor,* vol. VII (1872), p. 165, "Churches and Worship in California."

41. Ibid., vol. XVIII (1883), p. 88.

CHAPTER 22

1. Especially rich are reports in Archives Israelites, II Corriere Israelitico and in the Jewish newspapers in Germany.

2. *The American Israelite,* vol. XXXIII (1879), No. 21, p. 6.

3. *Der Israelitische Lehrer,* Jhg. X (1870), p. 295, "Amerika."

4. *Der Israelit,* Mainz, Jhg. X (1869), p. 779, "Salt Lake City."

5. *Jüdische Volkszcitung,* Leipzig, 1873, p. 70.

6. *Jewish Messenger,* vol. XXIV (1868), No. 18, p. 5.

7. *The Israelite,* vol. VIII (1861/62), p. 76.

8. "The City of Charity—an Appeal By Victor Tanno," *The Voice of the Fair,* 1870, No. 7, p. 4.

9. *Jewish Messenger,* vol. XXV (1869), No. 22, p. 2.

10. Ibid., vol. XXVI (1869), No. 3, p. 2.

11. Ibid., vol. XXVI (1869), No. 7, p. 2.

12. Ibid., No. 26, p. 2

13. Ibid., No. 3, p. 4.

14. T. L. Spalding, *The religious mission of the Irish People and Catholic Colonization,* New York 1880, p. 153.

15. *Independent Hebrew,* vol. I (1876), No. 9, p. 3.

16. "Our brethren in the West and San Francisco. By Dr. Lilienthal," *The American Israelite,* vol. XXVI, No. 22, 2. June 1876, pp. 4/5, No. 23, p. 4.

17. *The Hebrew Sabbath School Visitor,* vol. III (1876), pp. 309/310, "My second trip to California."

18. *The American Israelite,* vol. XXIX (1877), No. 2, p. 6, No. 3, p. 4; vol. XXXIII (1879), No. 13, p. 5.

19. *Jewish Times,* vol. III (1872), p. 12.

20. *Jewish Messenger,* vol. XXXIV (1873), No. 4, p. 3, "Judaism in America. An English View."

21. Ibid.

22. Ibid., vol. XXVIII (1870), No. 3, p. 1.

23. Ibid.

24. *Jewish Times,* vol. IV (1872/73), p. 565.

25. *The American Israelite,* vol. XXIX (1877), No. 3, p. 4, "Salt Lake City, Utah, July 7, 1877)."

26. Ibid., No. 11, p. 5, "Editorial Correspondence."

27. *Jewish Messenger,* vol. LV (1884), No. 1, p. 4, "Salt Lake City and Mormonism."

28. *The American Israelite,* vol. XXVII, No. 21, 15. Dez. 1876, p. 15.

29. *The Jewish Messenger,* vol. XXVIII (1870), No. 3, p. 1.

30. *The American Israelite,* vol. XVIII (1871/72), No. 15, p. 3, "The trouble at Salt Lake—What the Mormons say about it."

31. *The Occident,* vol. XVII (1859/60), p. 299, "Israelites in Congress."

32. *The Jewish Times,* vol. I (1869), No. 14, p. 7.

33. *Ben Chananja.* Szegedin, vol. III (1860), pp. 317–329, "Eherechtliche Studien," p. 317.

34. *Jewish Messenger,* vol. XLII (1877), No. 19, p. 1.

35. Ibid., vol. LIV (1883), No. 25, p. 2, "Baltimore, Md."

36. *The Jewish Times,* vol. IV (1872/73), p. 365.

37. *Israelitische Wochenschrift,* 1872, p. 289, "New York."

38. Franklin L. West, *Life of Franklin D. Richards,* "Salt Lake City 1924, p. 104.

39. *Der Zeitgeist,* Jhg. II (1881), p. 112, "Ein Vorschlag zur Güte."

40. *The Jewish Times,* vol. IV (1872/73), p. 630.

41. *Jewish Messenger,* vol. LV (1884), No. 26, p. 4.

42. *The American Israelite,* vol. XXVIII (1881), p. 61.

43. *Jewish Messenger,* vol. XLVI (1879), No. 7, p. 1.

44. Ibid., vol. LIV (1883), No. 25, p. 1, "From Ocean to Ocean." Rudolf Glanz, Jews and Chinese in America, *Jewish Social Studies,* vol. XVI (1954), No. 3.

45. *Jewish Messenger,* vol. LV (1884), No. 1, p. 4.

46. *American Hebrew,* vol. XVII (1883/4), p. 77.

47. *Jewish Messenger,* vol. L (1881), No. 9, p. 4.

48. *The Maccabean.* Chicago, vol. I (1882), p. 131, "The Times and the Manners."

CHAPTER 23

1. *De Bows Review,* vol. XVI (I–VI, 1854), p. 370.

2. *Salt Lake Daily Reporter,* 7. II. 18969, p. 2.

3. *Niles Weekly Register,* vol. LXIII (IX 1842–III 1843), p. 68.

4. *Baptist Home Mission Monthly,* VI. 1884, p. 271, quoted by Colin B. Goodykoontz, *Home Missions on the American Frontier,* Caldwell, Idaho, 1939, p. 315.

5. *Golden Age,* vol. IV, 4, VII, 1874, p. 6, "Utah and its people."

6. *De Bow's Review,* vol. XVI (1854), p. 372.

7. *Zweite Reise. Schilderungen aus Amerika. Eine Monatsschrift* bg. v. Heinrich Boßard, Zürich, vol. II, 1860, p. 179.

8. *The Edinburgh Review* vol. C (April 1854), American Edition, p. 191.

9. *Overland Monthly,* vol. V (1870), pp. 270–279, "Salt Lake City," p. 275.

10. *The Mountaineer,* 7, X. 1859, p. 2, "Greely in Utah."

11. *Handbook on Mormonism,* Salt Lake City, 1882, p. 9.

12. See Chapter XII, note 9.

13. *Journal of the Presbyterian Historical Society,* vol. XLVI (1946), No. 1, pp. 44–68, George K. Davies, A history of the Pres-

byterian Church in Utah, p. 64 (George Bird of American Fork in the *Rocky Mountain Presbyterian*).

14. *Southern Literary Messenger*, vol. XIV (1848), pp. 641–654, "Memoir of the Mormons."

15. *The Century*, vol. III (Nov. 1871–Apr. 1872), p. 400.

16. *Zeitschrift fur Völkerpsychologie und Sprachwissenschaft*, hg. v. Lazarus u. Steinthal, Berlin, vol. V (1868), p. 369–396, "Über die neueren Sekten in Nord-Amerika. Von v. Holtzendorff," p. 374.

17. *Onward*, vol. II–III (1869/70), p. 425.

18. *De Bow's Review*, vol. XVI (1854), p. 382.

19. *Los Angeles Star*, 11. II. 1871, p. 2, "Another Mormon Exodus."

20. *Jüdische Volkszeitung*, Leipzig, 1873, p. 70.

21. *Atlantic Monthly*, vol. XIII (1. VI. 1864), pp. 479–485, "Among the Mormons," p. 485.

22. George Arbaugh, *Revelation in Mormonism* . . ., p. 142, also mentions Cadman who wondered if Saturday should be the Sabbath and swine's flesh should be abstained from.

23. *Scribners Monthly*, vol. III (XI 1871–IV 1872), p. 400.

24. Fitz Hugh Ludlow, *the hearth of the Continent* . . ., New York 1870, p. 529.

25. "The passing of the Mormon. A. L. Mearkle," *The Arena*, vol. I (April 1890), pp. 378–389, p. 379.

26. Geo. Alfred Townsend, *The Mormon Trials of Salt Lake City*, New York 1871, p. 11.

27. *Harper's Weekly*, vol. I (1857), p. 257, "The Mormons."

28. Charles H. Brigham, "The Progressive Jews," *The Golden Age*, vol. I, 29. IV. 1871, p. 2.